D1421476

Studs Terkel is the author of ten books of oral history including *Working* and the Pulitzer Prize-winning *The Good War*. He is a member of the American Academy of Arts and Letters.

'One of the most important dimensions of Terkel's collections of interviews is that they give the lie to our inability to get beyond the anonymous babble of modern communications. Intimacy is their outstanding characteristic' *New Statesman*

'The book consists of the powerful, and sometimes harrowing, stories of sixty-three people who, in one way or another, have encountered death. Studs Terkel is extremely good at what he does. These conversations are, if anything, more about life than death, and Terkel's skill lies in encouraging people to talk about their most intimate, and often horrifying, memories. . .This is a truly heartening book' *Literary Review*

'Studs Terkel is the greatest interviewer in America' *The Times*

'This is a wise, moving, humane and generous book on a difficult subject. Studs Terkel is a remarkably gifted writer who has, over half a century, made the art of getting other people to tell their stories his own . . . full of surprises, this is a wonderful book' *Tablet*

'Terkel explores the simple nature of death with the added richness of dignity, acceptance and simple kindnesses. With Studs around, people talk and everyone listens. It's difficult not to' *Herald*

ACC. No.	CLASS. No.
2 50423	306. 9 TER
DATE.	CHECKED.
6/7/09	TKL

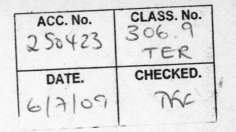

Will the Circle be Unbroken?

Reflections on Death and Dignity

STUDS TERKEL

Will the circle be unbroken? : reflections on
death and dignity

250423

Non-Fiction   306.9 TER

Royal Grammar School Guildford

Granta Publications, 2/3 Hanover Yard, London N1 8BE

First published in Great Britain by Granta Books 2002
This edition published by Granta Books 2003
First published in the US by The New Press 2001

Copyright © 2001 by Studs Terkel

The author is grateful for permission to reprint the following copyrighted material:
'A Bronzeville Mother Loiters in Mississippi. Meanwhile, a Mississippi Mother Burns
Bacon' by Gwendolyn Brooks, from *Blacks* by Gwendolyn Brooks, copyright 1987.
Reprinted by permission of Third World Press, Inc., Chicago, Illinois.

Studs Terkel has asserted his moral right under the Copyright, Designs and
Patents Act, 1988, to be identified as the author of this work.

All rights reserved. No reproduction, copy or transmissions of this publication
may be made without written permission. No paragraph of this publication
may be reproduced, copied or transmitted save with written permission or in
accordance with the provisions of the Copyright Act 1956 (as amended). Any
person who does any unauthorized act in relation to this publication may be
liable to criminal prosecution and civil claims for damages.

A CIP catalogue record for this book is available from the British Library.

1 3 5 7 9 10 8 6 4 2

Printed and bound in Great Britain by Mackays of Chatham PLC

Remembering Ida

You've got to cross that lonesome valley,
You've got to cross it by yourself,
There ain't no one can cross it for you,
You've got to cross it by yourself.

– as sung by Richard Dyer-Bennett

You've got to stand your test in judgment,
You've got to stand it by yourself,
Ain't nobody can stand it for you,
You've got to stand it by yourself,

– as sung by Big Bill Broonzy

We have loved ones gone to glory
Whose dear forms we often miss.
When we close our earthly story
Shall we join them in their bliss?
Will the circle be unbroken,
By and by, Lord, by and by.
There's a better home awaiting
Far beyond the starry sky.

– as sung by Doc Watson

. . . She's gone forever!
I know when one is dead, and when one lives.
She's dead as earth.
. . . Why should a dog, a horse, a rat have life,
and thou no breath at all? Thou'lt come no more.
Never, never, never, never, never!

– *King Lear*, Act V, Scene III

Contents

PART III

PART IV

Acknowledgments

My debts are owed to a legion of strangers, friends, and acquaintances. My first is to the heroes, unacknowledged in this book, though they have offered me their precious time and generosity of spirit. To them, my deepest bow as well as my apologies.

They are listed in alphabetical order, along with the scouts, who guided me toward them and toward the sixty whose testimonies are in the following pages: a burglar whose name I didn't catch, Charlie Andrews, Anndrena Belcher, Dean Alison Boden, Laurie Cannon, Susan Catania, Dr. Mardge Cohen, Tony Fitzpatrick, Tom Geoghegan, Jane Jacobs, Tony Judge, Dennis Hamill, Pete Hamill, Jim Hapgood, Claire Hellstern, Carol Iwata, Jamie Kalven, Soyun Kim, Donna Blue Lachman, Jack Lawrence, Alan Lomax, Bonnie Miller, Erskine Moore, Dick Muelder, Charlie Pachter, Andrea Raila, Bob Rasmus, Florence Scala, Dr. Gordy Schiff, Mary Schmich, Helen Shaver, Dan Terkel, Tish Valva, Rob Warden, Bob and Laura Watson, Yoriko, and Dr. Quentin Young.

To the Chicago Historical Society's president, Lonnie Bunch, and its staff members with whom I work, especially Usama Alshaibi, its demon engineer, who like an alchemist transmuted my slovenly, drossy tapes into gold.

And to the Big Three, who are most responsible for the book that has come forth. Sydney Lewis, who beyond being the transcriber, making sense of my indecipherable hieroglyphics in scrawled hand, was my chief scout and day-to-day colleague, offering invaluable suggestions. Were it not for Tom Engelhardt, the nonpareil of editors, who was uncanny in cutting the fat from the lean (something I found impossible to do) and who gave this work much of its form, I'd still be in the woods. And, of course, to my publisher and editor for thirty-five years, André Schiffrin, who conceived the idea of these 'oral histories' and who has been my cicerone through twelve such adventures, my gratitude.

Introduction

I've courted death ever since I was six. I was an asthmatic child. With each labored breath, each wheeze, came a toy whistle obbligato. At my bedside, my eldest brother, to comfort me, would whistle back 'I'm Forever Blowing Bubbles,' in cadence with my breathing. It was funny, and pleasing, but not much help.

That plus a couple of bouts with mastoiditis, head swathed in bandages, made my awakening the next morning a matter of touch and go. What troubled me was not that I wouldn't make it, but that I would no longer enjoy the whimsical care of my father and my two brothers. My mother was another matter; her hypertense attention more often than not added to my discomfort.

Death itself was too abstract an idea for me then, though I had, in a cursory fashion, become acquainted with the *fact* of death. For a week or so, there had been a warning sign on the door of the adjacent house: SCARLET FEVER. CONTAGIOUS. It was taken down the day after the girl inside died. She was my contemporary. Still, near as she was, I felt somewhat detached, only vaguely saddened. My ailments, though serious, were not of epidemic proportions. Nor did the unfortunate girl have two brothers and a gentle father who brought forth phlegmy laughter.

Of course, I had some difficulty, a fear really, of falling asleep. The idea of counting sheep might have worked had I been the child of a Basque shepherd in Idaho. I really knew nothing about sheep, not that I had anything against them. I was living in Chicago, where a fair south wind blowing in from the stockyards wafted the aroma of slaughtered cattle toward our rooming house on Flournoy Street. No, there was really nothing soporific in counting cows.

My brother, an assiduous newspaper bug, suggested counting celebrated names, names that made headlines. Charlie Chaplin. Caruso. The Bambino. Clara Bow, the 'It' Girl. Peggy Hopkins Joyce. In an inspired moment, he dropped the names of the celebrated lovers Ruth Snyder and Judd Gray, who had just been executed for bopping her husband on the head with a heavy, leaden window sash. Nah. It did nothing for my sleeplessness.

Astonishingly, it was my first awareness of baseball that turned the trick; at least, for a year or two. The Cleveland Indians had beaten the Brooklyn Dodgers in the World Series of 1920. Each night, the names of these new celebrities rolled from my tongue as I signed off. Stanley Coveleski, the Indians' pitcher, who had won three games. Stan-ley Cov-el-es-ki. Six salubrious syllables. The peerless Tris Speaker, who covered center field like a *comfortable quilt.* (A sports writer's apt phrase, my brother informed me.) Bill Wambsganns, the second baseman, who pulled off that unassisted triple play. Wambsganns. The name's slow pronunciation had the pleasant, slumberous effect of a Dutch hot chocolate.★

After a few years, when I had recovered from my childhood ailments, the effects of this nocturnal ritual wore off. Once again, I was in the thrall of sleeplessness. Now, a touch of fear that I might indeed die in my sleep distinctly possessed me. It brought forth a habit that still obsesses me. Whenever I'm about to doze off, I deliberately unclasp my hands and remove them from my breast. Every night. Even now.

Was it that photograph I saw on the front page of the morning Hearst newspaper seventy-eight years ago? The late Pope Benedict XV lay in state. On the catafalque, the pontiff's hands were clasped across his breast. It was the first image I remember of a dead person in a casket. From time to time, my young Catholic friends suggested a prayer. 'If I should die before I wake. . . .' No soap. I didn't want any Lord my soul to take because I obstinately insisted on waking up the next morning.

★Some thirty years later, when a television program with which I was involved, *Studs Place,* went off the air, I received a scrawled, handwritten letter from Cleveland. I remember a passage: 'I am sorry. I enjoyed your program because it gave me a feeling of *heimweh,* an old Dutch word for homesickness. I was once a baseball player. They called me Wamby.' It was signed Bill Wambsganns. I replied, though I neglected to tell him how he had helped me through my insomnia.

Fortunately, at the age of thirteen, I had a young English teacher in my freshman class at McKinley High School. With his scraggly mustache and tubercular mien, he bore a remarkable resemblance to Robert Louis Stevenson. He had assigned us Coleridge's 'The Rime of the Ancient Mariner.' And – bingo! – there was a five-line stanza that did the trick.

> *Oh sleep, thou art a gentle thing*
> *Beloved from pole to pole!*
> *To Mary Queen, the praise be given,*
> *She sent the gentle sleep from Heaven,*
> *That slid into my soul.*

For years, I mumbled those lines before sacking out. And it worked – after a fashion. (Ironically, my young Catholic friends had scored a point. They knew who Mary Queen was; I didn't.)

Now, at eighty-eight, after a quintuple bypass among other medical adventures, those words have lost their charm. Too many of my old friends, contemporaries, have died. Fortunately, I've discovered a new way of popping off to sleep. I count down the names of those departed buddies. Unfortunately, the list has grown exponentially during these last few years. Amend that: every month, every week, I spot more familiar names in the obituary columns.

Mordant though it may sound, it's not an unpleasant way of sacking out. I recall funny stories, jokes, and even imagined amours, especially after a few drinks, say, at Riccardo's, a favorite watering hole in Chicago, but now transmogrified into an 'in' place for Generation X. I have a good number of young friends, who are delightful company, generous-hearted, witty, and all that. Yet, there is that slight ache – *heimweh*, as Bill Wambsganns put it.

My fellow octogenarian Charlie Andrews explains: 'Have you heard the one about the old sport who married a much younger woman? It worked for a couple of years. One day, a mutual friend encounters him. The old boy informs him that they've split up. "She didn't know the songs."' My young friends do my heart good every time I see them, but they don't know the songs.

Naturally, when I pick up a newspaper these days, the first place I turn to isn't sports, or arts, or the business of business, or the op-eds. I immediately turn to the obituaries. The old doggerel with which many mature readers may be acquainted has replaced Coleridge as my mantra.

> I wake up each morning and gather my wits,
> I pick up the paper and read the obits.
> If my name is not in it, I know I'm not dead,
> So I eat a good breakfast and go back to bed.

This is the one book I never thought I'd write. It was too big for me; too abstract. It was more in the domain of the metaphysician or the minister. Yet the idea was put forth some thirty years ago.

Was it 1970? '71? Gore Vidal, at the Ambassador East Hotel bar in Chicago, suggested death as the subject for a book. I stared into my drink. No bells rang. My works had been concerned with life and its uncertainties rather than death and its indubitable certainty.

In all my books, my informants – mostly the uncelebrated, heroes of the 'ordinary' – had recounted, in their own words, the lives they had lived, the epochs they had survived. How did it feel to be a certain person in a certain circumstance at a certain time in our country's twentieth century? During the Great American Depression, what was it like to be that twelve-year-old boy seeing his father trudge home at eleven in the morning with his toolchest over his shoulder only to become an idler for the next ten years? During World War II, what was it like to be the mama's boy sitting tight in that landing craft crossing the English Channel, heading for Normandy? What was daily worklife like for the schoolteacher, the waitress, the spotwelder or the storekeeper? What did blacks in our society really think of whites or the other way around? How did the elders feel as they grew even more so in a society where their power ebbed as their span increased?

These were challenges I could handle, for better or worse – something I could put my hands on. In recalling actual experiences, my colleagues, the true authors of these works, found their own eloquence and poetry. Words from the seemingly inarticulate flowed like wine. At times they were as astonished as I was.

Consider the young mother in the public project. It was an

integrated complex of the poor. I can't recall whether she was white or black. The conversation took place in the sixties. The tape recorder had not yet become the household tool it is today. Her three little kids were hopping around, demanding to hear Mama's voice on tape. I played it back. As she caught her words, she gasped. Hand touching mouth, she murmured: 'I never knew I felt that way . . .' Bingo! A score for me as well as for her. An experience recounted, a revelation to oneself.

But what about the one experience none of us has had, yet all of us will have: death? Now in my late eighties, Gore Vidal's challenge of some thirty years ago had come back to haunt me. What is there to remember of a time and place at which none of us has yet arrived? Boy – what a challenge! I no longer stared at my drink. I downed the martini and the bells began to ring.

In what follows, you may be as astonished as I was, while scrounging around, to discover that we reflect on death like crazy much of our lives. The storytellers here, once started on the subject, can't stop. They *want* to talk about it; whether it be grief or guilt or a fusing of both on the part of the survivors; or thoughts about the hereafter – is it is or is it ain't? You'll hear voices offering all sorts of opinions: some are believers, others put forth the challenge, 'show me.'

For so many there's a recurring refrain, 'I'm not religious, I'm spiritual,' as though they sought separation from the institution, yet, as individuals, truly believed.

Invariably, those who have a faith, whether it is called religious or spiritual, have an easier time with loss. They find solace in believing there is a something after – that they will in some way, in some form, again meet or even merge with the departed one. Nonbelievers have no such comfort. They go with Gertrude Stein's observation in another context: 'There is no there there.' Nada.

All of the doctors I have come to know and respect, including my cardiologist, my surgeon, and my internist,★ have urged me to undertake this project. We, as a matter of course, reflect on death,

★Quentin Young has been our family doctor for the last forty years. I'm certain that his ebullience, his spirit of bonhomie, and his skills have been key factors in my living far beyond my traditionally allotted span.

voice hope and fear, only when a dear one is near death, or out of it. Why not speak of it while we're in the flower of good health? How can we envision our life, the one we *now* experience, unless we recognize that it is finite?

It is a sweet irony that my first book of the twenty-first century (possibly my last) is about death. Yet these testimonies are also about life and its pricelessness, offering visions, inchoate though they be, of a better one down here – and, possibly, up there.

My father and two brothers died in their mid-fifties. Angina. Bad tickers. I had a touch of it, too. It was in our genes, I guess. My mother, a tough little sparrow, fought out her last days in a nursing home. She hung up her gloves at eighty-seven.

From my fifties into my mid-eighties, the sublingual nitro pills were mother's milk to me. Whenever that tight fist would punch or grab at my left side, I'd slip a nitro under my tongue and all would be well. For a time. I still carry that tiny bottle in my side pocket. In 1996, while I was watching the Chicago Bulls and the Seattle Sonics in the NBA finals, a sharp zing stabbed me. It ran crazily up and down my left arm. I was perspiring freely and coldly.

The next day's angiogram was not that great. My arteries were a mess. My doctors were of one mind: unless something was immediately done, I had maybe six months to live. A quintuple bypass was suggested. *Quintuple!* I was impressed, though somewhat disturbed because I was in the middle of work on a new book.

'What are the odds?' Very good, the surgeon assured me. He had performed this one a number of times. He said something about ten-to-one in my favor. I liked those odds, and the procedure worked. Since 1996 there has been no sign of the fist, let alone the zing, and I've yet to touch the tiny nitro bottle. Of course, I'm aware that mortality is lurking just around the corner, waiting to pounce. One of my carotid arteries is shot, the other hangs in there barely, if obstinately. Stroke, stay away from my door – at least for now.

All in all, it's been a good run. Going on eighty-nine, I was born the year the *Titanic* went down. Who would want to live to be ninety? Churchill is reputed to have replied: 'Everyone who is eighty-nine.'

We are a greedy lot, aren't we? We old ones secretly sing the words of a little-known bard, Ralph Hodgson:

> *Time, you old gipsy man,*
> *Will you not stay,*
> *Put up your caravan*
> *Just for one day?*

These days I think constantly of my father and brothers. They died in what should have been their prime. I, the favored, sickly little child they loved (as did my mother in her own wild way), have had so much the better of it. Though I grieved when each of my brothers died, my father's death, the first in our family, brought upon me a heartache that was too much to bear.

At the rooming house my mother ran, my father was the invalid, bedridden much of the time. I shared that bed with him all of my preadolescent years. In New York, before he was stricken, my father had been a fine tailor. My mother, always nimble with her fingers and more so with her mind, was a magnificent seamstress. I still see her on her knee, pins in her mouth, fitting a neighbor woman into a new gown. I still see my father coming home from the sanitarium, wan, fatigued, gallant, insisting on going back to work. It was not in the cards.

In 1920, we headed out for the territories. Chicago. A fairly well-off uncle funded us into leasing a rooming house on the city's near West Side. It was in the heart of Chicago's huge hospital complex. Among our guests were student nurses, interns, a barber, and a hooker. She was a kid from Terre Haute. She was prohibited from having gentlemen callers. No tricks on these premises.

My mother was a cross between a harried Ruth Gordon and Eliza Gant, the mother in *Look Homeward, Angel.* I was bowled over reading it. Thomas Wolfe's mother, Eliza, was a dead ringer for mine, Annie. Eliza's boardinghouse in Asheville was Annie's rooming house in Chicago. They were both sparrowy, tough, and prevailing: living life at its flood tide. Too excessively, perhaps.

We had a crystal radio set, my father and I. It was at our bedside. Fooling around with that cat's-whisker wire scratched against the lump of silvery mineral, we caught Wendell Hall, the Red-Headed

Music Maker, on KYW, singing 'It Ain't Gonna Rain No More.' He played the ukulele.

We heard Hal Totten, on WGN, coming at us from Dayton, Tennessee; we caught fragments of the Monkey Trial. I swear we heard the voices of Clarence Darrow and William Jennings Bryan. Day after day after day, we followed the ordeal of Floyd Collins, the unlucky guide who was freakily trapped in Kentucky's Mammoth Caves.* Sharing the earphones, my father one and I the other, we were radio-hip to all that was going on. In 1925, the rooming house was sold. After a brief family breakup, my father refused to play the invalid any further, ailing heart or no. He leased a men's hotel on the near North Side, the Wells-Grand. For five years, even into the Crash of '29, he gallantly made a go of it. With considerations from our McKinley-Republican landlord, Henry L. Flentye, a fair man who admired my father's stick-to-it-iveness, we were making it toughly. Suddenly, in 1931, my father died.

It was I who found him in bed, his spectacles askew. It was the day we had planned to visit Mr. Flentye's three-step-down bare office on North LaSalle. 'H.F.' was feelingly fond of my old man. He was to offer more concessions. The new contract had already been written in Palmer penmanship longhand and was only waiting to be signed.

I was remarkably calm until, seated on the Grand Avenue street-car the next day, heading nowhere in particular, I surprised myself by breaking into uncontrollable sobs. Embarrassed, seeking to stifle them, blubbering despite myself, I hurried toward the rear of the car, ready to hop off anywhere, just to escape my show of grief.

It was not until sixty-eight years later — after up-and-down experiences as actor, disc jockey, radio commentator, book writer — that I was to experience a grief far deeper, though my manifestation of it was more muted.

*WGN's Hal Totten broadcast this one, too, earlier in the same year, 1925. It was a blow-by-blow account of Collins's twelve-day ordeal as rescuers tried to reach him. They were within earshot, but failed as another cave-in occurred. Both events, the trial and the guide's fate, were celebrated in songs by Vernon Dalhart, the most popular country singer of the twenties, in 'The Death of Floyd Collins' and a plaintive encomium to the martyred Bryan.

Those memories of streetcar grief came back to me when Antoinette Korotko-Hatch, a woman I was interviewing for this book, described an incident on a bus in which she came to the aid of a man having a heart attack. 'People on the bus,' she said, 'were mumbling about being late to work. I told the driver, "Get these people off the bus, tell them to take another one."' The man, she told me, though in pain, 'didn't want to be trouble.' He was embarrassed that he was 'holding up the whole bus.'

That man's embarrassment touched off the memory of that nineteen-year-old boy so uncomfortable at daring to grieve out loud for his father. Everything about this book became, unexpectedly for me, a journey into long-suppressed memories and all sorts of ambivalences in feeling of which I wasn't aware.

In her memoir of her mother's death, Myra MacPherson refers to 'disenfranchised grief.' During an interview, she said, 'I fell in this category. It means you're not supposed to feel it, certainly not supposed to show it. I was in my late fifties when my mother died. She was eighty-one. People came up with the usual platitudes. "After all, she lived a good life," "You shouldn't feel so full of grief."

'That's bullshit. That's why we really can't handle death very well. We want sort of drive-by grieving. Nobody wants you to carry on about it. They want you to deposit it like you do in a bank.'★

On December, 23, 1999, as I was beginning work on this book, my wife, Ida, died. She had been my companion for sixty years. She was eighty-seven. A few months later, a friend of mine, disturbed by my occasional despondency, burst out: 'For chrissake, you've had sixty great years with her!' Myra MacPherson was on the button.

Ida was seventeen years beyond her traditionally allotted time of three score and ten. On occasion, I'd hear her murmur in surprise, 'Why do I still feel like a girl?'

They were roller-coaster years we shared, since I first spotted her in a maroon smock. 1937. She had been a social worker during most of those tumultuous years: the Great Depression, World War II, the Cold War, Joe McCarthy, the sixties, the civil rights and peace movements. She had been, as they say, 'involved.' Garry Wills remembers

★Myra MacPherson, *She Came to Live Out Loud: An Intimate Family Journey Through Illness, Loss, and Grief* (New York: Scribner, 1999).

her greeting him, years after the Vietnam War had ended: 'Oh, we were arrested together in Washington.'

A year or so before her death, Laura Watson, a neighbor, 'looked out the window and saw this slim young girl in jeans, with a flower in her hair, plucking out weeds in her garden.' The girl looked up. 'It was Ida, of course.' Gwendolyn Brooks's bet: 'She could dance on a moonbeam.'

Yeah, she did live to the ripe old age of eighty-seven, but it doesn't cut the mustard, Charlie. I still see that girl in the maroon smock who liked yellow daisies.

Each week, there is a fresh bunch of yellow daisies near the windowsill. On the sill is the urn with her ashes. On occasion, either indignant about something or somewhat enthused, I mumble toward it (her): 'Whaddya think of that, kid?' Her way of seeing things had always been so clear-eyed. . . .

We've had one child, a son. Dan has become the good companion, the troubleshooter, the rock. There's a *lied* Lotte Lehmann sang, of a mountainside against which you lean when weary or bereft. My son is that mountainside.

One last personal note: The sixty-three heroes of this book, in offering me their bone-deep, honest testimonies, have been a palliative beyond prescription.

There was something of a 'poem' fraudulently attributed to Gabriel García Márquez. The novelist was understandably indignant. Nonetheless, the words of some ersatz philosopher, coffee-house pundit, or practical joker suit me fine at this moment:

I would teach the old that death does not come with old age, but with forgetting. . . . I would walk when others hold back, I would wake when others sleep, I would listen when others talk, and how I would enjoy good chocolate ice cream.

Hopefully, that's what this book is about: death, of course, but only by living to the full its long prelude, life.

PROLOGUE

Brothers

TOM GATES

A Brooklyn firefighter (retired).* During his earlier work years, he was a policeman. His words pour forth, stream-of-consciously.

I'm sixty years old! I just made a will out, and I feel *much* better. My son's going to be a lawyer and my daughter works in a courthouse in Pennsylvania – she's going to college. That's what I'm looking forward to, the kids.

Life and death? I never felt so alive as when you're a firefighter. To go into a fire with the heat and the fear and people's lives on the line . . . I remember sometime in July or August, summer, you'd be coming out of the fire and the sweat would be pouring off you, and you'd taste cold water and it was the greatest taste in the world. Better than any drugs, which I don't know anything about, but I know about cold beer and cold water and nothing beats it.

When you're dead, you don't know you're dead, right? So what's the big thing really, when you think about it? The ones that suffer are your family and your friends. They're going to be suffering with your memory.

I remember in 1956, when I was sixteen years old, we saw this man crying on a park bench. Prospect Park. He was about forty-one. He had a beard. We went over to him. 'What are you crying for?' He said, 'I just lost my mom.' We asked, 'How old's your mom?' 'Sixty-four.' We started laughing. 'Sixty-four – that's old! She lived a long time.' He looked up at us and said, 'Listen, it doesn't matter if your mother's sixty-four or a hundred and four, when she passes away, you're going to miss your mom. Don't forget what I'm saying.'

In 1981, I was coming out of the firehouse and there were these

---

*I first met him twenty-seven years ago. He appeared in *Working*, along with his brother Bob, a police officer, and his father, Harold.

teenagers hanging around the corner. I went over and told them to take a civil service test, become a firefighter or a policeman. You get security, you get a pension, and there's no better job than serving the public. As I walked away, another kid came over and asked his friends on the stoop, 'What'd the old man want?' Meaning *me!* It brought back the past, 1956, the forty-one-year-old man with the beard. . . . It was like a flashback. I turned around and said, 'Listen, like they say: as I am now, so shall you be.'

To me, life is like a relay race. You're tired, you hand the baton off to somebody stronger and fresher. That's what life is, right? The oldest thing in a human being is sperm, right? Sperm goes back to the beginning of time. I got a son now and a daughter, and they're going to carry on. Somebody said that the Earth is a spaceship and sometimes the ride, like yours, Studs, is lasting eighty-eight years. Me, I'm on a spaceship ride called Earth sixty years. Some people only ride it for one day. So we're lucky.

When you're sixteen, you don't know about death. Your friends are young, your aunts and uncles are only in their late thirties, forties. As I get older, half my friends are gone. My aunts and uncles are passing away. My father passed away, colon cancer, 1988. He was eighty-one years old. Before he died, he lived with me for two months. I got one of those wind-up beds. I'd wind him up and I'd lay down on the couch right across from him. A couple of nights before he died, every fifteen minutes he woke up, swung off the bed, and lit a Camel cigarette. He took two puffs, put it out. Five minutes later, Camel cigarette. All night. I said, 'What the fuck is *this?*' I don't want to curse, but I was going crazy. I said, 'Stop smoking.' He looked at me and said, 'You see the clock up there?' I said, 'What clock?' It was dark – four in the morning. He said, 'I was born at twelve o'clock. The hands are coming around and my time is coming to an end, and it's going to end at twelve o'clock.' It was unbelievable.

He was five-foot-six, a powerful man, a truck driver, longshoreman, a father – he was everything. He went from a hundred and fifty pounds down to seventy-eight. I remember changing his bag, cleaning it, and he was so embarrassed. I said, 'Dad, it's good in a way because it saves on toilet paper.' He ran out of the bathroom laughing. He said, 'Catch me if you can!' He was running around the kitchen and I was running after him. It was the first time I saw my father's legs in eighty-one years. They were skinny, the same size as mine.

I was up all night for days and days and I was starting to get mad because he was taking the life from me. I'm telling you honest, I loved my father – he was a great man.* He was just wasting away, wasn't eating . . . One night he was breathing hard and then he stopped. He was panting, then nothing for five or ten minutes. I said, 'Oh, my God, he's dead.' I relaxed. I says, 'I'm not telling anybody. I'll notify the family in the morning.' I wanted to close my eyes and get a few hours' sleep because I was exhausted. Just then, he started breathing again, I said, 'Son of a bitch!' That was my human feeling – I got pissed. He lasted two more days. I felt guilty, but I know he would have said the same thing. If it was me, I'd just want to let go, pull the plug – 'cause I don't want my family, friends, to suffer. My mother was in her seventies at the time. She's still alive at eighty-eight. I saw her starting to go. We're all going into the hole. A friend of mine committed suicide by Blockbuster. His wife and his son died. He kept renting videos all day and all night and just drinking liquor, scotch. They found him with the VCR running. He was only in his fifties.

When you're above ground and you're healthy it's great. My father used to have an old picture with all his friends on a Model-T Ford, sitting in the back on the rumble seat and on the step of the car. He was telling me, 'This fellow's gone, this fellow's in the hospital, this fellow's dead.' I said, 'Dad, you're sad.' He said, 'It's gonna happen to you. But it's great to live long because you're gonna outlive your enemies!'

I'll always have memories of my father. I was in a place in Pennsylvania and I saw a man that looked like my father. He was smoking a Camel cigarette and my father loved to blow the smoke in the air. It was like a dance. This guy had his back to me and he had a hat like my father, same size. I said, 'That's my dad!' I sat there and I looked at him, knowing my father's dead and the memories

*As a longshoreman, Harold Gates, a union man, was one of the independents who fought the thugs on the New York waterfront. He was the hero of a novel by the poet Thomas McGrath.

come back – old smells, old songs. Then he got up and he wasn't my father.

Like you, Studs – you look like my father. You know what I mean? I want to interview you. When are you gonna give it up? You're eighty-eight years old! *Unbelievable* . . . The great medicine now, you can go for ninety or a hundred. But you gotta have your faculties. You gotta be able to walk and talk and chew, enjoy food. That's the great joy of life, food and companionship and laughter. Laughter shoots chemicals into your blood . . .

Funny thing, memories. Looking back now, my mother was really the strength in the family. Five kids, and my mother kept us together. My father, he took off a number of times, but your mother's *always* there.

Let's talk about firefighters. January, 1976. I was on vacation when Charlie Sanchez and nine guys from my firehouse went into the basement of an A&P. Charlie Sanchez got killed, and they thought the other eight were dead. They heard the firemen crying for their mothers on the walkie-talkies and the guys outside were crying, too. The fire commissioner come down and said to give up, they were dead, turn off the walkie-talkies. They told the fire commissioner to get the fuck out of there. They're doing their job. They breached the wall with a battering ram, sixteen inches of brick. In the 1800s it had been a prison room for slaves. They grabbed the eight firemen and dragged them through the hole.

I went to the hospital and I remember Paul Matula, a big Polish guy – senior man, Ladder 131. Tremendous hands. I said to him, 'Paul, did you talk to God?' I don't believe really in churches. To me, churches is business – but there could be somebody out there. Paul said, 'Listen, I thought I was dying, so I gave God a couple of shouts.' You couldn't do better than that.

Gordon Sepper, the carbon monoxide was getting to him, and the smoke, he was falling asleep, his head down, knowing he was going. Just then, he says, a twenty-four-foot portable ladder appeared and he knew he could be saved. So he started reaching up, climbing up the rungs, and when he got to the top rung, his brain told his hand to grab the floor of the A&P there, because he was all carbon-monoxide-to-the-brain disorientated, right? Just then two firemen grabbed him by the coat and pulled him out. Another guy was Joe

Pennington. When the A&P was collapsing into the basement, Joe counted eighteen steps to the street – he knew enough to count the steps. They went down eighteen steps in the basement next door and breached the wall. I look up to those men. It was the greatest job you can ever have, a fireman . . .

Most firemen die after they retire, eight to ten years earlier than the general population. Cancer, emphysema, stuff like that. Smoke inhalation – it's cumulative. The chemicals, the plastics burn. My brother Billy was thirty-five years a firefighter – he's got a disability. He can't breathe. He's got asthma, emphysema – he never smoked. He was a marathon runner, twenty-six miles.

It's even worse than with the miners, who get everything, black lung, cave-ins, everything. I'm going with a woman whose father was a coal miner in Scranton, Pennsylvania. When she was a little girl, she remembers her father coming home with one finger chopped off from a mine accident. He took the finger, still in his glove, and threw it into the fireplace. A few days later, he went back to work . . . We've come a long way since then, but they're still my heroes, working-class people. My father instilled that in me.

I remember August 2nd, 1978. Six firemen got killed in Brooklyn. Louise O'Connor, with three kids, went to see her husband at the firehouse near Sheepshead Bay. They were going for a weekend down to the Jersey Shore . . . Just a routine fire. Her husband was on the roof of the Ward Bond grocery – he waved to her as the roof caved in.

I was on vacation walking on a country road. My father came running down. 'Six firemen just got killed.' It's like being at war and you're home. I said, 'I gotta go in. I gotta go in.' My wife says, 'Why do you gotta go in?' Because, I told her, this is my family, my second family. She said, 'You gotta stay here.' I said, 'No, I gotta go in.' I went in the shower. I didn't want her to see me cry. I put the water on and started screaming, '*Fuck! Fuck! Fuck!*' I went in and was missing for three days. I went to as many funerals as I could – 'cause it was two, three different churches. That was twenty-two years ago.

I ran into Louise O'Connor again in 1988 at the American Legion Post where another guy killed in a fire was being honored. She introduces me to her son, who's now a New York City cop. I said, 'That kid was a couple of years old when your husband got killed.' So the beat goes on. It never ends.

I hate guns. I wasn't a good cop because I used to walk around with no bullets in the chamber. I used to have them in my pocket and kid around saying if somebody starts in, I'll just throw the bullets real hard. [*Laughs*]

A few times I pulled my gun on guys. One time I went on the roof of this project and there's this big black guy, about six-seven, on top of the stairs. He had his back to me. I said, 'Hey, fella, turn around.' He said, 'Yeah, wait a minute, man.' I said, '*Turn around* and put your hands against the wall.' He said, 'Yeah, yeah, wait a minute.' It dawned on me he had a gun caught in his belt and was tryin' to take it out. I said, 'Holy shit . . .' So I took my gun out and said, 'You fucker, I'm gonna shoot.' He threw his hands up against the wall. He had his dick out and was tryin' to zip up his fly, and there was a girl standing in the corner, which I couldn't see. So here was a guy gettin' a hand job and maybe a lot of guys would have *killed* him. I said, 'Holy shit, I coulda killed ya.' He started shaking and the gun in my hand was shaking like a bastard. I said – I musta been cryin' – I said, 'Just get the hell outa here . . .' That's when I decided to quit the force and become a fireman.

My brother Billy was a fireman five years before me. He said, 'It's a different quality of life – it's great.' He was in a fire in a high-rise, knocking out windows in the bathroom. The bathtub gave way and he fell through the floor. They teach you when you fall to put your elbows out to your side. He caught on to the floor and the firemen come in and grabbed him. He said, 'No, let me go, I'll fall to the next floor and I don't want to take you with me.' The two firemen said, 'If you go, we all go' – that's the job.

I retired from the fire department in '88 and as a fire safety director in '95. Now it's just a memory. I just sit back and watch the world go by. Talk about dying – it affects everything I do. I feel life is like the twenty-four-second clock in a basketball game. I got the ball now and I gotta score. By scoring, I mean I want to travel, see the world more. I got twenty-four seconds left and I want to stretch it out. But if they hook up tubes to you and you're on a monitor and unconscious for months, they gotta be kidding. I'm outa here. Twenty-four seconds ran out.

We had a great fire captain, Bill Huber. When he passed away, I went to his wake, his funeral. He had a simple pine box, closed, with a picture on top of him in a fire uniform. That's what I want. In red pajamas, fire red. Then I want to be cremated. I want my ashes to be thrown into a beautiful pond in Jersey. I want somebody to sing 'I'll Be Seeing You.' [*Sings*]

> In all the old familiar places
> that this heart of mine embraces
> all night through
> I'll see you . . .

Isn't that wonderful? All the old girlfriends, the old neighborhood . . .

I remember years ago, a Laurel and Hardy movie, they're in the First World War. Hardy says, 'If we get killed, what do you want to come back as?' Laurel says, 'I want to come back as myself.' Hardy gets mad: 'You stupid, you can't come back as yourself, you have to come back as something else. You're gonna come back as a donkey.' They both get killed and Hardy comes back as a donkey.

I always said I'd like to come back as myself but with a great voice like Johnny Mathis or Tony Bennett. Well, this one time, I got off the subway train at Seventy-ninth by mistake, and there's a black man about fifty, in rags, with a bag to put money in, singing 'My Funny Valentine.' He sounded like Sammy Davis, Jr., a beautiful voice – unbelievable. I'm saying, *Holy Jesus* – I just wanted to come back as myself with a great voice and you can end up on the goddamn IRT, penniless.

Right now, I'm OK. My hearing's going, I got a ringing. My eyesight's going. The thing I still got left is my taste buds – I still love food.

These days I get out of a car like my father used to get out: grab the roof and pull yourself out. I got a bad back. My father passed the baton on to me, and I'm passing it on to my kids.

I'm not going to worry about any hereafter. A few months ago, my sister got a call at one in the morning. The police told her that they found her husband dead in bed. They were divorced, but they still loved each other and called each other up every day on the phone. I drove her in about two in the morning. My sister told me she had a dream a couple of days before that there was a hand coming out to her. I went into the bedroom where her husband was laying and he had his arm outstretched. My sister is strong, they got two sons. He was a young man, fifty-five. Like I said, it's a spaceship and we gotta keep going on.

So, here I am, a retired firefighter who almost died from drowning in the ocean. It was 1994, I was down in Bermuda, walking along this beach, hardly anyone in the water. It was a beautiful day. I went in. I'm not a good swimmer. Before I knew it, I was dragged out in the tide. It was up to my chest. The lifeguard was on a hill, couldn't hear me scream. I figured this was it, I'm going to die in Bermuda. Everything went through my head, the kids, memories – it's all over. The water was way past my chest and dragging me out. So I took a deep breath and dived toward the beach. My legs were kicking, hands moving, hoping when I came down I wasn't stepping on water, and when I got to the beach, I was like . . . [gasps] . . . heavy breathing. Barely made it. That was 1994. I'm sixty years old and I have a second chance. Yeah, I think about death more and more, but I can't do nothing about it. It's gonna come. Suppose somebody said, 'You can be alive forever, but you gotta drive through the Holland Tunnel for the rest of your life'? What would you do? Would you want to live forever driving through the Holland Tunnel?

BOB GATES

Tom's brother. He is sixty-one. A New York City police officer, retired for thirteen years, he was a member of the Emergency Service and then joined the Police Crime Unit, the homicide squad.

> Emergency Service is like a rescue squad. You respond to any call, any incident: a man under a train, trapped in an auto, bridge jumpers, floaters, psychos, guys that murdered people and then barricaded themselves in. We go and get these people out. It was sometimes a little too exciting. On a couple of incidents I felt I wasn't going to come home.

Ever hear of the Statue of Liberty job? We had a guy climb to the top of the statue, break through the center port window of the head, and stand on the top of the crown. For over an hour. He's there for a cause, and he's jeopardizing our lives by doing so. He was threatening to jump from the crown to the head.

After speaking to him for a while, my partner and I saw an opportunity and pinned him down, handcuffed him, and held on. We were tied in through a rope, but the tie was below us. If he had thrown either of us off, just the stress from the rope would have killed us.

Did I mention the World Trade Center job? That's a hundred and ten stories high. We had a guy, he defeated the tower security system. There was a rabbi there, with a priest on the way. The guy had climbed over the top of the World Trade Center and dropped approximately a foot onto a window washer's ledge, which was about four inches wide. My partner and I were looking down from above, trying to talk him into coming in. His problem is he was born a Jew and is now a Christian. He was mad at the Jews because, he claimed, they were responsible for the crucifixion of Christ. I said to him, 'Well, suppose they'd only sentenced him to seven and a half to fifteen years? We wouldn't be Catholics today.' He said to the rabbi, 'I'd like that officer to come down and talk with me.' They rappelled me over. I kept on talking to him. As I handed him a cigarette, I grabbed him in a bear hug and we both swung over, up on top of the World Trade Center. Besides being dangerous, it was *such* a beautiful sight . . . At a hundred and ten stories up, the East River is a half-inch wide. Talking to him, I just wanted to concentrate on him not grabbing me. I wasn't sure if he had a knife. At that point, it was life-threatening. I thought briefly about dying, but I had partners there to back me up – and it happened so fast.

You don't have time to have fear because you have to prepare psychologically, get focused on what you're gonna do – you got a job to do. With the sirens and the lights around, you're thinking about equipment, about who's gonna get the rope, who's gonna wear the Morrissey Belt, that looks like a safety pin . . . You're so hyped up, keyed up, you can feel and hear your own heart beating.

If it's a barricaded psycho, and he's got a gun and he's threatening to go out and kill somebody, you're focused on that person, on not killing him. They don't like the word 'kill' anymore – you're gonna *stop* 'em. But you're there to try and save his life. If not, you have to take other measures.

You always look at them as another human being. You try to get into a conversation and tell him what he's giving up, find out if he has a family. Sometimes it's not so good if he has a family, 'cause they're the ones he could be mad at. When they show up, that's when he may jump, or shoot himself.

Then there's the floater that drowns and eventually comes up. We pulled this kid out of the pond. You look at him with the hook in his eye. A woman asked me, 'What color was he?' I said, 'Lady, he's ten years old – what *difference* does it make?' She said, 'You pulled him out, you should know.' I just walked away from her. It never entered my mind whether he was white or black. He was a life that had to be saved, but it was too late. And people that hang themselves . . . if the body's there for a certain period of time, it decomposes. Sometimes we call that 'the smell of death.' You come into an apartment, the body's been there for a couple of weeks, and the acids are floating through the air. The body swells up and the gases inside penetrate the air and stick in your nostrils while you're cutting the person down. Maybe people should ride with emergency service, get into the shoes of a cop and see what it's like, see what they go through. The average life span of a cop today is fifty-nine years old – twelve years short of an average person.

Death . . . The most vivid case in my mind is a space case I had. A guy was caught by the train and rolled between the platform and the train. When we got there, the transit police were in conversation with him. He had a family, several children. He was caught in a four-inch space. The reason he was still alive is because everything was still intact above, keeping his heart pumping blood into his system. So you could converse with him while he was sitting there. There wasn't much else you could do. The medical people said the minute that we start to jack this train away from the platform, he would pass away. You could almost predict his death, but meanwhile you're talking to him.

I thought about the family as we jacked the car away from the platform with what we call a journal jack. You fit it between the supports of the train, the subway car, and the platform. As you start jacking, it pushes the train away from the platform, giving you another six inches to take the body out. The body is rolled like a bowling pin. He just went off to sleep, he passed away right there. Was he wondering, 'What are they gonna do to get me out? What's the story here?' I was talking to him: 'We're doing the best we can.' 'I don't feel my legs . . .' 'We're handling that now – we got people under the train . . . Where do you work?' – just questions to take his mind off what was happening.

We get to go in where your heart is pumping, your adrenaline is running and you've got your hand just off the hair trigger. You're in there because this is your job, and if you have to kill you will – but you don't want to. You have fear of accidentally pulling the trigger. You think about these fears afterwards. If you can save a life, you'll save that life. Thinking about the death end of it and your safety end of it usually comes after.

Since the time I first met you, I found spiritual solace and guidance. I stop off in church once in a while now. I believe in the hereafter. Yeah. But I have questions, too. Why do young people have to die? Why do people have to threaten to kill themselves?

One of the jobs I had was a private house where a man placed a twelve-gauge shotgun under his chin and blew his head off. Half of it went onto the ceiling and half onto the walls. We had to take the photographs and notes. I noticed the serenity of a death scene, how quiet. I was writing notes on this body, sitting at the kitchen table, when part of the skull and face drops onto the table and onto my shoulders. All I said to myself was that it was raining death, *raining death* in that kitchen. Sometimes you're a little annoyed because if somebody is going to kill themselves, why do they want to make such a mess? If they're gonna do it, if they made up their minds . . . [*Suddenly*] Police officers are one of the highest rates of suicides in the country – because of the strain, the stress, the problems. I knew a guy that committed suicide, a cop. I went to the scene. He was on top of the stairwell. He had a picture of his wife and kids leaning against the wall, and he shot himself in the head.

I never had that thought, thank God. But if I ever get to that point where they put the tubes in me, and the IVs, and I'm gonna vegetate, I want to have mind enough to tell them, 'Pull the plug.' If I'm put in an old-age home and I still got my faculties, I want my kids to bring me up some chocolate chip cookies, wipe my mouth, and wheel me out of the sun.

PART I

Doctors

Dr. Joseph Messer

Chief of cardiology at Rush–St. Luke's–Presbyterian Hospital in Chicago. Former chairman of the Board of Governors of the American College of Cardiologists.

I was born in 1931. Watertown, South Dakota, is thirty miles west of the Minnesota border. I lived there until I left to go to college in 1949.

Dad was an undertaker. It had been the family profession for five generations: all the way back to cabinetmakers in Maine. They were the ministers, the circuit riders who marked the trees for molasses. This was the 1600s . . . Their interest in wood led them to become cabinetmakers.

In small towns, the furniture business and the undertaking business were the same people. My father's father, going back several generations, had been in this business. My dad left it, being more interested in banking and finance. It was while traveling through Watertown that he ran into the town banker, who offered him a job. He married the banker's daughter. An interesting coincidence: my mother's side of the family were in the funeral business. My father gave up his banking interests and ended up in the funeral part of it. So I was raised as an undertaker's son.

We used to play in the chapel where the services were held, run up and down the aisles. I loved to play the piano. When I was about ten, eleven, my dad got a Hammond organ for the funeral chapel – I *loved* to play that. I was always admonished that I had to play somber music. A few times I would accompany my father – he had a beautiful voice – when he sang the old hymns at funerals.

By the time I was ten, I was working there after school, taking care of the hearses, the limousines. I attended a lot of funerals and, in time, I drove the coaches and the ambulances. In those smaller towns, the funeral directors ran the ambulances because the hearses were convertible. This was before the days of paramedics.

I grew up with grief, though I didn't experience it because I wasn't part of the grieving families. Having people die was a part of the life that I lived. I remember the enormous respect my father had for the deceased – he insisted that anyone in the funeral home share that respect. That was one of the important influences in my life. I remember going with my father to farmhouses where people had died. I would help with what we called 'removals.' He was on one end of the stretcher and I would be at the other end. I would watch my father interact with the relatives of the deceased, who were in grief. He treated people of all economic and social classes the same. I'm sure that watching him with people under stress, more than any other lesson, helped me become a good doctor – I hope . . .

I don't believe that I really felt grief until the boy who lived across the street was killed in World War II. I was about eleven, twelve. He was a wonderful young man. When we learned that he had been killed, it really struck home. It's my first memory of true grieving.

My father's real goal in life was to be a physician. He actually started to go to medical school, but had to drop out because his father contracted tuberculosis – not an uncommon disease in those days. That's what led him into business, supporting the family. He clearly had great respect for physicians.

I think he has lived out that desire vicariously to some extent because my brother and I became physicians; he's four years older. We were learning the bones of the body when we were six. I knew every bone in the body when I was seven or eight. He had all sorts of medical textbooks. He would teach me about blood vessels and veins and arteries. I saw him embalm many times. Preservative chemicals infused in order to replace the blood lost so that the remains could be preserved.

My brother and I were really programmed to be doctors. It turns out that my daughter, my dad's granddaughter, is a physician. [*Laughs softly*] I tried not to unduly influence her – I didn't program her.

My father was clearly trying to influence our career choices. I arrived at college with blinders on. There was only one thing I was going to do and that was to be a doctor. I probably missed out on some other things I might have been interested in . . .

Our major medical influence, our citadel, was the Mayo Clinic. That's where everyone from South Dakota went when they were seriously ill. I made innumerable ambulance trips for my dad from Watertown to Mayo. Lots of long-distance driving, about 375 miles. My dad was very interested in handicapped children. He had the dream that my brother, now deceased, and I would have the Messer Clinic, modeled after Mayo.

My brother was in the army toward the very end of World War II. He had heard of a place on the East Coast called Harvard – it was just a name to us in Watertown. We were going to go to the University of Minnesota, of course. But my brother decided on Harvard, much to my father's dismay. My mother said, 'If he wants to go there, let him.' I went to Harvard College, too. I stayed there for medical school, for my residency, and for my fellowship in cardiology.

After that, I worked at Wright Patterson Air Force Base. This was in the days of the astronauts – doing studies to get them up into space. Sputnik had gone up, and we were in a race with the Russians. I worked on human centrifuge – gravity and G-force. We would spin people around. That's how you simulated the tremendous G-forces of a rocket. It was a wonderful experience.

I went back to the Boston City Hospital, one of my favorite institutions in cardiology. Then I came here to Chicago, to be chief of cardiology at Rush.*

During the first eighteen years or so of my life, I looked at death as an objective event that occurs – I didn't get very emotionally involved. Now, at this end of my life, the other end of my life, I react very personally to the deaths of my patients . . . I sometimes become emotionally involved. I always seek out the families and talk with them and console them and give them my condolences. I'm very much helped by the memory of my father dealing with families in the funeral business. I don't deal with my patients' families as though I were an undertaker, but that ability to be empathetic, to share their feelings – I think it's because I watched my father do it.

As I watch my own colleagues respond to death in their patients, I see quite a variety of responses. A certain ability to separate yourself emotionally from the environment that surrounds a sick and dying

*Rush–St. Luke's–Presbyterian Hospital.

patient is important in order to maintain objectivity, to make intelligent decisions about the patient's care. I think you have to be able to separate yourself in that sense from your patients in order to be a good doctor. In some of us that ability is taken to an extreme. If you become caught up . . . that's why we don't take care of our own families, the emotional problem of dealing with illness in your own loved ones. Perhaps it's a defense mechanism so that we don't get embroiled. Sometimes it's absolutely heart-wrenching to see what happens to sick people. If you allow yourself to be subject to that kind of emotional trauma over and over and over again, it becomes a very damaging thing. There has to be a certain amount of insulation – but I think there can still be compassion.

A lot of it is experience. I was blessed in having the experience of watching a true master dealing with grief, my father, and maintaining that necessary separation – he had to do his business, he had to take care of the needs of that family. Dealing with death is a third-rail issue in the United States. We don't talk about death and dying as a societal problem, but it's going to become more and more of one . . .

It's a very delicate issue for many people – it probably conjures up all kinds of fear and anxiety in terms of their own mortality. But we need to do a better job of talking about it, thinking about it, preparing for it. As a result of that, I think the physician–patient relationship will be broadened.

Often when patients die, we know that it's inevitable. We know the condition they have is incurable, and there's no self-doubt. It's always 'could we have done better in the process of dying, in caring for the patient?' But, in some cases, you always wonder: there was a fork in the road in our decisions about a patient – surgery, no surgery. Surgery, we know there are certain risks but greater benefits. No surgery, lesser risks but lesser benefits. 'Should we have turned the other way?' Now, knowing the outcome . . . The retrospectascope – it's a wonderful tool to learn with, but it's a *vicious* mean tool to punish with when you look back and say, 'We should have gone this way or that way.' Of course we use it all the time in medicine and as well we should. You look back at how can we do it better next time – that's the whole basis of the postmortem examination.

When it came to Ida, I had about ten different feelings.* One was tremendous grief about her death, because I had enormous respect and affection for her. One was a sense of remorse: Had we made the wrong decisions in terms of recommending this particular course of therapy? Going back and doing a retrospect analysis. Did we overlook anything? What had gone wrong? One was: How am I going to confront you? I had learned that I was the one who was going to be telling you she had passed away. How am I going to break the news to you and your son? What words am I going to use? What's going to be your reaction? How are we going to interact in that terribly difficult period in your life and in my life? How can I help you after I've done that? What are the next steps? That's why I was so grateful to see that your son was there, that you had people with you.

A physician must be honest in dealing with a patient. If the patient senses a lack of integrity, it'll undermine the whole process. At times being honest means bringing bad news. What I try to do – I'm sure I could do it better – is to tell the patient what the facts are. Then to do my very best to point out that there are ways of dealing with this problem. It may be a palliative type of thing: we're not going to cure it, but we're going to lessen the impact. I truly believe that virtually every diagnosis we deal with today holds the hope of some breakthrough in the foreseeable future. I like to bring that to my patients' attention. Right now we may not have a treatment or a cure for disease X, but so much is happening in the field . . .

My son had Hodgkin's disease – it's a cancer of the lymph nodes. When we learned that, I was *devastated*. The wonderful physician who took care of him pointed out to me that things are changing so quickly in this field that you should have hope – and she was right! He's now seven or eight years after being treated and no evidence of recurrence. The number-one thing when you're dealing with an incurable disease is to give the patient a sense of hope without being dishonest.

Grief and guilt are threatening subjects, more so as we get older . . . Because we're getting nearer and nearer to our own mortality.

*Ida was my wife. She died after undergoing heart surgery. – s.t.

I think it's become more of a problem as our nation has become more secular. I noticed as a child, from experiences with my dad, how much of a role religion plays in dealing with this issue – the belief in the life hereafter, salvation and redemption, that sort of thing . . . The sermons given at funerals, the masses, the expectation of something beyond – these things sustained the grieving family through this terrible period.

My father was very religious, Methodist. He was a regular churchgoer and did all the things that religious people in small communities do in terms of contributions and the like. But his real religious expression was in the way he lived his life.

I raised my children in a religious environment because I'm convinced unless you have experienced this as a child, you cannot recapture a religious belief as an adult. But my science background makes it difficult for me to accept some of the assumptions of organized religion. My experience with some organized religions makes me doubt that they are truly religious in terms of their compassion and their concern for human beings and the needs of human beings. I doubt that there's a hereafter – and that's probably the first time I've ever said that. [Laughs] But it would be nice if there were. Though I can imagine the enormous complexities if there is a hereafter and all my ancestors are up there!

I think of people who have lost a loved one, as I have – my first wife died ten years ago – and then later remarry. How is that going to work out if we're all up there together with two wives? Maybe the Mormons were right. [Laughs] I don't mean to be disrespectful . . . But it does seem a little difficult to put together from a scientific, rational basis that there is a hereafter. I guess I don't really care. I think the important issue is the way we conduct our lives while we're here, and the impact we have on other people while we're here. And if it helps some people to think there's a reward in the hereafter for being good, Calvinism or the Judeo-Christian ethic, so be it. The motivation isn't as important to me as the solace it gives survivors.

I've always had an internal gut reaction against cremation. My initial experiences with it as the undertaker's son were emotionally repulsive. I don't know if I've ever gotten over that. When my wife passed away, my children felt very strongly cremation was the appropriate thing, and that my wife had actually told them that's what she wanted. She and I never discussed it . . . I don't know that I've really decided what I would want. I'll leave that to my survivors.

I think that we need to take a more active role in deciding about our own terminal care. If you haven't been able to talk about death and dying with your children, you've left them completely in the dark as to what you would like to have done. Most of us aren't able to do that in the last few months of our lives. Everyone has the right to a graceful death. Unfortunately, we don't have people die at home anymore, partly because there is this reluctance to engage in the process of dying. Many families don't want a sick person in the bedroom, dying.

Last week, I attended a play, O'Neill's *Desire Under the Elms*. There was talk in that play of the parlor, which no one had entered since the wife's body was laid out there. From that point on, the parlor was never used by the family. That's why often it's called a funeral parlor, as it was in the old days. The service would be in the church, but the remains would be taken back to the home, and the viewing, the wake would be there.

The issue of dying is a very sensitive one in our country. I think it's caused a lot of emotional stress, a lot of financial problems for people who haven't planned in advance. It's placed a lot of unnecessary burden on families because they don't know what the wishes of the parent might have been.

When I was a kid my mother said, 'There's certain things, Joseph, you don't talk about in polite company. You don't talk about politics, you don't talk about religion, you don't talk about sex.' She never said death, but I would add that – because there's a fear that you're going to touch a sensitive raw surface on the other person, that you're going to remind them of a recent death or stimulate their anxiety and fear about their own illness. I don't mean that's the next thing, but I think it is a topic that needs to be discussed so that we can get our fears and our anxieties out in front of us, take a look at them, and then begin to deal with them.

Dr. Sharon Sandell

We're in a high-rise on Chicago's near North Side. Her one companion is Juliet, a little Pomeranian. She's seen both sides of doctoring. 'I seldom go outside now. I have spinal problems, both neck and the low back. I've had repetitive spinal cord compression for three years. I've moved here because it's not safe for me to drive anymore. I don't have enough neck movement. Ten pounds is as much as I can lift, even and that's pushing it . . .' She moves about as carefully and gracefully as she can, but with obvious difficulty and discomfort.

I grew up in a part of Phoenix that was surrounded by wealthy people, but we were very poor, blue-collar poor. My parents were against education: they thought it was a waste of time for a female especially, and of course they didn't want to pay for it. My father actually set up my getting married when I was very young. He picked out a guy and arranged the first date. If I dated anyone else I had a curfew, and then there were a million questions – it was difficult. With this guy, I could stay out all hours, no questions asked. I married right out of high school, I was seventeen. It didn't last very long.

My goal was to get a college education. I just *knew* that there was more to life than being married. I wanted to know all I could know. I was very good in school. I excelled at everything. I didn't find out until I was in my thirties that I had been tested in kindergarten and my parents were told I should have been put in classes for very bright children. But that was kept from me – they didn't want me to excel in any way. I really do believe that they didn't want to have a child that didn't know her place. They knew their place . . .

When I started college, gee, it was one surprise after another for me. I was majoring in engineering after I found out how good I was at math. I was the only female in any of my engineering classes. I got national recognition for our project in engineering design. But I couldn't find work that I could do around the scheduled classes. That's when I started working through one of the nursing registries as a sitter, a baby-sitter for sick adults. That was good, 'cause I could stay up all night and study.

Then I found out I could make more money if I got six months of training as a nurse's aide – changing bedpans, getting vital signs, giving people bed baths. I had to decide whether I was going to finish engineering. I decided to stick with nursing because I was enjoying working with people more than with things and because there was still an incredible amount of prejudice against women in engineering back in the early seventies. I got a Bachelor of Science in nursing – that was in December of '78.

As soon as I graduated, I went to work for Maricopa County Hospital in the neonatal intensive care in Phoenix. I wanted to continue on to become a neonatal nurse practitioner – but, in order to do that, I needed a master's degree in nursing. I had to go down to Tucson to the University of Arizona. When I interviewed for the position in the master's program, they told me I had to have two years of medical-surgical floor nursing before they would let me in. Which meant I would have had to quit working in the nursery, which I loved doing, work with adults, and then apply to the master's program. I got angry.

The college of nursing was sitting right perpendicular to the college of medicine. After all I had been through I was so angry that a straight-A student wouldn't be accepted in their master's program without two years of nursing, that I marched over to the College of Medicine. I found the dean of students and knocked on his door – I said, 'What do I have to do to get in here?' I was thirty years old at the time. When I was twenty-three, I had been told I was too old to apply to medical school . . .

In eighth grade we had to do a paper on what we wanted to be when we grew up. I wanted to be a doctor. So here I was, turning down a good-paying job in nursing and struggling with putting myself through medical school? I worked as a nurse for the first two years of medical school, at night. Medical school was much easier than nursing school. I *loved* emergency medicine. Northwestern had the only residency program at the time where you could get board-certified in both internal medicine and emergency medicine. Now I'm ten years older or more than most of the students. At Northwestern there were eight hundred applicants for eight positions. I have no idea how I made it, but I was one of the eight. I'm really bright. I know that now, but I didn't know it for a long time.

I herniated the disk above one that had already been operated on in my senior year in medical school, in '83. I was working as the admitting resident at Columbus Hospital in the intensive care unit. And I got called down for a woman who was having massive rectal bleeding. They had put MAST* trousers on her. It was a procedure that called for all kinds of pressure on the abdomen, on the theory that it would save that blood for the brain and the heart. They don't use it anymore because it didn't work, but one of the cardinal rules was that once you pumped it up, you couldn't just let it down – it had to be let down very gradually or you'd kill the person.

I pulled the curtain back and I could see these MAST trousers on her, and she was just as blue as the sky. What I discovered was that while they pumped up the trousers, they were getting people in from another accident, so they were doing everything very quickly. They had caught the patient's gown in the trousers, so that when the nurse pumped up fast, it was strangling her. I tried to get the neckline free, and I was calling out for someone with scissors – I couldn't find anything. The only way I could make sure this woman didn't strangle was to actually tear that neckline, and that's how I herniated the disk. I worked my fingers under there and ripped as hard as I could. I knew something was wrong within minutes of having done that. I just about passed out from the pain.

It turned out that she should have never even been brought into the hospital. She came in from a nursing home with 'no code' written all over her chart. So they never should have brought her to the emergency room in the first place. I saved her life for no good reason. She probably died within a week or two.

What really did me in, though, happened in 1993 in Mesa, Arizona. I'm working in the ER, all these years later. A man had had a very severe heart attack and had been given thrombolitic therapy to thin the blood. Something that he was on caused his tongue to swell massively. The ER doc there for the night shift, who was

*Manually Adjustable Sphygmomanometric Trousers – a medical article long out of use.

trying to resuscitate him, couldn't get an airway in. She couldn't do a tracheotomy because of the thrombolitic. He would have bled to death. So I offered to help, to try to get a tube through this massively swollen tongue. I was pulling on that instrument; it's called a ringoscope. You get the tongue out of the way so you can see the vocal cords and put the tube through. I was pulling on it for all I was worth and my neck blew apart. I didn't know that the surgeon in '87 took out most of the joint at five–six to get rid of the disk material. So I had one joint holding it together. That blew apart. It was misdiagnosed for fifteen months. If I'd not been a physician, this would have killed me. I diagnosed myself. Finally, at Scripps Clinic I got referred to a surgeon who could fix it.

My biggest grief is the loss of a profession that I spent my whole life working for. It's years of my life down the tubes. Now it's a love–hate relationship. I'm not so sure I love medicine so much anymore. Maybe two months ago, when I went to see my doctor who's treating me now, I looked at the X-ray view box and I realized, 'I'm not a doctor anymore,' and I just broke into tears. The loss of my true love. It surprised me. I've had some people say things like, 'Oh, what a waste, all those years and you're wasting all that knowledge.' But if I hadn't been a doctor, I wouldn't be alive today – I'm the one who finally figured out what was going on with my neck.

Medicine is a big business now. It's not Marcus Welby, MD, anymore. HMOs and managed care don't let physicians work from their heart. I hate to see what's happening to it. There are a thousand things wrong, a million things wrong. Our priorities are so messed up. When you look at us spending thousands, millions of dollars on trying to save infants that are born way too premature and we torture these little beings for several months, and then they're either brain-damaged and have horrible, institutionalized lives or they die, and you look at hungry children out on the street who could have half a chance with the money that we're throwing away. When I was in residency, a lot of times we would see people we *knew* were going to die. I remember in particular one woman with terminal breast cancer who required almost daily blood transfusions. If she did not have insurance, she would not have gotten the transfusions. And what did we do for her, other than padding the pockets of the hospital? We kept her going for as long as the insurance kept paying.

There's a condition called a dissecting aortic aneurysm. The aorta is the first big, heavy vessel off your heart. An aneurysm is a ballooning out, a weak spot. If it ruptures it doesn't take too many heartbeats before you pump out all your blood and you're dead. Saving someone in the emergency room with a dissecting aortic aneurysm is a real coup. It's a very difficult thing to do. You're so proud of yourself as the physician who can make the diagnosis fast enough and get everybody doing the right thing at the right time. I did that.

When I was working in Mesa, I had a gentleman come in. I diagnosed him right away. Everything just clicked fine and I knew he'd made it, we'd saved him, and I was *so* proud of myself. About three weeks later, I was the ER doctor and suddenly got called up to reinsert the nasal-gastric tube in someone. It turned out to be this guy I'd saved. The minute he saw me he goes, 'You're the bitch that did this to me.' He was furious that I had saved his life, absolutely *furious*. He just didn't want to be alive, and he was mad I'd saved his life – he'd been robbed of dying a nice, fast, natural death. [*Laughs*]

Ultimately the patient, not the doctor, may decide life or death. Ultimately, who decides when you die is you. A colleague of mine had a patient in the emergency room on Christmas day saying she was sure she was going to die. The ER doctor did a complete workup on her and couldn't find anything wrong in the chemistries, blood gases, X rays, you name it . . . She still insisted she was going to die, but she really had no medical problems. The doctor called her attending physician who said this woman was not a hypochondriac. He knew her very well, had taken care of her for years. Even though it was Christmas, he was going to go in and see her. He looked at all of the workup that had been done, examined her, and there was nothing wrong with her. As he was in his car, starting to drive out, he got the page to come back. She was getting dressed to leave, had been discharged, and she died. Nobody ever knew why. She knew she was going to die. We don't know what she died of, but she died.

ER

DR. JOHN BARRETT

He is Chief of the Trauma Unit at Cook County Hospital, Chicago. He still has an Irish brogue.

In 1966, the Trauma Unit here was actually the first of its kind in the nation. It's dedicated to people who, more than being sick, are injured – patients who have been subjected to what we call intentional injury, violence. It's gunshot wounds, stabbings, personal assaults. Other trauma centers see patients who predominantly are victims of unintentional injury: automotive wrecks and falls. Our experience here has been inner-urban, lower-socioeconomic groupings; predominantly young, predominantly male, and predominantly penetrating trauma: gunshot wounds and stabbings.

I am the third of four sons. My father was a mail carrier, my mother was a dressmaker in Cork. The family really struggled to make sure that all of the sons went to university. My two elder brothers did science – chemistry and physics. I wanted to do something that was scientific in nature but more people-oriented. There was really no family tradition of medicine, but medicine seemed to fill my criteria. I can recall my eldest brother, Frank, saying, 'This is a terrible waste of time – you don't have to be intelligent to be a doctor.'

It's not as if it's rocket science. There's nothing terribly difficult to understand in medicine, there's just an awful lot of it that you have to remember. I always wanted to be a general practitioner. In my final year of medical school, I did a rotation with the then-professor of surgery, and I loved it. At the end of the rotation he said, 'Well, Barrett, what are you going to do?' I said, 'Well, Mr. Kiley, sir, I'm going to be a general practitioner.' He looked at me

and said, 'Barrett, there's the makings of a great surgeon lost in you.'
So that's why I decided to do surgery. I realized that what I really,
really enjoyed was the injured patient. It's such an acute event: the
patient is perfectly healthy, then something traumatic happens, and
within a matter of seconds they are injured. They're a great surgical
challenge because they're bleeding, they generally need surgical intervention. The epitome of those patients is the gunshot wound.
Despite all the terrible things you hear about Northern Ireland and all
the violence, where I was in the South we saw no gunshot wounds.
I actually had to come to this country to see gunshot wounds.

I have found that surgeons have a certain personality. They tend
to be very action-driven, very egocentric, frequently overconfident –
especially trauma surgeons who will act very quickly with a minimal
amount of information. That may not be the person you want to be
your lawyer or your priest, but that's the person you want to be your
trauma surgeon. They tend to be supremely confident in themselves, and that's why many people don't like them. They tend to
demean other people. It goes with the territory because you have to
be damn confident in yourself if your job is to start cutting people
open at the drop of a hat. People, when they hear that you're a
surgeon, they immediately look at your hands because they imagine
there's something unique about the surgeon's technical ability. That's
not true at all. People have said you can teach educated apes how to
operate – I'm not sure if that's true – but it's the decision-making
process, not the technical stuff.

If you ask me to talk about life and death, the first thing I would
think of is my patient. You begin to realize there's not a sharp dis-
tinction between life and death. When is a person alive and when is
a person dead? We have, for instance, patients who come in who are
clinically dead: their heart has stopped beating, they are not breathing,
their pupils are fixed and dilated. But we have them. The Chicago
Fire Department paramedics are excellent – they get them in here *fast*.
They've been without vital signs for a short period of time. You can
still resuscitate some of them, you can bring them back . . .

Was it two weeks ago? – we had a man who was stabbed in the
heart, came in clinically dead. We immediately opened his chest,
released the pressure from his heart, sewed up his heart, and he
actually recovered. He can't have been dead because we got him

back, but he was clinically dead. It's not a very firm line; there's a gradual blending from where you're alive to where you're dead. The people I see who are dead are in general young people who have suffered a calamitous event – they've been shot. You try your best. They're either dead when they arrive or generally die fairly quickly after they've arrived. You can't resuscitate them. The first thing that strikes me about it is, it seems such a waste . . . You're looking at a human body, and as a surgeon you know its intimate details: the anatomy and the sinews and the arteries and the veins, and they're now dead. This wonderful perfect machine is now no more. It's frequently the smallest thing that has killed them. A stab wound to the heart will kill one person and it won't kill the next. It seems to be such a capricious thing. What I really think a lot about is when children die. When adults die from trauma, you feel they have some degree of responsibility insofar as they chose to be in that place at that time. When a child dies, you think: *Why did that happen?* Five minutes' difference would have changed the entire course of events. And parents ask you the same thing: 'Why did it happen, doctor?' You try to explain: 'He was shot, we did the best we can.' That's not the answer they want. They want to know why this person who was awake, alive, and healthy this morning is now dead. You don't have that explanation as a surgeon.

The first thing I feel, I feel angry, angry that they died, that I haven't been able to save them. To me it's almost like a personal defeat. I know in a logical sense that's not true. I didn't shoot them. It wasn't my fault that there were guns on the street.

Remember how I characterized the surgeon? The surgeon is supremely self-confident. We whip them back from the jaws of death, we have the scalpel, we have the decision, we have the technology, and we have a system in this hospital that's supposed to save them. But you can't save them all. We don't lose a lot, but we do lose them. So initially I feel angry. That passes fairly quickly because I then say to myself: *What could we have done that we didn't do?* Actually, we talk about it as a group: Could we have acted quicker, recognized this quicker? Because even though this particular patient is dead, we may be able to improve care for the next patient. Then I think: *What a waste!* A total, absolute *waste*. Especially now. I'm fifty-five years old. It makes you think about your own mortality. We really don't realize what a precious gift life is. We take it for granted. I've always taken it for granted. My children are growing up, my daughter is going to college this year, I'm growing older, and I'm surrounded by people who are brought in, some of whom die. It is a very, very fragile thing we have that can disappear. The stuff that you worry about . . . Are you going to get the house painted? The basement floods occasionally. My God, the car keeps breaking down . . . It's all so trivial . . . We should really realize that the greatest gift we have is time, and that means you're alive.

When the patient comes in, you might see someone who's covered in blood. I don't see someone covered in blood, I see somebody who has technical challenges. A gunshot wound to the chest with hemothorax, we need to get a chest tube in, determine the rate of bleeding, and make effective interventions. So right then and there, I'm not thinking great philosophical thoughts – I'm in a mechanical, operative mode. You just go *boom, boom, boom* . . . It's like a very organized, choreographed dance. But then at the end, he dies. Then you say, 'Let's look back at the dance. Did we do something wrong, could we have done something better?' You do tend to become a little philosophical as you grow older. I'm convinced that the solution to all this violence is not surgeons. We need to somehow prevent it.

I come from Ireland, a country that has national health insurance. Every resident is insured. I'm an American citizen and I love being one, but I can't understand why we can't ensure that every resident of the country actually gets adequate health care. I'm so happy to work here at the County Hospital, because that's part of our mission statement: We will not turn you away. People refer to us as the hospital of last resort. I think that that's a very noble thing.

People say, 'Why did you stay?' It's so perfectly logical to me. Here's what I wanted: I wanted to be a surgeon who dealt with patients who required surgical intervention. Those are gunshot wounds. I also want to be able to teach people. I think it's important that you pass on your skills. And to even do a little research, to maybe improve the care of the patients. Patient care, education, and the research, all three things I'm doing here. The money isn't the greatest, and there are frustrations working in the public sector – but compared to what I've gotten out of it, I am one of the most fortunate people that you'll ever meet. I would actually pay money to do this job. They pay me to do what I love to do.

When you lose a patient . . . I think every doctor has their own way. It's not something they teach you in medical school, and they really, really should. Physicians and health-care people in general need to have a far greater degree of sympathy toward their patients, toward the patients' family. No one ever taught me how to talk to a family and tell them that their loved one was dead, especially in a trauma situation. It's one thing if a patient has, say, cancer and they become ill and then they die – it tends to be a process. You get to know your doctor, you finally realize the end is inevitable, you may have time to talk to your loved one.

Trauma is different. What happens in trauma is this eighteen-year-old leaves the house in the morning, perfectly healthy. Then the mother gets a call at two o'clock, it's the Trauma Unit at Cook County Hospital: 'Your son's been shot. Please come in.' When she walks in, she'll see me. She doesn't know me, she's never met me before, and I am now going to tell her that her son is dead. So how do I do it? The first thing that I do is I try to put myself into their situation. What they want to know is, is he alive or is he dead? I think you need to tell them that. Some people start telling them about he was shot and he came in and we did this and we did that. They're really trying to impress the family with the work that they did to save him. That's not what the family wants to know: they want to hear if he's alive or if he's dead. That's what I tell them. I say: 'You don't know me, I'm Dr. Barrett, I'm the senior surgeon here tonight.' They won't even remember my name. Sit them down. Sit down with them. Look into their eyes. If you can, hold on to them and say, 'It's bad news.' And they'll say, 'Is he dead?' Or they just look at you. You have to use the word, you have to say it: 'He's dead.' If you say he's 'expired,' he's 'passed away,' they don't hear that. You have to say he's dead. Then, then they react. They generally go into disbelief: 'No, no, it's not true – I can't believe it . . . How could it happen . . .' Or they say, 'It can't be him. Are you *sure?*' All you do then is you just let them grieve. I think it's actually helpful for them to come and see the body. I think that's important. He's all covered in blood, there's tubes in him. That doesn't matter. They want to see that person, they want to see that face. I say to them, 'It's OK to hold him, if you want to kiss him, if you want to talk to him.' I think it's important to do that because, afterwards, they'll go through that scene in their mind over and over and over again. 'I remember the night they called me from the County and I came in and this is what happened, and that is what happened . . .' It's very important to put yourself into their shoes, but you've got to say the word 'dead.' You've got to give them the finality of it.

I ask residents, 'How would you do it?' They're trying to explain to the family what they did: 'He came in, we intubated him, we did this, we gave him blood, we gave him CPR.' The family isn't even listening to that! They're *not* listening to it. After you've said he's dead, they won't listen to anything for a long time. Once they've calmed down, it's important to tell them the absolute truth. 'I don't know what the circumstances surrounding the shooting were, but as far as I can tell, he was unconscious very rapidly after he was shot. He never regained consciousness. I don't think he suffered.' Just tell them the truth, it's always the best thing.

When you die, you die. Your body rots. Everyone knows that. There's no argument about that. But there is a spirituality to us. If you want to call it a soul, you can call it a soul. I think of it more as the thing that allows us to choose to do good or evil. You kind of fall on one side or the other. You tend to be on the side of the good or the side of the evil. You can personify this as being God and the Devil. You can call this spirituality your soul, or not your soul, but whatever it is, I do believe it continues after your body is dead. I'm not sure that thing that's going to exist after I'm dead would say to itself, 'I am John Anthony Patrick Barrett and I remember everything about John Anthony Patrick Barrett' – I don't think it's that simple. I do believe in an afterlife, but I don't believe that it's up there in the clouds somewhere with angels flying around beating their wings, and God is an old geezer with a long beard.

Let me try it a different way. You do things that live on after you. Each of us, as we pass through life, influences others. You leave behind you a legacy of things you did and people you influenced. So even if you don't believe in a life after death, you've had an influence. And people say, 'I haven't had any influence. What did I do? I worked in a steel mill all my life, I didn't actually do anything. Got married, had a few kids . . .' Well, you did – you had an effect as you went through life, and it was either a good effect or an indifferent effect or a bad effect. That effect continues on. I have two children, and they're going to have influences on people and they're going to do things. I'm also a teacher: I've taught lots of people, hundreds, perhaps even a thousand people that I have influenced in a very fundamental fashion. Many of them are now surgeons themselves. There's little pieces of me that exist in all of that. So even though you're dead, you're not gone.

If you said, 'What do I think makes me different from other surgeons?' the short answer is I don't know . . . But I will tell you I think it's a word called 'empathy.' I have the ability to think and feel like the other person. I don't know where I got that, but it's something almost instinctive. Maybe that's what doctors need to have. If doctors are supposed to comfort, you've got to understand that the person is suffering; you've got to kind of live in your patient's shoes. I don't care if you're a Hindu or a Jew or an atheist, it's all fine to me. I certainly don't believe that there's only one true religion and one true God and only one way of getting to Heaven. If you believe in your particular belief, I respect that. You're gonna get to Heaven every bit as fast as I am, and in fact even faster probably.

I remember the first dead person I ever saw – my mother's father. I would have been probably four or five years old. I remember a big commotion in the house, getting dressed up and washed and cleaned and being on my best behavior. He was laid out in a morgue. I recall the body. He was in the casket. It was an open casket, and he didn't look like granddad. It was this pale waxen look – it wasn't him. The second one I ever saw dead was in Ireland. I think I was probably eighteen or nineteen years of age, and I was out on my bicycle. There was a guy who had crashed his motorcycle into a car. As I arrived at the scene they were getting the body out – and he was dead. And they were getting him out and I remember he was covered in blood. I haven't thought about this in a million years. I remember, as they took him out, he had his watch on. I remember the second hand of his watch was still ticking. Why do I remember that? I think it was the thing that I talked about before. He was fine, and now he's dead . . . but his watch is still going on.

If you had been born a hundred years ago, Studs, you wouldn't have lived this long. Yet you're still living a very productive and fruitful life. There comes a time when we really do have to balance that, though. Now, how do you make those decisions? These are actually not decisions that your doctor alone can or should make. Especially those of us who are technologically driven. If you were dying from something that I think I can cure by operating on you, I am going to try and convince you to have the operation. You may have a totally different perspective on life. I think medicine needs to acknowledge that. Sometimes it's not the patient, it's the patient's family who say, 'I want everything done.' How much of that is driven by them because they want to be able to say afterwards, 'Well, we did everything'? It makes them feel comfortable . . .

It isn't a huge problem in trauma because we really *do* try to do everything, because the patients are young. But if I am at the stage where I'm absolutely convinced that the patient is going to die but I can keep the patient alive longer, I think what you need to say to the family is not, 'What do you want me to do?' What I say to them is, 'If the patient in the bed could talk to us, what would he say, do you think? You know him, he's been your son or your husband. You know his approach to life. What do you think he'd say?' Then they begin to think: *What would he say?* They're surrogates. I don't want to know what they want to do because they're filled with guilt and anguish, and half of them want to do this and half of them want to do that. I want them to tell me what they think he would do.

Then there's the question about physician-assisted suicide. I can understand the sort of logic that says the patient is in absolute agony, the patient wants to die, and they want me to help them to die, but I don't subscribe to that. I think there's a huge difference between pushing someone into a river and having them drown, and seeing someone in the river drowning and doing nothing, letting them drown. If you look at the cases of physician-assisted suicide, man, you'd better be damn sure that you're doing the right thing. You need to be damn sure. I mean, surer than capital punishment. You need to be sure that whatever it is the patient has is totally incurable and cannot be relieved. You're dying because you're in intractable pain? We can take care of it, I mean, we really *can*. This feeling that they're turning to say, 'Kill me, doctor . . .' They're not depressed? There's *nothing* we can do to help that depression? I don't think I ever personally would feel so confident that I would do that.

I actually believe in capital punishment. It's rare for a doctor to say that, because doctors are trained in the preservation of human life. And it's probably even rarer for a professed Catholic doctor to say that. But I believe that there are some people who should be killed. There are justifications for taking human life – predominantly self-protection. If somebody is going to kill you and the only way you can save yourself is by killing them, then you are justified to kill them. That can be extrapolated into a just war, if there ever is such a thing. Now, let's go to the individual. I don't think we should execute people as a deterrent, although it is the ultimate deterrent for the person you've executed. I think there are some people in this world who are evil: they murder other people. So I would need to have a person who has committed heinous crimes, and I would include in those heinous crimes, rapes.

I also am very concerned about people who kill police officers, or even politicians, because they're protecting us. I would also need to know that there is no way to rehabilitate him. So that might mean that he has committed the crime many times. I would need to know that he continues to be a risk. People say, 'Well, why don't you lock them up for the rest of their lives?' I've seen these people. They will try to kill other inmates. They will try to kill their custodians. They will try to kill the guards. They are intrinsically evil. They cannot be rehabilitated, and they continue to pose a risk to their captors. They deserve to die because they are a threat to us, not because we're trying to frighten other people from committing the crime. They would have to be guilty much more than beyond a reasonable doubt. They exist – I've seen them. There are people like that in the world.

When I'm dead, there will be this thing that is left like the body of my grandfather. That I don't care what you do with it. It's like when I go to the barber, he cuts my hair. Do I worry about the hair? I don't give a damn what he does with it. You want to burn me? I don't care. Actually, whoever is left who's going to be responsible for my dead body, they need a ritual to bury me. So, sure, I'm sure there'll be a little ceremony and they'll be singing songs and ringing bells and lighting candles and smoking incense. I don't care what they do. Because that thing in that coffin, that is not me. Now that I'm fifty-five, I actually think about dying. I didn't think about it when I was twenty, or thirty, or forty. But I'll soon be sixty. And there's a whole bunch of stuff I intend to do yet. I've got big plans. My mother, she's alive and she's ninety years old; my father lived until he was eighty-six. I hope that I'll live a long time. But I can grapple with it now: I can see myself dying. I think the process would be messy, the actual dying, death. But I don't think I would be particularly bothered by the fact that death is inevitable. I'm not embracing death, but I'm not afraid of it. There are also the things you've done during the time you've spent on this earth that are going to remain behind, in some way, shape, or form, forever. If I'm dead and people come to my graveside and look at my tombstone, do you know what they're going to say? They're going to say, 'Who was he?' You want to know who I am? If I wanted to have anything written on my tombstone, I would have, 'Ask my children or ask my students.' I actually never thought of it quite that way. That wouldn't be a bad epitaph.

MARC AND NOREEN LEVISON

MARC: I'm a paramedic with the fire department for twenty-five years. I grew up in Chicago. Right now I'm a field supervisor.

NOREEN: I've been a nurse for twenty years. I moved to Chicago in 1979. I met Marc when I was working in the emergency room at Rush–St. Luke's–Presbyterian in 1981. He was a paramedic bringing the patients in.

MARC: The ER is where the most critical patients are brought in. That's the first entrance to most hospitals. Right now, it's the primary health care for most urban centers. The emergency room is a doctor's office. On top of that, you have paramedics bringing in the critically injured, being resuscitated, and some that aren't so critically ill. In Chicago, the fire department handles the living and the police handle the dead.

NOREEN: Being a nurse in the emergency room encompasses really everything from babies being born in the backs of cars to people taking their last breath of life. Usually people are in a stressful state, they're in emotional turmoil. We've seen a lot of people die.

MARC: The stress of the job caused us to have something in common. Noreen and I clicked. We understood each other's workday. I'm on a twenty-four-hour shift, and Noreen would do eight to ten hours at the emergency room. I spent thirteen and a half to fourteen years on the primary responding ambulance in the city. We get to the home before anybody, before the police, when the 911 call comes in. I've encountered death in the home and in the back of the ambulance. It was an honor to have the responsibility to go into the house first when they call – either the niece or the relative or the superintendent of the apartment building – and say, 'Well, we haven't heard from Mr. and Mrs. So-and-so in a couple of days . . .' We break into the house and there they are, they're passed away.

The nice ones, to me, were the ones where it was an older person in their eighth or ninth decade of life. You walk into this house and they're either on the floor or in their bedroom. They've been gone for maybe twenty-four hours. And it looks peaceful. There's all this stuff in the house. The pictures from the twenties and their wedding pictures of their wife that passed away, or their husband – and the kids. And the little certificates on the wall. That guy's laying on that bed almost like telling you, 'Hey, screw you. I'm living here, this is my life, and this is where I died' – instead of just a body on the bed that's got rigor mortis. This wasn't a violent crime, this was a natural progression.

When I was twenty years old I got on the fire department and we would get two or three of these a week sometimes. You'd just see the beauty of a person's life and it struck me that this is where they loved, either the Ukrainian Village or the West Side, and it didn't matter what color they were, what religion, or anything else – death is just about the same for everybody. When they died in a peaceful sense I always took in the room. You know, you don't disturb anything. You just take in the room and the stuff you can see, and it's just a beautiful thing to know that this person, the body was a human being and had a whole history. It might have been so insignificant to the rest of the world. But to this person it was a significant life. Everybody's got a significant life. And there they are, they're dead.

The violent deaths are a lot different. The violent deaths are the gruesome, the grim, the suicides. Most of the suicides, the gun still stays in their hand. They don't drop the gun. Oh my God, it's a nightmare . . .

Or the kid that's in the ambulance, the gangbanger that was a tough guy on the street two minutes before he took two nine-millimeters to the belly, and he's got maybe an hour to make it to County Trauma Center. And here's a little boy: you have to decipher, is he fourteen, or is he over fifteen years old and going to an adult trauma center. And the trauma centers weren't put into effect until about 1987. We used to just take them anywhere. Here's this kid that was the toughest kid on the street and now he's looking at ya, and he's got that look in his eye like, 'I'm a baby and I'm scared to death.' You start up the IVs, you've done what you can do . . . They're still awake, you're not doing CPR, they still have vital signs, but they're critical. You just might be the last person they see before they go into unconsciousness. Or when they hit the emergency room, that's when the physicians and the nurses have to really start going and maybe crack the person's chest right on the table. So you're the last person that he's going to remember talking to if he survives this incident. You gotta be careful what you say, you don't want to degrade this person – you don't want to pass judgment here. You hold their hand. 'There, there,' is all you can say. As he sweats and the blood pressure's dropping, the pulse is going up, and his respiratory rate is getting higher. You just hold his hand and say, 'There, there . . .' And he looks at you and you look at him. There's an exchange between eyes. He knows he's in trouble and you know he's in trouble, and you don't want to tell him, 'You're gonna die.' You say, 'I'm right here with you. We're going to get you there as quick as we can. And when you get there, they're going to be doing a lot of things to you, so you just hang in there.' There's no deathbed confessions from the gangbangers on the street. They don't say, 'Gee, I'm sorry I did anything.' They're just tough little kids that are trying to survive.

NOREEN: I'm the nurse there. I don't work in a trauma center, but we've had a lot of people come in where they're about to arrest. When I was a new nurse, you would have somebody come in and they would look you in the eye and say, 'I'm gonna die.' And I would grab their hand or I would try to comfort them. 'We're going to do everything we can for you.' But as I became a more experienced nurse, I realized that death is a part of life, and when they would look at me and say, 'I'm going to die,' I would say, 'Well, you may die. But what can I do now for you that's going to help? Can I bring your family in? Do you need to call someone? Do you want me to stay here with you?' I changed my whole outlook on how I work with people when they're dying, or when they feel like they know they're going to die.

When a person looks at you and says, 'I'm going to die,' they usually do die. That's what my experience has been. Somehow they know that their life is going to pass. What I found is going to help them the most is to be in there with them. From a medical perspective, we've always been taught to save everybody – get in there, resuscitate everyone. It's not always going to save them. Sometimes you're the last person they're talking to. What I've learned is: get that family member, get that husband, get the wife, get the daughter, get the grandson, whoever that significant person who's waiting in that waiting room so anxiously, get them in there. So their last few breaths or conversation can be with that family member – not with someone who doesn't really know them.

When someone comes in in an arrest, and the paramedics are pumping on their chest . . . Their heart has stopped. There's not too much we can do. You try not to look too deeply at that person's face because you know every person that passes by you affects you in some way. The people that stay with me the longest are the ones who die. Most of the people that come in in cardiac arrest die. What people see on TV is not what really happens. When they're laying there, after we're all done resuscitating, the nurses are the ones with the body, and they're the ones to bring the family in. You look at the person and you say, 'I wonder . . . what about this person?' Like Marc has the experience of being in their home and seeing the person. We don't have that until the family starts to come in. And even though they're grieving and it's terrible for the loss, you see that this person had significance in their family and in the larger world. The hard ones are the people where there's no identification. The junkie that comes in off the street and dies that nobody knows who they are. I think: *Oh, that's such a waste of life.* It's the people that don't have anybody. Those are the ones that have really struck me.

MARC: We're at such a high level. That's the thing that scares me about being a human. We're so highly developed, our emotions. You can't let death go without thinking about it. You have to intellectualize something like what happened here and who was this person. You don't have a heart unless you think about who was this guy, or who was this woman? But you can't dwell on it because the next time you go out the door, it's going to be another call. That's the best part about it. Emergency rooms are busy. Noreen has to clean the patient up and make sure that it's presentable for the family. But in the next two minutes, there might be another coming in for her.

What happens on our job and what happens in your personal life is completely different. My father died of lung cancer. Now I had cleaned the slate with my dad and had a great relationship with him. The day he was diagnosed, I got the call from my mom that they found he had cancer of the brain and lung. That's a death sentence – I knew that intellectually. I wasn't overwhelmed with this right away. He only survived two months after the diagnosis, which saved him a lot of pain and anxiety. He went on to wherever you go, peacefully in the night without too much suffering. My dad got out lucky. About forty-eight hours before he died we were at the hospital, Noreen and I, and something happened where emotionally I knew this was it: my dad was going to be dead in a day or two, and I'll never see him again. It just ate me up inside and I broke down and cried and cried for about a half hour. It was a terror inside of me. It dawned on me that this is it, and the daddy I had when I was a little boy, the smells, the feel of his clothes – the smell of the T-shirt he wore, even with the nicotine on it – that's what I identified with him. All the memories. It was the best thing that ever happened to me because I was able to hold his hand and say good-bye. But that terror that overwhelmed me was like nothing I ever felt before. It's so permanent. There's nothing the doctors can do, nothing anybody can do. He's going to die and I'll never see him again. I won't be able to call him on the phone, I won't be able to drive over to the house. Now, in my subconscious, he's with me more than ever because I think of him almost on a day-to-day basis. When he was alive I didn't think of him that much. That's the difference between the professional and the personal.

NOREEN: In our ER, someone dies and we also prepare the body. We take out the tubes and all the other things that we've done to the people, so the family can come in.

MARC: They don't want to see their loved ones with all the medical equipment still in there. That's a job that I would not want that Noreen has.

NOREEN: When the family arrives, the doctor will go in and tell them. Sometimes the nurse will come along, especially if it's a younger doctor that's inexperienced. A lot of times we have the chaplain there. When I was a brand-new nurse, I wasn't prepared for the response of the families. I had no idea that people would wail . . .

MARC: The death howl is indescribable. The mother that was just told that her kid is dead. It echoes through the halls of the hospital.

NOREEN: Inconsolable . . . The howling, the screaming, the falling on the floor, the almost seizure-like activity. That I had never experienced. We had a family of Gypsy background, and they laid their bodies on top of their mother. There's no consoling them. They were laying on the ground and shaking. A lot of times I find in the African-American community their reverend comes in. They always say, 'I'm going to wait for the reverend to come.' He groups the family together and they have a prayer around the body. That seems to really help in those situations.

MARC: I've had that happen. In the African-American community on the West Side they made a prayer circle around the ambulance as we're doing CPR in the back. I looked out, all of a sudden they're circling the ambulance, holding hands and praying. The neighbors heard about it, they came out of the church. I was struck by it. I almost didn't want to leave.

NOREEN: We see a lot of prayer. What can you say to people, other than you're sorry for their loss, you tried. There isn't much else for the medical person to say. But the prayer takes them away from the immediacy of death to a different place.

MARC: Different types of death cause different types of reaction. Somebody shoots somebody, half of the family wants to go get the guy who shot him, they want revenge . . . Somebody who's been run over by a car – they want that driver, they want justice. There's a *huge* amount of anger. Justice and anger. And they want to know what happened in that trauma. 'Couldn't you save them?' I've had that a couple of times, couldn't I do any more? I've never felt for one second that my partner and I ever did anything less than we could have. We always gave a hundred percent. That's one of the reasons that I'm able to close my eyes at night and love my job, because there's no slacking in the back of that ambulance.

Being on the front lines of death makes me more grateful that I'm healthy today. And when we have our arguments, as all married couples do, or I yell at my kids, it makes it a little easier to say I'm sorry quicker, to appreciate, 'Don't sweat the small stuff' – because I've seen some big fucking stuff happen.

LLOYD (PETE) HAYWOOD

We're at Stateway Gardens, a public housing project on Chicago's South Side. In its public squalor, it is incongruously surrounded by private affluence. On one side is the Illinois Institute of Technology, celebrating Mies van der Rohe's architecture. On another side is Comiskey Park, home of the Chicago White Sox. Overlooking the whole scene is the new site of the Chicago Police Headquarters.

Jamie Kalven, a freewheeling journalist, is my docent as we enter the shadowy, dimly lit precincts of the project. He is also the ex officio ombudsman for the residents – patently, the only Caucasian the residents trust. In the cold, dark corridors, we encounter figures, 'hanging out'; I cannot make out their faces. They recognize my companion, of course, and offer casual salutations.

We pause near the elevator. It is astonishingly small for a building so densely populated. We greet Pete, who has been expecting us. He indicates the lift: 'Here is where I been shot and left for dead.'

We rattle our way upward, toward one of the higher stories. His tiny apartment, in dramatic contrast to all else around and about, is airy, full of light, and painstakingly neat. There are puffy white pillows on the somewhat tattered couch. On the end table is a well-thumbed paperback: John Steinbeck's *The Pearl*. On the wall is a picture that immediately catches your eye. It appears to be a cemetery or some sort of memorial park.

'My family, my great-grandmother and my grandmother, yes, they attend church every Sunday. I used to oftentimes go with them.'

He had been a gangbanger. 'We called ourselves the Del Vikings.' He has since abandoned that life and is trying to find himself.

The night it happened, my grandmother gave me a rather large bill to play the lottery. Somehow I ended up spending the money. So I'd been out shooting dice, trying to get her money back, which I won a few dollars doing. Another guy ended up lending me the rest. But I ran into another friend of mine and we had went up to his house to drink some whiskey and smoke a bag of reefer. A girlfriend we grew up with, she was drunk. The guys, they was pulling up her blouse and my friend's mother, she came out on the porch where we was sitting and said, 'Would you all walk her home?' And I said to him, 'Come on, man, you know your mother's right . . .' We, like, carried her home because she was drunk. And upon doing this, the guys from the other end, they're known as the G.D.'s – [*Kalven interjects:* 'They're the Gangster Disciples'] – another gang. They were after us. She lived in a building where we had to go through their territory to get her home. I'd never had any problems until this night. It was about three of the guys from the gang. Something had happened earlier that day where they was like shooting out with somebody they said was from the end we were from. We walked her home and got on the elevator and got stuck. So I was trying to get off the elevator and hollering '*Help!*' for somebody to call the fire department.

The guys who followed us acted like they was helping us off the elevator. It was stuck on a floor. The door came ajar off the track. It was like six or seven people on the elevator. Could they get the fire department? The dude say, 'Hold on, we're going to help y'all get off.' So it was a lady headed into the hallway at that time, and the lady was asking, 'What's wrong, what's going on?' She said, 'I'll go up and call the fire department.' The guy told her, 'Lady, this is none of your business – we're going to handle this.' I knew then there would be some trouble. So the guy hollered back through the elevator door, 'Who all on the motherfucking elevator?' – excuse my cussing. So we're prying the door open from the inside, the door got about halfway open and a friend of mine, his name is Andre, he was stepping off, the guy shot him. They had guns out already. He shot him in the stomach. We didn't have *anything*. It was like a series of shots. Once one person unloaded his gun, it was like the next person, he would step through the door. And the guy shot him in the stomach and he flew back in such a way which I never seen nobody get thrown back like that. And after the guy shot him, he had the gun at my head, between my eyes. And it was this little dude on the elevator with us, another friend of mine named Howard, he tried to grab the gun from the guy . . .

I was in, I guess, shock. I couldn't move – I *didn't* move because it didn't seem real. And the gun went off, but it didn't hit me in the head. I guess the guy who tried to grab it got the guy's arm to come down and it hit me in the chest, which the other guy, from later stories I heard, thought he shot me in the head. It was like a scramble amongst my friends. We were trying to get to the bottom of the pile, and I was like, 'Well, I'll just lay here as if I'm dead – maybe they'll stop . . .' I was shot in the chest and in the hip, but I didn't know it at the time. I'm going to just lay here. Once one guy would finish unloading, another guy would step up. It was like they took turns. And through all this, I just laid there. And my friends, they said the elevator was dark. But I argue today that the light was on.

[*Kalven interjects:* 'Your friends say there was no light on in the elevator, but you saw light.']

I don't know if it was I was dying, but I remember saying, 'God, is it *ever* going to stop?' I wanted to call for my grandmother's name but I couldn't because I was trying to play dead, but with my eyes open so I could see whatever was going on. But the elevator was just brightly lit. Once the guys got through shooting, then it got quiet, and the only thing that you would hear was one of my friends, he was screaming, '*My eyes, my eyes!*' and the other one was moaning, 'My stomach . . . help me.' The girl that we walked down there, I had asked her to stick her head off the elevator to see was anybody in the hallway. And once she did that and I seen that nobody shoot, I ran over her to get off the elevator and go up in the building.

[*Kalven:* 'We came up in that little tiny elevator, exactly the same elevator where they opened fire on seven or eight people.']

Thanks to God nobody died. Me and Andre, we was the two serious hit. I didn't know that I had been shot, so my idea was, I was going to anybody's house, whoever would open their door. We was going to go into their house and weren't coming out until the police came.

And so upon running up the stairs in this building, knocking on doors *boom-boom-boom*. People: 'Who is it?' And I wouldn't say a name because sometimes people will open the door if you say 'me.' [*Laughs*] 'It's me – open the door. You hear them shooting out here.' But there wasn't nobody would open the door. We continued to go up the stairs, going through every floor. And my friend seen the police off the porch, we was on the eleventh floor. And my friend hollered down for the police – I guess they radioed to other police, and they came up in the building. But before they came up, I was feeling funny about my back, like if somebody were to hit you in the arm and put a frog in your arm – I was feeling that way on my back. And I was, like, more tired than I would normally be, and I was, like, '*I think I've been hit.*'

So my friend say, 'Let me see.' He raised my shirt up and he seen a hole in my back, a big hole in my back. He's like, 'Pete, oh man, you're gonna *die . . .*' OK, so I'm telling myself *remain calm*, but something was telling me *panic, panic!* I started getting weak. [*Laughs weakly*] I couldn't move now. I was like, *Oh my God, I'm fittin' to die!* And I remember the police coming up there: 'Put your hands up and lay on the ground.' I was sitting in the stairway against the wall. I remember telling the police, 'How you expecting me to lay down on the ground and I'm *shot*.' The police patted us and everything, they searched around to see did we have any guns. I was sort of mad and I was saying things, you know, 'Do you think if I had a gun I'd be the way I am now?' A couple of my other friends were saying things to the police: 'Why don't y'all just get an ambulance?' The hallway was filled up with a lot of people, people looking. And I felt myself going out, unconsciousness, but I didn't want to, I was trying to fight it. To keep from doing it, I was telling the people to pray for me, even though the people didn't know me and probably didn't care about me anyway. I was saying, 'Y'all pray for me,' 'cause I didn't want to die. At that time, that's when the paramedics got to me. That was a scary feeling – it's something I can't explain. Things were beginning to be blurry to me. Last thing I remember seeing at that time was a little girl, about eleven or twelve years old . . .

I remember looking down into this little girl's face, down the stair; when I asked everybody to pray for me. Things was beginning to get blurry to me. Last thing I remember seeing at that time was the little girl. I don't know if she prayed for me. She looked scared.

The paramedics, they worked with me or whatever they did with the little oxygen, and put me on the gurney and carried me down the stairs. When they took me past the little girl, I tried to reach for her, to say it's going to be OK. Once they got me in the ambulance, the paramedics was asking what happened, could I move, and do I feel certain feelings. I was telling them I could feel everything, but I was in so much pain – I was asking could they give me something for pain. They said, 'No,' because I had been drinking. I was like, 'Y'all goin' to let me die.' At the time, I had half a pint of whiskey in my back pocket. I said, 'Well, if y'all ain't gonna give me nothing, can I just take a last drink of alcohol.' I thought, if I'm going to die, I might as well die dead drunk. So they're like, 'No, we can't do that,' and they threw it away. I think I stayed in the ambulance for about twenty minutes or so before they moved.

They took me to Michael Reese.* During all that, I remember the doctors asking me, do I want to call my home, and I didn't want to call my house – I was afraid that might give my grandmother a heart attack. But one of the nurses did contact her, and I asked the nurse to let me speak to her. And I told my grandmother that I was going to be OK and not to worry. And I asked her to pray for me. Then she had got in touch with my father, and my father and my stepmother came to the hospital. I thought I was dying. The doctor was explaining to them that I should have been dead, or I should have been paralyzed, that they don't know how I'm alive or what's keeping me alive. But miraculously I came through – with no surgery performed on me.

Upon this Sunday after I got out of the hospital, I went walking. And as night came there was a group of people standing in front of my building – a group of girls and a few guys. I had happened to be paying attention to how they were pointing at me as I was coming across the field, going to this building here. It was, I guess, some

*A hospital on Chicago's South Side. For years, it was one of the most prestigious in the city. Since it has gone HMO, its reputation has diminished.

more of them guys. They were going to finish doing what they set out to do that night on the elevator. I wasn't familiar with none of them, so I had sensed something was wrong. I had a limp and I was already bent over, and I started staggering along, like I was drunk. And as I got closer, under each one of these buildings is like columns. As I was getting closer to the building, the guys, they, like, started getting on the columns underneath the building – and came out their shirts were *guns*. I noticed, but they didn't think that I noticed. They were waiting on me to come to the building. But me, by acting like I was drunk, and acting like I wasn't paying attention to what was going on, I had to think of a way to come out of it. So I said, I'm going to keep staggering, I'm going to stay along the path of this playground, coming toward the building that we're in now. At least to the corner, and then once I hit the corner, I was going to run to this building.

And when I got to the corner of the building, where I was out of their line of fire for that moment, I had started running. Even though I was in pain, I was running, and I looked back and I seen them coming after me. I ran through this building, ran through the first building on 35th and out Federal. And there, there was a squad car coming down the street. I ran out there hollering for the police. The police, they stop, and I'll never forget it, it was two white police. I said, 'Police, I just got out the hospital, I've been shot.' I said, 'These guys are trying to kill me.' I said, 'Could you please take me home.' The police, looking at the guys coming up behind me through the building, they seen the guys with the guns. The first officer told me I couldn't get in the car. And then once the guys got so close to where they was fittin' to fire, the guy told me to jump in the back. But once I jumped in the back, the officer, he said, 'We can't take you no further than Wabash' – which Kentucky Fried Chicken sat at Wabash. I said, 'What do you mean? I've been *shot*. You see them guys trying to kill me.' He said, 'We can't take you no further than here. I'm going to ask you to get out the car.' And he did just that, dropped me off right there. I didn't come back over here for a couple of weeks after that. I went back to my grandmother's house.

[*Kalven:* 'Pete, how long after that episode was it when you had the opportunity to get revenge on one of the guys who shot you?']

I stayed away for about two or three weeks. All this had took place in early August, so now it was like around Labor Day weekend in September – 1986 or '87, one of them years . . . There was a night where me and a group of friends, some of the guys were about age I am now, thirty-six, but they were guys just trying to gangbang still. The guy that thought he shot me in the head but ended up shooting me in the chest, he had happened to be on the stairs, and I was with a guy who seen him. So it was like, 'Pete, remember when you got shot? If you seen one of those thugs, what you would do?' And I was trying to be cool. I said, 'I don't know . . .' The guy said, 'Would you kill 'em? Because I don't like what they did to you and I think we should get them niggers.' I was under the influence of the drink. I said, 'Yeah, I'll do this and that.' So we had caught the guy that shot me one night, and we had trapped him in this playground. So the guy, he gave me his gun, he say, 'Pete, you got him, go on and kill this nigger.' And I looked at the dude – the guy kept saying, 'Go on and kill that nigger for what he did to y'all,' and I said, 'No . . .' I said, 'I like living and I love my life.'

I said I wanted all that to be over with and forgotten about because my God is forgiving and in order for me to be forgave of my sins, I must forgive – that's my belief. And I told the guys, I said, 'No, I don't wish nothing to happen to this young brother.' I said I just want to leave everything as is and to go on about my life and let him go on about his life. Hopefully that he would change, you know, in himself, after that night. Then the criticism came from the guys that I was with, 'Oh, you're a pussy motherfucker.' I said, 'No, I don't kill nobody 'cause you want me to kill them.' We got into a little argument and I left it at that. And I let the guy go. A few years later, I had got my apartment, my own apartment in this building in which I had started selling drugs. So the guy who shot me – I didn't know that I had knew his brother. His brother was coming around to my house.

So it was one day, we was up there, me, him, a few other friends, listening to some music and drinking beers, and I don't know if he had knew about the situation of his brother and me. He had brought his brother up to my house. I didn't see him when he came to the door. When I looked up and I seen that it was him, the same one I caught in the playground and let go, I found myself apologetic –

because it had messed up his understanding. You could look at a person and see the fear – he was trembling. I was assuring him that I was true to what I had said in the playground – that I would like everything to be forgotten about, that I forgave what he did and I'm thankful to be alive. He was relieved, even though I don't think that he fully trusted it at that time, because now he in the house with me and a whole 'nother group of people that I'm around. And I was letting him know it wasn't nothing. We sat down and we drunk some beers together and listened to some music. I still see him. We hold conversations, we talk for a few minutes at a time. But he's a busy person. He's a car salesman. He goes on about his business now.

There are things that I may not understand, but God, He's everything to me. My God is forgiving. He's jealous, too. My God is very jealous. I haven't served him right, but I continually ask him for the forgiveness of my sins because I know the things I do is wrong, and then I don't know things that I'm doing at that time. I ask God for forgiveness.

CLAIRE HELLSTERN

She has been a nurse for fifteen adventurous years. 'I studied at St. Mary's, Rochester, Minnesota, the Mayo Clinic, Northwestern University, and Ohio State. I took additional courses at the University of Chicago and worked at Michael Reese. At this moment, I'm at Advocate HMO corporate headquarters. I do physical assessment of patients from teenagers to seniors, a few of them a hundred years old. We promote prevention.'

I love this job, but it's not nearly as exciting as my previous one. I was the director of nurses for Northwestern University. It was called the Near North Adult Clinic, bordering Cabrini Green, one of the poorest public housing projects in Chicago. It was a rough neighborhood with people fighting hard to survive. I had many close encounters that could have resulted in my arriving in the county morgue on a slab.

I made a marginal salary. I couldn't afford a car, so I always took the bus and then I would walk two blocks. I'm walking with a black velvet cape, a yellow silk scarf. I always dressed very lively. And often these were maybe five-hundred-dollar outfits I got for twenty-five, thirty-five bucks – no one knows. When you're relating to gangbangers, poor girls, runaways, unwed mothers, I always want to provide a sense of hope: to teach survival techniques. If you don't look like a square Jane, you're more likely to get an open conversation and dialogue.

One time, I'm walking down the street and a young man about nineteen pulled a switchblade out of his sleeve. I had only seen these in movies, switchblades. It flipped open. I was kind of fascinated. He said, 'I want your wallet.' I handed him my wallet and he says, 'Only ninety cents?' I said, 'Buddy, I've had my purse stolen six times. Do I look *stupid?* I don't carry much money on me – I don't *make* much money. And I've got to go open the clinic.' He returned the wallet and said, 'Give me your whole purse!' I said, 'Young man, I *know* you don't use my type of comb, and you don't wear lipstick. I'd hate to have gossipers talking about you walking around with a lady's purse' – impromptu reasoning. I talked calmly and directly into his eyes, and I talked softly. He did not have the switch-blade up to my neck, he had it at the side of his body. So I knew from at least some street smarts that he was a novice. If he'd had it at my neck, I would have said, 'Take anything. Come, I'll do your cooking,' whatever, just to survive. When he realized that I wasn't going to cough it up, he was *stunned*. He bowed and said, 'Oh, after you.' I said, 'No, buster, after you.' So we're both bowing, like two matadors facing. He said, 'After you,' like a gentleman letting a lady pass. All of a sudden his manners kicked in. And we kept bowing and separating and taking a few steps backwards. And eventually he turned and ran. I turned the corner and then I had a few tears coming down my cheek. Not so much scared as ticked off. *How dare you?!* I've cut my salary in half, knocked myself out for this clinic and these people that I love, and I have never harmed a flea. How *could* you?

I was recruited by Northwestern and I wanted a fascinating job. I knew I could go the cushy route, make a ton of money, but it'd be boring. I love adventure – not danger, *adventure*. Here I could build from scratch. I consider myself a visionary. Even if you go to a job nine-to-five, you can still be visionary. I recruited student nurses, social workers, medical record students. I did marketing, I worked on grant proposals, publicity. We had Spanish and blacks and Caucasians. When the word got out, we got Asians, East Indians, multi-ethnic. We had no elevator – they had to walk up three flights of stairs.

I can remember several times when there was an elderly lady who needed assistance. There would be some young guys hanging outside, maybe gangbangers. I *really* didn't check their credentials. I'd say, 'Here, help me. You grab one leg, I'll grab the other' – they did. And another time one of them came in. He'd been stabbed. He told me he fell on a pair of scissors. That's physically impossible. He was like twenty years old. He said, 'I'm going to kill the guy that did it.' I said, 'Now, now. First of all, I don't have any money for daisies and you're going to be pushing up daisies. You go shoot that guy and you're going to be in jail or you're going to be killed. So chill out, take some deep breaths and the ambulance will be here in two min-utes. And then I want you to come back and talk to me after you've been treated. We're going to talk about this.' Like anger diffusion. I'll tell you one thing, they respected me.

I did have another incident. These fellas were selling hot stuff, stolen merchandise. I said, 'Gentlemen, we cannot shop indoors.' They were inside the hallway. We had a children's clinic, an adult clinic. We had a preschool. There was a gymnasium. Two blocks from the projects. My staff were African-American and Hispanic. And they were naturally afraid because they lived in the area, and we had no security guards. The doctors were only there so many hours a day. So it was always up to me.

I said, 'Gentlemen, you must exit the building – we'll see you after work.' So thirty minutes later, I get a call: 'Claire, what time do you get off work? We're going to kick your *ass* after work and Friday at four-thirty we're going to kill you . . .' So my mind went into overdrive. I could hear there were two of them on the phone. I said, 'Gentlemen, what did you have for breakfast? I think you had Jell-O and your brains sound like scrambled eggs. By the way, didn't your mother ever teach you how to eat a wholesome breakfast – you know, oatmeal, raisins, juice, milk?' I said, 'Now, I am *very* busy. I have a teenage pregnancy clinic and perhaps your girlfriend or cousin or sister is *here*. So, I'm going to give you two instructions. Number one, do not *ever* enter the building unless you have an appointment and you *better* be ill. Number two, I'm going to inform you that I'm saying good day, and I am now saying good day.' Bang. [*Laughs*] Nothing ever happened. [*Uproarious laughter*] You've got to out-psych the psychos and think fast on your feet.

This gentleman comes in, five feet tall. Everything he's wearing is black and white: his hat, his shirt, his pants, his belt buckle, his boots are all black and white. Now every patient that I have ever seen has always faced the scale when you weigh them. This guy faced me. Then he said, 'Oh, excuse me – I gotta take something off.' He takes like an *eight-inch knife* off the inside of his boot and lays it down. I said, 'Let me weigh you, and by the way, don't ever bring that into this building again. That is totally inappropriate. I don't want seniors fainting looking at that kind of stuff. What do you do, make furniture?' So then I do his history. 'Have you ever thought of harming yourself?' 'No.' 'Have you ever thought of harming somebody else?'

'Yes, I've thought about killing my father.' I said, 'Well, let's see the doctor and you'll come back out and we'll talk again and readdress that subject. I definitely feel you need psychiatric counseling.' So he goes in to see the doctor, and the doctor is African-American, six foot five. This guy's about a hundred and forty but short. I said, 'Doctor, please do not leave the premises until the young man has left.' Actually, he had to have an injection of penicillin. After the injection the guy gets dizzy, which was a con – he wanted to see if he could rip us off. I told the doctor, 'I'll make you some coffee, toast, juice, but you can't go anywhere until he leaves the building because we have no security guards.' He stayed put.

And the next night, the same doctor was there. Two guys come in the building who apparently had been using drugs. I got their names, addresses, and phone numbers. I say, 'I'm going to draw your blood,' and they suddenly split. The next thing we know, the doctor's car keys are missing – he drove a big old Cadillac. They'd been in his coat, which he'd hung up. This is like *frontier* nursing. So I'm on the phone looking out the window. It's about eight-thirty and it's getting dusky.

About a week before this, two bodies have been found in an abandoned freezer across the street. So I'm dialing 911 and I look out and here they come again. And I'm on the phone. 'Deputy, get over here on the triple triple double! They're coming back in this cotton-picking building and we have no defenses.' Somehow, some-body must have alerted the guys that we were wise, because they came to the front door and then ran around the building. A squad car shows up, they put me in the backseat and say, 'OK, give us the addresses.' And then they flash this big police light on the address 'cause it's dark now. I said, 'I'm going to lay down on the floor.' Because you know, if you're ticked off and you see the police coming at you and you might have a rap sheet, there could be cross-fire. Fortunately it was not the shoot-out at the OK Corral and we were able to regain the keys. I told the guys, 'It is not necessary for you to return.' Please realize the majority of our patients were just simple folks, sweet, churchgoing, wouldn't take a doily, very kind, concerned about their children going to school. Ninety-nine percent were angels – then you just have a few devils.

I had a few other situations. I visited the elderly. South of Taylor

Street, that was all black. I volunteer to see this lady who was ninety with a pacemaker. The program I volunteered for loaned me a Fractured Fender car, a piece of junk. I see three guys, young punks, and I say, 'Perhaps your grandmother's the lady I'm going to visit. Where is 209?' I want to make sure they know I'm not an insurance salesman or a policewoman. So I go see her. I come out, there's eighteen guys. I say, 'What a great day for a baseball game! I just covered the Cubs versus the Sox crosstown game as a sports reporter, but I'm also a nurse.' So we talked a little bit. I'm walking down the sidewalk by myself, and all of a sudden a five-foot metal rod is dropped off the top of the building right in front of me. God saved me. So what I did, I put my hand on my hip and tapped my heel. I stood my ground. I realized they could have outrun me, eighteen against one, and the guy could have shot me from the top of the building. So I just stood there. I actually wasn't afraid. Again, I was ticked off, angry: 'How *dare* you?! Listen, buddies, you're slowing me down!'

No one came near me. I just stood there for a few minutes. No one said anything, no one did anything. I know they thought I had a gun and might have been, I don't know, a white Pam Grier. [*Laughs*] Anyway, so I walk over the grass and get in the car and I drove the heck over the grass. I breathe a sigh of relief, 'Oh gosh, get me *out* of here.'

Then I go to a Hispanic neighborhood. INSANE UNKNOWNS is spray-painted everywhere – that was the name of a gang group. I promised to visit a post-op gallbladder, Hispanic lady. But in order to enter her house, you had to go down an alley and up the back stairwell. So I go to the corner and here's a bunch of winos. I happened to have anticancer literature in Spanish. I tell them, 'Buddy, guard me, hand this out, make sure everyone around knows I'm a nurse, and don't let anyone rearrange a piece of my hair. And when I come back I'll give you a candy bar and an apple.' And they did it. People, even if they're half-stewed, generally like to feel useful.

One of the most depressing things is to be in a clinic and see everyone with their head down, with no hope, with their life over at eighteen, fifteen, seventeen.

I think I've visited just about every kind of neighborhood in Chicago, and I find that if you acknowledge people, you know, if you look at them as just human, they always come through.

Ed Reardon

I'm a Chicago boy, born and raised on the North Side. I spent about fifteen years on the job as a paramedic in Chicago, working the streets all over the city. Ostensibly, you're the eyes and the ears of a doctor. When a doctor can't be on the scene, they'll send guys like us. I like to call us gutter medics because we work in the gutter – we work wherever we find a patient. Sometimes it takes you to some pretty strange places, strange situations.

The police don't have paramedics. Chicago's paramedics are strictly underneath the fire department auspices. We work twenty-four hours. We start at eight in the morning, we get off at eight in the morning. You take two days off, and then every fourth day you'd get a day off. That gave you essentially five days off in a row, so you had time to decompress. During a twenty-four-hour period, when I first started out, we could easily do twenty-five runs, be a minimum of one run an hour. No sooner would you put a patient down than you'd be picking up another one. You'd be going like that all day for twenty-four hours. So when you got off work in the morning, there really wasn't much left of you.

You spent your first day walking around in a daze. The day after that, you'd just be recuperating, and then you'd go back to work. That was the way it was for the first ten years I spent on the job. They would call us when they didn't know who else to call. They'd call us for domestic disputes. They'd call us when the police would have a problem that they didn't quite know how to handle. As paramedics, we would straddle the police and the fire departments – we had one foot in each one of their yards. We'd respond with the firemen to a fire in case somebody got hurt. We'd respond with the police department. In a domestic dispute, you've got a guy beating up his wife, you'd walk in on that. If you had a guy standing out on a ledge, they'd call us for that. They'd call us when they didn't know what else to do. If they had somebody crazy, if somebody said there's a bad smell in the hallway, they'd call us. They call 911. The police would arrive on the scene and they would request the paramedics, just in case it was a medical problem. Sometimes people would call

911 and instead of asking for the police they'd ask for paramedics. Quite often we would go and there would be no police there at all, and it would be a police problem, something that we couldn't even handle. Sometimes it would be a social-service problem: abandoned children or someone who wasn't able to take care of themselves. Sometimes, dealing with life and death . . . [*Sighs*] . . . trauma, medical emergencies, heart attacks, diabetic comas . . . [*Sighs*] . . . murders, stabbings, gunshots, car accidents. In a twenty-four-hour period you did it *all*.

There was a set protocol that we would follow. Sometimes life isn't black and white, it's all nothing but shades of gray. By law, we cannot pronounce someone dead. It takes a physician to pronounce someone dead. If you have a skeleton there, you know the guy's dead. Profound postmortem lividity – that's where the blood is all settled into the lower regions of the body and there's no resuscitating this guy. Decapitation: the head's cut off. Profound rigor mortis, where he's as stiff as a board and you're not going to budge him. It doesn't take a medical genius to spot someone who's dead. But by law we're obliged to at least make an effort. Sometimes you have to make calls that are really going to put you on the line. For instance, we were called into a home and the guy was dying of cancer. He was in his bed, he had his family around him, and you could see that the disease had completely ravaged him. He was unconscious but he was gasping for air, he was breathing his last breaths. I called the hospital and I said, 'Listen, here's what we got. The family doesn't want him resuscitated. There's no point. What should we do here?' They don't know what to tell us. They don't want to stick their necks out. They don't want to say, 'OK, do not resuscitate.'

This was before there was such a thing as living wills. I know that if we don't make some kind of a decision, this guy, his last moments are going to be *very* undignified. We're going to go through a whole resuscitation. That means doing CPR, cardiopulmonary resuscitation, on him, putting a tube down his throat. In a situation like this it would be debasing him. He's not quite a vegetable, but he's not going to be viable. As we're sitting there, he literally breathes his last breath. He utters out a shout and he stops breathing. I look around and I mean, I see, it's a Catholic family, we're a block away from the church that I grew up in, St. Andrew's Church. From my Catholic upbringing, I went to them and I said I'd already called a priest and he was on his way. I said, 'Why don't we gather around and say a prayer to St. Joseph?' – the patron saint of a happy death. St. Joseph is the patron saint of just about everything, actually, but a happy death is the one thrown in there. The family went with that, they thought it was a great idea. We kept them calmed down. We took the guy, we put him in the ambulance, and we took him to the hospital to be pronounced. Now, I'm wondering when I get there, am I going to run into some doctor or some nurse who's going to call me on this? As it turned out, the doctor understood our position, the priest was there. It was fine with the family. He was dead and he was going to stay dead.

Every situation is different. Not far away from here over at St. Joseph's Hospital, an old couple lived up in the high-rise just over-looking St. Joseph's. You could look out their window, see the back door of the hospital. This guy was a pretty vigorous-looking octo-genarian. He'd lived a very good life. On his walls you could see pictures of his family, you know, little things that you acquire that you bring along with you to remind you of where you'd been and who you are. We got in just as he was breathing, literally on the floor, breathing his last breath. We got on him right away, defibril-lated him, put the paddles on him, shocked him – it's an electric shot to the heart. Woke him up! Literally woke him up. His heart had stopped, there was no blood pressure, he wasn't breathing. So now he's talking to us and he's not in the best of moods either. 'What's going on? What are you doing?' We said, 'Relax, relax, we're going to take you down to the hospital.' 'Why? What happened?' So he's giving orders, right?

We're getting him on the stretcher and we've got him all bun-dled up and ready to go outside, get him in the ambulance. We've got an IV started on him so we can get some drugs in him if we need to. And we get to the elevator. There's me, my partner, the man's wife, and two coppers. We're going down in the elevator, and he looks at his wife, calls her by name, he says, 'I want you to know, it's really been great. Thanks an awful lot' – *bam*, dead. That was it: he breathed his last breath and no matter what we did to him, we couldn't get him back. We worked on him in the ambu-lance, we worked on him in the emergency room, but that was it. This man had gone. You wonder about it. He looked at his wife very purposefully, very adamant. Did he know? Did he see it? Did he have any inkling that this is what was going on? Five minutes before that, he was in charge, giving us orders, telling us, *no*, I'm *not* going to the hospital.

You try not to be affected by it. It's a reality you're facing, numerous times a day, it's part of your job, it's what you do. The body or the mind is a great layer of defensive mechanisms. You don't do it consciously – I think that you develop a thick skin as time goes on. You don't identify with that victim. He's not from your lifestyle, he's not from your class, he's not from your race. That would never happen to a member of my family, no matter how much they look like him because we wouldn't do something like that. You know what I'm talking about? There's a denial, a way of putting distance between yourself and the victim. You use every trick in the book. Because if you don't, you're going to wind up carrying some burdens that you just can't afford to carry. They're gonna get way too heavy. And I know a few guys, they couldn't handle it anymore. But there's a toll that you pay for building up that callus on your emotions. It doesn't come cheap. I've been off the job for ten years and I think that I'm probably free of it – I think I'm finally free of that thick-skinnedness that I had before.

You hear the humor that goes on in the back of a rig, the gallows humor. It's all very defensive. You'll see the same thing in cops, you'll see the same thing in firemen, you'll see the same thing in emergency room nurses, physicians. One of the things that was in our favor as paramedics was that we were hit-and-run guys – we got in and we got out, we didn't stay with a patient. For instance, I never had to be around someone who was dying on a long-term basis, like a hospice worker or a personal physician does. We would come in, we'd handle that patient, we'd be with them for a short period of time. Maybe the most intimate moments of his life we would be there for, but then we release him to other medics and we're gone, we're out of his life completely – that's in our favor. Other healthcare workers don't have that luxury. As paramedics we ride in on our horses, we're heroes, we drag them out, we get them to the emergency room, we drop them off. We say we never drop off a dead patient, which isn't true, but as long as we can try our magic on him, he's still alive. It's just a reality.

You can't afford to leave yourself, *any* part of yourself, with any one of these victims. Grief is grief. Denial is denial. I don't think anything used to make me more angry than suicides. The worst suicide that I ever saw wasn't gory or anything like that. It was really contained. It was a nineteen-year-old kid who took a shotgun, put it in his mouth, and pulled the trigger. For some reason, it didn't make a mess like you would expect it to. He sat in a very contained position against the wall. And it was the attitude that we found him in, the body, bare feet. He looked like a child, he looked like a kid. He left a suicide note on the counter. That was my big mistake – reading it. You separate yourself from things and you develop a thick skin. You try not to identify with the people that you have to deal with. Well, this kid left a note to his father and his brother about how he was tired of being treated as if he were retarded because he was very hard of hearing. He couldn't talk right and he couldn't hear. And that's what drove this kid to suicide. My big mistake was instead of looking at him and walking out of the room and forgetting about it, I bothered to read the note. And that's why it stuck in my head, it stuck in my mind.

We're the messengers – we don't bring good news. When you're the messenger with bad news, anything can happen. Did you ever see a war movie? You never hear anybody say, 'Medic, come here please.' It's always, '*Medic!*' – angry, urgent. It conveys a certain feeling, like *you* did this, *you're* responsible for this, do something to *fix* it! It's a feeling. You get over that after a while. You start to understand. But your initial response is, 'Hey, *I* didn't do it. Sorry, but it's not *my* fault.'

We have an energy that animates us, that, I think, sometimes reaches beyond our corporal bodies. You *know* the instant a person dies. You don't have to be a clinician to see the light leave their body, the instant that that body becomes inert substance. You just know it. Whether that body is comatose, whether it's a broken, traumatized piece of flesh, if you see the light leave that body, if you see the moment of the loss of animation, you know it. To me, it's a spiritual experience, like it or not. Aren't we this force, this life force that animates us? It always puzzled me how one thing will kill an individual and the guy right next to him can suffer the exact same thing and worse and survive it. I've had guys with conduit pipes shoved straight out underneath their chin, right out through the top of their head, and never lost consciousness. Another guy would be dead. I've had a man cut in half in a motorcycle accident who actually survived. I've seen people shoot themselves in the head and survive. And then little things. People die of them. Craziness. A guy bumps into the dining room table and an hour later, he's bled to death – simple little trauma, never knew he was hurt. Ruptured spleen. He just bled out. Never felt any pain. It truly is a mystery.

I think anybody who says they're not afraid of death is kidding themselves. I don't know whether we fear death itself, I don't know whether we have any understanding about death itself. That's what we fear about it: it's something that we can't possibly understand. What it's like to go beyond that door. No matter how many times we've seen it happen, no matter how many of our loved ones we've buried, people that we're tremendously close to: our parents, our wives . . . Not one of us has any understanding of what it means to go beyond it. We can say: 'I'm not afraid of death, it's just the other side of life. I wasn't afraid of being born.' In fact, Mark Twain, somewhere along the line, wrote, 'The only people who rejoice at births and mourn at funerals are the parties that aren't involved.' I think anybody who claims that they aren't afraid of death is either lying or kidding themselves.

Do I believe in a life after? I have no idea. I think of myself as spiritual. I really believe that what I am is not this body. I know how quick this body turns to garbage. You can't even make pot out of it. I'd like to be cremated and then shot out of a cannon during the '1812 Overture' when they set off the fireworks at Grant Park. That'd be a nice send-off. But really it doesn't matter to me. Get rid of me as cheap and fast as you can.

While we're alive, it's hope that keeps us going. That last laugh, that piece of cherry pie for today.

Law and
Order

ROBERT SOREGHAN

When he was seventeen years old – six years before he joined the
Chicago Police Department – he joined the Marine Corps. It was
during the Vietnam War. 'I spent eleven months out in the field.
We would be flown out by helicopter, and then we would search
and destroy our way back in for two weeks. I was young. It was an
adventure. Until you're over there for a while. Then the
excitement and the adventure seem to go away. It's a fear of the
unknown. You never ever knew where or when it was coming
from. There were no front lines. It was jungle warfare. It was all
around you. The most fear I had was of the unknown. It has never
gone away.'

I'm a fifty-three-year-old Chicago police detective, and I've been so
for the last thirty years. I deal with basically violent crimes. I'm married, I have two sons and two grandchildren. My oldest son is in the
police department now, and my youngest son works for an armored-
car company. We are practicing Catholics, but not as dedicated as
one might wish. I deal with any crime against a person: shootings,
stabbings, homicides, rapes, robberies, batteries – anything that one
person perpetrates against another.

I got into a shoot-out, 1972. I was returning from court down
at 321 North LaSalle on my way home, in uniform. I was on
Milwaukee Avenue, around Evergreen Street, and observed two
people chasing each other, down the street. One of them ran
into a storefront, Ben's Shoe Store, 1424 North Milwaukee. He
was followed by the other, who produced a gun and shot him
twice. I observed this. It was four-thirty in the afternoon, rush-
hour traffic, bumper-to-bumper. So I got out of my car, in

uniform, and drew my revolver, announced my office, and the individual that did the shooting turned and saw me and pointed the gun at me. I was fortunate enough to be able to shoot first, wounding him. Once I shot him, he dropped the gun and ran. He was about a quarter of a block down before he fell from his wounds. Just wounded – he didn't expire. I brought him back and he was arrested.

I had to talk very, very long to my wife prior to my interview to get on this job. She was scared to death. She married me before I got on the police department. I filled out applications for both the fire department and the police department. I'm still waiting to hear from the fire department. [*Laughs*] When I was notified by the police department that they accepted my application, my wife was fearful that something was going to happen – her fear of the unknown. But I talked to her and told her: 'I could go any time, anywhere – it doesn't necessarily have to be on the job.'

You don't see death all the time, but you hear of it. You monitor the radios and it's constant. The only thing that changes really is the degree. It could be something as simple as a minor domestic with husband and wife, it could be a simple battery, bar fight, all the way up to a hideous type of a murder. I try not to even think about getting killed. I had two friends of mine . . . [*Sighs*] Bill and Bruce were both policemen who worked in a Task Force Unit, and in 1973, we were patrolling up here in the twentieth district. They were patrolling up the street. This one individual comes out of a bar carrying a bag. They spotted this individual, he saw them, dropped his bag. They got out, looked in the bag, and there was a sawed-off shotgun. They ran back into the bar to apprehend him and he was hiding behind a portion of the entranceway. And when the first officer ran in, this offender, named Jacob Cohen, was also armed with a handgun. As soon as Bruce ran in, he shot him in the head. He fell down. His partner, Bill, ran in, grabbed him, and Cohen walked over and shot Bill as well. He killed both of them on the spot. We were the first car on the scene. We had just had dinner with them a half an hour before. They were close, close friends of my partner and myself. They were both talking about how they'd just picked up two new matching motorcycles. They were very close friends. And a half an hour later, they're laying dead on the tavern floor. That was very difficult to deal with. My partner transferred to another unit. It hit me really hard.

When I think of dying, I think *vault*. I don't want to be buried; that's just a personal preference. I'd rather they put me in a vault above ground. Maybe I'm claustrophobic, but I just don't like the thought of being six feet underground. I don't like the idea of being cremated. I have discussed this with the wife, and I think we're both agreed. You're still put in a coffin, but you're sealed in a concrete or marble vault. Or I could move to New Orleans. They're below sea level there, so all their cemeteries are above ground. My main concern is that I'm not going to leave those people that I love behind with any burden. I want to make sure that I can take care of them the best that I can and provide for them when I'm gone. My wife and I have talked about this: What if this happens now? We've laid out who to phone, who to call. I've got benefits with several different organizations – such as the army, such as the police department, the Masons, the VFW, the American Legion – all these groups I'm a member of, they all have these insurance packages, and I want to make sure that she knows where all these things are. I think our entire life, from the time we're born, is preparing for death. Somebody said and I heard it once, maybe it was in a movie, that from the time you're born you're preparing to die. That's pretty much the truth. It's a matter of living the best way you can and just preparing for the inevitable.

Delbert Lee Tibbs

He had served two years on death row in the state of Florida. He had been convicted by an all-white jury of rape and murder. Years later, the sentence was overturned by the Florida Supreme Court for lack of evidence.

I am a man of African and other roots: Indian, and no doubt European, as my research would indicate. A father, a citizen of the United States of America, and a man on the planet Earth. I was born in Mississippi, on a sharecropper's plantation, around sixty years ago. I grew up there until I was about twelve years old, at which time we migrated to Chicago, my mother and I. My mother had twelve children, like the twelve tribes. I was the last. Her baby, she called me. I went to Chicago public schools, from about the fifth grade through high school, and later I went to college for a bit. I went to the Chicago Theological Seminary from 1970 to 1972.

My mother was a black Baptist fundamentalist. I am spiritually orientated. I didn't go to the seminary actually to be a preacher – I went because I had fiddled around in school. I considered myself uneducated at the time. When I came up from Mississippi at twelve years old, I was practically illiterate. Black children were not expected to be educated – in fact, it was dangerous to be educated in Mississippi if you were black in the fifties. If you came from a black family, let's say middle-class, they would send you away to school. There you would be in danger just because of the fact that you were pursuing knowledge. That has always been something that has nettled me, the fact that my underpinnings were not good – that I might be an educated man impelled me to become a bookworm. I met a teacher in the fifth grade here and she started me to reading, and I never stopped. It also was an escape for me from the horrors of urban life. Reading became an escape from the squalor, from the gangs, when I was growing up here in Chicago. I started out reading anything and then, as time went on, I began to read 'significant' or meaningful works by whomever. I promised my mama that I was going to get an education.

One of the things that really got me going was that I failed English. I could do English basically from my reading, but I had no sense of the mechanics of grammar. I wrote a good paper, I read well, so the teachers would leave me alone. They didn't know that I didn't know any grammar. The same way with math, I just somehow got by. But when I went to night school, I flunked English, and that messed with my head.

In the meantime, I'm working a day job in the salt mines down at the old Lakeside Press, making telephone directories, Sears Roebuck and *Sports Illustrated*, *Time*, *Life*, and *Look*. It was one of the most racist places that ever existed on this earth. I also got a chance to read there all day – it kept me from probably leaping on one of those East Europeans and strangling him. I sometimes tell my son, 'Hey man, I don't know what your mama tell you about but I made a few sacrifices for you, because I wouldn't have stayed at that damn job for seven years and hated every single day of it' – I mean, with a *passion* that you can hardly believe. They were sued recently. Class-action suit for all of the years we were kept out of the unions.

I don't know if they knew I was going to school – it wasn't something you'd necessarily want them to know. I can remember a timekeeper. I remember him asking me to work overtime one day, and I refused. What he didn't know was I left there and went to school. If I had been a white boy, I could have told him that and he'd have said, 'Don't worry about it, go ahead.' But I just told him no, and then he said, 'Well, maybe eight hours is too much for you.' Of course I had a fit, I called him all kind of expletives. To myself, of course . . . [*Laughs*] I decided 'Fuck them, I ain't ever going back *there*.' But it taught me a lot. It taught me that if you have some heart, a little faith, God will take care of you. You might not always *like* the way He takes care of you, but He'll take care of you. So I quit my job. After a little hassle, I drew some unemployment, and then I went to school full-time. This was Delbert Superman – because, at that time, we thought education was the Balm in Gilead, education would fix everything. I mean, no more 'yassuh, boss.' It wasn't quite like that . . .

As a youngster, I wanted to be an adventurer, to live life to the fullest, go places that I'd never been. I used to tell people my ambition was to roam the world and make love to the various women of the world, drink the wines of Spain, the sake of Japan, and so forth. I leave Lakeside with nothing and no place to go. I'm twenty-three years old and I have a son who's four or five, and a wife that I'm separated from. The unemployment runs out before I can get my associate degree, and the rent man is banging on the door – so I have to go and find myself a job. And I did. I never read the *Defender*★ before in my life. I never would look in the *Defender* for a job because blacks ain't got no jobs that are going to pay me any money to take care of my family. But I do. And there's an ad for claims adjusters for the Checker Taxi Company. Hell, I don't know what a claims adjuster is, but I'm six feet three, I have all of my teeth, and my mind is sharp as a Toledo sword. [*Laughs*] So I apply for the job. And this Texan hires me. I look like I can take care of myself. At the time, the brothers are raising so much sand it's dangerous for white adjusters to go into the black community. So for the first time in my life, I got a white-collar job, right? I wear a suit and a tie every day. So I do this for two years, three years, and am very good at it. *Damn* . . . I speak very well, and my boss said, 'Mr. Tibbs, you know why you're so successful? Because people believe you.' I said, 'Well, generally speaking, I don't lie to them. I tell them what the deal is. I say, "Hey, I can give you three grand now, or you get five grand later and a lawyer gets a third of that and a doctor gets the other part."' That's my prejudice against insurance companies. So I would settle claims like that. And nobody ever came back and said, 'Hey, I got cheated.'

But the job was boring as hell. All kinds of other stuff was happening around human rights issues and so forth. I'm making good money, but that's only for me, it ain't doing nothing for my people. I'm not furthering my own growth, and so I spent a great deal of time afterwards boozing and carousing. After a couple of years, I met this beautiful young lady, Miss Julie Tyler, who was not at all typical of the young ladies I had met. She was a bourgeois black woman from Hyde Park. Her daddy was upper-middle-class. She had run

★The *Chicago Defender* has, for years, been the most widely read African-American newspaper in the country.

away when she was sixteen to march with Martin Luther King and became a member of SNCC.* I quit my job and she and I got a place in Old Town, and, as the youngsters say now, we chilled out for the next year or so.

At the time, the black clergymen in Chicago had gone to the white seminaries and said, 'Hey, you people graduate two or three hundred seminarians a year, but only one or two of them are black.' I found out about this three-year program where one could get an MAT, Masters in Arts and Theology. So they opened it up to selected black folks, whether or not you had an undergraduate degree. I was saying cynically, '*Yeah*, they're looking for somebody to stem the shit that's jumping off now. And yeah, I'll do that because I do believe that peace is better than war, that friendship and that kind of stuff is better than enmity. I ain't going to be somebody's Uncle Tom, but I will do what I can . . .' And so also I will have fulfilled my promise to my mama: I will have myself a master's degree. It was really beautiful because I could read all day and didn't feel guilty for reading because it was course stuff.

And then *crazy* stuff starts happening. I had about five friends pass away, and these are young guys, in the matter of a year or two. And it scared the piss out of me, if you will pardon the expression. Not to mention the stuff that's happening in the street. The cops going and shooting [Black Panthers] Mark Clark and Fred Hampton. I dropped out of the seminary.

And then I had an experience. I was at a friend's house, someone I was in school with, and I was drinking orange juice, and I think this guy put LSD in it. The story really gets crazy. I left his house and I was taking one of our friends home. I looked at the girl and her face had changed. I had this very violent verbal reaction, and I'm *not* a violent guy. I think I scared her. I dropped her off at home and my body started shaking uncontrollably, which acid will do to you. Something was happening with my body and I didn't know what it was. I drove my car all night because I knew I couldn't sleep.

I'd dropped out of the seminary and now I don't know what to do with myself. There was an agitation within my spirit, so I said, 'Well, I'll take off. I've never been anyplace except Mississippi, Michigan,

*Student Non-Violent Coordinating Committee.

Illinois, and Indiana.' I thought, you might not live that long anyway, so I took off and I took off walking. I wanted to go to California.

This was in 1972. I sold my car to my brother. When you're six-three and you're black, there are a lot of places you don't get no rides. So it was mostly walking, and then later on I rode freight trains. I'd get a job working by the day for two or three days, make twenty bucks a day. That would last me a couple of weeks. I smoke bulk tobacco, roll my own, and I sleep under bridges and in cars. I went all over the USA. I've been in all the states, except maybe three. So I was all over Florida. And when this crazy stuff jumps off, the murder and the rape thing – people say, 'You were in the wrong place at the wrong time.' Philosophically, I can't accept that. I was supposed to go through the experiences that I was supposed to go through for whatever reasons. I think God wanted me to disabuse myself of my fear of death, I really do. I think that's why I went to death row. I think God was saying to me, 'OK, I'm going to show you there's nothing to fear out here but me. I'm going to the House of Death' – 'cause that's what they call it, they call it the Death House – 'and I'm going to bring you out again.' [*Laughs*] And that's what happened.

During the time I was in Florida, this guy was killed, and allegedly this young white woman was raped. I really don't know what happened, because I wasn't there. But I do know I am not the perpetrator of it. I think what happened was this girl was like sixteen, and as pretty as you'll ever want to see, right? From Rhode Island. And she had been living with this photographer who was in his forties down in St. Pete.

A young white brother from downstate Illinois, who just got out of the navy, comes through. She says she had been smoking grass for several days, and I really believe this young ex-naval guy was maybe transporting. People did a lot of that back then, and Florida was one of the places that you could pick up really good weed. So this young guy, the guy who was killed, comes and stays in the trailer court where the girl was living in St. Petersburg, with her older photographer. And when the young guy takes off, she takes off with him. She runs away from her old man. At one point during the trial, my lawyer, from Chicago, he said to her, 'Isn't it true that you ran away from this guy? The photographer, he pursued you and caught you on the highway and then killed this young man and threatened to kill you if you didn't come back with him?' She broke down and went to crying. And the judge, great pale defender of white Southern womanhood that he is, called for a recess. And my old scary black lawyer didn't bring it up when he came back because he didn't want to make these white folks mad at him. And I understand it – I'm a Southern boy. My rationale to them for being in the state was just that I wanted to roam across the country, which is typical of writers and artists and so forth, but it's not typical of black people. It's all right for Jack Kerouac, but not for Delbert Tibbs.

There's another assumption: this is my country, I can go anyplace I like. This happened around the 4th of February, 1974. On the 6th of February, the Florida state police stops me. They asked me to let them see my ID. I let them see my ID. I told them I'd been down in southern Florida doing farmwork. They questioned me, I guess, because Ocala is, I believe, maybe two hundred miles from Fort Myers – which is near where the crime occurred. The cops questioned me and let me go, but before they do that, they ask if I mind if they take photographs of me. I say, 'No, I don't mind.' So they take four Polaroid snapshots. One of the cops said, 'Mr. Tibbs, I don't think you had anything to do with it, so I'm going to do you a favor.' In the meantime, they don't know what to do with this nigger. I've got ID in my pocket from the University of Chicago, and photo ID and that kind of stuff, and yet here I am in Florida with these work clothes on. He says, 'There's been a serious crime, and you're going to be stopped a number of other times because all the enforcement folks are going to stop people they see that are strangers.' He wrote me out a letter saying, 'This person, Delbert Tibbs, was questioned by me on the 6th of February, 1974, and I'm satisfied he's not the person wanted in connection with the crimes' – crimes, he never specified, which occurred around Fort Myers on such-and-such a date. And he let me go.

I think I got stopped once more after that. I go into Mississippi where I have an aunt. I tell her what I'm probably going to do is walk to Memphis, which is a hundred miles away, and stay at my uncle's house there. Then I'm going to call Roy, that's my brother who at that time was a lieutenant in the sheriff's department, and tell him to send me a hundred dollars. They think I'm crazy, 'cause I've left this job and I'm just roaming around the country. That's not typical for black young men to do. But I'm me and I don't always choose to follow the path that everybody else follows – which is what got me into trouble. I wasn't behaving – *quote* – the way a nigger ought to behave – *end quote*.

After a couple of weeks at my aunt's house, I get back on the highway. About ten miles from my aunt's house I see a Mississippi highway patrolman driving in the opposite direction. He goes past, turns around, and we go through the thing, 'Let me see your ID.' I show him my ID. He says, 'You're Delbert Tibbs? You're wanted for rape and murder.' He said, 'There's a warrant for your arrest.' I said, 'Here's a letter I have.' He said, 'I don't know nothing about no letters, I don't know nothing about nothing. All I know is there's a warrant for your arrest.' He puts the cuffs on me and takes me to the nearest jail, which is a little place called Clarksdale.*

I didn't know at the time, but the photographs had been sent to Fort Myers. Initially, the girl had given a description of the rapist and murderer as a black man about five-six or -seven, with a great big Afro. I had a small Afro and I'm six three and relatively light-complexioned. The police are desperate to find someone, because there's a black murderer-rapist running loose. The cops take the Polaroid snapshots of me and by now I'm sure they've scared the pee out of her because she ain't come up with nobody and here's the corpse here, right. And they said, 'Is this the guy?' And she said yes. So that's when the warrant went out. But now she's changed her description of the guy, right? I didn't know that at the time, but that's what's happened.

By then I had gone through a spiritual breakthrough where I almost didn't see people as black and white anymore. I had spent two years sleeping under the stars. I called it my 'wilderness' experience. Two years more or less at the mercy of the world. I was someplace one evening, sitting in the doorway of this freight train, and folks in their cars and pickups were pulled up waiting for the train to go by so they could cross the track, and I see this little boy. There was a

*Bessie Smith, the most celebrated of blues singers, was in an auto accident in Clarksdale in 1937. It is said that she was denied admission to the nearby white hospital and died on the way to another hospital.

guy sitting in a truck, probably with a rifle in the back, and this little white boy jumps out, eight- or ten-year-old kid, and runs towards where I'm sitting in the door of the freight train. I'm thinking, *What is this?* He's running to bring me a box of Kentucky Fried Chicken, 'cause his daddy done told him, 'Go take this to the guy, the hobo man, and feed him.' You know what I'm saying? What he saw was a hungry man, not a black man.

Incidents like that, there have been many of them – I saw individuals, I saw human beings. And that's both liberating and dangerous. So I think, *Why not go back to Florida?* Obviously, it's a case of mistaken identity. This stuff ain't gonna go away if I just sit here. If I were being pragmatic, I'd have let the states of Mississippi and Florida argue about it, and Florida would have had to prove that they had a reasonable cause to want me back. They didn't have anything except the girl said I did it. But I went back to Florida.

I should have known that something was crazy. It must have been a fifteen-hour car trip, handcuffed, chains on my legs. As we're going into the station, there's somebody out front with a minicam taking pictures. They take me in, fingerprint me, give me my blankets. Get up the next morning and they feed you the stuff they feed you, and I'm watching TV and I see myself coming into the station on TV. After that, they call me out to go into a lineup. I said, 'Well, shit, everybody in town knows what I look like now.' Sure enough, I go in the lineup with five or six other guys and the girl say, 'Yeah, that's that fucker.' That was her word. Oh boy, game's afoot now. So they have good cause to keep me. They bind me over, and I'm in Lee County jail waiting to go to trial for rape and murder. Irony abounds. My middle name is Lee and I'm in Lee County Jail. I spend the next nine months there. The first couple of weeks, I don't do anything 'cause I figure they're going to let me out of here, so I don't even bother my family. But that ain't happening. They say, 'Hey, shit, you're it.'

In a sense, I integrated the jail. This place was kind of like time had passed them by. This is Fort Myers. They do what they want to do down there. My presence there focused so much attention on it. This young woman I'd been involved with for five years, Julie Tyler, started the Delbert Tibbs Defense Committee, and they began raising money for lawyers. Folks started visiting me. A lot of my friends had been movement folks, so there was a lot of scrutiny on the town. They began to kind of get themselves together so they didn't look bad to the rest of the world.

I was slightly bewildered, but I still wasn't worried at all, which was stupid. I should have been. I had reached a stage in consciousness either where something deep in me knew that it ultimately was going to be all right, or where it didn't matter, kind of like Socrates . . . I'll drink the hemlock, ain't no big thing.

I was locked up for nine months and then the trial. All-white jury. In Chicago, my lawyer, he was with a prestigious law firm, very successful. But Chicago ain't Lee County, Florida. He was intimidated. He was scared, and I don't much blame him, because the judge was quite capable of locking him up too if he displeased him. When he had an objection, the judge would overrule it; when the prosecution had an objection, the judge would sustain it. It was obvious to me what was happening. We had one black person who made it through the peremptory challenges for selection on the jury and then got disqualified at the last minute. I think he said he didn't read or write too good and the judge maybe thought that was enough. You have this arrogant Negro dash nigger, from up North someplace, who tended to look white folks in the eye and who would not let them put words in his mouth. I can't stop myself. I said, 'Delbert, they see you as an arrogant, crazy nigger.' Actually, I was just being me.

The courtroom was packed. My folks had come from Chicago in large groups, probably every black person in the town had come to the trial because they knew about the brother from Chicago. The police department have marksmen on the roof because they think that some of these black militants might come down and try to bust me out. After a day and a half, they find me guilty.

At that time there was a moratorium on the death penalty and the judge said, 'Well, if the moratorium continues, then you will serve two life sentences consecutively. If not, then you are to be executed by the State of Florida.' Before that, there's a presentence investigation, where they check your background to see if you have a criminal record, if there are mitigating factors.

I'll never forget, one of the investigators came to see me after the trial and he asked me, 'Delbert, I know you say you dated white girls – did you ever have sex with one?' I'm saying, *Why would he ask me that?* I'm such a fool. I was inclined to ask him had he ever slept with a black one, but I answered his question, I said, 'Yes, I've had sex with white females.' He turned as red as your socks and again something said, *You fool – you were supposed to say no.* So I got sentenced, and then they shipped me off to the Death House. The electric chair is up at a place called Starke. Right next door is Florida State Prison, the regular penitentiary. The max joint is Starke and it's right next door to Raiford, the Big House. That's where the Death House and the electric chair is – Old Sparky, as they call the chair. Sometimes they refer to it as the Iron Lady. A couple of things stuck in my mind. When they got ready to take you from the county jail to the state jail, they always did it in the middle of the night. I remember reading about the camps in Germany, how when they'd come to take people to the gas chambers, they'd come and get you in the middle of the night. It was almost as scary because I didn't know where the hell I was going. For all I knew, they could have took me and executed me then. My rational mind told me they weren't, but it was just scary.

They put you in a van with no windows in it, and you're chained up, I would say maybe ten of us. Some guys are going to one place and some are going to another. I'm going to death row. There's a bench on each side and chains, one around your waist and another one around your feet, so you ain't going nowhere. I remember the guy saying, 'Well, you got five over here for Raiford.' He comes to me and says, 'What's your name?' I said, 'Tibbs.' He said, 'You're to go to the Death House.' The moratorium ended. Now the State of Florida's free to execute all the folks they want to. So they take me there and put me in my cell. The food was much better – cons always think about food.

I was there two years, until the Florida Supreme Court overturned the conviction. In the meantime, the Delbert Tibbs Defense Committee and Miss Julie Tyler, they're working. Pete Seeger did a concert for me. Angela Davis spoke at Operation Push and raised money. I sometimes tell people when I do lectures: If you really want to punish a guy, lock him up on death row for twenty or thirty years. After five years, he'll probably beg you to put him in the chair or strap him to the gurney. I have friends now, like Rolando Cruz, who did eleven years. I said, 'Man, you've got to be the *strongest* man on the planet.' Each day, each day . . . It was getting harder and harder by the time I got out. Each day it was like Sisyphus pushing that rock up the mountain. Tuesday might as well be Wednesday. The only kind of change was on the weekend, when people would come to visit.

I was convinced that they were not going to kill me. I didn't think that they were worthy of my death, to put it in those kind of terms. Somehow, deep down, I knew that that wasn't my fate. But, the reality is, in a sense, they *create* your reality. I am behind the bars, I have to ask to be let out, they feed me, they turn out the lights when they want to turn out the lights. I don't run *anything* there.

I had gotten so when I got up out of the bed about seven-thirty in the morning, I would reach for the TV. You automatically turn it on because it was something coming in from out there, and there were people on the TV, right? Then I'd eat breakfast and I'd sit up and watch TV, maybe doze off, go to sleep. At eleven-thirty, they serve lunch. And I would watch TV through lunch. Then some days I'd work out in the cell, do push-ups and sit-ups like most of the guys did. Then you look around and it's four o'clock and they served dinner. Everything was focused around mealtime. Because that was the only pleasant thing in your day, the food. You eat dinner and then you're up until lights-out at eleven o'clock. Turning on the TV was automatic. Before I'd go to bed at night a lot of times I would tie a towel around the knob on the TV, so that when I'd go to hit the knob, the towel would be there and I'd go, 'Oh, I didn't mean to turn this image on this morning.' It was one way of my taking control of at least that action.

When I meet people now, if they try to make a big deal about me having been on death row, I sometimes gently remind them that we're all on death row. The difference is that here the state's gonna do it, and at some point you're gonna know the date and the hour, but that's the only difference. I mean, if you're walking around here, *shit* – you're on death row, 'cause you're going to have to *leave* here. You're going to lay down and they're going to throw dust in your face. They never set a date for me. And I thank God for that.

The Florida Supreme Court finally overturned the conviction. They said that there was no evidence. The jury convicted me and they shouldn't have. The jury convicted me because a white woman said I had raped her. This is the politics: the state appealed the overturning of the conviction. But they had to let me out. They got every pound of flesh they could: they let me out on ninety thousand dollars' bond, so I would come back for the trial. The case was overturned a couple of times. I came to Chicago. In the meantime, the state was gearing up to retry me. At one point, there was a circuit court judge who overturned the whole thing and dismissed it. The state got the case reinstituted.

The case was overturned in 1976, I got out in January of 1977. That should have been the end of it. But the country was moving further and further to the right. Initially, when the sentence was overturned, it was a four-to-three decision. Four justices said we believe he's innocent, three said we believe he's guilty. All seven are very well educated people, why is it that these guys look at the same evidence, the same data, and come to diametrically opposite conclusions? It can't be based on intellect or reason, it has to be based on something else. I suggest to you it's based on that cultural conditioning. To folks of this particular mind-set, I'm guilty because that white woman said I'm guilty. And because I'm a big old black buck.

In 1982, the DA dropped the case. He said his witness wouldn't be credible before a jury because she had lived a life of alcohol and drug abuse and so forth. The girl admitted that she'd been smoking marijuana the day that the crime occurred. It certainly can impair your identification of somebody. The real reason he dropped the case was because, during the interview, the young prosecutor who had sent me to death row had said – this is the crazy part – I had made friends in Fort Myers. One of my white friends was talking to the DA's wife, and she says, 'What your husband did to Delbert Tibbs . . .' The wife said, 'What did my husband do?' She said, 'They convicted that man on just four Polaroid snapshots.' When he came home from work – he'd gone into private practice – she asked if that were true. And he said, yeah, but if he had known at the time, he would not have prosecuted the case. If we had gone to trial, he was going to be the first witness for our side.

I believe life is endless. We can't talk about life without talking about death; we can't talk about death without talking about life. I was listening to the Dalai Lama, I read his autobiography, and he says that Buddhists often meditate on death. That's total anathema to the Western mind, right? I think it has something to do with Greek culture, with its bifurcation of existence – this is life and this is death. I learned to meditate before I went to death row. That's one of the things that helped get me through, but it was very difficult. Otherwise, I read mostly, as much as I could. I can go home with a good book today and I'll spend the whole day reading it. On death row, I couldn't focus my mind on anything. I couldn't lose consciousness of my environment for more than forty-five minutes. If I did, I would find myself getting up, pacing, looking out of the bars. I remember saying to one of my homies who was executed by the State of Florida, I'd say, 'Hey, Shango, I believe there are spooks in this goddamn place.' He'd say, 'Well, if there's any such thing, Brother Tibbs, this is the place for it.'

What I've discovered is: All of the holy books are marvelous, absolutely so, including the Bible. The Bible has the most beautiful language of any book I have ever read. Not to mention the fact that there's something there. God is there. But I really do believe He's hidden. I believe the Jewish mystics who went into the kabala know that. I sometimes wish I spoke Hebrew because the words might not be the thing itself but they can lead to it. The *Bhagavad Gita* is the bible to three hundred million Indians and others who are not Indians. Thoreau and Emerson read it. Krishna says there never was a time when you and I did not exist, and there will never be a time when we cease to be. He said, 'This body wears out, like garments, and when a garment wears out, you take it off and you lay it down, and you pick up another one and put it on.'

One of the terrible things about executions is to jump people off into the universe like that. I think for a soul to be wrenched from the body is for that soul to be in anger and in pain and in hatred. I believe it impacts negatively on our world, that probably a lot of the calamities that happen are a result of that sort of thing. I mourn for the whole world because it's such a horrible place so often.

War

Dr. Frank Raila

A veteran of World War II, he benefited from the GI Bill of
Rights. He attended college and medical school. For a time, he
practiced as a GP in Illinois as well as in Brazil. He is now a
neuroradiologist in the University of Mississippi Medical School.
'I've saved lives, and it's a great feeling.'

My first memory of death was when I was a child on Honore Street.
There was ice, an accident, a horse cart and a vehicle. There was a
piece of this man's bone in the gutter with blood around it. I must
have been just six, seven years old. I remember seeing that rib-like
thing. That was the first time I ever saw something that belonged to
a human being . . . The next time that I saw violent death was in the
war. This one American was on his back. He was dead, but he
coughed up a lot of real red blood, and it was all over his face, down
both sides of his face. His skin was real white . . . that white and the
redness out of his mouth.

Another time, there was an American lying in the ditch near the
road. I had seen other dead bodies, Germans and Americans. But I
was real close to this one and the wind was blowing on his hair, and
the hair was moving. Movement is life, isn't it? This guy, his skin was
kind of a light greenish color, but that moving hair – it just struck
me. And the same day, we were going down this road into where
there were 20mm cannon shells laying around. I was trying not to
step on them because some of them are explosive. I was hopping
around a little bit. I almost landed on top of this man's upper jaw. It
was laying on the road. I remember it was very pink and it had a
complete set of beautiful white teeth. I almost broke my ankle trying
to keep from stepping on this guy's jaw. And there was red stuff
stringing off of both sides. His head was exploded and his jaw flew
out and fell on the road and I almost stepped on it . . .

I was born in Chicago. My father left Lithuania when he was fifteen years of age, came to Chicago, joined the army, and went back to the trenches in World War I. His son ended up in World War II. [*Laughs*]

I was trained in intelligence and reconnaissance and sent to the 106th Infantry Division. They put almost the whole division on the *Queen Elizabeth*, which was able to hold between ten and fourteen thousand troops. We were in a stateroom that was built for two people, and there were something like forty or fifty of us in it. They had bunks against every wall – they were only like eighteen inches apart. Most of us were seasick. We got off near Glasgow and got in trains that were all darkened. We ended up in the English Channel. We were all sick as dogs when we crossed it. This was 1944. I'd just turned nineteen. We got off in Le Havre. It was raining. We pitched our tents out in the field. It was muddy, rain. The next morning, we drove all the way into Luxembourg and it was snowing. We were on the trucks for days and nights, getting off and sleeping on the ground in between. We knew we'd be in combat, but we didn't know which theater we'd be in.

When we were in Belgium, we slept in the snow. We pulled down branches of evergreen trees and that was the floor of our pup tents.

We were put on a line. I was in the 423rd Regiment, Company E. We didn't realize that the Germans had thirty to forty divisions out there. It was winter, and we thought it would be a quiet front. And so they pulled out a very experienced division and put us in their place. These guys said, 'Oh, you've got an easy spot. We've got dugouts and everything's perfect for you. You're just going back to a nice warm spot, you've got nothing to worry about . . .' And then on December 16th, Germans attacked our lines with something like twenty divisions and had us almost surrounded. General Jones, our division chief, made the mistake of not pulling us back. He thought that the armored column that he had asked help from would come up and push the Germans back. But it snowed badly on the roads, the roads were packed. They never got to us. We were surrounded.

While we were going up there, 88s were exploding around us and we had faulty ammunition. There was a mortar squad ahead of us. The sergeant in charge would drop the shell in the tube and it wouldn't go off. And that shell in the tube is *very* dangerous, because you pull the pin out of it and all you have to do is hit that little nose and it'll blow up. So he had to lift that tube off the base plate and then slide that shell and catch it with two fingers and put the pin back in the nose and lay it on the ground and put in another one. They had, I'd say, three or four duds out of five. And all the time, we're all being shot at. The sergeant was standing up and acting as a point to show where to drop these shells and they were shooting around him. They had us zeroed in. The shells and mortars start dropping around us, and there were guys yelling for their mothers and screaming and being torn to pieces. I was right in the middle of it all. The ground was falling on my back in little chunks of earth.

One poor chap was screaming for his mother and a sergeant told him to shut up. We were so green, we were just laying out there getting pounded. I was very, very frightened. The thing that I think frightens most soldiers is not being brave in front of the other men. The fear of being cowardly in front of your men, I think, was greater than anything else, and kept you going. It's not the flag, it's not the country, it's not apple pie, it's the kid next to you – you can't let him down. I was really terrified. All of us were, but didn't want to show it. I remember being behind the second gunner, and he was hit in the hip and he was laying down right in front of me. Our foxhole was only about ten inches deep and it was filled with water and there was snow around us and ice. I can remember a bullet about three, four inches away from my head, hitting the dirt, and a little bit of dirt being flicked up in the air, and a little bit of steam coming out where the bullet went into the ground. That made me dig a lot faster, I'll tell you that. [Laughs] Six inches closer and it would have hit me right between the eyes. It's just chance, yeah, it really is chance . . .

Just before we pulled out, McBride told me to get some more ammunition and I went back down the road. McBride was my sergeant, the one that played for Notre Dame, a great big guy. I was the ammunition carrier. So I went back to the ammo place, a four-by-four truck. I told them I needed some rifle and machine-gun ammunition. Believe it or not, he asked me if I had a chit for it, a piece of paper for it. [Laughs] I said, 'Well, I don't have a paper, but there's a German tank coming up the road, you guys aren't going to be here very long.' So he gave me two boxes of ammunition and a bunch of boxes of thirty-caliber carbine ammunition. That was really funny, I never forgot that. We left all our belongings, all our packs in the woods. The Germans just zeroed in on those woods. So we left the woods with no tents, nothing except the first-aid kits and the shovel, and our bandoleers and a rifle. The Battle of the Bulge started December 16th and ended in January, like the 20th.

Every day there was something going on. I recall being in this field and there was a machine gun mass-firing at us. The officers told us to outflank the machine guns. There were actually two of them, they would fire in tandem. A German machine gun sounds almost like ripping cloth because it had a very high rate of fire. One machine would fire a short burst, and a machine gun on the other side would fire another short burst. It was hard to find out where it was coming from. But our guys came in and they attacked this machine gunner. They killed everyone there except a German sergeant.

They had this German in front of them and he was shot in the arm. He could only hold up one arm. The other arm was down because it was injured. The American behind him, one of the guys from our company, put a comb under his nose, like Hitler, and did the Nazi salute behind this guy. And this is when bullets were going! [*Laughs*] And we all were laughing at him like idiots. This is typically goofy American. A little bit afterwards, when that German came across and they put him in a first-aid station, all the guys all of a sudden turned around and pointed their rifles at him. I thought they were going to kill him right there. In my eighteen-, nineteen-year-old fervor, I got up and I said, 'Don't shoot him, we're Americans – we don't kill people like that.' Can you imagine? I was just a young greenhorn. It was almost embarrassing when I got through saying it. But it just seemed un-American to shoot a guy with his hands up in the air.

They stopped, and I took this guy and I came up to a barbed-wire fence and I told him to come with me. I don't know how I did it. The post that held up the fence, I just backed off and lunged into it like I was lunging into a football line. And I knocked that post down so he could walk over the barbed wire, because there was no other way he could get over it. I got to the road and told some people to take him back to the aid station. Then I went back to my machine gun squad. I don't think there were more than thirty, forty men making up our front line, and we had all these thousands of

Germans in front of us. I remember an American coming towards us, about a hundred and fifty yards away – he was limping, and McBride told me to go out and get him. Bullets were kicking up and stuff was flying around. And so I gritted my teeth and I ran out and I got up to the guy and he said he didn't want any help. [*Laughs*] 'Put your arm around me, I'm going to help you anyway whether you like it or not.'

McBride said that apparently the firing pin on the machine gun was broken. It wouldn't fire anymore. So he said, 'Let's go back and get the firing pin fixed, and then we'll go back to the front line.' When we got on the road and we were going through the village, here was our aid station. There was an American in there, he was crying, it was full of wounded men. There was a lieutenant on a table in front of a window who was shot through the testicles twice. You could see the fat and stuff sticking out of the holes in his testicles. And the German was lying on the floor on a stretcher. And the second gunner, who was shot and hit, was lying next to him.

There was one room that was darkened, the door was closed. I opened up that room and it was filled with very seriously wounded, dying. This one lieutenant was on the stretcher – I'll never forget – half his jaw was gone and he was gurgling something. And I got a water can and poured a little water in his throat. It kind of gurgled and I thought, well, that's enough. The bottom of the stretcher, there must have been about an inch of blood in it. He'd also been shot in the leg and had a splint on it. And there was an American sitting on a stool in one corner, sobbing. His hands and fingers were off. He had just gone crazy. He was just uncontrollably sobbing. There were other men that apparently were dead on the floor. I said to Mac [McBride], 'If we don't hurry about and get out of here, we're going to be trapped.' He says, 'Yeah, but let's help these people for just a few minutes.' And it was the few minutes that we lost that got us trapped. Because I was uncurling bandages on this man's groin, on his genitals, and I heard these hobbled boots outside. And all of a sudden this young German, nice thin mustache, kind of handsome – he was short, with a skull and crossbones on his hat. The window was open, and he stuck his rifle right through the window and had it pointed right at my chest. I thought he was going to blow me away. I dropped the bandages, I put my hands up and I said, 'Comrade is kaput.' And he said, '*Raus!*' They had us covered from the doorway. We got out and he motioned to us – I didn't speak German, just a few words – to take the wounded Germans out first. They had a captured American truck. Mac and I, with the German on the stretcher, were walking down this little street to the truck, and a German pops out in front of me, throws his rifle up to his shoulder, and takes a bead right at me. I stopped, 'cause I thought, *This guy's gonna kill me.* When I stopped, all of a sudden, the German in the stretcher wondered why. He put his hand out and started yelling German to the guy aiming the rifle at us. And he put the rifle down slowly and let us go by.

Now we were prisoners of war, and we went to a little churchyard and this was Christmas Eve. And McBride and myself and the first gunner Ray Russell and Delheim, the sergeant, we started to sing Christmas carols. And a bunch of guys got around us and were singing Christmas carols. And I guess this must have bugged the Germans because they told us to shut up or they were going to shoot us. [*Laughs*] We shut up. It was very poignant, this group of guys. We were covered with hoarfrost and it was late, twelve or one o'clock in the morning. And all these GIs in there sitting or standing around, decided to sing 'Silent Night.' And they told us to keep quiet – so we were silent. [*Laughs*]

We walked almost about a hundred miles with no food, no water, no place to stay. We laid down near the road, on the road, next to the road. Frozen. We were afraid that if we left anybody, they would be shot. So we helped everybody we could that couldn't make it. And then we were put in a building in Koblenz, Germany. Later on I found out it was for Hitler Youth. It was the only building standing. They put us in this building, and then the Americans bombed us during the day and the British bombed us at night. The German guards went into the air-raid shelters and left us up top in the buildings. We were in this one large room, I would say about twenty men. We put a mattress up against the windows because we thought that would keep flying glass from being blown in. And sure enough, these five-hundred- or eight-hundred-thousand-pound bombs were going off. Missed the building but blew the glass, the airframes, and the mattress into the room. We were laying down on the floor. I was the only guy sitting in a chair. When that thing went off it blew the frame, the glass, the mattress, and blew the door out into the hallway, and I went out with the door.

I was a prisoner for about four, five months near the end of the war. I didn't know when the war was going to be over, but I knew that the time to escape is when you're just first captured or when you're being moved. They decided to move us. They put us in a soccer field. There were English, Welsh, New Zealanders, Australian prisoners with us. And they counted us about a million times, like the Germans always do. They make one miscount, they count the whole thing over again. I had tried to escape once before. I didn't make it. There were about twenty of us living in a small jail. We had a toilet outside. They became more lax because we'd always come back. So I figured, I'd go this time. I had made contact with a British lad. I was to meet him on a bridge near Sandisdorf, and then we were going to take off together. Well, I go out there and I look for the food I had dug into the ground – there's nothing there. I go to the toilet and there's a guard there who escorts me back, and I knew that I was foiled.

I'd had it all planned. I'd gone this route before. At night, I'd go out to the toilet, jump on the side of the fence, and, with a leap, grab ahold of the eave, pull myself up, climb over the roof, jump to another lower roof, and then jump to the ground. Go to the place that had the carrots and stuff, put my socks around my pants, put the carrots in the pants and in my pockets, and then walk back, jump up this low roof, climb up to the low roof, climb up to the high roof, and then jump down, bring the carrots to the guys, and we would eat this stuff. So I did that about four or five times. One time I did it and I was trapped on a roof by air-raid sirens. The guard had come out the front door and he was crunching around on the gravel. I swear I thought he was going to shoot me right in my rear end. I had a watch on, and I put it in my mouth so he wouldn't hear the ticking. I don't know if he saw me.

Walking to Stalag Forbein was really terrible. We were put in box-cars and we had a short trip to Limburg. We got there just a few hours after Limburg prison camp was accidentally bombed by the Americans. There were about two hundred American POWs killed. We were being transferred to another place. I knew that I would like to escape again, so I walked very slowly. I was walking, say, two steps back for every one step everyone else was taking, so I could get back to the Brits. I met this same guy I was supposed to escape with, and he says there's something like ten guys are going to try to take off and if I wanted to go with them, I could go. So they herded us into this field; there was barbed wire around it.

The Brits had chocolate and cigarettes. When the fog came in, we were talking to the guards at one end, keeping them busy. And two Brits would go out under the barbed wire. I went with two Welsh guys. We were supposed to meet at a hayfield that we could see during the day. There was nobody there. We probably walked to the wrong hayfield. And so we walked all that night trying to find a place big enough for us to hide in. It was terrible because we had diarrhea. We finally found a place that looked like a big forest and slept overnight. The next day, we met up with a bunch of Russian slave laborers who had escaped. They had some vodka. I'd never tasted vodka before. They all got stinking drunk and I got a headache. Then that day they went and raided a German farmyard and got a rabbit. We split the rabbit up. It was three Americans and maybe eight, ten Russian slave laborers. And I remember they'd cooked the rabbit, and I got the head. It was delicious, I ate everything: the tongue, the brains, the eyeballs . . . protein tasted *delicious*.

The next day there are Americans coming up the road. It was an American reconnaissance column. I took my coat off and waved, I said, 'I'm an American, I'm an American, don't shoot.' The Russians were just in the forest, sticking their heads up. They were glad to see us, and then we got the British boys down and then the Russians came down. I gave them my coat and I asked the Americans if I could throw the Russians a bunch of Spam – 'Because they helped us,' I said. The guy said, 'Sure,' so we threw the Spam out, and there was some extra clothing too. They were really tickled pink.

Then they took us back to a little town and, since we were POWs, they sent us back to Camp Lucky Strike. And from Camp Lucky Strike, we went down to USS *Marine Devil*, and from *Marine Devil* to Boston Harbor.

I was always interested in being a physician, and so I knew I would see death. To me death is a part of life. I know that sounds contradictory. Death is only a portal, an opening to another type of life, a life that we can't explain or understand.

I know a P-51 pilot from World War II who, when he died, had his ashes scattered in the Pacific. You put yourself in the elements of the world a lot quicker. You become a rose, a tree a lot quicker. It doesn't make any difference once you're dead. Somebody asked me, 'What would you like to come back as if you were reincarnated?' I'd like to come back as an eagle. I would like to soar. I could see the earth from a far-off distance. When I've had dreams of flying, it was very enjoyable. And if I wasn't a physician, I would like to be a flier.

HASKELL WEXLER

A seventy-eight-year-old cinematographer, sometime director and producer, winner of two Academy Awards and nominated for three more. His commitment to socially conscious causes is reflected in many of the films he's worked on – *Medium Cool, Matewan, One Flew Over the Cuckoo's Nest, Bound for Glory.*

I tried to join the Abraham Lincoln Brigade, way back when I was too young. My Freedom of Information file refers to me as a 'premature anti-fascist.' Later, I worked with the Spanish Republicans. I was on one of the first ships that went into the Mediterranean. It was right after we invaded Italy, after the second front, after what Churchill called 'the soft underbelly.' It could have been '43, I think.

I was in the Merchant Marines and saw a lot of combat.* I remember being torpedoed in the Indian Ocean, and actually seeing friends of mine dying in the explosion and later from the exposure in the boats. Slim Houston, Cisco Houston's brother,† and I were shipmates on a number of trips. I saw him die. But even when death was around me and discussion of getting hit, as we called it, was there, I never felt I would die. I had a very strong belief in myself and in my ideas.

I know one time for a film I interviewed some Brazilian revolutionaries who were tortured. We tried to get at the sources of their strength and how they could withstand such brutal treatment. Every one of them ultimately came to the thought that their commitment, their ideas, their dedication gave them strength that far exceeded that of their torturers. I don't want to dramatize but I do think that, to

*It is believed that the Merchant Marines lost more people, per capita, than all the military forces combined.
†Cisco Houston was a popular folksinger during the forties and fifties.

this day, my own feelings or commitments make me feel, if not invulnerable, at least protected.

I ran mostly the North Atlantic, all the way to Murmansk, the Soviet Union. [*Laughs lightly*] About three years ago I got a medal from [Russian president] Yeltsin for being one of the defenders of Murmansk. See, the Merchant Marines were not considered veterans until a law passed about four years ago saying that if you were in combat zones as a Merchant sailor, you could have the benefits of veterans. Of course, you had to state what ships you were on and where you sailed. Fortunately, I had my Freedom of Information file. It was a very positive thing for me because I was able to look up what the FBI had recorded on me – so I knew what ships I was on, where the ships sailed, and not only that, but what books I'd been reading. And I find that I was a very well read young sailor because they had '*The Brothers Karamazov* written by a Russian.' I was able to present this information. So I'm a certified veteran thanks to the Freedom of Information Act, and many thanks to the FBI for their surveillance.

It was in the Indian Ocean when we were torpedoed Friday, November 13th, 1942. I celebrate that day every year. I was the last one to leave because I was on a 20mm machine gun. As the water was coming up around the gun tub, I pushed off. During that time, the periscope was circling. They didn't surface until I came off. Then I was able to swim to one of the lifeboats – it was *very* heavy with oil. When the submarine surfaced, there was a guy on there who was taking a movie with an Eymo, a little handheld 35mm camera. In later years, I often wondered where that footage was, 'cause they were filming us. The German commander was shouting questions to us. Ultimately my crew members hauled me into the boat. The sub kept circling us and they wanted to know what our cargo was and where the captain was. Everybody was just screaming. I was wounded in my left shin. A lot of guys were vomiting from swallowing oil.

The submarine just left. They didn't shoot us down. There were two other ships, the *Alcoa Pathfinder* and the *Pierce Butler*, sunk in the same area. Our ship was called . . . what the hell? . . . *American Fisher*. It was a ship made during World War I in Hog Island. So there were eighteen of us in the boat, and a lot of the really tough guys turned out to be less than tough. [*A small laugh*]

We had our organization on the ship. We had had to struggle to have mixed crews. Our ship was a checkerboard crew. The stewards department was black. In fact, the head steward had been an officer in the U.S. Navy in World War I. They had black officers in the navy in World War I. It was only in World War II that they didn't. Anyway, Milt McCord, a black guy, and I were the only ones who were together enough on the boat to help try to navigate it. The other guys are wounded and sick and we were taking a lot of seas.

They have a thing like a bicycle pump, which I was in charge of – and Gino, the mess man. I remember I told him just to hold the hose, because it had a curve in it, overboard and I'd pump until my right arm gave out, until my left arm gave out. This was in heavy seas. It turns out that this hose that Gino is supposed to hold over, clears back into the boat. This was the only time in my life that I ever felt like giving up, because I was pumping the water back into the boat, see. Then, God, a couple of the guys were actually in horrible withdrawal because there were no cigarettes onboard.

We were on that boat for fourteen days. You're talking about death. Our chief engineer was an old Irish guy. They were short on technician-type people to work on the ships, and out of patriotic reasons he joined. He had one leg and a wooden left leg. Finnegan, that was his name. He apparently swallowed too much oil or he was hurt, I don't know what. We figured he was dead, me and Milt McCord. It was important if he was dead to get him out of the boat because we were so jammed in. We spent something like three hours, like in the movies, when someone dies and someone reaches down and they touch them and say, 'Oh, he's dead.' We wanted to make sure he was dead. So we listened to him, we felt him. We also had a little metal mirror in the lifeboat to sort of signal, to make us discoverable. We put that over his face and then we weren't sure whether it was outside mist coming on it. Finally, we dumped him overboard. It was a very emotional and unemotional situation at the same time. It was like not really being there, I mean, seeing it happening to someone else, to dump a human being off the lifeboat like that. And it was a guy that we all knew, a marvelous man, a very patriotic man, a very humorous Irish guy . . .

I felt so strong in that boat and on that ship that nothing in the world could move me one way or the other. Actually, looking back, it was the first moment of my manhood, the first moment when I felt incredible strength. I was nineteen or twenty.

When we finally saw land, there were some black people on the beach. We were all white except McCord and a guy we called Cockroach, who was the steward. He and the guys started joking. Cockroach said, 'Don't worry fellows,' because they were afraid they were cannibals. All we knew was from what we saw in the movies. He said, 'Don't worry, they're my brothers – I'll talk to them.' We were landing our boats in South Africa. We landed at the Msubabu River. The coast was heavy, heavy surf, but we saw debris coming out, so we knew there was a river somewhere there, and we headed as best we could for that river. It was an area called Pondoland. That was the tribe. We lived with the Pondos. They looked upon us as curiosities beyond belief. These dark-skinned agricultural people in South Africa. They were fascinated with Cockroach. He tried to talk to them, and they thought it was so funny because they didn't know *what* the hell he was saying. And they took care of me, they put leaves and stuff on my leg. My leg had gotten a lot of ulcers all up and down it from the wound, like little volcanoes. [*He lifts his left trouser leg and shows off a long scar.*] I don't know if you've ever seen that. Pretty ugly. As a matter of fact, when I finally got back to New York I had to walk with a cane a little bit, and I wanted to get some official time off and maybe some medical care. I went to the Coast Guard, which was in charge of the sailors, and asked for some help and some time off. I said, 'Just look at this.' And the guy said, 'Well, so what? What, are you gonna be in a beauty contest or something?' I said, 'Well, fuck, you.' I went and I organized on the Great Lakes for the National Maritime Union.

I was also buzz-bombed in the United Kingdom when I was out hanging some clothes up. We were actually in port, and I had just closed this big wooden door and shrapnel went bing, right into the door. It passed my mind, 'Gee, that might have hit me.' You have to understand, I would *never* say, 'Gee, I might have been killed,' see – there's a difference. I wasn't scared. I don't know why. I think it could be that I dramatize myself to myself. I just felt that my life was a mission and nobody's going to fuck with me. [*Laughs*] Probably good parents give you that feeling. When they fill you with self-assurance, with positive vibes, with reassurance that you can do it, that whole idea that you're born to be a good person . . .

My father was a successful businessman. You know, 'I used to sell papers and look at me now,' I used to kid him. I'd struggled with my father a lot from the time I was a teenager. He owned a chair factory in Milwaukee, the chairs that are used by the Supreme Court. His workers went on strike. I remember sitting at the table and arguing with him and taking the side of the workers. And my father was furious. He said, 'After all I've done for them. They have all this and they have all that, and how can they go on strike now? All the other factories are moving down South where the labor is cheaper.' It was a very personal argument.

My mom was his conscience. Because of my father being as strong as he was, she didn't speak strong, but she always got her word in. I think she played a big role in all the causes to which he contributed. At the dinner table every night there were discussions on every subject. My dad never did forget that he came from very humble beginnings. His father died when he was six years old. He had to work to support his mother as a young kid. He went to school at night. He was of his generation, of those young Jewish guys, first-generation guys who really struggled, and he died . . .

I think a lot about death now. I read the *New York Times* obituaries and I take the average of the ages and I've been over the average for a couple of years. Yet I don't feel old at all. I have some signs of it, like forgetting where I put things and my hearing. And then any little thing that I might feel about my body, I think, 'Well, this is it. What about your will? Who's going to get one of my favorite cars? What about my grandchildren?' The main thing I think about is what I haven't done that I want to do.

I want to make a film that I wrote called *Obit*, incidentally. It's about a guy at a television station who's in charge of obituaries. He discovers that if you can complete an obituary of a person on film, before the person dies, it kills them – so he has the power of life and death. He has the ultimate moral problem. Since he can kill without anyone knowing who did it or why he did it. When Orson Welles died, the next night they were able to put on television an obituary with selections from Welles's films, a couple of recent

interviews. Immediately! It's on the air. In my film, after he com-
pletes his obit, he presses an electronic thing and that's it. It's a black
comedy, because this guy doesn't want to kill anybody, doesn't
want to hurt anybody, but everything in our culture says that control and power is success. Ultimately the CIA wants him to help kill
Castro's successor.

With my growing awareness of death, I have a completely different feeling of time. I have more immediate priorities. In past years,
I would say, 'Well, so I'll wait around for a couple of weeks . . .'
Now, I'm impatient with things I want to do. Usually it centers
down into relations to people, to human things. It's very hard to do
when you're on the track the way I've been: to write this article, to
make this little film, to make all those others. Wait a minute. What's
most important? Awareness of death may be liberating for some
people, but it makes me a little more tense.

I made a film called *The Loved One*. I was coproducer and cinematographer. It was very difficult to make because they were afraid
of making fun of the death business and exposing the huge racket
that existed, taking advantage of people who are vulnerable. Jessica
Mitford worked with us on it.

When my wife Rita's sister died, I was reminded of [James
Farrell's novel] *Studs Lonigan*, because I also shot the film of the
book. I had been at Irish wakes where the stiff is lying out there and
people are walking around eating hors d'oeuvres and drinking
whiskey. That whole attitude toward death that I've seen in the old
Irish way, I like that. I would like people to say at my wake: 'He
lived a hell of a life and he's not here anymore – let's get drunk and
eat and appreciate each other.'

This may sound crazy, but after my brother Jerry died, I had a
number of times where he talked to me. I am a very unbelieving
person of anything supernatural. Yet I got like strong messages and all
in good humor. He was not saying, 'Haskell, you better take care of
Mom because I'm gone . . .' It was jaunty, 'Now, look, kid, I'm not
here now, take care of things.' He was not like the adult Jerry, he was
like – since we were only two years apart – he was like the young
brother who spoke to me. He has done so a number of times, but
never in a negative way except to say of his daughters, who are suing
each other, 'Jesus Christ, why don't they cut that shit out.' [*Laughs*]

When it's happening, I keep saying to myself, 'What the hell's going on?' I could be scientific about it. But I enjoy it so much that I say, 'Fuck it, let it happen.' He died about seven years ago. Even when I'm talking to you now, I feel like he's listening to me. [*Laughs*]

TAMMY SNIDER

She is a psychiatric social worker at the University of Chicago Hospital. A *hibakusha*, a survivor of the atomic bombing of Hiroshima, she has written a memoir recounting the moment: *One Sunny Day*.

I've been noticing that people just don't think about Hiroshima very much anymore. If they could mark August 6th on their calendar each year, just to be aware and remember Hiroshima and what it meant to the human race. It has to do with the whole question of death.

August 6th, 1945, was a beautiful day, and it was a happiest day for me because I had just persuaded my parents to bring me back the day before, to be with them, to be home in Hiroshima. I had been evacuated to a remote village. We think of evacuation of the British children, but we hardly think of Japanese children being evacuated. We're both small islands. My grandfather, who had passed away a couple of years prior to that time, was an industrialist and had a large estate. We lived on this estate, our family and my father's elder brother's family, surrounded with beautiful, beautiful gardens, one mile away from the center of the town. So there was this dire contrast of the happy, peaceful, unsuspecting lovely morning suddenly turning into . . . entire destruction of all that was there . . . for me. The fire, the burning, the crushing . . . On that day, my mother had to go off to take care of business in the center of town. My cousin, who was like my brother, was also in the center of town. My father was away at the harbor of Hiroshima, so he was a few miles away from the center. I was in my room. First there was a warning that a few planes were on their way and then the broadcast said, 'Emergency is off, you can go back to work,' or whatever you were doing. So the people who were outdoors, a lot of them even took their shirts off. It was very sunny – a beautiful blue-sky day.

I was ten, going on eleven. I had just come home the night before, so I was catching up on reading that my cousin gave me which had something to do with a Samurai duel – a boy's book.

Then I had a little stomach trouble. My mother left me a little porridge to have. There was this simultaneous flash preceding the humongous sound of explosion, the kind of intensity that I had never heard before or heard since. And then there was the breaking down with the force of the wind and the shaking of the earth and the house breaking up. And then being covered with debris. The thing lasted for, I thought, an unending, infinite length of time. It was pitch-dark and I was just getting hit with all kinds of objects falling down on me. Even as a child it was the very first time in this midst of abyss, I said to myself, 'I'm going to die.' When I said that, something very quiet came through, and I wasn't completely falling apart – that was sort of curious to remember. It didn't end, the thermal wind and the force. It just went on and on and I thought it would never end. The words coming into my mind saying: 'So this is dying in a war. I'm going to die.' I was the one who was most surprised when it all ended finally. Everything became still, I found myself still alive and living and breathing . . . yeah.

It took some great effort to get out because I couldn't really move. Somehow, after I managed to get out, I saw the total changed scenery outside. First I thought there should be a great big crater in the middle of my grandfather's garden because I thought it was a direct hit by a huge bomb of some kind. There was no crater. So I stepped outside. Our house was raised up like a castle. So I stepped down to find people who were injured and the houses had collapsed and everything. Everything inside was just rubble. The first people I saw were two women and they were on the ground. Their clothes were bloodstained, and they were asking for help. There were others in the house trying to get out. They were covered with soot and hair all messed up, and later on I started to see en masse people who were hurt and burned.

I think we were all in a state of shock. All of us were raised in a culture that valued perseverance, not calling out with one's discomfort – that was frowned upon. So you persevere, and virtue is to try to cope with whatever comes along. You're not supposed to cry out with pain. Some people who just couldn't help it would say something, but for the most part people were very silent. They were whispering, like people who couldn't breathe, people who needed to be helped out . . . [softly] 'Please help me . . .' And that's much

more painful to remember, because you know they were in dire
agony. I think my sensation was sort of like a frozen statue. I knew
we were at war, and that this was part of the destruction of the war,
but I didn't know what happened. I kept on hearing explosions. I
think ammunition was exploding at the military base. Every thirty
seconds. The whole city kind of smoking up and people coming out
in this horrible condition.

So all I did was try to follow my mother's instruction – my
mother, who was afraid that incendiary bombs would surround us.
She always taught me, 'Get away and go to the river.' The river Ota
had seven branches, so there were plenty of rivers around. I tried to
get to the river. People were already trying to jump into the water
and drowning because they were just burnt to death practically, but
they were still alive and trying to relieve the pain of their burns. I
had no idea where my mother was, and had I known, I probably
wouldn't be here talking to you because I would have gone where
she was. Absolutely nothing would have prevented me. As it turned
out, she was crushed and burnt to death. Under a house near the
center. I would have died with her. I really would have stayed there,
I wouldn't have left her. There was no way I could find her because
I didn't know where she was.

After that very day, all of us went back looking for our kin.
Most of us didn't know where they were. So we had to go to
rescue stations. A lot of these were just people lying on the ground,
dirt, or floor of a chapel of one of the temples. I just couldn't stand
going by – person, person, person . . . So I would announce my
mother's name and then say, 'Oh, please answer me,' and no one
would answer but sort of stir . . . Even if I was so much in a state of
shock and desensitized myself, I tried. I just couldn't stand it, thinking *I can't find her, I can't find her, what am I going to do?* I want to see
her, but I don't want to see her in *that* condition. But if I can let her
know that I love her and that I want to be there . . . so, just playing with magical things in my mind, I started to sing some songs
that she taught me, that she loved hearing. [*With a touch of happiness*]
So I said, 'Please, God, carry this tune to my mother and comfort
her, because I can't find her.' That's when my feelings came back
and I just cried and cried and cried. But those are the scenes that all
hibakusha, the survivors, were subjected to. The powerlessness of

not being able to help or participate because we didn't know what dropped. Even those people who didn't have any burns and injuries started to suffer and drop dead because, you know, the radiation, how forceful it was there. It goes into the marrow of your bones and penetrates your brains and then changes your fetus, and malformed children are being born. We had no idea how to help ourselves or help anybody. So that kind of death is annihilation and death without dignity. Complete powerlessness. Not even a person being there, torturing you. It's invisible. Done to people, DNA, plants.

I gave you the four-leaf clover I picked. Just all over the bank of the Ota River. The clover's changed – to five-leaf, six-leaf, all over. I know – I picked them. Their DNA changed, for sure. Even people who weren't at the center, if you got wet with the black rain,★ it stuck to you – and we didn't know what it was. And all of us had to carry this – not just the biological effects, but mentally. For the longest time, it haunted me and tortured me. I think practically most of my young life. Even into my forties and fifties. Until I came to work in this hospital and saw death with dignity. I was trained in psychiatric services with many people, for this very precise challenge of understanding death.

I nearly died with A-bomb sickness at the time. I ran the highest kind of fever for days and I was delirious. I was out of commission for months. How did I recover? It was very slow. The peak time, when I was worst off, I wasn't expected to live. My father's younger sister came with a few living snapping turtles because she believed a living turtle saves a person's life. And my father and she struggled to sever the heads of the turtles with a decanter underneath it to catch the dripping blood. They made me drink it. Afterwards they made soups from it and they made me eat them. Probably the proteins from it were very helpful because most of us were starving. My fever started to go down. I didn't go to school the year after that. My best friend who was evacuated in the same class and also came back with me on the 5th of August – she was crushed to death. We were from the same village, same temple.

★Black rain – rain mixed with ashes from incinerated material and radioactive fallout – fell after the bombings of both Hiroshima and Nagasaki.

My brother-cousin, his body melted, he was burned to death. He was alive for several hours and somebody who saw him told us that all his clothes, including his outer skin, were gone, burned, scorched. He had lead bindings over his pants. Parts of that still remained, but everything else was burned.

Something in my gut, especially when I think about my mother and my cousin, how they met their end, something happens . . . It's a terror and it's a grief combined. And all of us who were there and who survived carry the imagery from it, the guilt. Grief is that you lost them and another grief is that you weren't there, you were powerless; you didn't understand what was happening; you were not warned; you weren't prepared. So, if you love your mom or if you love your brother, you wish that you could have done something, and even if you couldn't do it, you wish you could have been there to tell them, 'I love you, I'm sorry we can't do anything about your pain, but I am here . . .' We couldn't even give aspirin . . . we didn't even *have* aspirin, so what am I talking about?!

We couldn't even give water. In Japanese ritual, when a person is near death we always moisten the lips with cotton or something. Those burned people were begging for water. We couldn't give any water. People said, 'If you give water, they'll die, so don't give it to them.' You survived but they didn't. People went around saying, 'Oh, so-and-so died, and so-and-so died.' And then my grandmother was there. 'Hey, you make it look like all the people who died were good, but those of us who survived aren't.' And there was something to that, because we didn't feel good about having survived.

My uncle developed some kind of a swelling at the place where he had a gashing-open caused by glass. He was under my grandfather's factories that crushed him. It turned into brain cancer and he died. The aunt who wasn't there but brought me the turtle that helped me to survive – she was so close to him, and she died of grief. My other aunt, who was an older sister to that aunt, also died after taking a bath. My grandmother complained about abdominal pain for a long, long time, and then died also. My father, who lived for, oh, into his early sixties, he wrote me a letter and said, 'I am so tired every day, it's an effort.' And several days later I had a phone call: my father passed away. A lot of us had what other people called 'lazy sickness.' We were always easily tired, fatigue-prone. And we were cancer-prone. Some of the mothers gave birth to small-headed babies, so single women hid that they were survivors because, in those times, marriages were arranged. If you had a chance of giving birth to a defect baby, you were an employment risk, a marriage risk. You were vulnerable to unknown illnesses.

During the [American] Occupation, the press couldn't release any findings of these illnesses. They were not allowed to publish anything. So nobody really knew what was going on, and there was no treatment. Plus the fact that this was the first time the Japanese were defeated. And it was such a horrible war, and we suffered *so* much. Nobody wanted to be reminded of it.

Oh yes, it's etched in my mind like it happened yesterday. There is no way I can erase it, no way I can erase all the drenching memories and the terror.

I was driven by fear most of my life because of this – because I connected, identified death as annihilation. There was no respect to it. The memorial, the Peace Park, all of this, fine – but I saw it, I lived it. You cannot fool me that this is not awful, OK? I have to quicken myself to tell you that I don't feel the same way about death today.

This happened by an accident – I was led, like by the hands of fate, guided into this setting. My very first experience in terms of near-death conditions, my assignment was transplant. This was 1987. Fate is that my kids went to the Lab School,★ and I needed a place to work. I said, 'I've got to find work here on the campus' – and my first assignment at the hospital was a liver transplant. So I put on my sterilized gown and walked into intensive care, where a patient who had the transplant came out of the surgery. It's very serious, life-threatening surgery. I saw this person connected up to every possible life-support machineries, OK? My reaction to that was: How wonderful! Everything is being done to sustain this person's life in honor of her life. Unlike those people who were dying without aid, out on the dirt, on the floor, and no medicine, no food, no water. I said, 'This is so restoring to me, that this can be done for human beings.' For me it was a privilege to be a part of that effort to sustain life. The

★A highly regarded private school, part of the University of Chicago complex.

unfinished business and the regret that I could not help in Hiroshima, here totally different possibilities exist to honor human lives.

I began to let myself feel a little bit what I had been trying to suppress for years. I couldn't really look it in the eyes – I was too terrified. But after I saw other possibilities, I began to be able to start my process of how to think about death.

It didn't happen overnight. I trained with Elisabeth Kübler-Ross, I trained with Milton Erickson, I trained with Ken Moses. There was so much grief connected with my thinking about death. I was able to bring up the dreams that were shattered, questions unanswered because my mother died so suddenly and to express, really truly and fully, what had been on my mind for years and years. But you can't really share, maybe because I'm Japanese and very reserved when it comes to very private feelings.

My patients were the teachers, really. Like young women with young babies or children, feeling such great grief that they can't die, they can't leave these young ones behind. And I could feel how my mother must have felt, even momentarily: *I cannot die, I cannot leave this child*. It was so good to feel that it's a two-way thing. To lose a parent is hard, but for a parent to go is even harder.

Every single human being I met here who called themselves patients and allowed me to enter their lives and share in their deepest thoughts and feelings, I experience it. I've lived a thousand lives already, all of which enriched mine. Yeah. OK, here is what I learned from my patients: It's terribly important for us to have death with dignity. In annihilation, you have no preparation. Annihilation is simply a torture. What death means is saying good-bye to all your attachments, including things, but most importantly to bonds to people. For the person who's left, it's saying good-bye to that person, but for the person who's going, it's everything, it's global, saying good-bye to all that.

I love the music of Hebrew chorus in *Nabucco*,* the prisoners. I just loved it the first time I heard it. And then when I understood the stanzas, what they were saying, longing for their homeland, I felt so much in common with them because I had that feeling deep in

*An early Verdi opera.

my head. And I said, 'I understand that feeling, I long for my homeland too.' But when I really settled down in my mind and thought
about it, it's not the Hiroshima of today, the way it's rebuilt as a
sprawling megalopolis. I'm longing for my grandfather's garden,
I'm longing for my own home. I'm longing for the home where my
mother was. I'm longing for something that doesn't exist in a biological sense any longer. Death is going home. In our conscious
memory, we remember how we came down through the birth canal
and came out. The tape recorder of conscious memory doesn't start
until later years, but your cells probably have memories. I'm going
back to the home *there*, even beyond conscious memory. So I think
of death as being retired from this dimension, but moving on and
being transformed.

When I was sitting by the riverbank in my teens, so brought
down and distraught and confused – that's how I gathered all these
malformed clovers – sunset would come and the river is full tide.
The colors are reflected on the water that's almost still. Then when
it begins to recede and it's like, with the wind, dancing colors of
tranquillity, for the fleeting moment, even in those worst times,
there was a quietness that was Heaven. You bring me Heaven when
you understand what I'm trying to say. Being able to communicate,
that's Heaven. Being able to share feelings, that's Heaven.

When I speak of my home, it's closely tied to death. I took my
young adult children back to Hiroshima to visit and took them to
the markers of my life. Every time I went back I used to be so
depressed, feel so upset. This time it was a different kind of experience. And I never really entered the Peace Museum because I didn't
want any real things reminding me, but I needed my children to go
in to see, so I took them. And then I saw something I had never seen
before. It was a life-size screen across the center rotunda area with a
black-and-white picture of the *Enola Gay*, a millisecond movie
coming towards us before the bomb was dropped. And I just
unthinkingly put my hands out trying to stop it. Then I remembered how innocent and how well we were, even though we were
starving. And then I started to cry. I started to just cry until I was
choking. I couldn't stop. '*Oh please stop, please stop.*' And yet I knew
that it couldn't stop, it kept on going. And then it occurred to me.
In a way it's still up there: as long as we believe in waging wars

with the possibilities of using of nuclear weapons at some point. Because in all of mankind's history we've never possessed something that was not used. So that's when I found that, until my last breath I draw, I must address the consequences of Hiroshima because it was the very first time an atom weapon was used upon the human race. And that was a part of the family of man that it was used upon, and it was a part of the family of man that used it. So, please, remember August 6th and mark it down as the day of Hiroshima. And know that death and life are so tied together and so precious. And with life you can love, you can be loved; you can respect, you can honor; you can speak, you can sing, and you can celebrate until your last breath. [*Close to a whisper*] Not the hideous life and the hideous death that the *hibakusha* had to bear.

Mothers and Sons

V.I.M.
(VICTOR ISRAEL MARQUEZ)

He is a veteran of the Vietnam War.

When my big, fat grandmother died, I cried to myself. Like right now, I'm getting it in my eyes. Usually, I don't allow people to sit this close to me – usually you'd be over there. I see a psychologist and he knows he's got to sit on the other side of the room. But I'm doing this because I want to be truthful with you as much as I can. And it feels good because I feel like I'm opening up and releasing right now. Plus, I'm learning things too, because you've asked a few things I'm going to be thinking about for the rest of the day. [*From his wallet, he extracts and unfolds a report of his illness dealing with post-traumatic stress disorder.*] I carry this as a reality check. Usually, I don't bother anybody, but there are people out there that will bother you. And what I'll do is I'll take this out and I'll read it.

'V.I.M. (Victor I. Marquez), 52
DSM III-R
Post-Traumatic Stress Disorder
The attitudes of all contacts except the most intimate are so adversely affected as to result in virtual isolation in the community. Totally incapacitating psychoneurotic symptoms, bordering on gross repudiation of reality with disturbed thought or behavioral processes associated with almost all daily activities as fantasy, confusion, panic and explosions of aggressive energy resulting in profound retreat from mature behavior. Demonstrably unable to obtain or retain employment.'

I volunteered because I wanted to be a hero. I wanted to prove that I was an American through and through. In a way, I was aware of death because of the neighborhood I lived in. The chop-shops in the neighborhood – you deal with all the bad guys, you knew all the bad guys. And, yeah, there were three murders that I remember, right there in the neighborhood. Yeah, so I seen death. But it was nothing because it was like the guy deserved it.

A long time ago, when I was in the Marine Corps, there's an oath that you take, and it talks about integrity, family, God, honor to the Corps, the whole bit. I pretty much stuck with that my whole life. I found out that lying doesn't do you any good. Always tell the truth. I joined the Marine Corps on April Fools' Day, 1966. [Laughs] That was a real cool experience because I was so small, I weighed less than a hundred pounds and I was like maybe five feet tall. I thought there was no chance I'd be in the Marine Corps, but you know, they were snatching everybody. Like when they said 'Marine' like that, I was proud – I felt good.

I worked all my life. As a kid, I started off going around collecting bottles and stuff like that, like everybody else does. When I was about eight, I got a job on a fruit truck. That was pretty cool because at the end of the day the guy would always have a couple extra baskets of fruit and vegetables. He'd say, 'These are old and moldy, we don't want them anyway. See if you can save some of them.' It was all good stuff – that was his way of paying me extra. After that I started selling papers on Randolph and Wabash, where the El tracks are. I had my own stand there with a guy named Red. I don't know if he's still alive or not. In my senior year, I worked for Montgomery Ward's in their data-processing department – until I decided that due to the things that were going on during that time, all that atom bomb crap and everything else, and stuff like that . . .

I used to read the paper all the time, I was always interested in the news, and it was like I was gung-ho. I wanted to go over and I wanted to kick some butt, and I wanted to be a damn Marine. I knew the Marines were going to be in the toughest place, and that's what I wanted. When I say the word 'warrior,' a warrior can be anything, OK. In my case, the warrior in me was putting my life on the line to accomplish – because I needed to prove to myself at that time that I was a man.

Well, things happened real quick from there. I had already put my name on the volunteer list for Vietnam. As soon as I turned eighteen, the exact day, we mustered outside, they called my name, *boom!* Next thing I know, I was like packing up, getting all geared up. Me and these two other guys, one guy from the Appalachias, I forget his name, and a black guy, I forget his name – we had to go to Raleigh-Durham, North Carolina, to catch the plane.

That's the first time I saw discrimination, man. Halfway there we were hungry. Here we are just in our Marine Corps uniforms, and we told the taxi driver, 'Pull over, we're hungry. We'll pay for your food.' And he said, 'Well, why don't I just go in and get you some sandwiches.' We said, 'No, we're tired from sitting.' Went in there and they wouldn't serve us, everybody was looking at us.

We were in American uniforms, Marine Corps uniforms. You'd think they would serve us. When I went to the washroom, that's the first time I ever saw one of those signs: COLORED WASHROOM and WHITE WASHROOM. [*Laughs*] I came back to the table and I remember telling the black guy, I said, 'Man, you know what? I think we're in the wrong place.' So then the taxicab driver came in and ordered sandwiches for us and they wouldn't even take the money. We ate our sandwiches in the cab. Caught the plane, went to Pendleton, went through some jungle-training crap like that, and I was on my way to Vietnam.

When you're a new guy, it's like anything else except it's worse: you have to prove yourself. In the military, under warlike conditions, people can really be mean, all right. I wasn't really being utilized for about the first few weeks too much. I was so gung-ho, wanting to get into fighting and all that crap, that I was getting into fights with everybody else around me. So I was kind of a bad egg at first.

Actually, we had bodies coming in all the time, we were unloading bodies all the time. Dead bodies, American bodies. My first reaction? That's where I got my gear from, because they didn't have gear for us. When they were dumping the bodies, they were just throwing them off the chopper and they were throwing all the gear off – like knapsacks, ammo, rifles. Hey, I wanted to get as much crap as I could get, you know? Besides, they were dead anyway. I didn't really think about it much at that time. What did surprise me, though, was the very first time that happened, one of the body bags moved. It was some guy in there and when they unzipped the body bag he was swearing and swearing and swearing. They thought he was dead but he was alive. Somebody dropped him, and when they dropped him he came to.

My outfit, 3rd Battalion, 5th Marines, we were the only unit in North Vietnam, up in I-Corps, DMZ [Demilitarized Zone] area, fighting against the NVA [North Vietnamese Army] up there and no VC [Viet Cong] – NVA, real troops. We saw too much stuff in too short of a time. You didn't have time to even think about any-thing – It was like a survival thing. Death was on your mind all the time. It was for *real*. And I always had like a little thing in the back of my head: like when you're born, you're born with a disease, 'cause from the moment you're born, you're dying. [*Laughs*] I wasn't like a holy roller over there like a lot of guys were – a lot of guys, they prayed. Me, I did a lot of crazy things over there. I had to, because it was my way. I didn't want to be like anybody else. I really wanted to be a badass, I mean, the baddest ass there was around.

I was a little guy, so I was a tunnel rat. I'd go crawl in the holes in the ground, all through the caves and stuff like that, because I was so small. That was interesting work because you don't know what's in there. Like, I heard guys talk about taking flashlights and a forty-five. And I say, 'Nah' – we used to carry a K-bar and a light. When you're in complete darkness, a light only goes about this far. [*His hands span a short distance and he laughs.*] You can't see *shit*.

Love motivates a lot of people; with me, fear motivates me. Fear for me is something really hard to explain, because, like, if you say it in the wrong context it's weakness. No, I think you have to respect fear and understand it, accept it. Once it's accepted, it ain't nothing . . .

Fear of death. Death after a while, it was a joke. Guys that had been there for a while it was like: 'Hey, you know, before we go out, "Here, you can have my stuff."' And all the joking around between the dudes about trading off their girlfriends and stuff like that . . . [*Laughs*] Giving pictures of their sisters. Because everybody knew that we had a very good chance of, like, a lot of guys not coming back. So that was pretty cool. And then sometimes when we came back, we'd split up the gear of the guys that didn't.

I can't live without fear. I understand what fear is all about, and I will not allow fear to run my life, OK, except for the fact that I use it. Say, when you have an enemy, what's the best thing to do with an enemy? Learn all about your enemy. Once you learn all about your enemy, it's like everything turns into nothing.

Hey, man, those guys have been fighting for thousands of years. They knew jungle warfare really, really, *really* good. It didn't take us long to really get into it and learn just as well as they did. I have great respect for the North Vietnamese Army guys, OK. On the other hand, I'm not going to say that, yeah, I forgive everybody. No – they killed my whole squad. I had my whole squad wiped out on one particular operation I was on. The worst one, because I feel that it was my fault for making a wrong turn.

The first time I met the enemy I was point man, and I was walk-ing out of the jungle. Point man is the guy that leads, the front guy. You're supposed to watch for booby traps and all kinds of crap, and pick a path to go. And I used to volunteer because I liked it. Other guys would say, being a point man, being a rifleman, you only have a life expectancy of like ten seconds. Nah, I kind of figured out for myself, I'm a little dude, and I says logicwise to me, why would they want to shoot me just walking out real quick when they could wait for everybody else to come out and get everybody in the middle? 'Cause that's how you do an ambush.

That time I didn't actually see them, man. They were in these trees and they opened up on us. I just jumped in a rice paddy, but they got about maybe twenty-three guys on the first time. Not all of them died – there was more wounded than died. That was just one day. I went for two tours. In the first one, I was attacking a machine-gun nest that the NVA had, me and my partners were. And it wasn't quite successful: they got me before I got them. So I got wounded, I got hit by thirty-caliber machine-gun fire in the lower back and the shoulder, through and through. Actually, I thought I was going home. Medical gunship comes in and takes you to Da Nang or one of the places offshore. This was '67 – what all the guys call 'the shooting war.' The actual hand-to-hand-combat shooting war. I just blanked that out of my mind, it's sort of like I blanked the whole Vietnam experience out of my mind. What I really was doing was masking it, because at that time I was doing a lot of drugs and drinking. It was party time, early '70s.

This was my second tour. A big blank.

Once I got there and I started losing people that I knew, then everything that I went there for went out the window and it was survive . . . and make no friends. I mean, except for your right-hand man – 'cause they *die*. You don't need that kind of stuff over there, man, 'cause you gotta be on your toes. We had guys that broke down and stuff like that, and sorry to say, but we had to slap the shit out of them and kick them in the ass and straighten them up . . .

I was hardened. I faced death a lot of times over there. When I was a tunnel rat, you can run into just about anything: booby traps, people that are inside that tunnel. You'd be surprised – once you got to where you had to worm yourself in, they'd open up into big rooms, and you'd see American Red Cross supplies in there. [*Laughs*] That blew my mind. I was finding stuff from France and all the rest, all our alliances. It was like, *Jesus! No wonder they keep on going* . . .

I killed many of them. Because that was my specialty. I knew several different kinds of weapons, I was also a demolitions expert, OK? I also dealt with the flamethrower. I burned up bodies so that they were crispy critters. When they were in the cave and they wouldn't come out and stuff like that, you'd throw smoke grenades to try to get them out. And then you get up there with the flamethrower. That napalm will suck all the air out of that cave, so basically the people were asphyxiated before they get burned. And then I was told to throw more [napalm] jelly on them, because it was easier to carry them out. That would take all the liquids out of their body and they would be stiff. Like I said, crispy critters – you could stack 'em.

The truth is that we made a lot of jokes, like crispy critter, and that was probably to hide our true feelings. Everybody dealt with it differently. In the Marine Corps we have this really tight bond, we're all real brothers, not people who go around, 'Hey, brother' – we *are* brothers. That's the reason why we say '*Semper fi.*' And it's like we had to be one. It's just like life after death. I believe in life after death. I think we're all one, OK?

I was raised a Catholic and the whole bit, and I read the Bible and everything. But when I came back from Vietnam and I went to Holy Family, my first Sunday back I walked in there and they had these long-haired hippies sitting up in the front playing folk music and stuff. And people were standing in the aisles and clapping and, man, that blew my mind. [*Laughs*] And the people wanted to hug you and it was like, 'Get *away* from me.' No, man, 'cause I *couldn't* be hugged. After all this crap that I went through, you guys are gonna hug me?! No way!

I don't have any second thoughts because all I can do is talk about when I was there, and I knew in '67 that we kicked their asses. Que Son Valley had not been touched since the French were there, OK? Large area, skinniest part of Vietnam. Stronghold, OK? We went into Laos, 'cause the elephant trail came right through there. We never had a base camp, we were always on the move, we were always out in the bush, all the time. I know what the hell went down over there. It would take us ten thousand hours to talk about this, but just to lay it on the line, everything that was done, all the way from the top down or the bottom up, everything was done for a specific purpose, and that purpose was a political purpose – and it was scripted. This is how I feel now. After all these years, I've had a lot of time to sit down and do that retrospect thing. There's just too many times that we were sacrificed to bring the enemy out into the open. There was too many times that our own forces said they'd made mistakes and dropped bombs on us and crap like that. I mean, there was just a *lot* of shit. That was a *crazy* place. When they sent us out, all the morphine was gone. We didn't have morphine to even give to our guys because the guys in the rear took it. They were into that dope scene. So I'm lucky that I didn't get caught up in that. See, in my way of thinking, everything is scripted in life and it's long-range planning. You've been around a long time, you should know that.

Oh, war sucks, man. There's no doubt about it. There ought to be other ways of handling situations – it's just *too* bad. We're human beings, we're always going to be human beings, and as long as we have different religions, you know . . . We're the most dangerous things on this Earth.

Death's on my mind every day. But I don't fear death. You know what? I had several experiences. Like the time when I was caught between machine-gun fire and I went flying up in the air. I didn't see no white light or anything, but when I got hit, I know I went flying. It was completely black but I was still aware. I could hear shit going on, and it seemed like it lasted a whole hour or more.

I'm up there, and do you know what? You take away everything that exists right now, just try to imagine to yourself how good you would feel. Man, I felt so, like real *freedom*. I felt so at peace. Oh, so happy.

I think that we have a spirit, OK, and that spirit is going to go wherever the hell it's going to go. I don't know, because I don't know nothing about that. But I know that I'm going to like it. In the Marine Corps we have a saying and it's 'When you die, we'll meet you down at Hell's gates, we'll regroup, and then we're gonna call up God and say we're coming up to guard the pearly gates.' [*Laughs*]

Fear death? Hell, no. I've been through some of the worst crap in the world. Jesus, when you got something that people don't talk about . . . One of the things they were interested in over there was a body count. If you didn't have enough bodies, they'd go around, taking a machete, chopping off body parts, putting them in different bags so you have more bodies. Enemy bodies. Throw a couple arms in this one, a leg in this one.

I justify it this way: they were the enemy, I was their enemy. They were the same as me, as far as I was concerned. I was on this side, they were on that side. We were very good at what we did. Us, we took great pride in being victorious. We won all the battles. We just supposedly lost some stupid way. And that's because [President Lyndon] Johnson stopped the bombing in '68.

Do I have any regrets? No, I have no regrets. In fact, I'd go back right now. You know why? There's an adrenaline, there's a rush. Something that makes you feel really, really good. There's nothing like it, nothing like it in the world. It's like when guys start talking about hunting, I say, 'Hey, you want to hunt? Put me on one side of the valley, you on the other side of the valley. Pick our weapons. I want a shotgun, I don't give a shit what you take. And we'll go after each other.'

As for my fellow . . . I have not been able to speak to anybody. They're all dead, basically. I just got in contact with the captain of my company, from Birmingham, Alabama. Him and I have been talking recently. And a couple more guys. These are all combat guys. We will not talk to people that weren't in combat. These are real guys, I can talk to them. I learned a long time ago that once you start letting people into your life a little bit too much, for me anyway, I'll regret that I opened up.

I think my mother knows this, I've told my wife this, and other people, but I always tell the person that I meet, we may hang around, but there's going to be a time that either three things are going to happen. You're gonna get dead, I'm gonna hurt you, or you're gonna be in jail. And you know what? It's always happened. I'm getting used to it. I warn people now. So I figure, they ought to know when to back off – it's their responsibility. They're accountable for themselves.

I haven't slept straight through since '67. Except in the seventies, when I was drinking real heavy, but that's past now. I'm talking about real sleep. They just gave me some new sleeping stuff that's supposed to be really powerful and I actually slept for five hours. That is a record for me since '67. I'll sleep five minutes to half an hour. I get a lot of flashbacks and then they turn into stupid dreams, and the dreams turn into, like, man, it's like I got everybody in my life involved in the same crap. I keep a tape recorder and I keep a pad of paper with three sharpened pencils, and I never use the damn things.

I killed women over there. They were snipers, and they were chained to the tree. That's what they used to do over there, they were so *bad*, man. They would chain people to keep us under fire until we overran them, and then we'd find these people all chained up. The first time I felt funny shooting someone, though, was when I found this big Chinese guy after an ambush. We saw this big foot sticking out of the ground, so we started uncovering it. And this guy had to be like six-foot-two or -three, so we knew he wasn't regular North Vietnamese. The North Vietnamese are bigger than the South Vietnamese, but this guy was like twice the size. He had a little bag with him. It was the first time I went through somebody's property. The guy had a wallet just like mine. You open it up and he had pictures in there, like I got pictures in mine – pictures of his family, notes.

We all just looked at each other when we were passing it around. We had gone down there, what they call taking care of business: anybody alive, you take care of them right away. We started going through this guy's wallet, we all sat down and we looked through his wallet and we were all making comments. 'Wow, this guy had a good-looking chick.' And some of the pictures had kids. It was like the war didn't even exist. We were going through this man's personal life, and he was just like us. I thought that he was a good man. I thought that he put up a good battle. He just got fucked.

I kept my mom out of the Vietnam thing till about 1992. Now I think sometimes she tries to handle me with kid gloves, which I don't like – I would rather just be slapped around, you know? That I can understand. I have been working with a doctor, a psychologist, since 1991, going to therapy every week. He works with people with post-traumatic stress disorder. I have that and about twelve other things. It's actually called combat-related stress disorder.

Behaviorwise, on a scale of 1 to 10, as I told the doctor, we're at about a 9.5. We've still got .5 points to go before I become normal. [*Laughs*] This I want to give to you because I wrote this down this morning. [*He laughs as I read the paper he hands me.*]

Judge me not by the number of times I have failed, but by the number of times I have succeeded, which is in direct proportion to the number of times I've failed and kept on trying. V.I.M.

ANGELINA ROSSI

She is the mother of V.I.M., Victor Israel Marquez. She is seventy.
I have known her for many years; a strong, independent-minded
woman. She has worked as a bailiff in Chicago courts and as an
investigator for the Internal Revenue Service (IRS). She is now
retired.

Victor was a very sweet young boy, helpful – the neighbors all loved
him. He was the type of kid that would carry the groceries home for
the neighbors, sweep their yards or pick up their trash or dump their
garbage for them. He was the sweetest kid in the world. And then
he went to Vietnam.

He came back completely changed, an altogether different
person. Sometimes it's very difficult to take . . . for me. I'm his
mother, I knew what he was before. It's very difficult for me to see
him the way he is today. It's very sad for me. [*A long pause*]

I've had six children. One of them, his younger brother, was the
baby of the family. The other four girls were bossy, as most girls are.
They take after their mother, I'm pretty bossy too. I think he got to
the point where he just couldn't take so many females around him,
and he felt maybe he was missing something not having a man in the
house. And so he decided he was going to Vietnam. I'd been
divorced for quite some time. I never remarried. I'm not sure what
it was, but I think he just felt that he had to break out of where he
was and be in a more manly society. So he picked what he thought
was the greatest military service in the world, the U.S. Marines.

He's an alcoholic today. He does things that . . . I've never seen
him doing these things, but I've heard from others. He's one of the
people who has road rage or mall rage or restaurant rage or something. He doesn't seem to care about having any self-control. I am
completely confused. I have been very religious, up until five or six
years ago. Then all of a sudden, science, technology, the furtherance
of our minds has all hit me, and I think to myself, *How could this be?*
How could there be a Heaven? When we die, our bodies turn into,
the nice way to say it is, dust. We turn into nutrients for worms, for

other plant life. We evolve and we come back into a sprig of grass or a flower or a tree. And I think that's how we live on. [*She chokes up.*] I can't believe anymore that there is a Heaven. Am I going to see my mother? I don't think so . . . I am totally confused and scared. I'm scared because I think to myself, *What if I'm denying my religious beliefs?* What if I, for whatever reason, my age, the time of life, my thinking . . .

Maybe I want to be back as a six-year-old child. I want to just have my belief that there's a God, that there's a Trinity, that there's Heaven, that there's Hell. I think my Catholic faith has also got a lot to do with it, with my confusion. We have changes in what used to be laws: you couldn't eat meat on Friday night. Now you can eat meat on Friday. You couldn't be cremated. Would you believe I've already paid for my cremation because it's approved now by the Catholic Church. If the Catholic Church, or any church I would guess, is that correct and that right, then how can they change their rules in the middle of things? So I think to myself, *I've lived through so much life, I've seen things change, I'm realistic, I know what really happens, and I just don't know* . . . Is there a spirit that lives on? According to the Bible, we're all going to meet our maker, we're all going to be judged. Well, I don't have to worry about that. I don't think I'm going to be judged too badly. But I think to myself, how in the world can your entity, your human person come before a governing body, and they're going to decide whether you've been a good person all your life or a bad person all your life?

There's so many differences in people. Some people believe in having multiple wives. Our society believes, no, you only have one wife. Today our society believes you not only have one commitment to a person, but it could be a person of the same sex. You could marry another woman, you could marry another man if you're a man. I'm confused. Am I alone? Am I the only one? I find it very difficult to have any straight thoughts about anything because even though I say things, in my head is something else, something opposite is coming through.

We found that there are as many things beneath the ocean as up in the sky. How do we know what's there until we're there? The floor of the ocean is breaking up on the Eastern Seaboard. They don't know what's going to happen – might be horrible tidal waves that hit the shore. What if there's some kind of a living entity that comes out of that? Now we've got something else to worry about, something else to digest, something else to understand. Are we going to be the same like we are now with the crazy alien things? We're going to go out and kill them? They're human beings, or they're beings, whatever they might be. What if they have a religious background? What if they think there's life hereafter? As a child, there was no question – no question where I came from, where I was going to be, and where I was going to be when I died, I knew. When I died, I was going to Heaven, I was going to be in the arms of God.

I'm of the old school. Another thing that's changed with the Catholic religion is there's no longer a burning Inferno, there's no longer 'you're going to burn forever.' Today, the word is that Hell is you're just not in the presence of God – so that too has changed.

I grew up when the nuns used to hit your hand with the ruler or stick gum in your hair if you misbehaved. They did that to me for chewing gum in school. They didn't just make you throw it out, but me, they stuck it in my *hair* – and my mother had to cut it out. Of course, my hair was real long so that was *terrible*. But you believed everything the nuns and the priests told you.

I regret my innocence, I regret the absolute belief that I had, because it's making me nuts. I don't know what to think anymore. And this scares me – I'm very fearful that my whole life has been a sort of living – believing a fairy tale. And, I'm wondering: *Is there a supreme being?* And I have to cross myself . . . [*She crosses herself.*] Because there's the part of me that says, 'You'd better not be too sure about that, because what if there is a God?' What if all my life my beliefs *are* right? What if something has happened as I've grown older? An arrogance about myself that I think, *Oh, I know a heck of a lot more than the person on the street* . . . And then I think God can't hold that against me if He's for real. Because God made me. He knew what I was going to evolve into. He knew the person I was going to become. So if there is a God, then I have nothing to worry about. I think that's only because I'm as old as I am, and for me God has always been a male, a man. The pictures, the host, everything has always been he, he, he. Now, as far as I'm concerned, I don't care if it's a he, a she, or an it – it doesn't matter to me. If it's just a spirit, that's OK. If it's a force, that's OK too. Whatever it is . . .

I know I'm going to die. The only thing I hope and pray for is that I die quietly, that I don't die with pain and anxiety, fear. But I don't fear dying. I've lived. My goodness, have I *lived*. I have lived a life: I've raised six children. I've had a law enforcement career . . . I've been very happy, I've got very good friends. I can go at any time, it doesn't matter. And I'm all set for it. I'm all prepared for my death. I've got my funeral arrangements made. What little money I have is going where it's supposed to go. I hate to be very, very human right now, but I've got to tell you: I just cannot stand the idea of my body being infested with worms and maggots. I would rather be burned. After all, we go to dust anyway, according to the Bible: dust to dust. So I'm happy about all that.

I'm going to be seventy years old. Most people call this the golden years. I don't. For me, they're the rust years. Everything is rusting up — especially the knees.

When I go, I'd like some kind of closure for my family. I would like them to have a little memorial service with any friends that might want to come. A lot of my contemporaries are deceased now, so it doesn't much matter. [*Laughs*] I'm not a famous person, so there might not be that many people to come to my wake. If you're around and you've got the time, come on over and just say a few prayers for me. Because still I keep thinking, *OK, the person says a prayer for me, it works for me, so* . . . I would like to be remembered as a person who always did the best she could do, but who had a lot of faults. And forgive me for the faults that I had. For the most part, I tried to do the best I could do.

I find that the majority of people don't want to discuss death. I tried to speak to my family about what I want done when I die. I can't find anybody that wants to talk to me about it. I had to talk to my son-in-law . . . [*Laughs*] It's like it's never going to happen. It's like they're ostriches with their heads in the sand. It happens to everybody else, but it's not going to happen to us. See, that's not the way I think: I know it's going to happen. And I want to be prepared.

GUADALUPE REYES

She is eighty-two. She lives in Pilsen, Chicago's largest Mexican community, where she is recognized for her involvement in neighborhood matters. Of her eleven children, four daughters are community activists. Her oldest, Mary, was the one who got her started. 'I lost one child in 1983 – that was Bobby. He was retarded and physically handicapped. He was number six and became the center of our lives.'

Since Bobby was born, I always felt – and I think all parents feel this way – that we are responsible. You feel guilty. Maybe you weren't resting well or eating the right food or whatever. I used to get depressed. I used to take him outside for walks, although he couldn't walk very well, trying to make up for the guilt that I felt. I used to sit in my kitchen and cry, because I would see him sitting there, a big boy, playing with nothing. He was about twelve, thirteen.

They put a brace on him, so I would sit him on the table and swing his legs, put on oil, massage them and exercise them every day, in the morning. Then I put him on a tricycle, put on little elastic bands, and pushed him out in the hallway. Every morning or evening, when the kids were there, they would do it.

They told me, he may not talk because his vocal cords have been damaged.

I feel God was with me then. I read in the paper a little article that said blowing balloons would strengthen the vocal cords, so I taught Bobby how to blow balloons. These penny balloons. He loved it because he'd blow 'em up, then stick 'em with a needle. As he grew, I bought the five-cent ones, but now he was getting too expensive – he'd break them all. I thought of buying him a beach ball, but he didn't like that because it wouldn't pop. Bobby started to talk. I could hear sounds where he made noises. I was feeling my efforts were being rewarded. At the same time, I cannot say seriously that I made him talk. I wanted to cure him, but I knew it wouldn't happen, right? I was still trying. I felt I owed him something . . .

I used to call Mental Health and tell them to send somebody to help me with my son. It didn't work. I was going a little out of my mind. Finally, I decided to find out if there were other people who have the same problems.

I put a notice in the neighborhood paper, and I got about four people who had the same problems. We didn't know what we wanted to do, but I felt comfort that there were people who could talk to me. What happened was that other people joined these meetings: students from the universities taking Special Ed, community reps working with schools. Mental Health came around, curious to ask what I was doing. I said, 'We're just talking.' We didn't know what else to do, right?

The students were the ones who started it. They investigated places we might take our kids. That gave me a lot of courage. Mental Health would tell me, 'Lupe, just don't get disappointed if nothing happens, if things don't work out.' I said, 'Whatever happens will be better than nothing.' So I kept on working with these people. I had about fifty parents now that came together. We were just meeting in my house or in an office across the street.

One day, this professor came over, from some city college, and he says, 'I'll help you. We'll have a school going and you'll run it.' The hardest thing was getting parents to agree to let their children come to our school. Mary★ and I had to go to their homes and reassure them over and over and over. We were at all the meetings, asking people if they knew any handicapped kids in the neighborhood, getting names, addresses, telephone numbers, and making follow-up visits. We decided to open the school.

We gave the school a name, Esperanza – it means 'hope.' We started with a little pilot program of twelve kids. What happened to me is that I began to feel better when I started to do something for my son – no longer depressed. We had our problems, but Esperanza grew very well and is still going.

We knew that Bobby would soon have to leave Esperanza because of his age. Where will we put him? We didn't know nothing about adult workshops, so we set up a place called El Valor – it means 'courage.' It's a place where Bobby could stay forever.

Bobby was thirty-three years old when he died. This happened at

★Guadalupe Reyes's daughter.

El Valor. He usually had seizures, because he was an epileptic. He had a seizure there and didn't come out of it. Bobby was the center of everything we did. If we had a party, we counted Bobby in because he liked parties. He liked to dance. My granddaughter Anna used to take her guitar and say, 'Come on, Uncle Bob, let's sing.' They'd sing together. He gave us a lot of joy.

He was very funny at times. At my birthday party, Bobby wanted to give a speech. He started talking about Harold Washington and how we should vote for him. Washington was already mayor. We would clap for him and go along with it. He felt very proud and he made us laugh a lot.

When Bobby died, in a way I was thankful because he suffered a lot. He would fall and hurt himself – you couldn't watch him every minute. He could walk around and he could talk and he could run out the door, and he wanted to be the president and all kinds of things. But we had to be watching him all the time. My kids used to worry because I was alone and they said, 'When we marry, what are you going to do with Bobby?' I said, 'Don't worry, I'll be able to take care of him.' I said, 'God will help me.' That's why my faith is so deep . . . My youngest son came to me one day and said, 'Mom, I'm the last one here at home. I guess I'm going to be here now to take care of you and Bobby.' I said, 'No, you don't have to. The day you're ready to leave, the day you want to get married, you leave.' 'But, Ma, how about you and Bobby?' – because Bobby was hard to handle. 'Don't worry, son,' I said, 'God will be with me.' My kids all got married.

It's because Bobby was with us that my family was together. On Sundays everybody was there. Whenever I had problems, they would come right away to help me with him. He was a big boy, about two hundred and fifty pounds. If he fell, I couldn't pick him up – just put a pillow under his head and that was it. They were afraid that I would be alone with him. But Bobby and I managed very well. And he started to mature more. He started to be a little bit more calm, because there was no one there to tease him or yell or whatever. The television was his. My family didn't abandon us – they came every Sunday. They took him to McDonald's. He wanted to put money in the bank. He had about maybe a hundred dollars in the bank and he wanted to go to the bank every day to see his money. So my children would come on Sundays, take him for a walk to see the bank so he knew his money was there. I think Bobby also taught my children to love each other, because they cared about him a lot . . .

They used to get into fights with him because he was a nasty guy, but they were always there. So that taught me many things, too – compassion for people who have a problem like we had with Bobby.

Why suffer? After his seizure, they said, 'There's a pressure on the brain and we could try and operate.' 'What guarantee do you give me that he will survive?' 'None.' Ten percent or something. I said, 'Let him go.' They said, 'He has a right to life.' I said, 'I understand – but he also has a right to go.' I got my family together and I said, 'What would you like to do?' 'Mom, what do you think?' I said, 'For myself, as his mother, I have seen him suffer a lot and I don't want them to open his head and not even know for what or what will happen to him. But you're his family – you also tell me what you think.' They all decided to let him go. And we let him go.

The day that the Lord calls me, I want to be ready for everything that I had in mind. I'm Catholic, I want to have a priest, I want to talk to him and confess to him everything I have that may be bothering me. I want to be able to clean all that out. Then I want a very quiet time. I don't want any fancy things. I don't want to go to a funeral home where they keep you two or three evenings and people come to see you there. I want to be in my church because that's my home – that's God's home.

I will be with Bobby. There was this dream I had about him a few months after he died. He was very happy, laughing, and I heard him coming down the gangway. Then he was banging on the door and he pushes it and comes in. And he says, 'Hi, Ma.' I said, 'Hi, Bobby, what are you doing here?' Because in my mind I knew he was gone. He said, 'I came to see you. I don't want you to worry about me, I'm OK.' Now Bobby had a little problem with his speech, and he also limped on his left leg. He says, 'I'm OK, Ma, look – I can talk well now,' he says, 'and I don't limp anymore. Look at me. I don't want you to worry about me anymore, Ma, I'm OK.' I said, 'Bobby, why don't you come back to me?' He said, 'No, Mama, I just came to see you, but I'm not coming back.' And he started walking away. Then he came back and he gave me a big hug, and he says, 'Mom, I'm leaving, but I'm keeping an eye on you.' I said, 'OK, Bobby.' That was the last I remember. He was walking out, and I could still hear him laughing out there in the gangway. He liked to laugh a lot. I still hear him laughing in the gangway, banging on the door, pushing it open, and walking in and saying, 'Hi, Mom.'

POSTSCRIPT

Guadalupe Reyes died on December 31, 2000.

God's Shepherds

REV. WILLIE T. BARROW

She is chairman of the board of Operation PUSH. It had originally been called Operation Breadbasket, founded by Rev. Jesse Jackson. She is seventy-five.

I'm from a little farm in Burton, Texas, seventy-five miles from Houston. My daddy was a preacher. He pastored three churches for fifty years. Worked on a farm, had horses, cows, and chickens. He was Baptist, my mother was Methodist, and they got together, and chose the Church of God, and that's what I am. It's akin to Pentecostal. I was called to the ministry at age sixteen. I left Texas and stayed with my great-aunt in San Francisco, finished high school and college. And then went to Warner Pacific Seminary in Portland, Oregon.

I was really wrapped up in the music ministry, in the street ministry, and the prison ministry. I spent my younger life visiting prisoners and caring for them, taking them toothpaste and toothbrushes, preaching to them. I used to preach on the street corners, Saturday evenings, had a choir, had an organist and a whole orchestra on 47th, 63rd, 39th Street . . . There were thousands of people just gathered to listen to the message. That's where my ministry was, on the street. I preached that people can be transformed from the old life into a new life. I preached that you can live with yourself and with your neighbors. You don't have to cheat, you don't have to steal, you don't have to lie. You can live a life of Christ. The youth hour in our church became bigger than the regular eleven A.M. service because we recruited and mobilized them from the streets, lifting young people.

I came here in 1946, forty-four years ago. The labor movement was doing much of the work of the civil rights movement before

Dr. King. The packinghouse workers union, many African-Americans worked there. The stockyards. That's where I worked. I had a job packing sausage. I'd preach on Saturdays and Sundays. I used to stuff sausage and pack bacon and put Vienna sausages in cans. Before I did that, I had to work all the time. My parents weren't able to send me to seminary, so I worked my way. Guess what I was? I was a welder. [*Laughs*] In Vancouver, Washington, during World War II. Vertical, overhead, and flat. I was a welder out here in this so-called man's world.

Of course, I joined the union – United Packing House Workers of America. Then I got involved in organizing. I was both a preacher and a labor organizer. After that, I joined the Indiana Reconciliation Movement. That's when I went around the world and talked to Madame Binh – yeah, North Korea, South Korea . . . They wanted a black, they wanted a minister, and they wanted a woman so they found three in one! Then the civil rights movement, then Dr. King hired me. I worked for Dr. King eight years at SCLC [Southern Christian Leadership Council]. Then came Operation Breadbasket – that became Operation PUSH.

I got married in 1945. I married a guy from Belize, British Honduras. I had to adjust not just to a married life but to a different culture. When the doctors told me I couldn't have a baby, we adopted two children. One's dead now . . . Ten years later, I was on a mission to Jamaica. I had a whole two weeks to do preaching, so I thought I'd fast. After I came off that fast, I got pregnant. [*Deep chuckle*]

I have a hundred and four godchildren. My husband is a Pisces and I'm a Sagittarius. I got all this *fire*. I just move all kind of ways. And Pisces is very slow, very passive, and very quiet. One of the outstanding characteristics that he had and possessed was he enjoyed me being me, he let me be me. He never stopped me from participating. My son became an entertainer, and he was gay. This was my natural son, Keith Barrow. He had extraordinary talent. Sometimes I think when the scientists get through researching gay people, they're going to find that they are extraordinary, they're geniuses, most of them.

I really didn't know it until other people around there, they said they saw symptoms. I didn't know it until he was about eight years old. He went to college and got his PhD at twenty-two – this was at New York University. Keith wrote music and he got a big contract with Atlantic Records. Then he was getting ready to go to perform and he got real sick. Every time before he would go on stage, he would call me no matter where he was and ask me to pray with him. And I would pray with him. That night he called me, he said, 'Mama, I don't think I can make it – I've got to go to the doctor.' The doctor put him in the hospital. That's when they detected he had HIV. I flew to New York, was with him in the hospital for over a month. And it went into AIDS like three years later. He was twenty-seven when he died.

My husband died July the 7th – he'll be dead two years. Keith died in 1983. He's been dead over seventeen years ago. Me and my son, we were just very close. And now with him going, and my husband going after fifty-four years . . . Fifty-four years to the same man.

My mother died very suddenly. She was out in the yard working and she felt real sick, came and laid down on the bed and died. She had a heart attack – she was sixty-two. I was a grown woman then. My father died, he was on his way to service, to church, and a drunk driver was driving and ran into him and killed him. I have seven brothers and sisters, and my oldest sister died at birth, and then my oldest brother, he's dead. My middle brother is dead. My baby sister is dead. And my baby brother is dead. Nobody's living but me and my older sister – she's living in San Antonio. But the worst in all the deaths was the death of my son. It's a strange hurt. It's a hurt that you can't scratch, it's a pain that you can't grunt it out.

You can't scratch, you can't rub it. But I'm finding out how grief works. I've never done a lot of crying. Only after I leave my house, get in my car, it comes down, it just comes down on me. I think about my son, I think about my husband. My husband just had presence, and that's what grieves me now. But the real grief all coming together affects me to the point that I don't want to do nothing. Like some of the goals and aims that I have in life, I'm sluggish. That's what I'm trying to cope with right now.

Even seventeen years later, even two years later . . . Especially since I don't have no other family and my husband is gone and my child is gone, I got to put my whole house in order. It's difficult for me to make that start. It took me over a year before I could remove my husband's clothing. It doesn't diminish. And I've now finally got enough courage, aspirations to deal with his clothing. To even send the death certificates out that my husband is dead, I got to change the names. That kind of little business is very difficult. When I get really down low, I just go back to the Bible and I repeat those things that have kept me going. He promised us that He would be our mother, our father, our sister, our brother, and I just keep going over that. You promise to be with me. Keith is gone. Honey is gone. My husband – we called each other Honey. Now, Lord, I don't have nobody but you, you've got to come and lift my spirit.

I talk out loud. I just talk to the Lord. And I get refreshed in my spirit. And then I share a lot with my friends. I have friends who have lost children and who have lost husbands. So we share with each other. I have a list of people that I talk to that have lost their mates. I got their telephone number, I say, 'I had you on my mind this morning. How you feeling?' Sometimes I call up those that I feel are much stronger. I say, 'I need your help this morning.' And they'll call me – just like the Fourth of July. They'll call and say, 'I know you're going to miss Honey, and I just want you to know we're here for you.' One of the things that I believe is that there's a hereafter. And I try to live right. So even in my marriage, I never went to bed angry. If me and my husband had a problem, I would clear it up. We made a promise that we would never go to bed angry with each other. That's why I don't hold any grudges, I don't carry any hate in my heart. I get it out. I say, 'You know, what you said to me yesterday, I didn't like it and I want you to know 'cause I got to try to go to sleep tonight.' [*Chuckles*] I keep a clear conscience. Because I believe if you want to go to Heaven, go to a place where you know that God is prepared for you, things gotta be right.

I believe the ultimate Heaven is where all good people will be. Ultimate Hell is where all bad people would be. But there is Heaven on Earth. When you've got trust, and loyal friends, and when you can help people that need your help, that's Heaven – that's Heaven. The most challenging words my son said to me were: 'Mommy, don't cry over me unnecessarily. I know you and I are close,' he says, 'but remember the Scripture that Paul says. He said, "For me to live is death, but to die is to live again." Mama, if the Lord healed me right now, if I continue on earth, I may not be what I am today. If I die, I know I'm right. If I die now. But suppose I be left here for another thirty or forty years. I don't know what I would turn out to be.' He said, 'So, Mama, let me go. Don't hold on to me. Let me go.' And that's the thing that consolated me more than anything. He said, 'If there ever was a time that God would perform a miracle, I'd rather die than He perform a miracle. Because if I lived a long time, I may not live right.' And that just comforts me.

POSTSCRIPT

If I'm preaching a sermon on someone's death and I don't know anything about the person, I preach to the living, those that are at the funeral. I say to them, 'It is appointed unto man or woman once to die, you only die once. Are you ready to die? You that are left? I know you're here grieving over your loved one. But he or she is gone. Are you ready to meet your Maker? And if you're not, it is time. Are you holding grudges? Do you hate? Are you abusive? Then you need to change your mind. Because we too got to go this same way.'

'You gotta stand your test in judgment.' You know that spiritual?

[*Laughs*] That's right, you got it.

White people sing, 'You gotta cross that lonesome valley, you gotta do it by yourself.' And black people, 'You gotta stand your test in judgment, you gotta do it by yourself.'

[*Picks it up, sings*] Nobody here can do it for you. You've got to stand all by yourself. Yeah, you know it! [*Laughs*]

You know that song 'Will the Circle be Unbroken'?

[*Sings*] 'Will the circle be unbroken, by and by, Lord, by and by. Will the circle be unbroken, by and by, Lord, by and by . . .' [*A chuckle*] Good God Almighty, you just turned me on. [*Laughter*]

FATHER LEONARD DUBI

He is the pastor of St. Anne's, a Catholic church, in Hazel Crest, a southwestern suburb of Chicago. It is a lower-middle-class congregation of white and black parishioners. He had been, in the early sixties, an outspoken advocate for civil rights and had, on occasion, challenged the city's highest authorities, especially the elder Mayor Daley.

I broke out of the womb at 8:21, July 9th of 1942, and last Sunday was the first time I ever said Mass at the exact same time that I was born, at 8:21 – and I had this pious thought that this is what my life is about, it's about living and dying. When we're celebrating Mass, we celebrate Jesus dying and rising. And I'm born at that time.

I turned fifty-eight years old last Sunday. On the 13th it'll be my mom's eightieth birthday. She's dead twelve years. I've been thirty-two years a priest.

No, I didn't go to Catholic school. I was really marginally Catholic all my life until I went to the seminary. The reason I'm a priest is because of Mary Buckley, my teacher at Bowen High School. Recently, she called me up to tell me she was dying. It was the very day you called me about your book about death. I got a shiver when that happened. It tells me there is some higher power involved in this coincidence.

I've been involved in social justice most of those years and believe that that's the central way that we worship God in our world . . . in the action. That's the action for justice. That's the way that I show I love Jesus. I believe that Jesus talked about the reign of God and that's got this worldly part. If we want to go to the otherworldly part, we gotta do the this-worldly part: helping people in very concrete ways.

The way that Jesus lived and related to people is the way I believe God lives and relates to people. When I die, I believe that I will see Jesus. But I believe I also need to see Jesus right now. You know Sister Helen Prejean? *Dead Man Walking*. She asks the guy, 'Patrick,

do you want me to be there with you when you're being executed?'
And he says yes. And she says to him, 'Well, Patrick, when you look
at my face, I want you to see in my face the face of Jesus looking at
you and loving you.' And the last face that he saw as he was executed, he looks at this Sister Helen. Now that's what I believe about
Jesus. I mean, he now exists in people who keep that spirit alive, and
Sister Helen's face was the face of Jesus.

As for Heaven and Hell, I know people who live in Hell right
now. They don't know it, but they live in Hell. They're miserable
people. They're just living for themselves, they don't care about
anyone: it's only for *me* that I live, *me* and *mine*, and the only ones
that they're concerned about are their own children or their own
blood relatives. They're just concerned about possessions or grasp-
ing for things – they want more and more things. That's Hell. I've
been in my own kind of Hell. I'm a recovering alcoholic, as you
know. Eighteen years ago, I went into recovery. It was the last
time I got drunk. I had a blackout and I got arrested a block away
from the police station. It was up in Michigan. I was on my way to
see the family of a dear friend of mine who had died. I didn't know
he was dying, so I missed the opportunity of being with him when
he died. I was feeling real guilty. His folks greeted me as I think
that he might have. He liked to drink too. I had a couple of cock-
tails and it didn't affect me and I said, 'I'm not an alcoholic – I can
drink.' The next day I had a couple of more and I went into a
blackout – I was driving on my way back to my motel, and I was
stopped. Instead of going to jail, I went into treatment. So it was
the death of my friend that gave me a new lease on life. So that's
what death is. Death is opportunity, death is a doorway you walk
through.

I don't fear death, I fear the dying. [*A deep sigh*] I fear the kinds
of dying that I've seen people experience, terribly painful moments.
Moments when they're alone. I've been doing this kind of breathing every day. I started inhaling on the count of four, exhaling for
the count of four, holding it for two. I'm up to twenty-eight or
thirty now. Sometimes I get to the point where I'm afraid I'm
going to stop breathing, and it reminds me of dying by suffocation.
When that happens, how frightening that is. That's the way Jesus
died on the cross, he suffocated, he couldn't breathe. That's what

that horrible instrument of the cross was. He died being faithful that there was still meaning and purpose in life.

Both my mother and father died right in my presence. My father died in my house. My mother died in her house and I was there. Both of them died of cancer. My mother died first, twelve years ago. She died with great dignity and she was there with my father who said, 'Mom, you can go.' As soon as he said that she expired and she looked, she looked beautiful.

My father died of cancer of the stomach. I said, 'What are you gonna do, Dad, when you can't live alone?' He said, 'I'm going to move in with you.' [*Laughs*] So he moved in. He couldn't eat anything so he went down from oh, about a hundred and eighty pounds. He was less than a hundred and ten. He died at my house. I had him upstairs in my living quarters. He couldn't stay in the bed because that was not comfortable for him, so I got these inflatable air mattresses. And we'd blow them up and we sat there and he had my remote control and he watched the ball games.

He's dying, but there was a lot of humor in it. I have a couple of cats, and they're declawed, but whatever they were doing they had put their vestigial claws in that air mattress and it deflated. He says, 'Those goddamn fleabags!' [*Laughs*] We laughed at that. And he continued to decline. We had the hospice nurse come in. He didn't want to see anybody, any medical person. I remember picking him up. [*He's been going along quite easily, but now he strains, and fails, not to cry.*] He's a hundred and twenty, less, pounds, and he's got his arms around me like a little, little boy. I carry him downstairs and put him in that bed. And I thought about the reversal of the roles and how this man who is my father, he's now like my child. And he was dying, and I was able to be there for him and care for him. He lost control of his bowels. He wouldn't have any nurse do that. 'You're gonna do that for me.' So I did that for him. And how close, how close we got. And that was so good because for a long time in our life I couldn't be close to him.

Death was a healing. I did the services for my mother and my father. My mother . . . We gave her a round of applause at the end. She was a lady who grew up in the Depression, and she was *always* afraid that she was not going to have enough. She was always concerned about saving. She had plenty – I mean, working-class plenty. They had their own house, they had their own car. They had enough money if they wanted to take vacations, which they didn't. Now she has no more to worry about. She has gone home. My father had some struggles that I shared with him, with the alcoholism. Yet what a wonderful man he really was, he had insight into people and service. He was like the mayor of the block. When he was in health, he had a snow blower and he'd blow the snow of everybody on the block. Lots and lots of people came to his wake.

The death of close relatives, when it's hopeless it's always a very difficult decision for people. I always listen to what they're saying, and I try to reflect with them. If there's any glimpse of how the person wouldn't want to be this way, I try to balloon that and help them to make that decision. Ultimately, it should be that person's decision. If the loved one doesn't see it in the words or the thoughts of the dying, you can't really persuade them to do that. I hope that everybody would come to an understanding that they don't have to keep a person alive using all these extraordinary means. I know I wouldn't want it. I have my living will. I don't want to be kept alive.

The doctrine of the Church is that we cannot be for active euthanasia. But passive euthanasia, allowing somebody to die without having any kinds of extraordinary means, that's certainly acceptable. You *can* pull the plug.

One night I was coming home. This was about twenty-one, twenty-two years ago while I was still in my cups and I was driving home. I took my car flying off a bridge. I went down thirty feet. The car was so crushed that they had to take it away on a flatbed. [*Laughs*] I walked away with just a scratch. My little toe and my one finger, that was all. I was hardly hurt. As this is happening, I was thinking to myself, *I am not going to die, I'm not going to die, I'm not going to die.* I remember thinking that.

They took me to the hospital. A friend drove me back to my rectory, and I remember going past the scene of the accident and cars were backed up for about two miles and I thought, *O my God, I'm so sorry.* I'll never be able to make amends to those people, you know, for doing that . . . But I also remember thinking, *I'm not going to die.* That's the closest near-death experience I've had.

When I was a boy, I remember diving into the lake at Rainbow

Beach. And I came within just inches of hitting rocks. I guess, as I'm thinking about it out loud, death has not been a stranger to me. I believe that I'm in the right vocation. I really believe that I was meant to be a priest – and part of being a priest is dealing with this, to give people hope that death is not the end but a new beginning of sorts.

I'm not God, but I know that when I'm acting in a good way for justice I'm acting God-like. I believe that same power that brought me here, that brought everything else here, will continue afterwards. I don't believe that all these bonds we've had, all these life experiences with people end with death. It continues, if nothing more than the memory.

I can find understanding but I don't agree with suicide. It *hurts* other people. I think that what the Church teaches is that the presumption that suicides are not in their right mind, either because of their depression or because of their anger . . . I want to give them the benefit of the doubt. In the past, it was the sin of despair, so they couldn't be buried in the Church. Now it's a much more compassionate way. A very sick alcoholic drug addict who married a friend of mine left a real nasty, bitter note. It was to his family. I didn't read the note publicly, I just burned it. I wasn't going to lay that trip on people who loved him. He wanted to hurt them, yeah . . . I wasn't going to let him do that. I had a kid from the parish who went to the bedroom and shot himself. His mother – she'd had a hard life and she sacrificed for him. The kid was so nasty and he took his own life, and it made me so *angry*. I like the image of the caterpillar for life, death, transition, always – and I use it every single Easter. The caterpillar is this creature who crawls around on the ground or up in trees and eats leaves. At a certain point it spins a silken cocoon. If you look at that, you'd think it was dead. It hangs there in this cocoon. After a certain amount of time, instead of dying, it's being transformed. It opens up that cocoon and out of it comes the butterfly that can now soar. Instead of eating leaves, it can drink nectar. I think that death is that process when we are transformed from one state into another. I find that it's a simple image, but it touches something deep in me. It summarizes a lot of what I believe.

RABBI ROBERT MARX

He is rabbi of a Jewish Reform congregation: Hakafa (a Circle). It is in Glencoe, an upper-middle-class suburb of Chicago. He is, as well, a founder of the Jewish Council on Urban Affairs, devoted to work in the have-not communities in the city.

I listen to the voice of the prophets. Amos speaks to me. And Isaiah. When Isaiah spoke of Yom Kippur, the holiest day of the year, he understood that you can't fast without doing righteousness, without doing justice. Without thinking about the orphan and the widow and the disinherited of the earth. In my rabbinate, I have tried to teach people what Judaism has to say about justice, whether it's economic or social or political.

Martin Luther King quoted them very often. He studied the prophets when he was in divinity school and knew that they had some important things to say in the civil rights struggle. I don't think you can fight that battle without being aware of the message of the prophets, and of how difficult it was for them to enunciate a message in which they were seen as attacking the power structures of their times. They were attacking the priests, they were attacking the kings, they were attacking secular rule – and, above all, they were attacking an unequal distribution of wealth. Amos, for instance, in a beautiful passage, says, 'They lie on beds of ivory,' criticizing those people who had conspicuous consumption as their motto, who didn't think of those who were poor, who didn't take care of those who were unjustly treated by their society. They're very modern.

I was one who my teachers thought would have been the least likely person to be a rabbi. At an early age I was expelled from religious school because of disrespectful behavior toward my elders. In the midst of that time in my life, something happened to me, and I decided – it was as if a voice came to me and said, 'You will be a rabbi.' I had some grandiose visions in those early days. I thought I could save the world. Now I've come to understand there's very little I can save, but I can add my voice to those who would try to make this world a little bit better place in which to live.

Silence is not inaction. It is doing something: silence is *acquiescence*. When you acquiesce to injustice, you are contributing to it. The hardest thing in the world is to help people find the courage. In that process, finding it yourself is not always an easy task. You have to say that I'm willing to be inconvenienced, I'm willing to march in that parade, I'm willing to sign that petition. I am *willing* to go down to a prison and visit somebody who has been wrongly imprisoned. I am *willing* to have rocks thrown at me, as has happened.

I have a congregation called Hakafa. It means 'a circle.' We have a group of people who study a great deal, who are not content with just using the external trappings of religion. We are unusual in that we have no building. We want our resources to be used toward taking care of people, in running social projects, in doing things that will make life a little more pleasant for the world. Our congregation is made up of all kinds of people, from social workers, to doctors, to attorneys, to writers, to people who take care of homes.

We are Reform Judaism. We don't regard ourselves as being in a process that has been completed, so it is Reform. There is also Orthodox Judaism – and Conservative Judaism, which stands between the liberalism of Reform synagogues and the traditionalism of Orthodox synagogues. In an Orthodox synagogue, most of the service would be conducted in Hebrew. Men and women sit separately. In a Reform service, much of the service now is in Hebrew, but there's also a great deal in English. Men and women sit together. From a traditional point of view, the Torah, the entire law, was given to Moses at Mount Sinai. For most Reform synagogues, the law is a process of progressive evolution, of an insight that was given to Moses and is constantly unfolding before us.

My father was an attorney in Cleveland. I admired his strength, I admired his moral courage – I wanted to be an attorney. One day, I was talking to my father about this and the thought came into my mind that there were other professions. I mockingly said, 'Suppose I were to become a rabbi?' And I laughed. In the midst of the laughter came the existential *ah-ha!* . . . that's what I wanted to do. Nothing in my background had really prepared me for that. I knew very little Hebrew. Tradition was not part of our family. My father, though not a Hebrew-speaking or even -knowing Jew, was a deeply pious Jew. Used to say a silent prayer at our dinner table every night.

Went to our Reform synagogue every Sunday morning and ushered in his frock coat, because in that particular congregation things were very formal. It happened very quickly with me. This sounds self-aggrandizing, but I wanted to help people to think about changing some of the attitudes they had. I liked to talk. So I became a rabbi.

I was fifteen years old when I entered college, Western Reserve in Cleveland. I wouldn't call myself precocious, I simply worked hard. I became a very young student at the Hebrew Union College in Cincinnati, Ohio – and studied for many years at the seminary. Then took a PhD degree at Yale University in philosophy. That's what put into shape some of my social action ideas that I was able to express through creating the Jewish Council on Urban Affairs here in Chicago. I get very emotional about it . . .

The Council provides help to community groups, usually of the poor, in the city of Chicago. We never do anything unless we're asked by a community. We are different from so many city organizations in that we have no answers. We don't come in and say, 'This is what you ought to do.' We provide help to groups that want to help themselves – the people who are fighting slum landlords, people who are seeking to prevent urban renewal from destroying their community, we provide staff for them to do it. We're doing pretty much what Amos and Isaiah were talking about. About life.

Death to me is the antithesis of everything I've given my life to achieve. From the very moment that we begin to mature, we human beings become aware that death is what lies before us. We meet death by doing a variety of things. People make a big mistake by avoiding thinking about it, by avoiding understanding it. As a rabbi, I'm seeing most people are afraid of death – they think it's an enemy. They're terribly, terribly fearful of what looms before them. I, when I understand a commitment to life, have to also understand that I'm fated to death, and that death lies before me.

Judaism, my faith, has always been ambivalent about death. Judaism in a sense simply says: Death is a reality. There are ceremonies that we deal with in terms of death. We say the Kaddish prayer when somebody has died. Yet Judaism has always been leery of defining too sharply what happens to us when we die. There's a difference between what my religion allows me to think about death or how often it allows me to think about death and *my own* thoughts about death. Judaism does have an idea of Heaven, it does have an idea of life after death – that is very clear.

Again, there are differences between Reform and Orthodox Jews. We all tend to say we believe in the immortality of the soul – something of us lives on. We don't die. Orthodox Jews tend to say there will be a Messiah come someday; and with the coming of the Messiah, the dead will be resurrected. I'd like to believe in resurrection – I find that hard, though. But I do believe that life goes on, that there's something that happens to us after we die. I believe that very strongly.

I lost a son many years ago. He died after a long illness. I go to a cemetery and visit his grave. At the grave I stand there as if I'm going to call him up to me. He will come forward and be with me. I often feel that he's in some holy spot, with God, and that I will see him someday – and we will be together. The thing that troubles me is that when I think of Heaven, I think of a place that lacks the one thing I feel is more important than anything else, and that is free will. So when I think of my son, I think of him lately as being able to do the things that he wants to do. I'm standing at his grave and it's as if some bureaucratic official far away is calling him forward and saying, 'David, come from whatever you're doing' – and it takes him a long time to leave what he's doing and join me in spirit as I stand at his grave. I know this sounds surrealistic, and I also know that I can't defend what I'm saying rationally, but I believe it. I believe that David is somewhere and that someday I will be united with my son. We will be together, and we will talk, and David will lay his hands on my forehead, as he once did when I had a headache, and he said, 'I'm so sorry you have that headache. I'm so sorry . . .' When I think about death, I don't think about something abstract, because that defies all logic. I think of the concrete people I know, and of the possibilities for me someday being united with them in some way that transcends anything that I can possibly imagine.

I think the most beautiful things in my life are things I can't prove. I can't prove why I feel being a rabbi is important to me. I can't prove why I believe in God. In my rational moments, I've tried to do a taxonomy: a classification of God so people can know how many different ideas of God they're really talking about. When somebody says to me, 'I don't believe in God,' I always say, 'What do you mean by God?' They talk to me, and I don't believe in that kind of a God either – but I do believe in God.

I'm a variety of pantheist: I'm a panentheist. I believe – and this is very personal – I believe that God is in everything, that in *this* moment God is here. When we talk, when we meet. In each of us there's a little bit of God. I also believe that there is an element of God that is outside of us. That explains why I can pray. If I were God, or if you were God, there'd be no sense in prayer. But if there is a part of God that is outside of us, then we can reach out and say: 'Let me do the best that I can do. Let me be the holiest and noblest I can be.' I do not believe this God is all-powerful. I don't believe that I'm going to be punished by this God, or that I'm going to be rewarded. Here's where traditional theologians disagree with me: I take away omnipotence from this idea of God, though I *do* say that there is something that is there, that is outside of me, to which I can turn and find strength.

I think Hell is within us. I don't see a physical Hell any more than I see a physical Heaven. My Heaven is metaphysical. It is a place where spirits are. I know this is so illogical, but I accept the discontinuity. I believe in some sort of ideal Heavenly time frame in which the people I love exist eternally. I don't believe in a place of punishment. I believe Hell is what we make of our own lives by the selfishness or by the corruption that we tolerate or foster in our own world – in the relationships which we destroy through our thoughtlessness and carelessness, through the love that we shatter. That's Hell. We don't need another place. I believe that there's also Heaven in us, too, but I believe there's Heaven that transcends us. That's where my panentheism again finds expression. *I'm talking about what we do on Earth.* I'm also talking about something that takes place in us and through us after our life is ended. I think we need a completion: our lives are not complete. We are preceded in life by our mothers and fathers, and I think we, in turn, give something, even in our death, to those people who come after us. There's a wonderful Hebrew tradition about the Kaddish, that the Kaddish is a way not only of saying a prayer in which we remember those who have gone before us, the memorial prayer, but it's also a way of redeeming our parents and those we love. There's a connection between the living and the dead. What we do in our lives is make a disconnect between the living and the dead – we separate. I think that's a very dangerous thing. Our fears make us separate like that. I don't think we need to be afraid of death. I see a continuity, and I see life is something that includes death.

I talk to my son very, very often. I capture him as he was at the age of fourteen. In my conversations with David, he is eternally fourteen. We talk, and his memory is a humanizing blessing to me. It teaches me to understand the pain of other people who have lost. I feel their pain as I think of my son.

That was in 1973 that he died, almost twenty-eight years ago. He died on a Jewish holy day. He died on the Festival of Purim. It is a day in which things are reversed. I'm just having an insight now that I've never had before. In Purim, people dress up and they are the opposite of what they seem. In Purim, they wear masks. It is a festive day – it commemorates the deliverance of the Jews. It's the Book of Esther in the Bible, in which Jews were delivered from the king's adviser, Hamen. For the first time I see that, as we dress up and change things around on Purim, the day of his death may be the day for me of his life.

For many years I led a group of parents who had lost a child. There were moments when I envied the Catholics who were in the group – because they could say, 'My child is with God,' and they believed that with absolute certainty. Other members of the group were uncertain about what they could believe. Their uncertainty led them to feel alone in their time of solace. I'm not for a moment suggesting somebody should accept a belief that they cannot really, really understand or believe in. But I *am* saying there's a function that we have tended to ignore – the role of solace that an organized community provides. That's very important for people to have.

PASTOR TOM KOK

It is a beautiful June afternoon. We're seated in the rectory of the Peace Christian Reform Church in South Holland, a suburb of Chicago. He, the pastor, is forty years old.

My wife and I have three children. The eldest, Tom, is thirteen, named after his dad. The second one, Jedidiah, is eleven – it's the name God gave to Solomon. My little girl, Amanda, is going to be ten soon. They mean a lot to me, and I spend a lot of time with them, enjoying their company.

The people of the Christian Reform Church actually came over to the United States in the early 1800s, and originally joined with the Dutch Reform Church. There was a difference over a few issues, so we broke away from the Dutch Reform people in 1857. Basically, our tenets are the same.

The community of South Holland has a rich heritage. The motto of the town is 'Faith, Family and Future.' The people who founded this town have really worked hard on making their faith part of their life. We take what we believe and weave it into our daily lives.

It is a changing community. A number of the traditional Dutch folks have moved out to other areas, and we have new people moving in of a variety of ethnic backgrounds. But, still, for the most part, South Holland is a churchgoing community, definitely conservative. The people of Harvey and Dolton, next door, are probably a majority African-American.

When I was about ten years old, I sang in the church choir, the kid's choir. A great time in my life, by the way. It was in Grand Rapids, Michigan. My father was pastor of a church there. I remember one day when we came to church in the middle of the week to sing. I was vaguely informed that a little girl who was my age had been killed on her bicycle. I hadn't really put two and two together. Before we sang at the church, we had an opportunity to walk through the vestibule, the entryway to the church, where the casket was. That was probably the first time that I came face-to-face with death. A little girl, my age, laying in a casket – I saw her there. I was as close as you and I are to each other. I felt a little fear. If somebody that age could die that easily and that quickly, so could I. Confusion, a little bit – not really understanding death. In our faith tradition, we baptize infants, and the big reason we do that is we want our children to know from a very young age that they belong to Jesus Christ. My parents taught me that very well. My grandfather was a baker, and he was one of the most godly men I've ever met in my entire life. I was learning very early on the songs like 'Jesus loves me, this I know . . .' Prayers like: 'Now I lay me down to sleep, I pray the Lord my soul to keep. If I should die before I wake, I pray the Lord my soul to take.' I prayed that a lot when I was a kid. We were taught in those prayers that death was part of life. It's a way of accepting death.

Death is the great unknown. It's something that none of us has experienced but all of us will. I will fear death when it comes, but that fear is not going to be the overwhelming emotion that I experience. I believe that, at that time, my childhood faith, that faith that lives in me now as I go from here to there, that Jesus Christ is going to be with me, He's going to hold my hand, and He's going to walk with me through that valley of the shadow. I've seen that a lot. Because I'm a pastor, I have been present at the death of a number of my members. I get called in at the last moment when the machine is unplugged or when people are feeling that the time is coming near. I can't express to you the feeling of peace that these people have as they face this great unknown. They're not wanting to go, because of family. But I have had a number of godly saints say to me, 'I want to go home' – they see it as home. One of our basic beliefs as Christians is that this isn't really our home, that God puts us here to train us in how to live and how to love him, but that there's a better thing coming.

When I talk about God I talk about him as a friend of mine, because He is a friend of mine. The big question that comes up in a lot of people's minds is if somebody kills himself, can he go to Heaven? I know that there are certain faith traditions that say no – because you don't have a chance to repent. This past weekend, as a matter of fact, I did a funeral for an eighty-three-year-old man who committed suicide. And I believe that man died in despair rather than in comfort. I've been talking to a lot of people about that this past week. You want me to talk to you about that? This gets at the heart and soul of my faith, in that I believe with all my heart – and the Scripture teaches – that once I belong to Jesus Christ, He doesn't let me go. I do a lot of stupid things in my life. If I, say, am driving down Cottage Grove here and I'm distracted and I run the stop sign and I hit somebody and he's killed, does that mean that I'm disobeying God's will? God's will is that I obey the governing authorities. If I disobey the law and I die, am I not going to go to Heaven? No, I don't believe that's the case. I believe that God knows – in fact the Bible says He knows – how we are formed, He *knows* the thoughts that go through our minds, and I believe – and Scripture says very clearly too – that God is gracious.

So you believe that that old man who committed suicide will go to Heaven?

Yes, I do. I believe so because my understanding of Scripture is that it's God who gives me salvation and not myself. It's not what I do, it's what He does. One of my favorite passages, if you'll allow me to quote it, is Ephesians 2, verses 8 and 9, which says: 'It is by grace you have been saved through faith; and this is not from yourselves, it is the gift of God, so that no one can boast.' It's the salvation that comes completely and fully from what God does. He just gives it to me as a gift.

Does God forgive everyone?

Everyone who asks for it, yes, yes.

What if one commits a heinous crime, brutally?

Yes, he, too, is forgiven – I believe so. Salvation by grace is a basic teaching of the Reform faith. The Christian Reform Church, really, I don't think has ever taken an official stand on it. This is something that I came to from my own understanding of Scripture. We are sinners, but God forgives us in spite of ourselves.

Do you believe in a Heaven and Hell?

Yes, I do. Heaven is being in God's presence, living as we were intended to. The Bible teaches about Adam and Eve and the Creation. The Westminster Shorter Catechism, which is the expression of faith of the Presbyterian Church, begins by saying this: 'What is the chief end of man?' And the answer is: 'To enjoy God and glorify him forever.' That's what we were made for. There's a God-shaped hole in all of us that we seek to fill.

A God-shaped hole? There's God within us?

Not really within us, no – God is not within us. But there is within us a *need* for God. We were built to have that peace in us. When we walked away from God in the Garden of Eden, we lost that peace.

Can you set the scene of Heaven?

I often think of Heaven, I think of a choir that is singing the praises of God continually. I think of a lovely garden, like the Garden of Eden must have been. The Bible talks about a new Heaven and a new Earth. I tell my kids all the time, I'm looking forward to walking in the grass and playing baseball. My golf game probably won't be any better, but I won't care. A new Heaven and a new Earth, that's the promise of Scripture.

What about Hell?

Hell is the opposite, it's a separation from God. Hell is the place where all the goodness of God that we take for granted today is gone – the fact that day follows night and my heart continues to beat and gravity continues to work. I believe that all of these things are the direct result of God's constant care. And when those things are taken away, it's Hell.

Do you think some people go to Hell?

I do believe so, yes.

Who would they be?

You're asking me to make a judgment that I'm not sure I want to make. But that's OK ... I would say there are people who have heard the message of salvation by faith and Christ and who have determined not to accept it. Persons who maybe grew up in the Church and who know the truth, and yet who have chosen to live otherwise and not to put their faith in Christ.

What of someone who is not of that Church and of that faith?

The Bible actually talks about that, too. It talks about how God has built a basic law into people's lives: the law of right and wrong, the law of good and evil. In every society, as far as I know, there are the laws of right and wrong. But I do want to say here that God is much more gracious than I could ever possibly imagine. And I believe there's a whole lot more people in Heaven than people would dare to guess.

What about an atheist?

You're asking a tough question. Biblically speaking, I would have to say that they wouldn't be able to go to Heaven. To reject, to willingly *reject* the God who created you and who sent his son to die for you is a grave mistake. But again, I want to qualify that by saying my God is gracious –

Even to an atheist?

It's very possible.

Otherwise I'd be going to Hell. Is there an in-between Heaven and Hell?

No, I do not believe in a purgatory. I believe in a judgment that takes place. There are two basic judgments. The first one is when we pass from this Earth and we go to the place where we have chosen, and the other is a judgment that comes when Christ returns – and that will be the final judgment.

When was a time you grieved, really grieved deeply? Has there been such a time?

I would have to say no, not grieving deeply. Mourning the loss of a loved one, somebody that I really cared about – my grandfather passed away when he was about eighty-eight. That was about ten years ago. He was a godly man, a wonderful man. I mourned because I would not see him anymore. But I couldn't grieve, because I knew where Grandpa was.

So that's a vaccination against grief.

To some extent. We still deal with the hole that's left in our life from somebody who dies. When somebody dies, we come to know how much they meant to us. How many times we stopped by to see Dad or Mom or whatnot. And so we do have that grief. But there is, in a sense, for the Christian, an incredible joy. My grandfather's funeral was actually a celebration. There was a reading of Scripture. The Bible has some marvelous things to say in it. Christ says, 'I am the resurrection and the life. Anyone who comes to me will never be turned away. I am the way of life.' First Corinthians 15 is a marvelous passage about the Resurrection: 'As in Adam all die, so in Christ shall all be made alive.' And then we sing songs from the faith. This past week we sang a song called 'When Peace Like a River': 'When peace like a river attendeth my way / When sorrows like sea billows roll / Whatever my lot though has taught me to say / It is well, it is well with my soul.'

Was there any weeping at his funeral?

Oh yes, of course – there's always the weeping for those that we love. I've had some close friends here at the church pass away rather suddenly from heart attacks, and the tears are always there. And the pain – you cannot avoid the pain . . . There is no immunization from the pain. If I see people who are immune from the pain, I know that there's probably something going on in their hearts that's not right or real: they're denying. But it's not the mourning without hope.

There's a Southern song called 'O Lovely Appearance of Death.' In a way that's reflected in what you're saying – going home.

Going home, yes . . . yes. I feel that burial or cremation doesn't matter. God had the ability to create bodies out of nothing when the world started, and I believe that when Christ returns and the resurrection of the dead takes place, God's going to be able to re-create those bodies with the same power that He made them with. So you can burn 'em, you can mash 'em, you can spread 'em all over the place if you want to – it doesn't matter.

We have the Heidelberg Catechism, a summary of Scripture written in 1564: 'What is my only comfort in life and in death?' And the answer is: 'My only comfort is that I belong in life and in death to my faithful savior Jesus Christ.' We teach that to our children very, very early on.

Is God personified to you?

Yes. Jesus gives us permission in the Bible to call God father. I see him as the ultimate parent.

Him? Why?

Him, yes. The Bible talks about him as a him, as the father. Though the Bible does use some mother-type imagery for God – as a hen gathers her chicks under her wings. The terms of compassion that are used are very feminine terms. The Bible presents him as male. I'm not going to argue with the Bible.

You see him anthropomorphically?

As having a lot of human traits, yes: compassion, love, anger. The Bible talks about God being angry. You can hurt him, you can grieve him.

Do you ever get angry at God?

A while back we were, as a church, looking for a second pastor to help out with the work around here, and we had a young man who was just fantastic. And we called him to come. At the same time, another church issued a call to him asking him to come, and he chose the other church over us. I was very angry with God . . . Why? Why? Just this past week when this elderly man killed himself, *why?* What's going on? Why are you allowing this to happen? Yeah, I've been angry with God. But then I usually learn afterwards that God had a good reason for doing what he's doing. Because since that time, we have hired another gentleman, my associate, Pastor Jim Lester, and I couldn't have asked for a better man.

You said you feel angry at God at certain moments. When a child is killed, or an old man is a suicide, do you feel it's God's will?

No. I believe that the bad things that happen in this world are the result of Satan's prompting and human choices. I do believe that God can take everything that happens and work it for good. One of my favorite texts also is Romans 8:28, where it says, 'We know that in all things God works for the good of those who love him and are called according to his purpose.'

You believe in Satan, the Devil?

Certainly. Scripturally speaking, Satan is an angel – a fallen angel. He may have been the greatest of the angels, the highest form of creation that God ever made. But Satan decided that he knew better than God, that he wanted to be equal with God and he challenged God – and was thrown out of Heaven with his followers. But he is alive and well. And powerful.

Where does he live?

Wherever Hell is. [*Laughs*] I'm not going to say down or up.

How would you like to be remembered?

I would like to be remembered as a man of God – a man who found his hope, his purpose, his strength in loving and serving the Lord. In the way that I love and serve my wife, the way I love and serve my children, who, by the way, come before the church. My priority scale is God, my family, the church.

Church is second to family.

Yes, I believe so. God has called me to be the minister of my home before he's called me to be the minister of this church.

You'd want a celebration?

I would love there to be a great deal of singing. I love to sing. I grew up singing around the family piano. 'How Lovely Is Your Dwelling, O Lord of Hosts, to Me . . .' 'It Is Well with My Soul' – what a great song.

Those songs that you sang, did they also deal with death . . .?

Yes. One piece, 'Like a River,' does talk about when death arrives. I know it by heart:

> Oh Lord, haste the day when my faith shall be tried
> The clouds be rolled back as a scroll
> The trumpet shall resound and the Lord shall descend
> Even then it is well with my soul.

It's good. There's a Dutch word that's the equivalent for *shalom*. I have a *shalom* pen holder over there. *Shalom* is this idea that everything is right. It's not just peace, but everything is as it ought to be. The Dutch word: *gezellig*.* My dad is sitting in his chair at home and he has some food and the family is around and he's enjoying the grandchildren . . . he'll say, 'This is very *gezellig*' – everything is as it should be.

And death, too, when it arrives.

When we get on the other side, it's very *gezellig*.

*Pronounced 'cchz-zelicch.'

Rev. Ed Townley

He has been an actor, director, and set designer. He is now a
pastor at Unity Church.

I'm a fifty-six-year-old Unity minister, here in Chicago. Before that
I was in theater for a number of years. I divide my life in two parts:
before age thirty, when I had a death experience, when I was
declared dead, and then everything that's happened since then. It was
at age thirty that my life really turned around. Twenty-six years ago
this October, as a matter of fact. I'm a recovering alcoholic. At that
time I was not recovering – I was very definitely a full-blown. By
age thirty, my life was *totally* a mess. Alcohol and drugs and all that
that can do to you in every way. I have slept on streets and in door-
ways. I was in New York City then, and I was taken to a hospital on
Long Island. I had just collapsed. I hadn't been eating. All of the
physical things that alcohol can do to you, it had done to me. I was
turned away from one hospital because it was a Friday night – it was
very busy, they didn't have time, and I wasn't going to live anyway.
So then they had to race me across Nassau County to another hospital. The doctor came by. It was a very busy night. He said, 'He is
not going to live.' He signed my death certificate and said, 'Fill in the
details when it happens.'

And I had one of those experiences. Now, you've got to remember that this is 1974, before Kübler-Ross had become really well
known. I could hear them talking about the fact that I was going to
die. I had pancreatitis and bone cancer and just *total* destruction
from alcohol. The doctor said to the nurse, 'He's not going to live,
and I may not be able to get back.' I could hear it all. I was, like,
floating above myself. I could look down on my body and I could
hear them . . . [*He pauses, a little choked up.*] I don't talk about this
very much. I knew that I was dying, and I knew that that was just
fine because all of the pain was down in the body and I didn't have
to deal with it anymore. It was like I was tethered in some way. I was
drawn toward a light. This is really going to sound weird . . . I felt
like I was on some sort of spaceship or flying saucer or something,

but I was surrounded by beings. Without really talking in words, they told me that I had to go back, that it was not time. I didn't want to go back because I'd made too much of a mess of it – I just couldn't go back to *that*. And they said: 'You really need to. You have to because we really need you to go back. Rest here for a while and we'll talk to you again.' So I rested. I didn't die. I was in a coma in intensive care for about ten days. At some point, they came back and they said: 'It is really important that you go back – you have work to do. We will promise you it will never be that bad again.' I finally said OK, and I came back and I recovered. The doctors said, 'You are absolutely a miracle. We don't know how you are still alive. But as long as you don't drink again you'll be fine.' I guess the first sign of health was when something within me said, 'I don't know how to do that. But if I go back, I know what's going to happen.' So I started my process of recovery, and I've been sober and drug-free from that experience to this day – twenty-six years.

These spiritual beings, they stayed fairly anonymous. They were sort of distant. They didn't want me to get too comfortable there. I've never tried to understand the whole thing. If you talk to other people who have had near-death experiences, I'll bet they say the same thing. From that day till this, I have never been afraid of death. I'm afraid of lingering and being in pain, but I've never been afraid of death itself. I didn't see any of them. I remember being very annoyed because I felt their presence from everywhere – there was no up and down. It was like the yardsticks had vanished and I was just embraced in this energy. People ask me how did they communicate, did they speak English? I don't know . . . I didn't hear them – I just knew.

I was in the hospital for another month. They released me from intensive care and I went into a treatment program for ten days. Honestly, I had no intention of not drinking. It didn't occur to me that I might be able to do that. I thought, *If I'm going to die, I'm going to die*. But somehow, the days just began to string together and pretty soon sobriety became a way of life. It's not like I lived happily ever after. I've had more pain and more anguish and more challenges in my life since then than I did before. What I understand them to mean when they said it will never be this bad again is, I've never felt that *total* despair, that real *belief* that there is nothing and I am lost.

I was not at all spiritual at the time – I was agnostic, I had no belief. Once you start in recovery, you need some concept of a higher power. Nothing worked for me. I tried various churches. After I came out of the hospital, I started getting sober and tried to live that life. And then somebody took me to a Unity service, and it made a whole lot of sense. To think that I was dealing with a power within me greater than I had ever imagined made a whole lot of sense, 'cause *something* was keeping me sober – it wasn't me. I had at last found security.

Unity is what would generally be classified as new-thought Christianity.* It places its emphasis on the presence and power of God in every person – that what we are here to do is to release and express that God within us. So our prayer work is more internalized than it is to a God somewhere in the distance. We're very Bible-based, we're based in the teachings of Jesus. It's a very empowering, loving energy.

I had worked for Joe Papp in New York at the New York Shakespeare Festival, Shakespeare in the Park and then down at the Public Theater just when he first opened it. It was a very exciting time. Once I got sober, one of my fears was that the creativity is in the bottle. I think everybody worries about that. I found that wasn't the case. So I continued in theater, but my life really began to center around recovery. I got very active in AA.

I happen to be gay. I met a lover and lived in Detroit for a while, and then moved to Chicago and worked at Wisdom Bridge Theater. But the spiritual dimension that had opened up in my life became more and more dominant. I just felt this calling – it really was a *calling*. So, at age forty-four, I went into ministerial school.

I had always felt so totally different, so totally stranger-in-a-strange-land. I'll tell ya, we gays have given ourselves quite a road . . . I didn't even admit it to myself. I just was in deep, deep denial. But what would happen is that I would get drunk and then I would act out sexually. Once I stopped drinking and using drugs, I had to come out of the closet because I really had to give myself permission to be who I am, if I was going to survive at all, much less accomplish anything with my life.

I was about seventeen or eighteen years sober by the time I entered

*It is not New Age; Unity was founded in the late 1800s.

the ministry. I was ordained when I was forty-six, so I'm coming up on ten years. I *know* that there is life after death – I believe that life is continuous. I don't believe in a hereafter any different than this. I believe that we are spiritual beings and, as spiritual beings, this life-time is part of a larger continuum. We were somewhere else before and we will go somewhere else afterward. The experience of death and the experience of birth are almost identical: they're a letting-go of one dimension and moving into another dimension.

Unity has no dogma. I believe in God. Somebody asked Jung, 'Do you believe in God?' and Jung said, 'I don't believe, I know.' I know that there's a dimension to life beyond what we're experiencing. I believe in reincarnation. It's not a basic Unity belief, but we just believe that if we are eternal spiritual beings, then eternity doesn't begin when we die – we are part of eternity now. We must have been somewhere before we were here. I don't spend a lot of time worrying about whether I was Cleopatra in a past life – that was then and this is now. I do believe that we grow, that we have more than one opportunity to make the choices that will align us with that spiritual energy so that we're more powerful. Once a woman offered to do a past-life reading on me. I just said, 'OK, fine.' She said, 'You weren't on this planet in your last life.' I said, 'Lady, I haven't been on this planet for most of this life! That doesn't surprise me . . .' I don't really worry about it too much.

Being a gay minister, I do a lot of work with persons with AIDS, and have done a lot more memorial services than I'd ever care to. That really is the most comforting thing that I can offer, and the most empowering: it's not that you die and you are judged and you are punished, it's just that life goes on. The truth of who you are cannot die, and so it will find another way to express itself.

Oh, I've been to Hell, done that. One of my metaphysics teachers says that Hell is useless, unnecessary suffering that we put ourselves through. It's what we do to ourselves by judging. What was the one thing Jesus said more often than anything else? *Judge not.* Judge not. And what's the one thing that his followers insist on doing in his name: judging. Exactly what he told them not to do: judging others.

One of the things that makes it possible for me to be a Unity minister is that we don't have doctrinal opinions. People say, 'What is Unity's stand on abortion?' We don't have one. We honor the guidance within you and we support that. And that's why there are so many gays and lesbians in my church, because we don't judge. We don't say you should be straight but we'll love you anyway. We say: Be the best gay you can be, be the most compassionate. That's what you're here to do.

As for death . . . I have no question that people have the right to say, 'This is enough – I want to go now.' But there's so much we don't know. There was a woman I visited recently in a nursing home and she said, 'Why is God letting me linger? I want to go. This is expensive – I'm in pain.' And I said, 'We have no way of knowing. Your being here may be affecting another life in some significant way. You may have one little thing still to do, one little piece of forgiveness still to accomplish. And if you do it now, you don't have to come back and live another life to do it again. You can just do it now.' I certainly would never judge them or condemn them.

In some religions, they almost freeze-dry the grief and just keep you in it forever. *Of course* we're going to grieve – that's part of the process. I can't think of anything more unkind to do to somebody who has just lost a loved one than to say, 'Gee, I hope he goes to Heaven.' It's just . . . a life is completed and that's to be celebrated and grieved and learned from and we move on. To just make it such an occasion of judgment and finality is too cruel.

The most powerful death experience I've ever had – I was a minister by then – I was living in Portland . . . This was my best friend. A brilliant actor, wonderful talent, who died of AIDS at age thirty. He gave me the greatest gift anyone has ever given me. At the end, when he knew that he had very little time and it was affecting his brain, he called me and he said, 'I want you to be part of my support team while I go.' I was present in the room with him when he died. To be part of that experience . . . It was definitely scary, definitely frightening, just as birth is frightening – that's why we scream when we come in, because we're moving into the unknown, and that's *always* scary.

We walk in one door and walk out the other door, and the experience is the same: we're afraid to move to the next dimension. The womb is a nice safe place to be – but you can't stay there forever. When I became a minister, my greatest fear was that I wouldn't be able to handle death, I'd just collapse, I'd just be too moved, be too grief-stricken, I wouldn't be able to . . . Maybe it's because of my own death experience, but it's one of the great gifts I have to offer and one of the richest experiences in my life is to be present when somebody makes a transition. Often this is the role I play with the person who's dying and *knows* that he or she is dying while the family is in deep denial. And you show up and they say, 'Doesn't he look better today? And next year on vacation we're going to go . . .' This poor guy, all he wants to do is talk about what is going on for him. Sometimes I'm the only person to whom he can say, 'You know, I'm dying. I'd like to talk about what this is going to be like.' Everybody else around him thinks that by refusing to discuss it they are somehow cheering him up. It's just the opposite: they're making it so frustrating for him to try and bring some kind of closure that will let him go in peace. The dying man says to me, 'I want to tell my wife about the safe deposit box, but every time I do she goes nuts and says, "You're not going to die!" I *know* I am, and I'm OK with it. Please, help us communicate . . .' That's what I do more than anything else, is just bring people together and say, 'Let's talk.'

I'm not eager for death. There's a lot I want to accomplish here. I'm just starting to get the hang of this now. [*Laughs*]

The Stranger

RICK RUNDLE

He arrives by bike. He is a forty-five-year-old 'hoisting engineer' for the Streets and Sanitation Department; he works in graffiti removal. He lives with his mother and a younger brother, John, who has Down's syndrome. Just the previous month he had donated part of his liver to John Husar, a columnist on the outdoors for the *Chicago Tribune* and a member of his parish congregation. Theirs is the only white family in a black community on the south side of the city.★

My family was always religious, but I think anyone's faith, it ebbs and flows. For a true seeker of answers, it ebbs and flows. So I can't say I always had strong faith – I'd be lying. But it's not the hour you're in church, it's all the other hours you're not in church that truly show who you are.

I went searching for different parishes to get what I needed. The parish that I settled on is Old St. Pat's, down on the near West Side of downtown Chicago. It's the oldest public building in the city of Chicago. I had slowly become a Eucharist minister, a liturgical minister, one that does the readings and passes out the bulletins. About three months ago, at the end of the mass, the priest made an announcement that there was a parishioner who was looking for a liver transplant. Five of my close friends have come down with hepatitis C, which is a chronic liver disease – lifelong friends that I've known for years. So I was somewhat familiar with liver disease. The

★His mother says she finds it more comfortable now than she did before the neighborhood changed from white to black. 'In the old days, when Johnny would amiably pat a woman's bottom, she'd angrily mutter, "Why don't you have him put away?" Today, when he touches a black woman, she turns around, smiles at him, and says, "How ya' doin', honey?"'

odd thing about hepatitis C, it's pandemic. Probably more people are going to die of hepatitis C this year than will die of HIV in this country. Because it's a silent disease, it's a disease that takes fifteen to twenty years to incubate and once it does, it affects different people in different ways. The only known cure, and it's not even a cure, is a liver transplant.

John Husar wasn't a friend. I'd see him at church and, of course, I enjoyed reading his column.

I wanted to see him live. I wanted to give him a chance at a life that was being denied him. I knew my friends who had hepatitis C, and it's not a good existence. It's a lot of sleeping, it's a lot of times you don't even feel good enough to get out of bed. And I met a priest who got the last liver in the previous millennium, 1999. He talked about how much it did for him and how good he felt.

Everything has a purpose. By meeting people, you make an equation and make your own decision. So I met this Carmelite priest, oh, he's got to be close to seventy or older. And he said to me, he goes, 'I don't know why they decided a person like me should get the liver. They should give it to a person who was thirty years old. But I guess they see that I have a purpose in life, that I can do something with this life of mine.' I saw that without a liver, John Husar had no hope, that he was going to die. There was no ands, ifs, or buts about it.

I felt it didn't have a risk to it, but the doctors told me it had a big risk to it because there's a number of complications that could have happened besides me dying on the table. I gave one pint of blood in case they needed it during the operation, which I was told would take six hours. Then the nurses told me the operation would take nine hours. Then it took twelve hours. So it's a very long, complicated, sophisticated operation. Because of all the bile ducts and arteries and veins going into the liver, because of filtering properties of the liver – it's a more complicated transplant than the heart or the kidney. What happens is, they take the right lobe of your liver – they take over fifty percent of it. But the unique thing about the liver is, it regenerates itself. The liver you have right now will not be the same liver you have three weeks from now – it'll totally disintegrate, let's say – and replace itself within three weeks as long as you're healthy and there's no fevers. So my liver is back to full strength, though the scar is still there.

It was about a month ago, but it still feels like somebody whacked me with a paddle or a cane right across my abdominals. As soon as you get out of the hospital they tell you . . . Well, I like to golf: so no golf, no sailing, no strenuous exercise. And, of course, no drinking. So all I've been doing is reading, listening to music, and taking naps.

I did it because it would only be a couple months of me not being able to work or do what I want, and this is something I could do in my life. I could give life to someone else, give them hope, give them the chance. I minimized the risk in my mind. For years I used to race a sailboat and not be a good swimmer. I rode a motorcycle for years and was in a lot of close accidents. You take a chance any time you get on a bus or an airplane or a train or a car – so everything is risk. But if you're not willing to risk, you truly don't own it, do you? So I thought: *It's my life*. You have to risk your life, and especially for someone else, to give life. We're all part of this human community, and if you're not willing to give of yourself, then you're held captive. To me, God is unconditional love. That means to love someone, no matter what they do, how they are, how little you know them, but to help someone with all they have.

I got this belief through years of listening to the sermons at Old St. Pat's. And also from my mother. She's eighty-two years old. She went to work for the city in the Health Department, in the Water Department. She met my father in the late forties and had five children; then as my younger brother, John, was old enough to be put in day care, she wanted to go back to work and make money. So then she taught high school for twenty years in the Catholic high school system. So I get a lot of this doing from her.

She believes in people. If she didn't believe in life, in the dignity of life, whatever life there is, she wouldn't be that way to my brother, Johnny, who has Down's syndrome.

Life is sacred. And if you can help someone in a time of need, you would not even think twice about it. It's what they call a no-brainer. I got it, I don't need it. You get by with forty percent of your liver. Right now my liver is back to full strength. The right lobe was taken out and now it's back to a hundred-percent volume.

The surgeon came to me right before they were going to put me under and said, 'If you die on the operating table, you're not going to come back and haunt me?' He says, 'If you want to get out, get out now.' He wanted to make sure that I knew the consequences, or the ultimate risk, and that I was doing this of my free will. He wanted to challenge me one more time and tell me that I could get out. I said, 'I've had a good life these forty-five years. And if I die, I'm at peace with myself. But if I don't take the risk to help this person, I'll forever look back at myself and say, "Why didn't I?"' So I told him, 'I do this of my own free will, I'm at peace, and I wouldn't haunt you. Don't worry about me.' This is one thing that I could do and would do and feel good about doing it.

My mother said, 'Well, Rick, I think it's OK because you're going to do whatever you want anyway. You've made up your mind.' It wasn't until my mother met Laura, who is John Husar's daughter, that she actually understood what it meant to John's family. John had been on a transplant list for the last two years and gone to the hospital as a standby, but never got it. Five times he was prepped for an operation. I'll never forget: we were at a meeting a couple of months before the operation and the doctor looked at him and said, 'I give you six weeks on the inside and six months on the outside. If you don't get a liver by then, you'll be dead.' That's really looking down the barrel of a gun.

I didn't really make a will. I contacted a lot of people that I thought would be upset, through e-mail and telephone, to let them know that I was doing this and there was a small amount of risk there. A lot of times in life we try to play down our own risk, you know what I mean? More people told me there was a risk than I believed there was. I don't know if it was my strong faith or my vitality.

Now, from what I learned there's a ninety- to ninety-five-percent success rate for the recipient. The donor – they've only lost I think two, three donors. There's always complications of bleeding, of bile, and infection. But I didn't see it coming my way. Of course, I have a scapular on. It's a thing that was given to St. Simon Stock, who was the head of the Carmelite Order, by the Virgin Mary. Basically, it says whoever wears my scapular will never suffer the flames of Hell.

To me, Heaven is no pain, seeing the people you want, having the questions in your mind answered. People are always nice, they're always altruistic, you only have rainy days if you want them. You see the people that you haven't seen that are in the other world. To me, it'd be like a big picnic. Whatever you're missing in this life, you're made whole. My brother, who has Down's syndrome – I would probably not even recognize him. He'd be able to talk and we'd converse more than we would now. Johnny as a whole person – not handicapped, no wheelchairs.

When it's time for you to go, when you're near there, they say it's usually someone from the other world who you know who will come and get you. And not that I wouldn't mind seeing my sister, who's been dead for twenty years or so – in that automobile accident. Or my father. But I see now that it'll probably be someone like John Husar. And in your mind, Studs, you would be at a radio station, doing a radio show of fifty years ago. And you would see someone that you haven't seen in a long time. And they'd say, 'Studs, where have you been? I've been looking for you. We've got another show to do on the other side of the river.' I see myself, I'd be in the St. Patrick's Day Parade, either on the South Side, on Western Avenue, or downtown on Dearborn. And this guy will come up all dressed in white, and it'll be John Husar. And he'll have the torch – he ran with the torch in the Olympics one time – and he'll say, 'Rick, I've been looking all over for you. It's time for you to run with the torch. We've got somewhere to go!' Or I'll be sailing my boat and out of the corner of my eye I'll see this rowboat will be trying to catch me. I'll try to get the boat to go faster because rowboats aren't supposed to catch my sailboat. And I'll see it's John. John will say, 'Rick, I've been looking for you. Come on, get in the boat. We gotta go rowing.'

POSTSCRIPT

When John Husar died, it's not that I was mad at God. I was just like: *How could this be?* How could this be? Because here was a person who, although I'm sure he looked at death, wasn't ready to die. He didn't write his final column. The day he died, the bass came into Chicago, the fish – that's something he worked at. So I'm thinking to myself, he has to live so he can cover the Bass Masters Tournament – it was where they came from all over the country to fish for bass in Lake Michigan, around Chicago. He always had a Sunday and Thursday column and I went out to buy the newspaper, like I had expected to see his column there. *Can't be.* Couldn't be. Can't be. 'Cause I tried to give this person life . . . If you put a new set of tires on your car, you figure you get another fifty thousand miles out of it. You put your money in the tollbooth, you figure you can at least drive to the end of the road. But see, that's the odd thing. Life is so precious. Life is not the given. Death is the given. Death is the certainty. Life is this gift. Life is kind of . . . we make it as we go along. For every birth there is a death. The real thing in life is the journey. Now that's an odd thing in America where you think the goal is how much money we make, or the car we drive, or the position we have. We're getting away from what life is actually about. A lot of times I see the person selling *Streetwise*, the magazine put out by the homeless, and I talk to them. You have to give people dignity. The dignity you give is the dignity you see in yourself and you carry yourself.

I usually pray in the morning – usually a Hail Mary, something like that. But there's this one website I go to, the website for Henri Nouwen. He was a Dutch priest, a theologian. He taught at Notre Dame University, Harvard, and Yale. At the last part of his life he was with people with Down's syndrome. I met him once, and his books are just phenomenal for me. You look at the computer and there's a thought of the day, a prayer of the day. He would write whatever thought was in his head for that day. A lot of times, even in this past struggle that I've had in the last month, they really spoke to me. I'll never forget the day that John Husar died, Henri Nouwen's thought of the day was about the Good Samaritan. The person that crosses the road to try to help the other individual. They say that my kind of transplant was a Good Samaritan transplant because it wasn't within the family and it wasn't a close friend. So it spoke very profoundly to me for that day.

PART II

Seeing Things

Randy Buescher

A former carpenter, he is an associate at a Chicago architectural firm. He appears at the door, somewhat gaunt, bearing a stuffed briefcase. On occasion, I'm told, he uses a cane. Not this time.

> I have a younger sister, two years younger. We were raised Presbyterian, which always seemed so bland that I could never figure out what it was. We quit going to church when we were kids when the minister wouldn't stop talking about donating more money to the church.

I had very, very severe cancer, I was diagnosed at the age of about thirty with advanced Hodgkin's disease. I was working as a carpenter, I was raising a kid by myself, and I was running a crew of about five guys. So I wasn't paying attention to my body real well. I had these night sweats and I had these fevers. But my big concern was really to raise my daughter. I'd been divorced for a year, and I'd taken that pretty hard. My wife had run off with somebody else. In the long run, that was actually a very good thing. I somewhat attribute the cancer to the fact that I was so depressed and I was having such a hard time trying to raise this kid by myself.

I had won the custody battle. It was unusual to be a man raising – especially – a daughter in that day and age. This would be about fifteen years ago. My daughter Amelia's eighteen. I'm now forty-five. She was three at the time. I finally said, 'I have to go see a doctor.' This poor man came out and he was *white*. He said: 'I need you to go get an X ray. Your blood counts don't look very good – you need a chest X ray.' So I went in and had a chest X ray and he saw it. He said, 'You've got to go get tests done right away.' I said, 'What's the matter?' He said, 'You've got cancer, and not only that, it seems like it's fairly full-blown.' My biggest concern was to find out what was going on. I didn't really worry about the fact that I was dying as much as I wanted to know what you could do at that point – that was really the concern.

When the doctor told me the news, there was a certain amount of relief because it made sense why I was having the night sweats. So what do I do about it? My take on these things has always been: Let's get some information, we'll figure out what to do. Once I got diagnosed, other people's reactions were really interesting.

I had this group that I used to see at the Gare St. Lazare – that was sort of our bar hangout. A group of probably thirty people that were real close. It was a drinking club, let's face it. And the owner was one of my close friends, but he was the most morose guy. He would say things like [*in lamentory fashion*], 'I know how you're feeling . . . Oh, oh . . . It's OK, Randy.' I'd say, 'No, actually I feel OK this week.' '*No, no, no, no* . . . No, I really *know*.' By the same token, my closest friend, who's this theater director, we sort of got through it more by joking.

At one point I went through a biopsy, they took out a big lymph node in my neck. Then they sent it to all these doctors across the country. I was an anomaly because it happened fast. They weren't able to quite pinpoint what kind of stuff I had and it went to all these different people. And the first doctor I went to see gave me odds on survival. He said, 'Well, you have maybe a sixty–forty chance' – whatever it was, it was less than fifty–fifty. I said, 'I can't believe that somebody would give me odds. What a depressing methodology!'

Once I had gotten diagnosed, I had a lot of doctors. This one doctor, this oncologist, was a real beaut. He looked at my charts and said, 'You've got it bad. It's very advanced. There's only four stages and you're already in stage three. It's throughout your whole body, down to your abdomen. It's spreading rapidly, your spleen is enlarged.' I remember because I didn't have anybody else to help me along, I asked, 'What do you think my odds are?' And he said, 'They're not very good. You might have a fifty–fifty chance or less to make it.' Something clicked. I said to myself, 'I need to talk to somebody else.' I didn't tell him – I just left. I thought: *Do I want somebody taking care of me who doesn't think I'm going to make it?* I was of the belief, if you don't have a real positive attitude, there's not a chance in Hell you're going to get through this thing. So I asked around. I had some friend who was a nurse and she said, 'If I had cancer, I would go to this doctor.' So I called this guy up and he said, 'Look, I'm a surgeon and you don't need surgery – you've already had the one lymph node removed. What you need is *treatment*. I'd go see this guy at Evanston Hospital. Because if I were sick' – this is the doctor saying it – 'the only guy that I would let see me is this guy.'

I went across the street right then and met this guy. He looked at my charts and he said, 'Ah, we gotta start doing treatment now . . .' I said, 'What are my chances?' He said, 'I wouldn't give you chances – I wouldn't give you odds. We have to start treatment and we'll see results and we'll see what happens. But I'm not going to give you odds.' He says, 'I've cured people who have had your condition and I haven't cured people who have had your condition. Everybody is different. It depends on your personality, your strength, your fortitude.' And immediately I said, 'OK, you're the guy.' He said, 'OK, you need to start tomorrow.' This was going to be massive and very heavy chemotherapy. I said, 'I can't imagine doing that. I have a little girl, and I don't want her to see me this sick if she doesn't have to. She goes to her mom's house every other Friday for visitation. Could I wait till Friday.' He said, 'Yeah, you could.' I said, 'Well, actually, I'd like to get another opinion.' He said, 'Look, we don't have time for this.' He said, 'If you don't start treatment now, aggressively, you're not going to spend Thanksgiving with your daughter.' I was at that point in Stage Three B, and Stage Four? Most people don't get turned around in Hodgkin's Stage Four. He was determined for it not to get to that next stage. So I said, 'OK, fine, I'll start on Friday.'

I didn't have a wife at that point, somebody who could have been sort of standing by your side. I had a good group of friends, but it wasn't really the same. So I actually had to do something that I hadn't done in years: I had to go back to my parents. I had to call my mom and say, 'I need some help. I'm going to be going through this treatment and I'm going to do it on the weekends, but you're going to have to pick up the pieces with Amelia. I want my daughter to stay here. I don't want her world to change.'

I didn't know what the results were going to be. I knew that my hair was probably going to fall out. I already knew that I was looking pretty bad and I thought, you know, *why make it any worse?* So the first thing I did was to go cut my hair. I said, 'If my hair's going to fall out, I'm going to take my hair out myself.' So I went to this really pretty woman who'd been cutting my hair and I'd been hitting on for a long time. I decided I would shave it to a crew cut. I had heard that if your hair was really short, it didn't fall out. I just thought, if I can minimize the downsides to this whole dying part, maybe it'll make it a little better. At that point, I knew I was dying. It wasn't like when you're a kid and they tell you you're going to die someday. It's not like even when you're an adult and you're worrying about getting older and your friends are dying. We all know we're dying somehow. But in my case, I was dying quickly. Something was going to happen. I was really concerned about leaving this little girl. And I have to tell you, that was actually what kept me going. I really didn't want Amelia to be left alone.

So, I thought, *I'll do something* – I'll see if I can stop myself from dying right now. Buy a little bit of time . . . I also knew that people who survive cancer don't always survive a whole lot longer. But in my mind really I was thinking that if I can get Amelia to some age where there was a stable environment . . . For one year we'd messed up her life. The worst thing you could do, the way I was raised, was to get divorced. I aggressively pursued the divorce when my wife stepped out and wasn't interested in her daughter. I aggressively pursued putting an end to that so that Amelia's life would be a little better. And now I'm dying . . .

When I found out I had cancer and I let the world know, my ex-wife called me and she was real upset. I said, 'There's nothing I would like better than to have had somebody by my side right now. But what do you care? Move on.' I didn't have time for that. I talked to my parents and I said, 'I'm going to try to take chemotherapy on Fridays.' I was doing a hybrid chemotherapy. They were always experimenting because chemotherapy is really no different than bloodletting – it's just a doctor's wildest guess as to what might work. And if somebody else has something else that works, they try to blend those things together to see if that works better. The first cycle I go through is a Friday and then another Friday, then I'm two weeks off. And then the next time will be a Friday, skip a week. It can work on a four-week schedule. If we can have Amelia be with her mom during that period of time, maybe she won't see the worst effects of the chemo. 'You need to come down and take care of me,' I told my parents.

The chemotherapy was as bad as you can imagine. I couldn't take the antinausea drugs. I tried them, but they made me want to kill myself. Interestingly enough, I'm trying to save myself from dying and the antinausea drugs made me want to kill myself . . . Two percent or something of the people who take those on that day had these suicidal tendencies. I literally tried to jump out of the car on the Eden's Expressway – I was trying to open the door up! The drugs made me *so* anxious . . . They made me feel like I had to get out of my body, I just wanted to jump out of my skin.

So I had about one hour from the time I took my chemotherapy to get home before I started violent vomiting. I would vomit for about eight hours straight. This was on Friday afternoon. Saturday I would recover a little bit. I tried everything. People said pot is supposed to help, so somebody gave me some pot, but that didn't help. My parents were around and I was stoned with my parents looking at me. That made me more paranoid. I tried everything I could do. By Mondays I was back to a somewhat normal existence.

I tell you, the haircut is probably the best one I ever had because it was cut by this woman. I'd tried to date her, unsuccessfully. She liked me, and she was real pretty. She'd been cutting my hair for several months and I said, 'I want you to take the buzzer, put it down to an eighth of an inch, and cut all my hair off.' I had fairly long hair at that point. I said, 'I want to get a crew cut.' She said, 'What's going on?' I said, 'Don't worry about it, really. Just give me a crew cut, it'll be OK.' She said, 'No, something's wrong, Randy, I can tell. What's going on?' I said, 'I've got cancer, my hair's going to fall out when I go through chemotherapy. I don't want to wake up with my pillow full of hair. Just cut the hair off. I thought it would be a good ritual if I came to you, even though I'm paying fifteen dollars for a haircut. I can get this from the barber for three bucks, but I thought it would be nice to have you cut my hair off.' So she took the buzzer and she started running it across my head. This was a really fancy salon down in Old Town. She's running this thing through, and there's wisps of hair coming back up again because it's not taking it all off. I've got all these chunks of hair standing out. Another hairdresser walks over and he goes, 'Be careful, he looks like a chemotherapy patient!' She got so embarrassed she dropped the buzzer on the floor, and then it was doing this snake dance across the floor. I just broke up into hysterical laughter. She broke into laughter. The poor guy said, 'What? *What?!*' Toni looked at him and she said laughingly, 'He has cancer.' [*Laughs*] And the guy, 'Oh, I'm sorry sir, I'm very sorry, I'm very sorry . . .' At that point, I actually realized that laughing about it was a much better approach than worrying about it.

That theme carried through about a week later when my friend Bob and I . . . My spleen was incredibly enlarged, and they were hoping that the chemotherapy would make my spleen go down in size, because otherwise they would have to do a splenectomy. And it hurt. I was in the apartment one day with Bob, and he was, 'How ya doing?' I wasn't doing that well, and he was trying to help with Amelia too. He'd come and help cook, goof around. I was in the apartment and we were looking at each other and I said, 'God, my spleen is killing me.' And then we both realized what I'd said and broke into hysterical laughter because, in fact, my spleen *was* killing me. We were literally on the floor, one of those laughters that you can't stop laughing. That's the poignant part. I told you about this friend of mine in the bar who would get so depressed. It wasn't about feeling bad for yourself. It was actually better feeling good about yourself, and that's what I'm convinced sort of pushed me through the whole thing – laughter.

The humor and laughter got me through it more than anything else. That happened time and time again. I went to a party at the Gare toward the end of my chemotherapy run – it had been going on for like eight or nine months. It was going to be a Halloween party. I didn't feel like dressing up too much, but our friend Martha Redhed walked in and she was wearing a bald wig. My hair had never really fallen out because I'd cut it. So Bob said to me jokingly, 'You know, we never got to see you bald. What a bummer. We should have actually seen bald Randy!' So I asked Martha if I could borrow the skinhead and I put the thing on. By that time my hair was maybe an inch long. I wasn't real well, but I was seasoned. There's a certain amount of time you go through chemotherapy, like anything else, you start to get used to it. Believe it or not, you actually get used to sort of the dying, the pricking, the X rays, the CAT scans. If you tried to tell anybody else, they would *never* believe it. To this day, if I go into a cancer treatment center, I can taste and I can smell the chemo drugs which nobody else can smell when they walk in. They're in the air, but you have to have had them in your veins. So I put this bald wig on and we started laughing because it was hilarious! I wasn't feeling well anyway, and with the wig on I probably cut off all the oxygen to my brain. I got really sick to my stomach and I went to the back room and lay down on the floor – because I felt *really* bad. My friend, the restaurant owner, came back and saw me laying on the floor and of course he thought maybe I was dead. He got right in my face and he said, 'Are you OK?!' I said, 'Actually, I'm not OK, I don't really feel that good.' And he goes, 'OK, be calm, it's OK, really . . .' He got real nervous and he was really in my face – it was uncomfortable. I remember Bob came back and made some stupid joke which Francis thought was just awful, but again, we were laughing. Time and time again, that thing sort of changed the way I felt about trying to stay alive.

Actually, my responsibility a lot of the time when I was sick was to make other people feel better because they felt so bad for me. I realized that I was better at making them feel better than they were at making *me* feel better. There are those that just feel so bad because they're so frightened about dying themselves. The laughter was life-giving. People have told me, 'God, Randy, I don't know how you got through all that.' I'm convinced that a lot of it was that my bent was really toward the positive and all the funny things that were said – because I was a wreck, an absolute *wreck*. I mean, I cried for weeks and months. I couldn't figure out how this could possibly happen to me. I'm convinced, if there's anything in your body that's not quite right, and something bad happens and you dwell on it, it can make you sick. The bad marriage . . . We were young, stupid, but we had a wonderful kid. The stress played a role. Laughter was the antidote.

There's the other things too: my out-of-body experience during this whole thing . . . I don't know what to believe. Anytime I tell anybody I get pretty emotional about it. Through all the chemotherapy, I lost most of the veins in my body. The veins got burned up and scarred. Now they do these little ports in the heart area, but in that day they just would give it to you intravenously. The drugs were so bad they would burn your veins and they couldn't use the veins again. It got more and more painful as I was taking the drug. One of the things they gave me was Prednisone, a steroid which everybody's on. In that day, they gave it to you in *super*-high dosages. When you came off of it you had like a heroin withdrawal. Nobody told me about that . . . The other consequence, because it was a steroid, you tended to bulk up on foods even though you weren't hungry. So I was eating like *boxes* of mashed potatoes.

I don't remember exactly what happened that day, but I called my dad and said, 'I'm sick. Something else is wrong and I gotta go to the hospital.' At *any* cost I would avoid going to the hospital. My goal was *never* to stay overnight in a hospital – I thought that if I could stay out of the hospital, I could probably stay well. But at that point, I don't remember if it was that I was constipated or what, but I went to the hospital and the doctor said, 'You don't look well. I can't get ahold of your oncologist right now – he's not on call. They want to admit you to the hospital at once. You're dehydrated.' I said, 'I don't want to have an IV because I just can't have you poking my veins. How much liquid do you need in me?' The guy said, 'I need *gallons*.' I said, 'Fine – I'll drink it. I'll be willing to drink as many gallons of water as you want not to have to have an IV.' And the guy said, 'No, you can't drink enough.' I said, 'Let me *try*. Tell me how fast you need.' He said, 'You need to put down two gallons in the next hour.' I said, 'I can do that.' He brought the water in and I started drinking. I started drinking cup and cup after cup after cup of water . . . I'm in the emergency ward, and I'm behind one of those curtains. I'm not in the cancer-care ward, but I know where I'm going the next day if I stay there, and I know they're going to throw an IV in me. They're going to try to convince me to have chemotherapy out of synch. I *don't* want to stay the night. And I'm a fairly convincing guy – that's been one of my strengths, I can talk my way out of just about anything. So I convinced this doctor I could drink the water, which I did. I convinced him to let me go home and the reason he needed to let me go home is that my daughter was now at my mom's house, and so that she wouldn't wake up frightened that something had happened to her dad the next morning, I needed to go home to my parents' house. I'd always spent every night in my own house when I was having chemo-therapy. I said, 'If you let me go to my parents' house, my mom and dad can watch me, and if there's any problem, my dad will certainly bring me back to the hospital.' I was apparently convincing enough, because the doctor said, 'Against my better judgment, I'm going to send you home.' In hindsight, he probably should have kept me there, but I was adamant because I didn't want Amelia to wake up and not find me there. Amelia knew what was going on – she was only three years old, but she knew her daddy was dying of cancer. She could see it. If you see the pictures of me from then, I look like I was an Auschwitz guy: I'm just completely sunken in, my jaws, my weight, I'd dropped down about twenty pounds. I felt she'd been through enough.

We got back and Amelia was already asleep in what had been my sister's room when I was a kid. I got in bed and was laying there and I thought: *It's a good thing to be home.* And somewhere in the middle of that night, I woke up and I noticed I was looking at the bottoms of my feet. I appeared to be sitting up, but I was seeing the bottoms of my feet. And I thought: *Well,* this *is very odd . . .* I was on a lot of drugs, but I was able to pull back to where I was up at the ceiling level. My head raised up – but it really wasn't my head, it was just my eyes, and I could see my whole body laying in the bed. And I said, 'Oh, jeez, I think I'm dead. There's my whole body laying there and I'm not in my body right now.' I had what appeared to be a vision of the room. I could see the two walls to the side of me, I could see the bookcase in front of me, I could see the foot of the bed, I could see myself on the bed. I couldn't see my hands . . .

I couldn't do anything with the body that was down there on the ground. I thought: *This is a bad dream.* I said, 'I gotta prove that it's a dream, I gotta prove that this isn't real.' I said, 'What can I do? I can't possibly know all the books in this bookcase –' I hadn't lived at home in years. My whole body is laid out. I was *outside* my body. I thought I was dead. But I gotta prove it . . . The worst thing was, Amelia's down the hallway and I'm thinking about Amelia. I said, 'I've got to do something empirical that will prove this or not prove it to myself.' I thought: *OK, I can't possibly know all the titles of all the books in this library – I'll start reading the titles.* I went to the left-hand corner and dammit if I couldn't read the first book. I read the second book title and the third and the fourth. I went all the way down the line, and I read *every* goddamn book title in the place.

I'm trying to prove to myself this isn't real and I got through the whole place and I said, '*Shit*. This *is* real . . .' Then I tried to get my body, this vision I had, to move around. I said, 'I *can't* move it.' I was like stuck right there in that spot looking at my dead body, looking at the books, and I *can't* move my body. I can't go down the hall-way – I can't float out. None of these things that you would hope, that there is some sort of a spirit that moves around. This one's not moving. I said, 'Jesus, I'm trapped in this stupid room and this is not where I want to be dying . . .'

Then I realized that my daughter was always the first one up – Amelia was going to wake up first. [*Fighting tears*] She was going to walk down the hallway and she was going to come in, and she was going to find me dead in the bedroom . . . [*Sighs*] I said, 'God*damn* it . . . Everything I've done to try to insulate this kid from me dying, and I'm going to die in my parents' goddamn house and my *kid's* going to come and see me.' [*Crying*] I said, 'Fuck. I've done *every-thing* else I'm supposed to do right and now I come back here *stupidly*. I could have died in the goddamn hospital and she wouldn't have seen me. And I would have had a chance to live, 'cause they could have done something.' I said, 'God*damn* it. She's going to see me. What am I going to do now?' I tried to yell, I tried to scream, and there was no sound . . . nothing . . . nothing. I tried to blurt out something and there was nothing. Then the *weirdest* thing hap-pened. Instinctively, or whatever we do in our world, we sort of go back to our parents or something. I wanted to call my dad. So I said [*plaintively*], 'Dad . . .' And I didn't hear anything, but I could feel a little bit. I said, 'Dad' – and goddamn if I didn't hear a sound. I said, 'Dad . . .' I got another one out. Then I heard footsteps coming down the hallway and I felt my dad touch me on my back, and all of a sudden, I was facedown in the bed, I wasn't above. He said, 'You're cold – you're *really* cold, Randy. Are you OK?' I said, 'Yeah, I think I'm OK, Dad . . .' I didn't want to freak him out. I got up and I went down and I saw Amelia in bed and I kissed her and I climbed in bed with my parents. I'm a thirty-year-old man climbing in bed with my parents, and I cuddled up with my dad. And I slept the rest of the night with my dad.

I honestly believed for a moment I was not alive in that body and there was something that made me – and it was Amelia, it was the agony of a three-year-old girl who had already been through enough in the last year, who didn't need to have her mother gone and didn't need to have her dad die and didn't need to be waking up and finding her dad dead in her grandparents' house. That pulled me back.

I've always tended to be a believer that there's bigger issues. I was reading what people called alternative sorts of religious things in the sixties and seventies. I had other weird experiences. But this one was very poignant, and it seemed real. And I actually thought somehow after that point I might be able to beat the cancer completely. At that point, I thought: *If I've died and I've come back . . .*

Amelia's eighteen now, she's going to college next fall. She remembers these years very vividly. I never insulated her from anything I did, but I don't think she knows about this one particular night. She knew about my cancer – it's very much a part of her life. And all the hip surgeries because of the damage the chemotherapy did to my bones. It was a turning point. In fact, the cancer was always getting better. I don't know how much you know about chemo treatments and cycles and that sort of stuff, but I did eleven cycles of chemo – eleven months of chemotherapy. That's a *long* time. And I did three months of radiation therapy after that. I went through a lot of pain. I still can't get blood drawn. My veins are all scarred. But I will tell you something: there *is* a regenerative power, and a year later they said, 'You're virtually free of it.' I went through five years of coming back on a regular basis. I had no sperm count.

I met Janet. I was reluctant to get married, because I thought I had so much baggage. I said, 'Here's a young girl who wants to marry a guy that's not only got a young kid but he's having hip operations as a result of the cancer. He's got no sperm count so he can't really give her children . . .' She's the best thing that ever happened to me. We actually have three more kids. They say that almost never does a sperm count come back on people. Part of the chemotherapy is that it just wipes out everything, your testicles are one thing . . . and it never comes back. I'm convinced that I came back in a real big way. I went down in a real big way and I came back in a real big way.

POSTSCRIPT

As he was about to leave, I made a casual comment about the hereafter. 'If there's a hereafter, I hope to God I'm not stuck in a room somewhere reading my parents' library books over and over again. That would be Hell. If there is a Hell, I think I've seen a little glimpse of it.'

Chaz Ebert

A lawyer. She is married to Roger Ebert, a film critic.

I'm a black woman who's a mother, I have two children – I'm a grandmother, too. A wife, a daughter, a sister, a friend, a lawyer. Dad was Baptist, but Mother was spiritualist. She went to the Spiritualist Church – that's an actual religion. Mother believed in communication with people on the other side. My mother was a prophet, a seer, a psychic, and a minister. Dad worked for the packing house and was also a union organizer. I'm not really religious. When I was in college I called myself first an agnostic and then an atheist. But even when I was slightly atheist, I still said my prayers at night just in case – I wanted to hedge my bets. I don't know what I believe. I live my life according to certain laws of physics. I believe that for every action there is an equal and opposite reaction. Our soul, our bodies, everything, if it's all matter and molecules and it can't be destroyed, it goes somewhere. Some religious people think that's Heaven or Hell. I think that we still exist, even when we die. Something of our soul or spirit or energy, matters of particles. I think we exist somewhere and I think we can be reformulated.

This sounds really crazy, I know, but I've had lots of experiences. For instance, the grim reaper came to me one time – and I *never* believed in the grim reaper, I thought it was just some mythological thing. My first husband's father was someone that I was very close to. He was dying. He was very sick . . . In the middle of the night, something woke me up. I opened the door of the bedroom, and there was this figure, about seven feet tall. It had the monk's robe and the whole thing, like the grim reaper. I looked into the face but it was no face – it was just all dark. There were kind of lit orbs where the eyes should be. He communicated to me telepathically. He said, 'Don't be afraid, I didn't come for you.' He said, 'Go over to the bed.' I look in the bed where my husband was asleep, but it wasn't my husband anymore. This coffin appeared, and my father-in-law was in it. This lasted for a few seconds, then it all disappeared. Then my husband was there again and I woke him up and I told him that the grim reaper was there and about his father. He said, 'I think you were dreaming.' I said, 'No, I *wasn't* dreaming, I'm awake!' So we go to sleep, and the next morning we call and they say his father died. His father died at the same time that the grim reaper came to my house. So I think that there's something more when we die. I don't know.

Too many people have had these near-death experiences. Some scientists say these are hallucinations. They say that when people have near-death experiences and they talk about seeing this bright white light, those are things that are already in our brains. That they can make you have a near-death experience while you're just sitting in a chair in a lab if they stimulate certain parts of your brain. That may or may not be true – but I don't think it's a mass hallucination.

See, I . . . wow – it's really hard for me to say . . . I believe that there's something. Let's say energy – energy after death. I do believe in that. It takes various forms.

Even as a kid, I was always interested in what happens to us when we die. I think most people are. I don't shy away from it, because I just lost my mother in November. Within the last five years I lost my two oldest sisters, and watching them die . . . I was very close to my sisters. Both of them died around the age of fifty-nine. I sat with them, and they were very courageous. My oldest sister, Carrie, was not afraid when she was dying. And it's not that she welcomed death – she just wasn't afraid. She said there was something very beautiful waiting for her. It's not just her faith that told her that there was something – she learned that in church. But she saw it during the time she was dying, so she wasn't afraid. That took away my fear of death, watching my sister . . . My other sister, Martha, who was actually more religious, was afraid to die. She didn't want to go to sleep because she said she might not wake up. That confused me, because I thought the more religious you are, the more you should welcome death – because that means you're going to be with God. But no, she wanted to stay on the earth. It did confuse me.

There were ten of us. Three dead, seven living now. I had four sisters and five brothers. I don't recall my first awareness of death; I just always knew that there was something. I was fascinated with my mother's stories about how when she was growing up in Georgia, when someone died they would have their bodies laid out in the parlor for a month – for a long time. She told me that everyone wore black, and you had the house darkened. The body would just be there and people could visit with it. It's not like today when we're afraid of corpses and we're afraid of bodies and nobody wants to go to a funeral. It seemed like they were more comfortable with it. Back then, death was accepted as a part of life. Now we can prolong life – people live a lot longer. Then, not only was death more accepted as a part of life, but the generations living together were more the norm. I think that's why death was accepted, because if you had all these generations living together, someone was going to die, and that was just a part of life. My mother died right around Thanksgiving. Because she was a member of the Spiritualist Church, and because she was a prophet and a seer, I fully expected her to come back. So I asked my sister if she had seen my mother yet, and she said no. This was after she died. The rest of my family believed. We didn't talk about it a lot when she was alive. When we were kids, we thought our mother was a witch because she had these meta-physical powers. And so we fully expect to see her come back. We do think if it's possible to come back, Mother will come back in some form. We don't know what form she'll take.

In December, 1999, I was out in California and I had this dream about my mother, about meeting her. In the dream I got up to leave and I realized – I looked at her, I said, 'Oh my God, this isn't a dream! I'm meeting you somewhere. This is, like, some way station and my spirit is meeting your spirit.' And she said, 'Yes.' I said, 'Mom, this isn't a dream because you're not really here, you're dead.' She said, 'Yes, I am, and I can only be with you just this one night, and then I don't know when you're going to be able to see me again.' After that, she didn't communicate by mouth anymore – she started communicating telepathically.

Even if I cease to exist forever, I realize that some of my energy will be reconstituted. Not that I will be reincarnated, but some form of energy will go somewhere. It will live on somewhere. I'm not scared. Not anymore, no – but I don't want to be cremated. Roger would like to be cremated. I want to be buried. Cremation – that bothers me. I was in a fire, my dress was on fire when I was a little girl. I still have the scars. I'm very fascinated with fire as a result of that. But I don't want to be in anything where I'm burning again, *ever* . . . That's what I don't like about cremation. I was already in a fire, I was already burning. I can still remember what my flesh smelled like when it was burning, when I was on fire. I was running down the stairs and my dad had to tear off my dress and roll me in a rug. I just don't want to be cremated. I don't want to go through that anymore.

Sometimes when I go to sleep I say, 'Well, I might not wake up.' And I say, 'If I don't wake up tomorrow, am I satisfied with my life right now? Do I think I did a good job? If there is a God – if I'm wrong and there really is someone who's going to be waiting up there to judge me – do I think that I have more checks in the plus side of the book rather than in the negative side of the book?'

I used to live in the John Hancock Building, and this happened in 1987, I believe . . . I was living by myself on the eighty-second floor. I was divorced, my children were away at college. Again, it happened at night – I was asleep. I had been sick, I was dehydrated and that caused me to lose my sight and my hearing for a very short period of time. They took me to a hospital in an ambulance. My sight came back, my hearing came back. I was in bed, this was a day or two later. In the middle of the night something woke me. There was a bright light in my room and there were twins. I call them the twin Virgin Marys. They were on my wall. One was the Black Madonna, as I've seen her in pictures, very similar to the one who was venerated in Latin America and Poland. The other was the traditional picture that you see of the Caucasian Madonna. In front of them were three infants. One was Caucasian, one was black, and the one in the middle was a mixture of all the races of the world. And they said, 'This is the true one, and he hasn't come yet' – kind of a Christ child. These Madonnas communicated with me telepathically – their mouths never moved. They said, 'This is the true one, he hasn't come yet, and we are entrusted to take care of him until such time as he is coming.' That made me think that if there is a Christ, he hasn't been here yet . . .

I think Roger deals with death much better than I do. He's more pragmatic about it: he knows that people are born, they die. When they're gone, they're not coming back. He doesn't expect to be reunited with them again – even though he was raised Catholic. That's why he wants to be cremated. He doesn't think there's anything more. Cremate him and spread his ashes in all the places he loves: London and Venice and everywhere.

Some Buddhists think that you can choose when to die. I fly a lot, so I might die in a plane crash. If I do, I hope that Roger is sitting next to me and we're holding hands.

My mother died in November, and she had a very beautiful funeral. When I looked at her in the casket . . . to me, that wasn't my mother. Sometimes people will kiss a corpse. I can't do that because that wasn't my mother. Even though that was her body, embalmed and looking not like her at all – to me. I still feel my mom around me, so that's why I think that there's some energy, something that happens. When you die you're not completely gone. But I do think some people disappear completely. Some people don't leave a trail of dust or anything behind. I know this contradicts what I said earlier about energy not being destroyed. I think people who went timidly through life and really in their souls did not want to leave a mark . . . I think that people are born with different amounts of cosmic dust. Cosmic dust to me, it means a lot of things. It means our thoughts, our actions, what energy we had before. I think that you can expend your cosmic dust by doing good deeds. People can do bad deeds and still expend it. But they leave something, and they make an impression on other people. But one thing bothers me. I'm still grieving over the deaths of my mother and my sisters. If that energy or matter somehow goes on, why am I still so sad?

Antoinette Korotko-Hatch

She is the development director of the ninth-oldest Catholic church in Chicago. 'I'm in charge of raising fifteen million dollars, so they can renovate this church. The buildings are quite old. The parishioners are mostly African-American. The school is a hundred percent African-American, with eighty-five percent of the children non-Catholic and below the poverty line.

My father was a widower with four children when he married my mother. She had married before and was pregnant when her husband died. So, at their marriage, they had five children. I was born twelve years later – I'm the youngest.

All my siblings were half. I never thought of it that way until our parents were dying. It was amazing to see the change in family. All those years . . . nobody ever talked about 'my mother,' 'your mother,' 'my father,' 'your father.' It was always 'our mother.' As my parents became ill and my father died, slowly I could see it was happening: 'your father,' 'my father,' 'my mother,' 'your mother.' By the time my mother was dying, the family was really splitting up. It had been very cozy. It was the death of our parents that split us up.

One sister would start talking about her First Communion – my mother sent her to school the next day in ankle socks – that my mother was a cruel stepmother for not realizing children weren't supposed to wear ankle socks. It was against the school rules. Another sister talking about when her mother died, they were put in an orphanage. What does a man do when he's got four children under the age of four in the 1920s?! You might put your children in an orphanage for a month to get your bearings back. But memories just suddenly became *bad*.

I was raised Roman Catholic. My father was a very religious man. I would come home from a date, and he would be at the kitchen table saying a rosary. And I'd say, 'Stop, I want to talk to you about my date.' He'd stop – and then he'd take it up again when I'd go to bed. I went to church regularly. My father went to mass more than just on Sunday. Tuesday-night devotions. I had three cousins who became priests. That didn't always have the happiest of endings. One of them became an alcoholic and left the priesthood and died an alcoholic. Another's parents – my aunt and uncle – were millionaires. They built a shrine in Michigan which allowed their son to leave the Franciscan order and become a secular priest, so that he could inherit the money.

In college, I was beginning to question more and more, and to doubt more and more that there was anything after this life. Once the Second Vatican Council came into being I began to think, *What happened to all these people who supposedly went to Hell for doing this and it's no longer wrong?* Eventually I came to believe that there wasn't anything – that we were born just as our pets are born, and that there is nothing after we die. I firmly believe that. This doesn't give one license to do whatever one wants. I still believe in the Ten Commandments, really. I just don't think there's going to be any reward for having followed them. I simply don't believe in Heaven or Hell – or God, for that matter. I can't believe that there's somebody watching over all this. How could anybody judge what people have been doing? How can you judge a young man in the projects who commits murder? How can you say, 'That's a mortal sin – he's going somewhere'? There's so much that played a role into his committing this murder. My friends always say to me that if they ever are tried with some major crime, they hope I'm on the jury. [*Laughs*]

I had been married to an African-American law student at Harvard. At first, he was concerned that I was not religious enough. By the time he left me three years later, he said I was too religious. I hadn't changed at all – I was the same person. He had problems. I have three grown children. One worked in China for six years. She's now back, got her MBA, and is now, between jobs, traveling in Burma. One son went to Harvard. He's trying to break in as a screenwriter in California. The other, who went to Princeton, worked with children with aphasia, and is now working with mentally challenged adults in psychiatric units.

I raised my children my way. People would say to me, 'While

they're young, can't you get them to believe?' I'd say, 'You're putting God on the level of Santa Claus.' You believe one thing when you're young and something else when you grow up. You either believe or you don't believe.

I think you just die. That's it – there's nothing. There's been some need with humans to feel that this can't happen to them, and therefore they have to think that there is something else. It would certainly make me feel a lot better if I thought there was something else, but I just don't. When I was young, we were taught that you went into Heaven with the body that was when you were at your peak. When you get older and you start thinking about that, well, what about newborn babies, guys? Is that the way they go to Heaven and they stay with that mentality forever? Even now, at the church where I'm working, they talk of a force: you're aware that you are dead and you're aware of what has gone on. But few have really come back to this old-fashioned belief in Heaven and Hell. And to say that you're going to see somebody that you knew before . . . Take a look at my father with two wives, my mother with two husbands . . . [*Sighs*] How will *they* get along up there? [*Laughs*]

As a child, I was very aware of death. When I was a little girl, we were very good friends with a family that owned a funeral parlor. There were many in Milwaukee, my hometown. They had a family similar to ours – older brothers and a younger boy my age. We would go over there and play in the funeral home. We would make hopscotch marks on the rugs and make marble rings and play right there. Sometimes there was a body there. The father would come out and say, 'Come on now, we have to clean up this rug.' We would be shooed out because the funeral was going to start. This never bothered me.

My father went to a lot of funerals because of the church and being active in the community. Sometimes he would take me to the undertaking parlor and I would sit in the back. Then we'd go off for ice cream. I don't think he was really aware as to what effect this was having on me. I would be *terrified* when I would go with him at night. I could have been playing in that room with that same body in the afternoon. I had visions of the body coming to life, of the head turning and the eyes opening.

We lived in a house that had two stories. If I had to go to the bathroom, I'd go as fast as I could, running down the stairs *terrified*. I had cousins a little bit more savvy than I was, telling me all these tales that I took very seriously, and scared me. So I was always aware of death. Always, with my father. I thought about death a lot, actually, when I was in boarding school: I'd be sitting at the bus or at the train and looking at my father, who would have taken me to the station, and concerned that maybe I wouldn't see him again. The feeling would pass once I got to school . . . It wasn't something I dwelled on. But in those brief moments on the train or the bus I'd look at him, and I often felt that I would not be able to get through his death. This was something the undertaker's son and I would talk about when we were both kids. We would sit there on the rug, making things from branches in the lilac bushes. We would talk about who did we want to die first, our mother or our father. Way deep down, as much as I loved my mother and didn't want anything to happen to her, it was my father I was most concerned about. I didn't think I would ever get over his death if he did die. It was my father who died first . . . I went to that funeral in somewhat of a numb state. I never really truly cried about my parents' deaths. There just was no time: I had three small children and no husband. It didn't mean I loved them less.

It was one of the times my husband got back in touch with us and he wanted the children to come to California . . . They didn't know him – they were very little when he left. I wanted him to come to Chicago to introduce himself at least, before I sent them to a total stranger. This was 1979. I had cancer surgery, and I didn't want to cause any problems. I was doing a lot of crying, a lot of smoking, and I sent them off. The next night I suddenly felt *very* tired. I was trying to read and I kept going to sleep. Tired and weak. I couldn't walk across the room. I got *horrible* back pain. I went to the closet to get the heating pad, which probably would have killed me, but the pain was so bad I couldn't reach up. I remember just putting my head against the door and thinking, *I can't get it.* So I went to bed. I woke up the next morning and the first thing I was aware of was this back pain, but now I also had hand pain – I could barely move my hands. I called the pharmacist and I said, 'What could this be?' He said, 'I don't know – call the doctor.' So I called the doctor. I had a lot of drug allergies – I couldn't take penicillin. I couldn't take *any* antibiotics. And they were afraid of the anesthetic when they did the cancer surgery. The doctor said, 'You've got so many medical problems, I don't want to guess. Just go to the emergency room.' I almost stayed home to clean the bathroom instead, thinking, 'This is my imagination.' I got to the emergency room and I tell this young doctor, 'My hands are hurting so I can't stand the pain.' He made a *classic* statement – he came up to intensive care later to apologize. He said, 'Do you make it a habit of coming to the emergency rooms on weekends for attention?' He later said, 'You're young, you're thin, you're a woman. I didn't think anything was wrong with you . . . But you taught me a lesson.'

They took my blood pressure and they couldn't *get* a blood pressure. They did an electrocardiogram and he came to me and said, 'I think you're having a heart attack. It's different from the electrocardiogram from your cancer surgery.' They took me up to intensive care, and I started gagging – you know how you gag when you're having a heart attack? They left me in the room. I was monitored. All of a sudden, everything went *black*. My first reaction was: *The pain is gone*. And then I saw my three children – it was like a portrait. Anthony was in the middle – that's my second child. And Zachary and Jane were on each side of him, just as you would pose children for a picture. When everything went black, I had had a cardiac arrest. They told me later that everything started ringing down at the nurse's station. Everything went black. But my mind was working and I said to myself: 'The pain is gone.' I saw my children as posing in a picture, a picture for a formal portrait. Now I can talk about it . . . I can still feel the sadness. The sadness that I was dying, that I had died . . .

Let me jump ahead. When they brought me back, my chest was *completely* burned from the paddles, the electric shocks. My chest hurt from all the pounding that they had done. This happened in August, and my chest was as sore as late as December, Christmas – if I hiccupped or coughed, I felt like I was being thrown across the room. They had to really work on me to bring me back.

When it happened, I have never felt this sad in my life. All I was thinking was, *I never had a chance to tell my children to be happy* . . . I'm going to cry, Studs . . . That it's OK that I died, that they should just be happy. I wanted to have a chance to tell them, but now it was too late. I kept thinking, *If I could just get over into complete death, there would be nothing* – I wouldn't know how sad I should be. I was pushing. Because I had *no* thought that I was going to come back. I thought I was in the process of dying, and if I could just push myself completely over, there would be nothing . . . I was still aware, which is what amazes me, because obviously my heart was not going – but my *mind* was *going*. Evidently they hadn't tied down my arms – they probably didn't take the time, they were just working fast. Suddenly I saw this green ball on my stomach. They told me later that was what they were pushing air into my lungs with. And I saw a doctor or intern, a black man, at the foot of the bed. I remember I threw my arm back and I touched somebody and I looked up and there was another doctor there and I said to him, 'Is this a dream?' And he said, 'No, it's not a dream – we're trying to stabilize you.' He said: 'Just stay calm. And stop screaming about your children.' And then everything went . . . I just sort of became unconscious, but I wasn't dead.

I never went back to hospital records, but obviously, it couldn't have lasted more than four minutes. I was in the intensive care ward for about a week. My children are in California with my ex-husband. The first day after, I wanted to try to talk but I was very weak . . . The next day, my own doctor came back and said, 'Well, what happened?' And so I started to tell him the story. He said, 'No, no, that's OK – you don't have to tell me.' And they sent in a psychologist with a nurse to talk. She said that she was working with somebody on these experiences and, you know, *what happened?* And I started again, but nobody ever heard me completely through. It was, 'OK, yeah, we've got enough. We'll come back later – you're probably too weak.' They really didn't want to hear it. I had the feeling they were uncomfortable. There was all this talk about a light and going to the Creator, going to God, this beautiful light and coming back. I was talking about how there was going to be nothing. One woman did say to me, 'Now, what about this light?' And I said, 'I didn't see anything. There was no light.' I said that if I got completely dead there would be nothing. They began patting me . . . and walked away. Later on, I would find that if I talked about this, they would say, 'But of course now you believe, don't you?' – because I'd experienced death. I'd say, 'Well, no. *I* haven't changed.'

'You mean the experience didn't make you want to believe?' And I said, 'No.' I think they were annoyed. It's sort of like the man who is leading a horrible life and then he comes close to a tragedy and says, 'I'm going to change my ways . . .' They expected that because I came so close to seeing death, I should change my ways.

It was full cardiac arrest. I should go back and ask for my records. They didn't like the fact that I thought there was going to be nothing. I've just done some reading on people's experiences, and I've never heard *anybody* say that there was going to be nothing. If they believe in a certain afterlife, this is what they're going to see; if they believe there is nothing, this is what they're going to see also. Which makes me think even more that there's nothing. You see what you expect. You see what you want to see. I mean, it would be nice to think that you go on, and that all this wasn't for nothing. The psychologist was the same as everybody else. In fact, *nobody* really wanted to talk to me about the fact that I had died. That whole hospital stay, *nobody* talked to me about the fact that my heart had stopped, that I had this chest that was so burned, and was hurting so much. About three months later I ended up back in the hospital because I was having strange feelings. They put me back in intensive care to observe me. A nurse came in and said, 'I remember you.' She said, 'I was the one who found you and started the CPR until the cart came.' That was the first time anybody . . . I would ask in the hospital, 'Who were the people?' 'Cause this is a *big* event – I could have been dead! *Nobody* talked about it.

Whatever study the psychologist was doing, maybe it didn't fit the pattern of where she wanted it to go. My question is: Does the mind continue to work after the heart stops? You know how people talk about going way above their body? I never saw that. So let's say even that my heart had stopped for two minutes. I might not have seen the vision of my children until it got started again. But that first thought, the pain is gone, must have occurred after the heart had stopped beating. It happened so fast . . .

My children being left alone was very important to me. I was amazed later when the doctor had said to me, 'Stop screaming about your children.' I had been in an arrest and, somehow, my voice was coming out afterward about them. They were twelve, eleven, and ten at the time. It was the fact that I hadn't had a chance to say anything to them, that it happened quickly . . . When people say, 'I hope I go quickly,' I say, 'Why would you want to go quickly? You only die once. Wouldn't you want to go a little slowly so you can think about it and talk about it?'

I used to read the obituaries as a child. I don't know if it's because I knew Tommy, who was the little boy from the funeral home, or what. By the age of nine, ten, I was reading the obituaries as a matter of course. I notice my children don't read them. I still do.

KAREN THOMPSON

She is currently a graduate student at Northwestern University. She was in a coma for two years. She appears to have recovered somewhat, though she still takes a considerable number of medications. She no longer has a walker or carries a cane. She is preparing to move to Berkeley to attend the University of California's course in screenwriting.

I'm fifty-one, an African-American woman. As far as I know, my father is dead. My mother died when I was sixteen. My mother was an architect. I'm the fourth generation of architects in my family. My grandfather was Albert I. Cassell. He built most of Howard University. My mother worked seventeen years on the gothic National Cathedral in Washington, D.C. – she was one of the chief engineers. She did the Rose Window and the south transom. She was a graduate of Cornell University, *magna cum laude*. At sixteen, I came to Chicago to attend IIT [Illinois Institute of Technology]. I had studied a great deal with my grandfather and my mother, so I really knew a lot about architecture before I came here. I was pulled out of school and apprenticed with Mies van der Rohe. Oh yes, I knew him. He was quite a character, very taciturn, very dry kind of humor. Then I worked for C.F. Murphy Associates, as well as Skidmore, Owings, and Merrill. I went to Perkins and Will for a while, too. For a year and a half, I worked for Milton Keynes overseas. Then I came back to Skidmore. It was about '82, '83. I was working sixteen, eighteen hours a day . . . A lot of the times I would stay overnight, underneath my drafting table. [*Laughs*] And then I got sick.

It was stress. I was very ill. I was malnourished. And I had walking pneumonia. I had taken some over-the-counter medicines, you know, Primatene and Robitussin, trying to keep going. After several months, I realized that my whole condition was much weaker than it ever had been. I had just moved into a new apartment. I had a respiratory failure. I called the ambulance and I told them, 'I'm having a very difficult time breathing, please come at once.' They came and got me to the hospital. They stabilized me and gave me epinephrine and injections. I was on the inhalator for a while and I was taking cephalin, and after a while they said, 'All right, you're OK, you can go home.' They gave me a penicillin prescription. When I got home, I was at my kitchen counter, and I was feeding my cat, and I realized, *My God, it's happening again – and this time I'm going to die.* I don't have anyone. No one – I'm by myself. This was 1986. I didn't wake up until April of '88.

I know people describe the white tunnel and all of that, but I did see what looked like a blaring white light. It looked like a lightning flash. I felt faint but I felt very charged. It made my knees buckle, but it was like a surge of energy. I felt like I'd been struck by lightning. It didn't feel like a heart attack or anything like that. It just felt like this is *it*. I didn't see the white tunnel, nothing like that . . . But I saw something quite different inside the coma. That's a very long scene . . . [*Sighs*]

First of all, I have always been a Buddhist. I was born into a family that had been Lutherans and Baptists and Episcopalians. In the meantime, my mother, since she was dealing with battling death all the time, with cancer, began to investigate Buddhism through people like Alan Watts. We would talk about perception and how you view yourself and whether there's a soul.

So when I was standing there at the kitchen counter, I wasn't afraid. I wasn't afraid, not at all – 'cause I'm not afraid of dying. I've been here before and I'll be here again.

You believe in reincarnation?

It's not a matter of belief, I *know*. I *know* I've been here before – that was what was confirmed inside the coma. And I think it was probably the greatest blessing in my life. It was like being reborn.

The coma lasted how long?

Two years. From 1986 to April 1988, I was hooked up to machines and tubes in a hospital. And it's a good thing that I didn't have relatives because they told me later, after I'd been out of the coma, that if you have relatives, they can sign and they would cut off the life support and I would be dead. Most of the time, if you're poor, after a very short time, all of your medical insurance is used up. Because I didn't have anyone to vouch for me, no one came . . . [*Laughs*] They didn't think I was going to ever wake up. I was very, *very* lucky not to have anyone. [*Laughs*] It kind of reinforces the idea that you really are here *alone*. It's wonderful to have friends, but ultimately you're here by yourself. You're a spiritual being who has come for this particular journey. Also, inside of the coma, I was shown other lives that I've had.

The last thing that I remember inside the coma was: *Don't explain.* As soon as I came out of the coma I started to try to tell people because it was so astonishing to me, even though I was a so-called Buddhist. It's very hard to deal with these tight, compartmentalized definitions of religion. I couldn't walk, and I didn't remember very much. I looked like I had cerebral palsy. I was shaking, everything was atrophied. The doctors were just astonished. They couldn't believe it. No one can . . . [*Laughs*] It's a blessing.

What did you see inside the coma?

Oh, I remember very vividly. I was conscious of it happening to me while I was inside the coma. It was incredible darkness. I've never had a darkness that surrounds you like that . . . But very, very, *very* comforting. A soft darkness. In this soft darkness, I had the sensation of flying. After I recovered in '92, '93, I went to a Tibetan monastery and institute in Ithaca, New York. I told them in great detail. They were interested and they believed me completely. And they were telling me what it meant. Inside the coma I was shown all the different lives that I've had to this point. For instance, one of my questions had been: *Why do I have bad lungs?* What happens is all the various lives you have had, you die at a certain point. If you believe in reincarnation, your soul lives forever. Death is part of life. Life is not separate from or in opposition to it – there's not the duality. As humans evolve, they will realize it's not either/or. It's not lack of light. It's not good or bad. It's many things at once. You have to learn to deal with paradox. And not to have to find the answer. You have the answer – it's just, you have to listen for it.

I'm not afraid of death at all. It's *part* of life. So I will continue. I will come back as another form of human being. I hope it's as a black woman. [*Laughs hard*] This is the first time I've been a black woman.

You think you've been someone else before?

I know it. Why do you keep saying 'think'? I've been an Irish woman, I've been an Egyptian boy. I've been an Inuit Eskimo Indian. I was in Africa – a young boy. I have not been a black American woman before. One of the reasons I have bad lungs is because of my life as an Irish woman. [*Laughs*] I was also the Egyptian boy who died in the 1600s. I'm not competing with other people. I'm trying to be a better soul myself. I'm not trying to beat someone or get the highest this or do the highest that. I'm just trying to be the best person for myself. We belong to ourselves. You have to be personally responsible. It's a spiritual thing that we're all going through.

Did you feel this way before the coma?

Yes, but not as articulately. I was on a great deal of medicine when I came out of the coma. And a lot of it made me sicker – a lot of it was steroids. That was supposed to help my breathing but they made all my muscles ache, they made my adrenaline go haywire, they made my immune system collapse. So I slowly but surely got off of all the steroids and all the medication, but I can't get rid of the weight they put on me. I was slim, very slim. People used to say, 'God, you're as thin as six o'clock!' [*Laughs*]

The doctors told me at the time that I would never walk again. I was scooting around on my butt for a long time. It's 1988, twelve-something years ago. Gosh, I was in my late thirties, thirty-eight. I wasn't what they would consider young, so I wasn't given the option of the Rehab Institute [of Chicago] or anything.

I taught myself. I got them to give me a walker. I didn't have any assistance. I did get the social workers to help me with getting disability, because I wasn't able to function at all. It's been an uphill battle. For instance, trying to find any kind of work at all. They always associate any kind of disability with your being mentally handicapped. It took nearly three years for me to be allowed to go to school. They kept telling me that I was so severely handicapped that I couldn't function. I was living by myself. My landlord at the time – I was incredibly blessed in so many ways. He took care of my cat that whole time. I still have the same cat.

At one point there were three different visiting nurses I got to come. The first one stole from me. The second one would bring the forms and say, 'I'll be back a week later.' She had some *huge* amount of cases. She said: 'Just fill out the forms – I need it to get paid.' The third one wanted me to become a Christian. She said I had gone into a coma because I hadn't been saved by Jesus. She got on my nerves more than anything. [*Laughs*]

When you were depressed, did you ever think of suicide?

Of course I thought of it – many, *many* times! [*Laughs*] But what would be the point? I'd come back . . . It's not as though you escape. So, OK, I kill myself and then I have to come back and deal with all the angst and the pain and the suffering of having killed myself, and I have to deal with it ten times over because I've hurt all these people. I have about five or six really good friends that I've had for thirty years, twenty years. Suicide is self-defeating.

When was the first time you felt grief over death?

My cousin Bobby had died when I was eight – the one who was lynched outside of Montgomery. There were other deaths in my family, but the one that touched me the most was Bobby's.

When was your first awareness that there was such a thing as death?

Oh, when I was about two.

You go back that far?

I remember when I was born.

What was it like being born?

Very difficult. [*Laughs*]

What about organized religion?

I dislike it *immensely*. I think it's done more harm than good. I think it's been more divisive than anything. I can recognize the need for people to have some way to organize their fears. That's what it's about: you need a spiritual fix. There was a time which was a turning point. People call it your satori – when you feel that things are getting darker and darker and darker, and more and more horrible, and more and more difficult – it's just before a point where you come into your own in another way, at another level. You reach a certain kind of epiphany. I thought I would never walk. I would invent this whole regime of exercises and I would get myself down the stairs – it would take me half an hour. I would walk from my apartment to the end of the block, and then I'd walk back. Every day.

One of these times, I was on this walker and I had *almost* gotten to the corner. It was just *such* a struggle. And it *hurt*. I was very depressed, very low . . . A whole truckload, an open flatbed truck, of white young males came along and went into the gas station. In my mind, I associate it with my cousin Bobby – these rednecks. The whole idea of young white men on a flatbed truck: *danger*. I just kept on walking. I was with the walker, struggling. It was *painful*. All of a sudden, they were standing up, all of them, and they were whistling and giving me claps and applauding and cheering. I was terribly moved. I'm still moved by that. It still brings tears to my eyes . . . [*Emotionally*] I can still feel how much it meant to me at the time because it was so transforming that these young white males recognized the enormity of my challenge and appreciated what I was trying to do. I still cry because it meant *everything*. That's what I call chance. That's coincidence. People say there is no coincidence – everything happens for a reason. I happened to be there, they happened to be there, they didn't have to pay me any attention . . . They didn't have to recognize me. But they *did*. I responded. I waved and thanked them – because they gave me something tremendous. It was an *enormous* gift.

I believe I was ready for the coma. I needed to have it. I really needed to have that knowledge. I was Buddhist before, but now I'm not so concentrated on trying to make this life work. A lot of times, you worry whether you're doing the right thing. I don't have to worry about that anymore because I know I am. I can relax about the kind of person I am. I don't worry about whether people like me or not. I worry about things like justice and whether people are treated fairly, things of that sort. But I don't have to be concerned about whether someone likes me.

You have friends?

Yes, I'm just much more selective about it. More women. I don't talk about these things anymore, because people either don't believe you or they want you to tell their future. I'm not a fortune-teller.

DIMITRI MIHALAS

He is ebullient, scholarly in appearance, and, incongruously, wears a ponytail. 'My second wife took me to my first Quaker Meeting. The first time I was there, I felt very comfortable. The second time I was there, I became aware that something was going on. Nobody said a word, but something was going on. And by the third time, I was hooked.' Since then, he has been a devout Quaker and frequently attends gatherings.

He works as a physicist at the National Laboratory in Los Alamos, in the desert of New Mexico. It is a village unto itself, an enclave of scientists. It is a legendary spot that has become a piece of American folklore. It was here, in 1945, isolated from the rest of the world, that they created the atomic bomb.

I never thought about death until 1985. And I was already forty-six years old. Now I'm sixty-one. I was living in Colorado, a member of the National Academy of Sciences. I had just finished a book on radiation hydrodynamics, published by Oxford University Press. I was riding at the peak. I was living in a beautiful house in the hills west of Boulder. I was sitting down in my study one night. I was feeling serene, listening to classical music playing, looking out at the night sky and thinking, *This is really great.* And then I had an utterly alien thought: *How do you get from where you are to where you must be when you die?* It was the first time I had ever really seriously thought about death. And I said to myself, *huh?!* – here I am at the peak, sitting up on this little needle point, and I'm thinking about *death!*

I found the answer out later that year. September 1, 1985, was the precipitating day. We moved from Boulder, pulled up all my roots because my wife had lost her job. She got a new job at the University of Illinois in Champaign. For years I had suffered from bipolar disorder. Suddenly I crashed into what the doctors in their very neutral, scientific language called major depression. It's deadly – I got nuked. I realized that what I had done, all my life, to protect myself from all of the things that I feared in life was I had built a huge steel-reinforced concrete shell around me. I made that son of a bitch *so* strong that *nothing* was going to get in there. No illness. No disease. No fear. No loss. No pain. No death. No *nothing*. But when you get nuked, it's gone . . .

It was a downward spiral. I had only been a little bit depressed before, little up-and-down waves. I'd go a couple of years where I'd lie low. Next couple of years, I'd feel a little hypomanic. I would write all the papers – I wrote *six* books. Then I'd get a little low again. In Champaign, my whole foundation was gone. *All* my friends were gone. We'd moved to this strange place, alien surroundings. I hate the Midwest – I *hate* the color green. I was born in a desert. I live in a desert now. What happened was that my shell didn't crumble, it was vaporized. And there I was naked. I was obsessing constantly about killing myself. Every minute, some quiet little voice in my head would say to me, 'This is impossible to sustain. There is only one solution' – *death!* It's the only way out.

I actually did try once during that year. I kept a gun at home – it was a 9mm automatic. I was sitting on the floor thinking about it for about three hours: *What should I do?* I finally got up and I said, 'I can't handle this. I only see one solution.' I used to keep the gun stuck in between some blankets in a closet in the bedroom. I reached in, there was no gun. Pulled the blankets out. No gun. My wife, on the advice of the doctor, had taken the gun out – she had removed it. She took it apart and she gave different pieces to different people all over the county. If she had not removed it, I absolutely would have shot myself. When she came home, all the blankets were back. I didn't say a word about this.

I was so broken at the time, I couldn't even think of another good way. I could have stuck the car in the garage and turned it on and kissed the world good-bye, but I didn't think of that. I just limped along.

About two weeks later, she and I went for lunch, like we usually did, at Wendy's, then I went one way to work in my office, and she went the other way. It was snowing pretty hard. I went along for about ten paces, and all of a sudden, out of pure impulse, I stopped. I turned around and I watched her walk away from me. She was wearing light-colored slacks. She had on a blue parka and a white knit stocking cap. You watch things disappear when the snow is falling and you start seeing snow and you don't see them anymore.

So her cap disappeared, and then her trousers disappeared, and the last thing to go was the blue parka. All of a sudden, it was just a sheet of white from the snow. I couldn't see her . . . I had this tremendous pang – I was almost in despair – I said: 'Jesus Christ, *what* would happen if she were gone tomorrow? *How* would I go on living?' About a minute later, another thought popped into my mind. And that was: *What would happen to* her *if you were gone tomorrow?* I stood there in the snow for a long time. I finally realized that it was unethical, immoral, to take your own life. I've had people say to me, 'It's my life, isn't it? If I blow it away, what do you care? What does anybody care?' That's wrong. Because your life is *not* yours. Part of your life is part of everybody else's life who loves you, who cares about you. I thought: *If I kill myself, I would kill that part of her that she had invested in me.* And I would kill that part of everybody else I knew who knew me as a friend, a teacher, whatever. And that's murder. Suicide is one thing, murder is another. I can't murder. All I could do is plead for relief, but I can't murder some piece of someone else.

So I found myself in the position of standing on the edge of a deep, black canyon. All I had to do was take one step forward and I was gone. But I couldn't do it. So I hung on. And about a month later, I began to have this totally irrational feeling, that in some sense I was being held, protected by a higher power – that I was being spared. Yes, I'm a scientist. But I'm a mystic, too. I believe that there are things beyond science. I am a card-carrying scientist and I am a card-carrying mystic. Call it God, call it the laws of physics, I don't know . . . Whatever it is that gives this world its incredible order. Look at this flower – the daisy there on the table. It's a sex organ of a plant. Its sole function is to attract insects to fertilize the plant. But it's beautiful. It has symmetry, it has elegance. Why? Why couldn't it just be an ugly little thing that exudes the right scent to attract the insect? You don't know. I don't know. My conclusion is, there are layers and layers and layers and layers of articulation and organization in this world that go far beyond anything that you and I can either perceive or understand.

I finally got back to Boulder. My friends had arranged for me to get a one-year fellowship back there. Really, it was to get medical treatment. The doctor started me on a new antidepressant, medication that worked, and within three weeks, I was up and running again. I had been spared. That taught me that sometimes, even though things are so utterly black, you can be spared. Five years later, I was sitting in Quaker Meeting, meditating, and I asked myself: *Why is it given to us, some of us, sometimes, to have to go through the deepest darkness?* Is it a test? Is it a trial? Is it a punishment? All of a sudden, I got the answer. It's a child's answer, the kind of answer that only a kid would know: When you are in the deepest darkness you can best see light. It is a *gift*. This whole thing exploded in my brain: *Hey, I'm an astronomer!* If I want to go look for a galaxy at the twenty-third magnitude, so faint that it can only be seen with the largest telescopes, I don't go out at noon, I go out in the deepest darkness. It's in the *darkness* that if you can look in the right direction . . . Then I realized that in Quakerism we talk about God's Light and our inner Light, that part of God's Light is reflected in us at all times, but we have to *follow* this inner Light.

In 1996, ten years later, I got cut by the other edge of the sword – not depression, but mania. It wasn't just this benevolent mania where you become very energetic; I was in a really *manic* state. It's the difference between a saber-toothed tiger and a house cat. The classic mania pulls your guts out. You're doing stuff that is just off-the-wall *crazy*. I was spending money, I was having an affair, I was doing stuff that was professionally damaging – I was just *totally* out of character. There have been really manic people in the world. Look at van Gogh – he was bipolar. In the last year of his life, he painted two hundred masterpieces, almost one a day. He would work on ten or twenty at once, just to get the light right as he was working on them. William Blake. He's as crazy as they come, man. He was off the *wall*. But he was crazy in a very intelligent way. Mozart was bipolar. When he was up, he could write a symphony in an afternoon; when he was down, he couldn't write anything. He died wanting to finish his Requiem.

In 1997, I was driving from Boulder to the Denver International Airport and I ran into the end of a guardrail. I ran smack-dab into the end of that guardrail going over *eighty* miles an hour. And I don't remember *anything* – because when you get a traumatic brain injury, it's gone. I was unconscious. People tell me you can still see a great big cross on the back of my head, where the scars are. Blood was pouring out of my head and arm. There were two people who came and found me. They did two things: they had a cell phone and they called the police, and they also bandaged up my arm to help contain the bleeding. Passersby. And then, apparently, they vanished. They were *not* there when the police came. My daughter says they were angels. What do I know? Maybe there *are* angels – I don't know, you don't know, nobody knows. All I know is that they called the police, the police got me to the hospital. I was there for maybe a week. They did MRIs, they determined yes, there was injury to the brain: there was blood on the frontal cortex, there was blood on the occipital lobe. But there was nothing life-threatening. I don't remember *any* of this . . .

Then my daughter moved me here into the Rehab Institute of Chicago. All of a sudden, for inexplicable reasons, I went into a deep coma, a psychotic coma. I was thrashing around constantly, I was screaming all the time, I was struggling to get out of bed. They had to tie me in. I was having all kinds of wild psychotic dreams. They said, 'Your dad's got encephalitis.' They took me to Northwestern and at their radiological center they did three sets of MRIs. They sent them back: no sign of encephalitis.

The doctors were puzzled. My daughter had had five years of chemistry before she became a lawyer and so she started reading the medical literature. What she found is that I was showing all the classic signs of lithium toxicity. They had me on lithium to control the mania. I was taking it, but it had just stopped working – that happens. While they were feeding it to me, I was getting dehydrated, so the lithium level in my blood went up and up and up. She got a nurse to show her my chart. My lithium level was three times therapeutic and twice toxic. She *convinced* the doctors to stop the drip. Later a staffer told me, 'At that point, your estimated time of arrival for the big airport in the sky was forty-eight hours.' So I was that close – forty-eight *hours*. I would have died . . . My daughter saved my life.

The Rehab kept only minimal staff at night. My daughter was afraid I'd still try to get out of bed, fall on my head, and do more damage. So she hired Lydia to look after me at night. A big black woman from Bermuda. Lydia used to read to me every night before I went to sleep, just to put me off into dreamland. She would always start with Isaiah 43. It says: 'I am Yahweh. I created you, Israel. I created you, Joseph. Fear not. I have redeemed you. You are *mine*.' She always used to emphasize that. 'You are *mine*. I have called you by your name. And when you are in the water, you shall not drown. And when you cross the river, you shall not be swept away. And when you are in the fire, you shall not be burnt. And the flame shall not consume you. For I am with you.' So every night she would read that. It took me maybe a week to understand it. And longer to believe it. When I did believe it – and I still do – I started getting well. This really pushed just the right buttons. I just said: OK, He says I am his, He's called me by name, I will not be swept away by the river, and I'm not going to be consumed by the flame. So what the hell. I began to *heal*. [*Laughs*]

You pop out of the womb and into this hostile world and you start crying, that's *it*. That's life. You've got it right up to the moment when death comes and the brain goes flat. That's death. In between, there are things we call *living* and *dying*. Those are active words. They're not nouns, they're verbs. We make a choice: every moment of our life, we can either choose to live or to die. I know people like you, who are a lot older than I, who are so *alive* it's unbelievable. And I know people who are thirty years younger than I who are dead. Death hasn't come yet, but they gave up. It's terrible to see . . .

I have had psychotic experiences. When I was still detoxing from the lithium, I was wildly psychotic. I was convinced that I was in a hospital because I was mentally ill, not because of an accident. It was all hallucinatory. I'd hear people talking at night, trying to make a plan to overthrow the hospital administration. While I was totally out of my head, I had a series of psychotic dreams. They were like visions – horrible ones. One is burned into my memory: I was walking along in a place that was like a jungle. I saw in this clearing two gigantic figures that looked like pre-Columbian gods. They were running a big machine that had a great, big, old-fashioned hopper on top, taking things that looked for all the world like human brains, and throwing them in. There would be a grinding sound and out the other end was coming something that looked like a gigantic white river of pus. I finally screwed up my courage and asked one of these guys, 'Who are you and what are you doing?' This guy is *awesome*. He looks at me real fierce and says, 'It is given to us to take the souls that have not made it beyond this point on their path to enlightenment, and to facilitate their reincarnation into a new soul.'

I said, 'What must a person do to avoid this particular stop on their path to enlightenment?' He said, 'You must understand that there is only one human emotion that has any value whatsoever in this world.' I said, 'Oh . . . what is that?' And he said, 'Compassion.' At that point, the dream faded.

I went to see a doctor in Albuquerque. I was getting suicidal again. At the end of 1997, my brain chemistry was so altered by taking Depakote instead of lithium that my old antidepressant failed. He said, 'You're in danger. You should go into the hospital tomorrow. It's the best thing you can do.' I thought: *Holy shit!* If I do, that's on my record: I've been hospitalized for mental illness, all this crap. I'm going to be working at Los Alamos, security problems. I *don't* want that. Then I said: *Hey – listen to yourself.* You're doing the same damn thing that you've told other people with this disorder *not* to do . . . You're listening to the stigma. This illness is the most stigmatized illness in the world. So I said, 'Screw it! I'm *not* going to be stigmatized. I'm going in the hospital.' And I did. Ten days later, I was released. The doctor said, 'You're OK now. We expect you in every day as an outpatient.' I showed up the first day. We're sitting at a great big oval table, fifteen, twenty people. I recognized a lot of them from on the ward, people detoxing from alcohol, from drugs. There were some drug pushers there. There were some prostitutes there. There was one guy who was a Vietnam veteran suffering from extreme post-traumatic stress syndrome.

I'm sitting there thinking: I'm a distinguished professor. What's a nice boy like me doing in a place like this? I was being priggish. Then they started talking. These were the women who had been raped repeatedly by their fathers or their mother's boyfriends or an uncle from practically the minute they were born – they became prostitutes. And these were the boys who had been beaten repeatedly, within an inch of their life, by their fathers, their stepfathers, their mother's boyfriends. These were the people whose lives had been *destroyed* when they were young – very, very young and helpless. I realized that this is where compassion comes in. This was the fulfillment of the dream. And then I said to myself: 'You know what? This is just like a Quaker Meeting.' Because in a Quaker Meeting, people stand up and talk about their deepest spiritual and emotional experiences. And when they do that, they are standing naked spiritually and emotionally, in front of the Meeting, and asking for the compassion – not just of the Meeting but of God. So I said to myself: 'You're in a Quaker Meeting, behave accordingly.' I sat with those people for three weeks, I learned from them, and I taught them what little I could. It was quite an experience. That was a real healing experience – that was a big one. Out of the darkness has come the Light.

These days, in the morning when I wake up, my cat is up on my chest purring. I open my eyes, it's light out, and I say, 'Hey, I got another one . . . and it's a freebie.' Because I've already been dead four times. Twice by suicide I could've been dead. Twice as a result of the accident and then the coma. *Four times.* So what am I gonna do? I'm going to get up and I'm going to use the gifts that I have been given. They are very considerable gifts. I have a lot of intelligence, I have a lot of understanding now. Not really about people, but how what I do here locally does perturb the Universe. You put van Gogh in front of the canvas and he knows what he has been given to do. He doesn't think about it – he just does it. You use the talents you've been given. And while you're at it, you be as nice as you humanly can be to everyone around you. That's the bottom line. My illness has become my greatest gift. My life has been touched by Grace. I know it.

A View from the Bridge

HANK OETTINGER

He is a retired printer. He spends most of his retirement days reading all sorts of magazines and newspapers and visits his favorite alehouses. His obsessive avocation has always been and still is writing letters to the editor. He has written thousands.

My grandfather Adam Oettinger fled Germany after the German liberal revolution failed in 1848; he settled in Wisconsin. They're called the forty-eighters, and they were the basis of Wisconsin's liberalism, up until the days of Joseph McCarthy. My grandmother was a member of a Catholic sect from Bavaria where the priest became disgusted with the pressures that were put on him by politicians – and he took his parish, congregation and all, and settled in St. Nasians, Wisconsin, close to Fond du Lac. He set up a Catholic-communist settlement. It became quite famous in Wisconsin history. One of the members of his congregation was my maternal grandfather. He was married, and they had five children – they settled in Peshtigo. My father was born in the last year of the Civil War. So I am a second-generation American.

My family consisted of eleven children – I'm number ten. The first four died in infancy from scarlet fever. The other seven were remarkable in their survival. I'm a good example of that because I am now eighty-eight years old. All seven and our parents survived until I was sixty-four years old. There was not a death in that family. My mother died at the age of ninety-six, and my father at eighty-eight. All the rest of the brothers and sisters were in their high seventies or eighties – a great survival rate. I have never had any disease except mumps when I was maybe six or seven years old. Never had any major operations in my whole life.

Believe it or not, I was never vaccinated. I probably picked up immunity from my older brothers and sisters who probably had some of those diseases. I don't have any troubles physically. I'm drinking my beers every day at the Old Town Ale House and Billy Goat's and sleep well.

But there's one thing: I can feel the approach of Alehauser's disease – that's my name for it. I can see that it's starting. The loss of certain memories that were usually so clear, fast, in my mind. But nothing to worry about. There was only one case of Alzheimer's in my family, and that was my father. In those days they called it the 'insanity of the aged.'

I was brought up a very strict Catholic in a German Catholic family. My father had the job for years of ringing the church bell for Angelus at six in the morning and six at night in the little town of Crandon, Wisconsin, way, *way* up. He would oversleep too often, but Father Schmidt didn't care about the morning Angelus anyway. Eventually, my father got confused and sometimes he would ring the Angelus at four-thirty in the afternoon . . . [*Laughs*] My mother had me pegged for the priesthood. From the time I could talk she taught me the responses for serving Mass. I was so religious I even set up a little altar with a statue of the Blessed Virgin, and said my night prayers before I went to sleep. I was *disgustingly* religious.

In 1926, when I was fourteen years old, I started at the printer's trade on the weekly newspaper. Started out setting type by hand before I got a Linotype. About two years after that, here I'm still strict Catholic, an old German printer by the delicious name of Engelbert Schimmelvennick would talk to me and give me hints. One day I mentioned that I was going to go to communion, and he says, 'Oh, you're going to practice theophagy.' I said, 'What are you saying?' He says: 'God-eating. It's very common in many ancient religions, they eat their gods or symbols of their gods. You're practicing theophagy.' So that started me. Then he would give the other examples. He had me going – and he recommended readings.

In high school, I am the champion orator. I win contests all over. It comes time for the contest and the principal says, 'Well, Henry, have you chosen a subject for your speech this year?' I said, 'Yes, I'm very interested in Robert Ingersoll.' 'What?!' [*Laughs*] Ingersoll was an atheist. I think one of his sayings was an agnostic is an atheist without the courage of his convictions. I wanted to make up my speech from the writings of Robert Ingersoll. The principal says, 'That damned atheist! No, no, no, no – that won't do.' So I gave up the idea.

The next year was the crash, 1929. We moved to Waukesha, which is rock-ribbed Republican – the *most* Republican county in the whole state of Wisconsin. There I joined the Typographical Union and became an officer. In 1934, I was secretary general of the Typographical Union, really active in union work. I was working on the *Waukesha Daily Freeman*, a rock-ribbed Republican paper. I started my letter-writing career around 1937. One of my first letters, which appeared in the *Milwaukee Journal*, was about Bishop Shiel of Chicago, who made a famous speech when there was a surge of anti-Semitism in the Midwest, led by Father Coughlin and Gerald L.K. Smith. He said, 'Spiritually, we are all Semites.' I publicized it, even in the *Waukesha Freeman*. As a result, the German American Bund, which was *oh* so strong in Milwaukee – they'd have rallies at the auditorium with those swastikas on their armbands – twice sent me death threats. They signed with a swastika. And my mother said, 'Oh, Henry, please, *please* stop writing letters – I don't want them to kill you.' And now I was well on my way to being an atheist.

My mother was such a sweet, darling old lady, and I would hide it from her as much as possible. Wisconsin had liberal drinking laws regarding Sundays. While Chicago wouldn't open until noon, in Wisconsin they opened at ten o'clock in the morning. So I'd get up and I'd make believe I was fixing up for going to High Mass at ten o'clock. I'd go down to Louie's Tavern and at noon wander back home. My mother was satisfied.

My father was as strict as an old German could be. I was the only atheist in the family. While working at the *Waukesha Freeman*, I set up type for the *Carrollville College Echo* and for the *Waukesha High School Cardinal*. These kids would bring copy for their papers to me and I would indoctrinate them. It finally got to the point where the president of Carrollville College put out a law: Students may not go to the composing room. They'd leave the copy in the front office. Louie's Tavern was a half a block away. I'd meet the kids out front and further indoctrinate them. Finally, one guy raised hell with me. I think he was the district attorney. He said I negated the work of

Bishop Fulton J. Sheen by converting these kids to atheism. [*Laughs*] I was responsible for more conversions than he was!

Has there *ever* been one single tiny bit of evidence that there's a hereafter?! Never once. There is *no* evidence! There is *never* anybody that's come back, that I know of, from after death. I think that religion has been a detriment to humanity, not of benefit. The earth is here, we're here, the animals are here, the birds are here and . . . [*Sputtering*] Why do you need God? What for?!

When you die, you go back to the earth from which you arose, that's all. You're dead, that's the end – *kaput!* That's all. If there was any chance, Clarence Darrow would have come back down to that little bridge down on the South Side.* He said if it was true, he would come back. He died an atheist.

People try to convert me, try to get me back to religion. One was a bright young man about twenty-five years old, from Moody Bible Institute. He accosts me at North and Wells and hands me a pamphlet. I said, 'No thanks, I happen to be an atheist.' He says, 'You can't be an atheist.' I says, 'I can't? I figure I've been an atheist for about fifty, sixty years. Why can't I be?' He says, 'Who made you?' I said, 'You mean to say that you attained the age of twenty-five and nobody explained the facts of life to you yet?' [*Laughs*] He took his pamphlet back, but he laughed – he got a kick out of it. I ask people, 'Do you believe in the Noah's ark story?' Two each of everything. 'Yes. The Bible says it's so.' I says, 'Well then, tell me, what did the anteaters have for their second meal?' They're dumbfounded. There are two ants there and two anteaters . . . [*Laughs*]

After I die, I'm going to the medical school of the University of Chicago, because they feature studies of the skull and the brain there, and I don't want to deprive them of a great prize example. I've been signed up for that for years. Afterlife does not exist. It is not necessary. Life goes on on Earth, and we have our memories. The only life that is necessary is the one that we're enjoying now.

Nobody figures he's going to go to Hell. He doesn't in his heart believe that even a mean old man like God is going to make somebody burn forever. Everybody figures he's going to Heaven. Again,

*There is an annual ritual in Jackson Park on Chicago's South Side, during which nonbelievers whimsically await the return of Darrow.

there's no evidence, no proof, no sign. Religion started out of fear. There's no question about that. Fear of death is the basis of religion, because they can't imagine themselves not existing, so they project themselves as a spirit that leaves their body and lives on forever. I don't know if I'd want to go to that Heaven in the first place. Jerry Falwell's going to be up there, and Pat Robertson . . .

There are many sins, but they aren't theologically based – starving children, antiblack sentiments, disease – they aren't based on any God. Capitalism is a sin! It is my firm belief that capitalism and Christianity are incompatible. They are *absolutely* antagonistic to one another: the idea of Jesus, certainly, and the Christian ethic, there's no question but that it's good. Can you imagine Jesus coming back to Earth and having a meeting with Bill Gates and all these millionaires? Now they got *billionaires* having a conference with right-wing senators! He would ask them, 'Did you *ever* hear of the biblical injunction to sell what you have and give it to the poor? Did you *ever* hear that wealth is bad, that war is bad?' He said, 'Love your neighbor.'

I have absolutely *no* fear of death. I know that one of these days, *poof!* I'm done, I'm gone. But I'll live on in the memories of a hell of a lot of people that I affected. Because I feel that if anybody should go to Heaven, it should be me. I've spent my whole life working for the laboring man, for farmers, for the poor, against war, against racism. Organizing the unorganized workers back in the thirties and forties. I just happen to think I am a saint. [*Laughs*] So I'm not worried . . . That's the only way we're going to live on, is in memories. That'll be enough.

In fact, I know when I'm going to die. I made up my mind, oh, say ten years ago. I'm going to die in the year 2008, around November. I figure that when that year comes, I am going to borrow money, sell everything I have, which is *nothing*, accumulate as much money as I can, and bet the whole thing that the Cubs are going to win the World Series. Because it would be one hundred years since they did, and I figure they have to do it once in a century. And when I get that sum of money, I'm going to throw the biggest party at the Ale House and at Billy Goat's, and that's enough.

IRA GLASS

He conducts *This American Life*, a weekly Public Radio International program.

> I just turned forty-one. I grew up in Baltimore, went to college for two years at Northwestern, and graduated from Brown. My parents are first-generation professionals. My father was an accountant. He grew up working in a family corner grocery store and struggled to make it through college. When I was nineteen, I talked my way into an internship at National Public Radio in Washington and just managed to talk my way into one job after another.

I think about death every day. Last night I was watching *The Sopranos* and at the end of the show they say, 'Next week . . .' The first thought that I have in my mind is, 'If I live that long . . .'

I don't know why I have that attitude, but I think about death all the time, and I always have since I was a little kid. My earliest memory is lying in bed as a child – I grew up in the sixties, I was born in 1959 – and the Vietnam War is going on overseas. And at some point my uncle Lenny went off to Vietnam. I was convinced that the war would go on forever, and that I would get called up and I would be sent to Vietnam, and I was *sure* that I would die in Vietnam. I was sort of a chubby, round little kid and was terrible in all sports. If I was terrible in softball, I would be terrible at running across a field with a gun. [*Laughs*] So I just took it as a given that I would die. So my earliest memory is lying in bed and trying to picture what it would mean to be dead . . . forever. I would talk myself through it. I would think, *OK, what it means is that all of forever will go on, but I will not be there . . .* Things will happen and I won't even know about it and it won't even matter to me because I won't exist. And I wasn't a very gloomy kid either. I think I was a pretty normal kid. I didn't have a bad childhood.

The first person I actually knew who died was a girl in my junior high school named Bonnie Goldschmidt, and she died in a car crash. I remember that. I was about thirteen, fourteen. A bunch of us went out to the junkyard to look at the car. A side had been completely smashed in. The seats were all bloody from these kids who had died. One of the places that we would go all the time, my friends and I, was this cemetery – one of these beautiful park cemeteries. We would ride our bikes around the cemetery. We would get off and walk up to the tombs. We'd look at the markers. Me and my buddies from around the block – just your average suburban kids.

It's funny because the intensity of fear that I had about death as a child, I don't have anymore. I went through several phases of trying to come to some understanding of what I believed. I was raised in a Jewish household: I went to Sunday school and Hebrew school three times a week. By high school I would argue with the rabbis. Judaism, once you get down to what the actual religion teaches, is very vague. What Judaism teaches is that you are good because it is good, because good is self-apparent. You treat other people the right way because that's the right thing and that's that, not because you'll get a reward for it. But on the question of what happens after you die, it's utterly vague . . . there's nothing there. So, starting in my teenage years, I became very interested in Christianity – because it had such a paradigm for what would happen, and such a reassuring paradigm.

My access to Christianity was through the recordings of *Jesus Christ Superstar*. I would listen to those records over and over. My first introduction to Christianity: *Jesus Christ Superstar* . . . I was obsessive about it – it was what I thought about all the time, though I believed none of it. OK, you're the creator of the universe and you're going to set it up so that human beings will be born onto this Earth and they'll be born into sin. They have to believe in this one religion, that this one guy died on the cross, and if they do, they go to Heaven but if they don't believe that one thing, they go to Hell. Even as a fourteen-year-old I thought, *If that's the system, then the system is rigged and I don't care – I'll go to Hell!* But it was so simple – it was really attractive. Any Jew who expresses even a mild interest in Christianity, Christians will come forward to lead you by the hand towards it. The first girl I kissed was this girl who took me to Christian Bible study.

Those of us who were children during the sixties were raised in an environment where it was clear that the way things were going didn't make a lot of sense. I was more of a leftist as a teenager than I've *ever* been since. And the way it would come to you as a child was from the news and everything around you, the television shows and *Laugh-In*, through all these pop-culture things that I think to adults were just candy. Like *Mad* magazine – it had a politics to it that was *so* iconoclastic, yet that doesn't quite capture what it was. There was a politics to it that questioned everything. Even *Spider-Man*, a comic book, was about somebody his society couldn't understand. Every part of culture seemed to be about something terribly wrong in the way that society is set up. There was a real urgency in what I think a lot of us were feeling. I was very strict about what I thought was right and wrong in a way that I don't believe anymore. I think that things are more of a muddle now. It's hard to see clear to what solutions would be to the problems that we see all around us. As a reporter, I see the people who are doing good work with people are people who are doing it on a very small scale. There are a lot of people who are really committed to making things better.

I'm an atheist. I haven't believed in God since I was a teenager. About once every year and a half, I'll get very close to some religious people in the course of the reporting. This summer I went with a group of kids on their first missionary trip. They went to West Virginia to help the – *quote-unquote* – underprivileged. I spent a week with these Christian kids and it came up all the time. I adored them – I loved them. They were wonderful kids. I don't agree with them . . . [*Laughs*] . . . about Heaven, Hell, the hereafter . . .

I think of death coming all the time. I feel like something happened to me four or five years ago, where the future vanished. I see the way that I live my life: I don't have enough time in it, I don't really take the very best care of myself. I've been to a doctor once in the last fifteen years. I think it's because I don't believe in a future for myself – that it could just end like that. I'm just trying to get through this day and get through the next day.

I fear death, but not the raw sort of visceral, gut-wrenching fear I felt as a child. I don't want to sound callous, because I'm glad I'm alive and I don't want to die. But how many more friends are you going to make? How many good conversations can a person have? How much ice cream can you eat in a lifetime? I've been lucky: I get to spend my day doing something that I choose to do. Most people can't say that. That's an incredible thing. I don't imagine myself living to fifty.

KID PHARAOH

He is seventy-three. During his vintage years, he was 'a collector.' I first ran into him about thirty years ago. He was standing on a corner, chewing the omnipresent cigar. He wistfully indicated the Chicago skyline. 'I should have owned some of those buildings. Instead, it's in the hands of thieves, incompetents, and triple-faggots.'

Today, I am a social, economic, and biological failure. I had expectations but I took the wrong road. I met the right people, knew what I was doing, but there was some compunction of self-destruction about myself that I had, and I never got to where I was really going. I'm Assyrian. My paternal grandfather was the private mentor of the King of Persia. He was multilingual in thirteen languages and was educated in Paris. He could read and write and *spoke* the lost languages that Jesus Christ spoke. This is the truth.

The reason my father never got an education was, he was the last son, and the mother had nobody home and she wouldn't let him go. To get even with her, he ran to America because she wouldn't let him get an education. He met my mother, who was an Ohio missionary. There were immigrants coming to America and she was their Bible teacher. There were four of us: a sister, two brothers besides me. My sister died at birth. My brother, he went to the penitentiary. I hustled like hell: peddler, set pins, picked up bottles off porches during the Depression to get two cents to buy candy. I'd go to a craps game. I didn't do anything constructive.

I've lived in the Webster Hotel forty-one years. I'm the residential emeritus. I gave them a quarter of a million dollars in rent. What's interesting – I never had a job. How did I get the money? It's just the crazy acquaintances and things that I did. If people had problems and they couldn't solve them, I solved them. I took money away from people who should have had the money taken away from them. Some didn't deserve what they had. If they'd have a problem, somehow I'd get into it. I always went in small, but it got bigger and bigger. By that time it accumulated, and they couldn't stop giving it to me for fear that they wouldn't get what they really had given me. I went on and on and on. I had six of them, money people – my clients. The bad luck is that all six died on me. All the money people that I knew that were good to me. They had problems. Either money they loaned out wasn't coming back – and it was my job to get it back – or their business was in some difficulty. I was an ex-prizefighter: I would be the guy that would go after whoever it was and straighten it out, whoever had to be straightened out.

I always walked in and I always told them my name was Rocky. I gave it a Mafia image. When they hear that they sort of think twice – how should I put it? – less reluctant to pay. I even collected for Charlie Finley, the baseball owner. He had a problem in Indiana. A guy had fucked him out of five or six thousand, and he sent me there. I'll never forget it. I went to LaPorte, Indiana, and he wasn't there. I called Charlie back and he says, 'Go to his house' – he gave me an address. I had a guy with me. We rang the doorbell. No answer. My guy walked around and he says, 'I swear to God, there's a guy in the kitchen under the table, 'cause I see his feet.' So I says, 'Leave me look' – and, lo and behold, there was a guy, under the table with his feet. He was hiding. I pounded on the window and I says, 'If you don't come out, I'm coming in.' He came out. 'Who are you?' 'I'm Rocky.' 'From where?' 'Chicago.' 'What do you want?' 'Charlie Finley sent me for the money.' 'Oh, I've got it here – all the time I've had it here.'

I could've been a somebody – but I distracted myself. I was taught right by the greatest teachers in the world. It's like Walter Lippmann at Harvard in 1907, with the greatest tenure of professors in any university of all time. He had George Santayana, he had James – not the faggot Henry James, his brother, William – and two or three other mental giants who educated him. I had the great teacher Jack Kearns, who managed Dempsey and Mickey Walker. Kearns knew Jack London, Wilson Meisner, and all them guys. I sold out wherever I went. I was a good club fighter, but I wasn't ranked.

I just fell into collecting. I was very friendly with the boys [the Mob], but I worked independently – as an independent contractor, so to speak. I never understood how these marks, who didn't exactly impress me as representative of the intelligentsia, accumulated this money . . . till I read the book *The Peter Principle*,★ where certain people reach the height of total incompetence. Years later, I look back in anger, and I say to myself: *What did I do to my life to destroy it?* These guys that were handling money had *no* right in the world to handle money.

Just once I got in danger. I was in a restaurant eating, and some guy had a banquet there. The restaurant guy said, 'Go up on Peterson's, on some street. He didn't pay the bill. He's got the money.' I walked in – there were nine coppers waiting. The guy who sent me set me up. The coppers said I threatened the guy with a baseball bat. I never even seen the guy. Went to Reed and Company, polygraphers on Michigan Avenue, took the test and cleared. In other words, in a court of law. They put me on probation. Almost sent me to jail for something I had nothing to do with, never did.

I'm against burial and I'm for, a hundred percent, cremation – because I believe that funerals are barbaric. Loading a guy in a box with a necktie is the most barbaric thing in this century. Haven't we smartened up yet? My God. Shakespeare teaches us it's all a fraud . . .

You're not a religious man?

Not at all.

Was your family Christian?

Yeah, Christian. I'm not Christian.

Do you think there's something after death?

Shakespeare, a great line: 'Death is an undiscovered country from which no traveler returns.' Nobody comes back. Where are they? Where are those guys like Lincoln and them guys. What happened to them? They're in a box? Where? Give us some clue that Jesus is

---

★Laurence J. Peter with Raymond Hull, *The Peter Principle: Why Things Always Go Wrong* (New York: William Morrow, 1969; repr. New York: Buccaneer Books, 1996).

coming back . . . Give me a *clue!* What year is he coming? So we can be prepared.

What about reincarnation?

Fuck no. The great mystery to me is metamorphosis – how that fucking butterfly comes out of a caterpillar. *Unbelievable.* One of the mysteries of nature that they don't write enough about. How interesting, how it goes from one life to another. The caterpillar goes and dies, comes out another one.

Do you believe in God?

I'm from Missouri – you better show me.

Are you afraid of death?

Hell no, but I'm pissed off that I wasn't a success and I didn't leave a legacy of money for my nieces, or a name for myself. Not to go out as a number but to go out as a mensch – a guy who did something constructive, someone who will be remembered. *You!* Who the fuck is going to remember *me?*

Isn't somebody going to remember you?

They forget – people forget.

You're in a couple of books.

Because of *you!*

You feel you were a failure, is that it? What is a success?

Economic security, not necessarily social stature. To be generous to people that came short of the glory of God, you might say, just didn't make it and had the ability. Many are called, few are chosen.

Where do you get these literary phrases?

I've read Walter Lippmann's *Twentieth Century* twenty-six times – he was the smartest. I read the *New York Times Book Review* section to see what they're publishing. I pick it up every week.

You buy it?

Who said anything about *buying* it? One example, somebody had written on *Amos 'n Andy*, the radio show, in the review. The reviewer apparently didn't do his research. If he did, he should have put it in there because it was interesting: the theme song of *Amos and Andy* was the theme song that they played in the theaters on the organ for D.W. Griffith's *Birth of a Nation*. That was a tidbit. How come this reviewer, or the author of the book, didn't have that in there? There's another occasion of the Peter Principle. They reach the height of total incompetence.

Did you ever see people get killed?

Do I know hit men, professional killers? Of course I do.

But you were never in danger?

They knew I had sponsors. That avoided any conflict.

You told me once you don't go to weddings? Why not?

I'm not that type of guy. I don't dance, I don't drink, and I don't flaunt myself like some others I could name. I go to funerals. I never look. Even my own brother died, I never went up to the casket, or my nephew, or my mother, or my father, or my sister – I *never* look. I find it disgusting, absolutely disgusting. I was hustling rugs years ago, oriental rugs. So I went to a funeral home. I had a phony book in my hand. I told the guy, 'I have an oriental rug and I don't want to bring it back. I'll make a deal with you. You want it? Buy it and I'm on my way.' So he took off his gloves and came down. He says, 'Will you take a check?' I says, 'I can't take a check – I'm giving it to you for a price. You want it or you don't.' So he says, 'Follow me to the bank.' He gave me cash. I would sell undertakers.

They'll take a hot stove. Those are the *biggest* thieves in the world. They push the wife over this way to buy the most expensive casket because she would be in grief. And the husband, they got him busy at the other end of the thing. She would sign for the most expensive coffin. But they never sold it to her husband, always to her. Undertakers are the most thieving sons of a bitch on the planet Earth. They're worse than stock manipulators. I tell these guys, 'Here, I'm giving you a fucking bargain, *take* it. Throw me a bone.' I had a big markup with it. They'd come down. But I always showed a profit.

Now, at seventy-three, I can't do much of anything – my spine. I went to the doctor yesterday, he gave me a new pill to help me. I can't walk too good. It's a terrible thing for a man to go out a complete failure. The one sin of nature is that we grow old and die. The great gift of life we got is that they gave us that gift to be a fucking failure. After they give to you good health and good common sense. Now, I don't fear dying. The great fear I have is dying a *failure*. We all go. I don't want to go out a nothing. I want to go out a man among men.

Quinn Brisben

A retired public school teacher. He and his wife are the only white family in an African-American community. His appearance is a cross between the traditional Santa Claus and Colonel Sanders. 'I was a schoolteacher for well over thirty years. I have been active in every progressive cause I could get into from the fifties on.' He's been teaching primarily African-American children. 'I've had three generations in one family sometimes. Some of the worst deaths were when students died. It happens now and again. There was one girl whom I liked very, very much who got shot in a drive-by in the late nineteen eighties. And we've had them go to dope . . .' [Quinn hands me a card.] 'I have donated my body to medical science. Embalming, autopsy should not be performed. An executor will arrange with a funeral director to remove my body to the Anatomical Gift Association of Chicago.'

I think death's going to happen to me. [Laughs] It happens at the rate of one per person. There's no way out of it. I'm sometimes tempted when I see someone jogging in the park to yell at 'em, 'You're gonna die anyhow.'

I am not religious. I've been told all my life I was going to Hell. Fortunately, I read a very good book when I was eight years old, The Adventures of Huckleberry Finn. Huck says, when he realizes he's one of these dirty abolitionists that everybody hates, and that all the preachers in town say you're going to Hell, he says, 'All right, I'll go to Hell, then.' You know, there are things more important than satisfying the religious conventions of your time. And ever since I read Huckleberry Finn, I've believed that.

I think the Greeks were right: you're alive as long as your friends remember you. Now, you've got all these books, Studs. The thing is, you are probably going to be remembered not for what you say but for what Lovin' Al, the guy who parked the cars, said in Working.★ He's

★Studs Terkel, Working: People Talk About What They Do All Day and How They Feel About What They Do (New York: The New Press, 1997 [repr.]).

the one that I happen to remember best. You're going to be remembered for what he says. We both know who Kid Pharaoh was, and he's going to be remembered as Kid Pharaoh, not by his real name.

The thing is that I teach history, and you remember these things. You teach them to students. George Washington led this army. You don't tell them the names of the privates and the corporals, even if they were an important part of this, because nobody can remember everything. Bertolt Brecht wrote this marvelous poem: 'those people that built the Great Wall of China – where did they go for lunch . . .' The more you study something, the more you tend to downgrade the achievements of individual celebrated people and realize how much help they had.

This really got to me when I'd just gotten out of jail in Columbus, Mississippi, in 1964. I'd been in jail for about thirty-six hours, and they released another guy at the same time, a guy by the name of House, from Detroit – some relation to Son House, the blues singer. He had been in for two weeks and he got lice, as it happened. Those were not ideal jails . . . 1995 or '96 or something, the ACLU sued the state of Mississippi and they'd had to tear down half their jails as cruel and unusual punishment. Anyhow, we got back to the Freedom House and I got one of these long combs. You've got to have a fairly fine-toothed thing for this job, combing out lice. You dip it in kerosene and you pull it through the hair – and you've got to get down to the scalp, that's where the louse eggs are. That, in my opinion, is the original for the phrase getting down to the nitty-gritty. So I was doing that with Stu House. This was 1964, and the length of his hair of course was a political statement. He was wearing, I don't know if they called them a natural yet, a 'freedom bush' I think was the name in '64. He was a *nappy* rascal. This was hard work, pulling the lice out with this fine-toothed comb. We had the television on and we'd been kind of left behind.

All the important people were at the Democratic Convention in Atlantic City. It was a great day, the day that Fannie Lou Hamer had testified before the credentials committee. Mississippi Freedom Democratic Party. The Southern Christian Leadership Conference had been part of our group all summer, but Dr. King personally had not endorsed the Freedom Summer Movement. And Goodman, Schwerner, and Chaney had been killed, and a thousand of us had gone to jail – and still no word from Dr. King. Now that we were a complete success, that day Dr. King endorsed Mississippi Freedom Summer – late August. Stu said to me, 'Do you know, you and I are going to go down in history under the name of Martin Luther King.' Well, we have. The civil rights movement takes a whole page and a half in a high school textbook. They mention King, they mention Rosa Parks, they'll mention Malcolm X as the loyal opposition, sort of. They don't have time to mention even Bob Moses, let alone all of us privates and corporals. I wouldn't have it any other way. Martin Luther King absolutely deserves all the honors he's got . . .

I am very grateful to the women – it almost certainly was women – who invented agriculture twelve thousand years ago or so. I don't know any of their names. I don't know a lot of people's names who have contributed to all kinds of things that I enjoy. Somebody invented that machine that even you can operate, the tape recorder, though you *are* notorious for goofing up . . .

There's two things you can do wrong in your personal life. One of them is that you don't prepare for death, that you don't think it's going to happen to you. The other thing is that you don't prepare for living on. I went into a spell, a very severe depression in the late sixties. Most of it was just my personal thing, but the civil rights movement was grinding to a halt, the Vietnam War escalating, Richard Nixon becoming president. I'm sure this added to the troubles. I ended up in a mental hospital with severe depression for about six weeks or so. The thing is, Dr. King had been killed, all kinds of other people had been killed. There were assassinations all during that period. Some people I knew had been killed, like Mickey Schwerner. And I hadn't been. In other words, I was a *failed martyr.* I'd gone out there and risked my ass and there were no takers. I'm this awful failure . . . The thing is that I hadn't prepared: What happens if you *live*? How do you keep on living? I've lived thirty-some years beyond that. So I've got to prepare. There could be a headline in tomorrow morning's *Sun-Times*, Studs Terkel and anonymous die in car crash. That's OK, I'm in your books. I'm going down in history under the name of Studs Terkel, too, just like Lovin' Al and Kid Pharaoh.

I taught high school history for thirty-two years. All of these people who I taught about, whose memory I preserved . . . Every year I taught U.S. history I talked about those guys in the 54th

Massachusetts, charging up on Battery Wagner and getting slaughtered and proving that blacks were willing to fight for their own freedom. I preserved their memory. As for my depression, for one thing Richard Nixon helped. He went steadily down and I felt better because of it. My mother would have said that was un-Christian, but that was the way it was.

Then, I had a family, I had a loyal wife, I had two nice children. I did it better than my father: I'm friends with my grown children. My grandchildren like to be around me. This helped. The school administration never liked me much, but I was popular with the students. There are things I've got left to do. It's important to have things left to do. After you die, other people live on. You saw my card. I am *very* happy to have my physical existence helping some third-year medical student learn something about the human body by cutting me up. That will be it. Oh, maybe I can still achieve martyrdom and there'll be a memorial meeting. Bernard Shaw used to say that martyrdom is about the only way that you can achieve great fame without having any ability. [*Laughs*] The best book that helped me was by Albert Camus, *The Myth of Sisyphus*. He says that you do not want to break off your encounter with the absurd – you keep going on. Also, I'm with Nietzsche on this. He says, 'I love the thought of suicide, it's gotten me through many a rough night.' [*Laughs*] You know, you've always got *that* out if the pain or the humiliation gets too much. But you really don't want to break off that encounter with the absurd – you want to keep going.

I will learn again from Richard Nixon. If that man couldn't be humiliated to death, that's the kind of toughness we all want. Actually, if your favorite organ, the brain, is dead and beyond hope under our present technology of resuscitation, by all means cut your bill to Commonwealth Edison – pull the plug. It's just that I don't want anybody putting pressure on me to pull the plug. I've been active with an organization run by my friend Diane Coleman, who's been in a wheelchair, I guess, all of her life, and it's called Not Dead Yet. She's against this assisted suicide because, if you're running up bills in a nursing home, the temptation is for the management to increase their bottom line by putting pressure on you to pull your plug. Really, people should *not* be talked into suicide. The obligation of the medical profession and everyone else is to talk them out of it, to keep them going on and countering the absurd. If I'm not talk-ing back 'cause my brain is dead and there's no hope of reviving it, that's fine, pull the plug. My favorite nineteenth-century Manchester economist is Ebenezer Scrooge. He used to say, 'If Tiny Tim is going to die, then let him do it and decrease the surplus population.' Nobody's got a right to tell that to Tiny Tim.

KURT VONNEGUT

A writer. Among his more celebrated works is *Slaughterhouse-Five*,
a novel inspired by his experience as an American POW in
Dresden, during the Allied bombings. His most recent sardonic
work is *God Bless You, Dr. Kevorkian*. He is honorary president of
the American Humanist Association.

My first American ancestors had been born Catholics in the north
of Europe, around Münster, Germany. Vonnegut is not a noble
name. There's a stream right outside of Munster which is about the
size of a table, about three and a half feet wide. It's called the Vonne,
the stream. And 'gut' is a piece of property.

My ancestors, educated people, came over before the Civil War.
One on my mother's side of the family lost a leg – I forget what
battle. They settled in the Middle West, founding cities like Chicago,
Milwaukee, St. Louis, and they forgot all about Europe. They didn't
forget about the music, and they didn't forget about the poetry, and
they didn't forget about the language, but they really lost all interest
in German politics.

My ancestors settled in Indianapolis. My paternal great-grandfather arrived with some money, looking for a business to buy. He
bought a brewery. These were well-heeled opportunists, educated
opportunists, as compared with Irish immigrants or Italian immigrants. They arrived here before there was an Ellis Island, before
there was a Statue of Liberty. They were here to settle down and
become American nobility.

My grandfather, Bernard Vonnegut, was born in Indianapolis.
His father, Clemens Vonnegut, the immigrant, had founded a successful hardware store. He was selling rifles and axes and all that. He
had three brothers. They all loved the business, they were making a
lot of money, but Bernard was so unhappy. He wanted to be an
artist. They hardly knew what the hell *that* was. Apparently they had
never had one in the family before. They talked to a guy who knew
something about art. He did the lettering on tombstones, and he
was also a sculptor. He said, 'This boy has to go to Europe.' So by

God, his family sent him. [*Laughs*] He had a hell of a good time. So they told him to come home.

He was stagestruck – theater. He wanted to design sets, but there is no such trade that anybody gets paid for. So he went to MIT instead and took a master's degree in architecture. Then he went to New York and founded a club of young architects, meeting at the Salmagundi Club. His family said: 'Enough is enough! You're having too much fun – come home, get married . . .' So he did. He became the first licensed architect in Indiana. As for religion, my family were rational people, and they decided the priest didn't know what the hell he was talking about. What really shook them was Darwin. That sounded exactly right to them, and it put the Bible out of business. To them, this country did have religious documents: the Declaration of Independence and the Bill of Rights. They had no expectation of an afterlife. They were freethinkers. The Germans were so hated in the First World War, never mind the Second World War, that the freethinkers simply disappeared. They became Unitarians.

My father was partner with his father, my grandfather in Indianapolis. He was an architect who became my grandfather's partner. A lot of buildings in Indianapolis were done by one or the other. But Father was a businessman, and so he had to join Kiwanis, because the people pass around business in Kiwanis insurance and architecture and law and whatever. But he also had to have a religion, because *nobody* wants to deal with a guy who isn't anything, has no religion, which means he's just a wild man. So Father said he was a Unitarian. That was OK. He and his father designed the Unitarian Church out there in Indianapolis. You had to be *something*.

What the freethinkers were are now called humanists. I am one. A humanist believes, because of Darwin, whose truths were so shocking, in making the most use of good science as possible. Humanists behave well without any expectation of either reward or punishment in an afterlife. We serve, as best we can, our community. When I was growing up, nobody ever said anything about Heaven, about an afterlife. They said that this life was enough.

I have experienced what happens when I die, and so have you. We call it sleep. We had a fire in our apartment in New York last February. I was unconscious for three days, in a coma, and I had a near-death experience. I had already written *God Bless You, Dr.*

Kevorkian at that time, and I was talking about the blue tunnel into the afterlife. People who are interviewed on TV every so often tell about their near-death experiences. Some talked about the blue tunnel and it seemed like a good, funny idea to me. It's not a blue tunnel, it's a railroad train – probably because railroad trains used to play such a big part in our lives. When I left Indianapolis to go to the University of Chicago, I got on a train to Chicago. When I came home from the army, from the war, it was on a railroad train – so they're very important symbols. It was parked near the hospital. I could see it. There was a railroad siding. It was just a regular passenger train with a diner and all that. There didn't seem to be any people in it, but it was all lit up inside. I knew that if I died, I'd be put on a gurney, I wouldn't have to walk to the train. Off I'd go. It wasn't a terrifying image at all.

I wish I'd died on D day, it would have saved a lot of trouble . . . [*Laughs*]

If you'd died, we wouldn't have had Slaughterhouse-Five, *we wouldn't have had . . .*

You would have had *so* many good books. [*Laughs*]

My parents certainly relieved me of all terror of death just by their own attitudes. They never made death seem a threatening thing at all. And, you know, I look at the Sistine Chapel, with people going to Hell and all that, I have to wonder, *could a man as intelligent as Michelangelo believe this?* [*Laughs, wheezes*] It's hard for me to give credence to that. But as a humanist, I've never tried to talk anybody out of religion. We don't proselytize at all. My particular war buddy, who's dead now, is a guy I put in a couple of stories in the book, Bernard V. O'Hare. When you're in the army, in the infantry, you're essentially married to somebody else, you look out for each other, you pair off – particularly prisoners of war. O'Hare was a Roman Catholic, but when the war was over O'Hare gave up on Catholicism. We parted company in Newport News, where the troopship finally put us to shore. He said he was through with God and with Catholicism. I didn't think the war was that bad, and I knew that Catholicism was a very nourishing, helpful thing. And honorable. I was very sorry to have him take the war that hard. He lost something

I'd never had. God is a shorthand for everything. Like *tout le monde*, there's the whole universe. What I've said about humanists is that we sure as hell know something very important is going on – we just don't know what it is.

Einstein's $E = mc^2$ is an extraordinary concept. So radical: matter and energy are two phases of the same sort of general stuff. There's only one other idea that radical: Forgive us our trespasses as we forgive those who trespass against us.

The whole idea of revenge was so reputable that Hammurabi, a great leader somewhere in the Middle East, wrote the Code of Hammurabi: an eye for an eye and a tooth for a tooth. Somebody pointed out this was in fact a peaceful proposal. He wasn't recommending that somebody take an eye for an eye or a tooth for a tooth. He was saying, 'Take that much and no more.' [*Laughs*] But then came this radical idea: If you are injured, don't avenge yourself. What kind of a person is that who doesn't seek revenge? $E = mc^2$, try this: Forgive us our trespasses as we forgive those who trespass against us. The Lord's Prayer, of course.

You were a prisoner of war, and you were in the cellar there in Dresden, being bombed by the Allies. Weren't you scared?

There's no point in being scared – you're just asking what kind of animal is a human being? You just sit there with hands over your head to avoid the plaster falling. And try not to start crying or yelling or anything. The reason we didn't suffocate is the slaughterhouse was full of open areas for penning the animals. So there wasn't that much combustible there.

About five years ago I got a letter from a woman who said she was about to have a baby and did I think it was a terrible thing to bring such a sweet, innocent animal into a world this terrible. So I replied that what made being alive almost worthwhile for me was saints I met – people who behave decently in an indecent society. They're all over the place. I ran into them in the army, and I ran into one just today. Think about the saints you meet in the course of an ordinary day. And then I tell people, 'Perhaps some of you will be saints for this woman's child to meet.'

You know what Sartre said? 'Hell is other people.' It's a threat. I have said that inconvenience is other people, and inconvenience can be *Hell*. People are in the way all the time. That's Hell enough.

Andrew Lloyd Webber set new music to a requiem that came out of the Council of Trent in 1500, something like that. The Reformation had begun, and the Catholic Church was really quite pissed off. This requiem came out. It was at St. Thomas Church – this is on Fifth Avenue in New York; it has its own boy's choir. It was by invitation only. I had to wear a tuxedo, my wife had to wear an evening gown. We were lucky enough to be invited. We sat there and heard these boys singing in Latin. These lovely high voices, boys whose voices hadn't changed. They were looking up at Heaven and loving God so much and everything. I happened to look at the English translation of what they were singing. Terrible things were going to happen to people after they died. [*Laughs*] One line was, 'Even the innocent may be punished.' People were going to be fed to lions and thrown into lion pits and all that after they were dead. And the sheep were going to be separated from the goats. It was a horrible, sadistic document and there was no reason to love God at all. So I went home and that night wrote a new requiem, a secular requiem. In it I said there will be a moment of great hilarity when people find out that nobody's going to be punished. There are people who want a whole lot of people punished and then they get to Heaven and there aren't going to be any punishments. [*Laughs*]

What about a guy like Hitler?

In one of my books, I wrote about Hitler's last words. As he's down there in the bunker and the Russians are right up above him, and if they catch him they're going to put him in a cage and show him around and humiliate him, piss on him. So he's definitely gonna have to kill himself. The whole question is what his last words should be. There are other witnesses to hear his last words. Goebbels is there, and Martin Bormann, to hear what this great man's last words are. And Hitler says, 'I regret nothing.' Goebbels points out to him that this is in fact a song by Edith Piaf. People are going to see the similarity. She was called 'the little sparrow.' His last words are going to be the same thing the little sparrow says. Finally he says, 'I never asked to be born in the first place.' And he blows his brains out. What are you gonna do? You know what the punishment was for counterfeiting in the time of Henry VIII? Being boiled in public. [*Laughs*] That was how much they didn't want anybody to mess with the currency. [*Laughs*]

The fact that forgive us our trespasses as we forgive those who trespass against us isn't honored more – I blame that on writers. Because the easy story to tell is the vengeance story, and it's known to satisfy. This guy shot my brother. How's the story gonna wind up? And what does a reader think? OK, that's settled. So it's just the easiest of all stories to tell. So it in fact encourages, makes *reputable* vengeance.

What about physician-assisted suicide? Your view of Kevorkian is, of course, an affirmative one.

Yes, because I think that's good medicine too. There's no murders prevented by our keeping doctors from putting people out of their misery. My mother committed suicide right before I went overseas. She was so unhappy she thought it was time.

Has the thought ever occurred to you?

Of course. I have attempted it. One of the legacies is that suicide is a way to solve problems. In one of my books I said, if Farmer A can harvest seven pecks of potatoes an hour, and he's joined by Farmer B, who can harvest three pecks of potatoes an hour, and there are one thousand potatoes to every square acre, how long will it take Farmer A and Farmer B, working together, to harvest five acres? My answer is: I think I'll blow my brains out. [*Laughter*]

I've told my lawyer and I've told my oldest son what I wanted for a funeral service. It's not to be in any holy place, it's not to take place in New York City. I don't want a Viking funeral where they put a guy on a boat with treasure and set it on fire. I want it to be on Cape Cod, where I raised my family, and I want to be cremated and my ashes scattered over Barnstable Harbor.

I've seen grand funeral services in New York City, even with videos and famous people speaking and all that. If I'm to be remembered, the work's all been done, that's the final ceremony. [*Laughs*] I just want a farewell.

In *Slaughterhouse-Five*, every time somebody dies, and when a bottle of champagne loses its bubbles and is dead, I always say, 'So it goes' – that's all. Whenever anybody has died – and this would be my sister, my brother, my father, my mother, and I was nearby for those events – that's how I felt . . . That was that . . . I had nobody to appeal to, to get mad at. [*Laughs*] When somebody dies, it's wholly unsurprising and so it goes. What could be more ordinary?

The Boomer

BRUCE BENDINGER

During the seventies, he was a wunderkind in the world of advertising. He had been Gerald Ford's creative director during his 1976 campaign for the presidency. Our first conversation was in 1986: 'I'm a hired gun for a couple of companies fighting the warfare of the marketplace. I'm an eighties version of Paladin. The battlefield is corporate America. I'm still fast on the draw and I'm quick to pick up trends. One of the things is called pattern recognition: it's the ability to pick up quick little bits, out there in the environment, and come to the right answer ahead of the rest of the pack. They pay me enough to do it that I can't afford to take time off and tend my garden.'* Today he is the director of marketing 'for a company that stands a good chance of making a bit of money in the new economy.'

My mother's generation, there you're really watching just everybody kind of wear out. My stepfather is a retired submarine captain. He sank boats in World War II – he was a hero. A bright man, a smart man – burned out. There's just a lot of parts that are not happening. Some of the software's going in the system – you know, memory. When I'm talking about software, I'm talking about the software between your ears. My stepfather can talk to you about how atomic reactors work and battles he fought in World War II, but he can't remember what time his doctor's appointment is. It's just, the stuff's wearing out. I think that we're all gonna be, as a species, living a little longer, a little healthier. But some of it, we just . . . Right now, my generation is seeing our parents' generation just wear down. And we see that as our fate, maybe, but we still think we're thirty. I'm not sure that we're really aware.

*Studs Terkel, *The Great Divide: Second Thoughts on the American Dream* (New York: Pantheon, 1988).

My generation has been a self-absorbed one. It's totally unprepared for this next stage of life – leaving life. You have a drink or two in the evening and somebody talks about what's really on his mind, the end of some career path, the end of unfulfilled expectations. They're really very much at sea as to where things are going. It's something I see all around me.

From a marketing standpoint, our generation has been the straw that stirs the drink. Every moment in history, whether it was new schools for the new baby boomers, new colleges, new cultural changes, new voting blocks, new markets moving from Volkswagens to SUVs, is determined by the boomer generation's taste, conditioned of course by very media-sophisticated marketing people. It is absolutely startling to me how marketing has taken over our society. What you do in marketing is: you plan for next year. Whatever business you're in, whatever plans you make, the conclusion for next year is always: Do it faster, more, cheaper. It's always some intensifying of what's going on. The frenzy in which we live is, in many ways, a result of this kind of increasing flywheel effect. Everybody's multitasking. Things are flying by. You got a hundred channels and nothing's on. The pace of life right now has been accelerated past our ability to live it.

I was born during World War II, a baby boomer. We've had our foot on the gas for fifty years. And now, as we hit the twenty-first century, we have really accelerated past, I think, what is good for people. What the baby boomers have done by putting all of our children in front of *Sesame Street* with channel changers in their hands and then in their heads, we have made intense but disconnected audiovisual images, just like MTV, the dominant mental processing of this generation. We're getting these children to have these short, disconnected attention spans – not verbal, highly stimulated. Television is like calorie-free food: everybody sitting in front of the television has only one thought, *I wonder if there's anything else on*. You're not really thinking. So how can we think about such a thing as death? Suddenly we start to lose people our age. These things are coming closer and closer to us. This is something that's happening to this particular demographic. Because of the speed of things, if you are of a certain age and you haven't been able to regularly update your software, you're in a *lot* of trouble. If your only skills are in old industries, you've got yourself a real situation. If you didn't update your software, you're still running old programs, you're not going to be having a very good time.

Right now, the topic most people deal with is either an upcoming retirement or seriously aging parents. A lot of us right now are in the role of parenting our parents. Both ourselves and our parents are a little startled at this new set of circumstances. I think we're making the best of it. In many cases it's a chance to get reacquainted with our parents in a whole different way.

My first memory of death was in fifth, sixth grade. The biggest, strongest kid in the class, Peter Jansen, was going to be the fullback. He got blindsided by stomach cancer at about the age of twelve. And I watched the strongest kid on the block leave us. It wasn't the last time I cried, certainly, but that was the moment where it all really got nailed for me. I was eleven or twelve. He didn't even have time to have a prime of life. I'm startled by how vividly and clearly I remember sitting on the living room couch and coming to grips with the strongest kid on the block being gone. A good-hearted kid – he wasn't a bully. He was the guy that would have protected you if somebody was trying to push you around.

If there's a spirit, if there's a God, you know, hey, I'm a fan. I don't know if there is a God – it's not central to me. I believe in life, I believe in how we should live. I believe we're here, each of us is here, to answer the big question – which is to figure out why we're here. I look at you, and I've figured out why you were here. I talked to you earlier about various times you touched my life, really, from like sixth, seventh, eighth grade on . . . How I got touched by *Division Street*. How I got touched by *Working*. How you touched my life was part of why you're here. Why am I here? I've got my own little job to do. I do books that help the young and women learn about the business that will help them make a living. It's like I'm teaching people how to fish – I'm teaching people how to fish in the marketplace. How to stay in touch with a world that has gotten dangerous and fast-moving.

I wrote a book about an advertising guy who died, Howard Gossage. He was one of the founders of *Ramparts* magazine.★ He

★An irreverent monthly out of the West Coast. Its vintage years were the sixties.

introduced Marshall McLuhan to the world. I was involved with the trail he left, putting together the puzzle of his life. Howard had disappeared from sight and from the minds of people in the ad industry. I put this little book together, and his memory lives again. They named the hundred top people in the advertising industry in the twentieth century, and a guy who was off the charts four years before we put the book out is now the thirtieth most important person in advertising history. His daughter was six months old when he died. So thirty years later, this book shows up. She said, 'If it weren't for your book, I never would have known who my father was.' That's a good reason to figure out why I'm here.

I believe there's something going on out there that's bigger than us. Just the whole mystery of life is, like, *holy smoke!* The way people are built, the way our minds work, the way our hands connect with our eyes and our brains, the amazing creativity of nature . . . I make my living in what they call the creative department. What I do to sell a box of detergent – it's really incredible. I don't know what Hell is down the road, but it's Hell on earth if you hate how you spend your days.

I had a very good friend, this guy – well, let it ride . . .

We live in a world where you've got to keep updating the software. I think we're finding out that a lot of what we thought were defects of character, it's really that you got yourself dealt a little bit of a strange hand in terms of your body chemistry, your mental chemistry – a bug in your software. If you're schizophrenic, you've got an organic software, a problem in your brain that doesn't have anything to do with you having a bad attitude, or how Mom and Dad raised you.

We're all going to be victimized finally when this wonderful life we have just kind of wears out. I'd say that if you're getting towards that age, write something down and take the burden off the people who love you.

Instead of a headstone, I'd like to have a bench somewhere with a pretty nice view, where somebody could just sit in the middle of their day. Nobody's going to be doing that in the middle of a graveyard. I could just give somebody a nice moment in their day. They could park their butt down on a bench and take a deep breath and think about things. If you want to be immortal, have a kid. Go to a sperm bank. That's another path to immortality: have a kid, hope you're lucky. Don't have too many expectations in this world because, at a certain point, you get the immortality but you don't necessarily get to write the script of that next person's life. And that's that.

One other thing that is interesting about the software. We all seem to operate better when we believe in something. If you look at people who have some sort of religious belief, whether it's humanistic or some particular lodge hall, people who have some sort of belief live longer – they operate better. Life isn't just about them. If you want to live longer, believe in something and feel good about it. Today, we live in a time where we have to keep reinventing ourselves, and I've reinvented myself. I was in advertising and, at a certain point, they want to see some young guy there. So either you send in a young actor to play you in the meeting or you go find something else to do. Exit laughing.

PART III

PART III

Fathers and Sons

Doc Watson

A blind folksinger. He was born and raised in Deep Gap, North Carolina. 'I feel that music is an expression of people's joy and sorrows and all the in-betweens that come along in life.'

Was my family religious? I've heard people call Dad's religious approach to the Almighty *fundamentalist*. He wasn't exactly that. He wasn't as strict as a lot of people. Some of the people there used to skin me alive. I was playing with a dance band in the fifties. A cousin of mine, a Baptist preacher, he used to say, 'Doc, you shouldn't play that music – you ought to play gospel music all the time.' One day, right after I moved out with my sweetie on our own, he came up to the house and I *knew* he was going to get on the subject in about two minutes. I said, 'Brother, you were talking to me the other day about music,' and I said, 'I've been thinking about the good old book that you and I both love.' I said, 'In that book, it says the man that provides not for his own house is denied the faith and is worse than an infidel. I figure if I can get out there and earn a little of that money them old boys are blowing on booze and beer and the slot machines at the VFW clubs and help my sweetheart raise these two little children, I don't think I'm doing too bad. Can you help what they do with the lumber you cut at your sawmill? They may build beer joints or houses of prostitution or whatever.' He says, 'I never thought about that.' I said, 'Well, you better think about it.' [*Laughs*]

Music covers everybody trying to find their way.

My dad was a singing leader at the church, but he made me my first little stringed instrument, a homemade banjo, when I just had turned eleven, in '34. I took it to the School for the Blind over at Raleigh the first year, with me. A little later on I said, 'Dad, pick me another piece on the banjo. You showed me a few things.' He said,

'Son, you can pick it better than I can.' He handed the banjo to me and he said, 'Here, learn to play it real well. It might help you get through the world.' The best thing he ever did for me, Studs, was put me to work on the end of a crosscut saw when I was fourteen. I didn't have to sit in a corner, and he knew it.

He had a little hillside farm where we grew about what we needed to eat. He also did a lot of work when he wasn't in the fields on Public Works jobs – everything from having built some of the buildings at ASU College in Boone to doing work on the highway. He was what they call Freewill Baptist. My mother – there were lots of hymns, too. Mama knew a few of the old ballads. She'd sing some of the sweeter ones to the little children when she'd rock them to sleep. Somebody said to me once, 'Did your mother play the guitar?' And I said, 'No, she raised nine little brats – she didn't have time to learn it.'

From the time I can remember, I was vaguely aware of death. My first memories of music, in the form of singing, unaccompanied singing, were at the church. I was sitting on my mother's lap, I must have been about two, and they were singing 'The Lone Pilgrim' and 'There's a Foundation Filled with Blood.' 'The Lone Pilgrim' speaks of death. I can remember thinking about the fellow who went to the old boy's grave and stood there in contemplation of the man's life: 'I came to the place where the lone pilgrim lay and intensively stood by his tomb.' I think that headed me in the right direction to a little later think about death for what it really was, because they took us to funerals from the time I was just a little boy. Death was talked about, and Heaven, and the danger of being lost. They didn't fully understand how to clarify the truths to young children. I had to learn about that later, the truth of the gospel. But death was certainly there, very present from the time I was a little boy.

I believe in the presence of the Almighty and spirit in our lives – I believe that with all of my heart. If I hadn't, I don't know what I would have done when we lost Merle.* There was times on the road

*Merle Watson, Doc's son and colleague for many years – 'and a very able musician' – died in 1985 at the age of thirty-six as the result of a tractor accident.

when I had to go to my knees at the hotel rooms after we'd do gigs. Me and this boy over here, Jack Lawrence, and T. Michael Coleman that played bass with us – it was tough. Without that assurance, I don't know what I would have done.

Three weeks before Merle's fatal accident, we were coming back from Nashville. I said, 'Son, I'm not the best candidate I can think of to talk about this with you, but if old death was to slip up on you, how is it between you and the good Lord?' He said, 'Dad, I've been on my knees in the woods and I've made my peace with him – I don't have to worry about that.'

His mother, Rosalie, taught him his first chords when I was on the road in '64. Ralph Renzler called me and told me Merle had started playing the guitar. Man, I was in seventh heaven. I couldn't wait to get back home and hear him. I got back and he was already doing some finger-style things. He started doing occasional jobs in the summer in '64. His first trip was to the Berkeley Folk Festival. We worked together a long time.

When I first heard of Merle's death, I was numb emotionally. I couldn't cry for a long time. Even when I was by myself, I couldn't cry. It was so unbelievable, so unreal. When you're in shock . . . There was scrap paneling that I was going to use for kindling left over. I worked a whole day the week after his funeral cutting that stuff up with a little, tiny saw. And all I could think about was his laughter and his enjoyment of a trip we did in '68 to Africa. Especially the sounds, and how we talked about the different birds, the mynah birds and things that were in the wild and their natural calls. And I could hear all of that. It was just as real as if he was standing there by me. The hurt didn't come down fully, the full hurt to where I could really shed some tears and lift the load, for oh, two or three years, or four. I wasn't fittin' to be amongst man nor beast for a long time. It's the hardest . . . I can't describe it.

I guess, if I can be honest with you, I overcame it with God's help. I don't think *I* did it. I think I just leaned on the promise that He'll get you through if you trust him. I'm as honest with you as I can be. I'm not a saint, Lord knows. Faults, just like me and you and everybody else has got. I just . . . He helped me through it, that's all I can say.

Between his accident and the funeral, I had called my manager and told him to cancel the tour we were about to do, I wasn't going back on the road. But financially we had just built a new house and my family was in need and the savings was gone. I dreamed that night that I was in a desertlike place, and it was *hot*. Like quicksand, I couldn't go any farther, and I could feel the darkness, it was so awful. And I thought, *I just can't make it*. And that big, old, strong hand reached back and said, 'Come on, Dad, you can make it.' And he helped me out to where it was cool and it was sunny, and I waked up. And I knew God sent him. His resting place is right close to our yard. It's our own family cemetery, immediate family. We fixed it with the state. I've already taken care of our immediate family's funeral expenses.

Merle's son Richard does occasional jobs with me, festivals, whatever. He plays mainly blues. His dad taught him some blues licks before the accident. But he waited a long time before, one day, he said, 'Pa, I'd like to play some music with you.' So we began to work and we did a little tape first, and then recently we did a CD called *Third Generation Blues*. We used Merle's guitar as the stand-in for him in the cover picture.

I think the good in our lives, if you will, is gleaned out and left to live in our offspring. I believe in an afterlife, but I don't believe in reincarnation. I envision an immortal soul that's us, that goes on, besides what we leave here in our offspring as immortality. When we're young fellas and newly married and the little ones come along, we don't think about how strict an example we need to set and the gentleness we need to instill in our offspring, rather than being a bossy daddy or mama and all that kind of thing. All of that has to come down, and it's a shame that it comes down too late in our lives most of the time. [*Laughs*] I look back and see so many things I left undone with Merle – little things that would have mattered so much. I could have done a better job of living rather than talking about it to Merle and things like that. I was angry at God because I thought I needed Merle worse than eternity did. But then I thought about it. I'm not going to go into detail about this because we don't need to. [*He pauses and sighs several times.*] Merle, as far as his domestic life and his love life, had one hell of a rough time. And the road, because of his emotional depression and his load, was too hard on the boy. He was about to get mixed up in some things that would have utterly destroyed him. We found out from a paper that Merle got from the specialist where he was examined in Winston-Salem some months before his accident that he had a brain tumor. It probably caused the accident. Instead of giving it to the family physician, he left it hid in his files at home so Rosalie would find it some time after his death and know that that was the probable reason. Merle knew he was going to die, he didn't know for sure when, but he knew it as good as the Almighty knew it. He never told us. He didn't want to worry us with it – he was like that. He knew that we'd pamper and baby him, and he didn't want any part of that. He wanted to live as near normal as he could possibly with his load of problems. I understood that, though. It took me a while. I eventually said, 'Lord, I guess you knew it was time for him to check out and get out of this trouble.' But it sure left us with a load. Will I overcome it? It will be here as long as I am. His memory is so richly celebrated with that annual Merle Fest where all the top folk artists come. Fifty thousand people show up annually.

My life's been seventy-seven years long with all its problems and misunderstandings and regrets in some cases. To me, Heaven is a place where everything will be perfect. There'll be no sickness, none of that – all will be good. It's a utopia that mortal man dreams of making upon this earth which, in my book, will never happen. Because we're mortal and all of us have misgivings about everything.

I think the flames of Hell is a representation, but I think it exists as a place without the knowledge of God. A place of total mental darkness and regret. A mortal mind couldn't even comprehend the awfulness of it. I think it's reserved for those who become totally evil, all the way to the core – I really do believe that. Because if there wasn't, how could there be a Heaven? If everybody got in there and the bad ones who have no thought of caring for other people or don't care who they kill or what kind of misery they cause, how could they be let in the gate? You have to call Heaven out too, if you don't believe in Hell. I have thought and wondered if – Merle was such a fast-learning, good musician – taking him on the road with me affected his life and caused his problems. But I've sorted it out to the best of my ability and asked for guidance from the Almighty. And I've come to the conclusion that Merle's problems could very probably have been worse if he hadn't gone with me. Because he had the music, he found a lot of friends, and he loved the music. The road was, as the old saying goes, tough as the devil on the boy. But there's some things I have thought, maybe I shouldn't have done it. And that thought hurt me. And then I'd begin to use a little faith and a whole lot of reason to think about all the problems he had. And I put it aside. I don't let that trouble me. I think Merle's life on the road with me was meant to be, I think it was in the cards.

POSTSCRIPT

When I think of you and Merle, I think of the old hymn 'Will the Circle Be Unbroken?'

I've always loved that song. It's an old hymn, long before A.P. Carter did his arrangement of it. Let me give you the lyrics that was probably in an old hymn book:

> *We have loved ones gone to glory*
> *Whose dear forms we often miss*
> *When we close our earthly story*
> *Shall we join them in their bliss*
> *Will the circle be unbroken by and by, by and by*
> *There's a better home awaiting far beyond the starry sky.*

In this other version, the last verse says: [*sings*] 'We can picture happy gatherings around the fireside long ago / And recall the tearful partings when they left us here below.'

It's just as real as life itself for those who believe. Whoever wrote it was inspired to write it because of the way they felt about life and death and the hereafter. [*Sings*]

> *Oft they told us in our childhood of that happy land above*
> *Pointing to the dying savior as they told us of his love*
> *Will the circle be unbroken by and by, by and by . . .*

I may do another gospel album sometime before I lose the old voice and age takes the vocals down to where I can't sing. I have some allergies, but I told the boys on the festival, I said, 'I can still croak 'em out pretty good, boys.' [*Laughs*] I love to sing gospel and hymns I heard when I was in church. I get a lot of enjoyment out of that.

VERNON JARRETT

He retired as a columnist for the *Chicago Tribune* as well as the *Chicago Sun-Times*. He had begun his newspaper career as a journalist for the *Chicago Defender*. For years, he conducted a weekly television program on Chicago's ABC affiliate.

Deaths were quite frequent in the black community. The life expectancy of black men and women was anywhere from ten to twelve years less than whites. It seemed as though somebody was always dying. The old folk used to sit around at nights, before we had radio, before we had record players, and certainly before television, and remember when old sister so-and-so died, and how she looked. Older people always explained predilections about how they would like to die and warnings of death in the clouds, or in the shadows at night that the moon liked to give. [*Laughs*] As little boys and girls in the South, you grew up sitting there listening because you weren't permitted to talk. Our entertainment was relating to each other at night great moments in your personal histories. Some of these stories you heard over and over and over, until they became real to you . . . About how a friend died right after a big picnic in the country. They used to say, 'He died from indigestion,' when he was actually having a heart attack. I used to hear that all the time.

I remember when B.B. died, one of my little playmates. First grade. Because people were very poor, when my dad took me to the wake, he didn't have a casket. He was laying on what they used to call the cooling board. It took a little time for them to raise money to get him a little casket. I remember going by and there was little B.B. laying up there. I blamed God for this. Why would God do this to a little boy? A little innocent *child*. Do I believe in God? The whole God concept is unavoidable. Whether you believe there was an identifiable God, as we grew up believing, is too heavy for us. I don't think our brains will ever be able to understand the idea of a God. So we make it up. The human being has the capacity to create situations to make up for what you don't know. So we are going to create a God. Who knows?

My paternal grandfather used to come and live with us in Trenton, Tennessee. Two thousand people. My maternal grandmother used to come, too, because they were very old. They sat around and talked all the time. She would read the Bible to him. He couldn't read, but we didn't know it. He claimed his eyes were bad – actually, he was illiterate. Both of them were ex-slaves. They talked about dying, and they remembered specific deaths all the time. How some people saw signs in the sky predicting death – sometimes the image of it was on the clouds. They were saying, 'That looks like old man so-and-so. We don't know whether he's going to make it to next year.' [*Laughs*] They had me believing all that too. Shadows that were on the outhouse in our backyard had the configuration of the moonlight through the clouds, and these configurations might take the shape of some face that they knew – and people would become worried. Especially if you were already ill, usually somebody old. They didn't see any for young people.

My grandfather was very strict, very stern. I didn't like him too much. He didn't like it when I asked him questions. He was a runaway slave. We learned later that he didn't know where he came from. He just ran north. One Sunday morning, I went to Sunday school and I was mad at him. He had pushed me around a bit, whupped me, because I talked back to him once. I asked the Sunday school teacher, 'Who was God's father?' She said, 'You don't believe in God, little boy?' I said, 'Yes, I do – but I would like to know who was God's father.' She made me go sit in the corner and reported me to my parents . . . [*laughs*] because I was entertaining atheistic thoughts. I guess I couldn't have been over seven. Finally she said, 'There's God the son, the father, and the Holy Ghost, and that's all you need to know if you are a true believer.' I just swore I was a believer. I said, 'OK, you told me who God's father is, but who was God's grandfather?' I thought about that all my life. I'm grandfather-conscious. I wanted to know. She couldn't tell me who his grandfather was. Then I asked her, did God's grandfather ever give him a whipping when God was a little boy? [*Laughs*]

The question reoccurred when my son died. I had a hard time, even when I was a strict churchgoer, believing that a loving God – a God that everybody says is such a loving God – would make sinners burn forever. I remember one time I burned my finger on the stove when I was a kid, and I said, 'Oh, this is awful!' I said, 'I wonder what it must be like to burn for an eternity . . .' What kind of God is this that would make somebody burn forever because they didn't believe the same thing that somebody on earth said? I said, 'This whole thing is outrageous. I *cannot* believe that any God would do that to anything that He made!' If you knew we were going to burn, why didn't you make us different? These are questions that used to go through my mind as a kid. I used to have conversations with God. I'd say, 'Why would you do a thing like that?'

People have to have something to hang on to. Black people say, 'We identify with the Supreme Being. We're not worried about you white folks here now, because you're gonna get yours.' That's the way the older people used to think – God is going to take care of you guys, you people who are brutalizing us and lynching us. Our day is coming. God is going to see to that, because we're God's children.

My son, William Robert Jarrett, I took a special interest in. He was my firstborn. I have two sons. I named him after my father. When his son came, he named his son after me. This is a reverence that we learned early to have for our elders. When he died, he was forty-one. Let me tell you what happened to me. Despite the fact that I had dismissed the idea of Heaven or Hell, I didn't have the gall to say there's no such thing as God. I think you have to be very careful to say what is not. For somebody to say there is no God, well, what is there?

When my son died, I started getting these wonderful phone calls. 'Brother Jarrett, you will see your son again, in glory, in Heaven. God has a way already mapped out for us, and this is just one phase of our transition.' One person, whom I had high respect for, who is in the sciences, said something about our being just like the butterfly, maybe one thing in one world and maybe a worm in another. Mostly, it was, 'You will see your son again in glory.' You know, that made me feel good. That's when I realized I needed to hear something like that. The thought, even today, of never, ever meeting again is an awesome thing. *Never!* You can call this fiction all you want to, but we need to create these bromides to make us feel better, like you need a drink . . . or like some people smoke a cigarette. You need something to give you the lift to continue on. Because if you conclude that this is all there is . . . You know that song, 'Is That All There Is?' You say, 'Is this all there is to it?! You mean we're through?' – then you leave the door open really for everybody to go out and exploit everybody else if they want to, say, 'Let me get mine.' Or kill themselves. This is the law of the jungle. Why do you want to live? There's no aftermath. It's only a matter of time before I'll be forgotten, everything I'm doing will be forgotten, so why bother?

I think this is the genesis of all the religions. People need something. Can you imagine being a slave in America, where you don't see any future at all for your physical being? So what you have is a spiritual being that is going to outlast the rest of this. I used to hear my grandmother and the other old ex-slaves sit around and sing 'When the Saints Go Marching In': 'I want to be in that number.' Suppose they didn't have that song . . . They *couldn't* say: 'This is all. This is it. There's nothing left.' So you have to create something to make you want to bother with just being here.

I remember the first Christmas Eve after my son's death – he died in November. I went out to the graveyard in the afternoon – it wasn't sunset yet, but almost. Ice was on the ground, and snow. I didn't see any cars or anybody near Oakwood Cemetery. I parked right in front of my son's grave and I said to myself, 'It's just wrong to say he's out there in the cold ground. If he is living, and I hope he's living, it's going to be through me or his brother or his friends or his mother, and his grandchildren.' I just had to disabuse myself of the thought that he's out there in the cold ground. That's how my mother used to think. When my dad died, she spent a big chunk of the insurance money on an expensive vault. You know why? She said, 'I just don't want my husband out there wet in the cold. I want a leakproof vault where, on the coldest days, he will be dry.' She felt so much better spending that money. I think that thing cost us two thousand dollars.

When my grandmother Harriet Jane Thomas died, she suffered for three or four days. The word got out in the church and in the neighborhood that she was dying. It was a simple ailment. Today it would have been knocked out in no time – gallstones. She had lost consciousness. There was a little ritual in the semirural South. After they have decided that you are beyond hope, they take the pillow from under your head. I remember my brother, when he heard that, he said, 'Don't *ever* take the pillow from under my head!' I said, 'Me either! Leave that pillow under my head because something may happen that I come back to life!'

I can remember all the specifics of that afternoon when my grandmother died. The people in the neighborhood would come by and pat her on the hand and say something to her. It took a little of the edge off of the suddenness of death. I think she was about three days out of it. People would come by, and they'd pray and they'd bring stuff to the house. When she finally died, somebody called a mortician from another town, because we didn't have a black mortician. The white morticians then did not want to do black funerals or burials. This man came over with his assistant and they left my grandmother in the room where she died. That evening, while all the other older folks were in another room around the fireplace talking and eating their dessert, I went outside and peeked in the window. I saw them begin the embalming process. I remember they put this jug right up under her arm and they cut a slit in her arm and put a tube in the vein, and the blood started coming out. That's when I left.

They used to have the wakes in the house. The casket stayed open. The speech-making was at the funeral. I grew up going to funerals all the time when I was old enough to walk. I cried at all the funerals – I didn't have to know who it was. My brother used to get on me. He'd say, 'You little phony – you don't even *know* these people.' But you learned to accept the things for all mankind. I used to feel real sorry for whoever was dead. The older people would take you there because they wanted you to get accustomed to the fact that you can die, that you're not going to live forever. They really drilled that into your mind. I'd go by the coffin and try to peep up and look at them or pat them.

There was one other death too that put much on my mind. I watched an execution here in Chicago. I was a reporter for the *Chicago Defender*. The guy who was supposed to write the story said he just couldn't go out there because he'd been following the trial. It was a young man in his very early twenties. This could have been '47. I'm young, I'm just starting. It was 26th and California – Cook County Jail. We left everything we possessed, maybe outside of a pencil and a notepad, with the guards. The guy had killed a store owner. I said to myself, 'I'm sitting here awaiting a human death.' It was the strangest feeling in the world – that we could take life quite that lightly. I was so traumatized by it, and I didn't write the story: I missed my deadline, I went to a tavern, I just sat there, I didn't even talk to anybody. I didn't know what to say. Two men brought him in blindfolded, his head had been shaven, and he stumbled a little and they sat him down in the electric chair. They braced him up and he made one or two little moves.

The thing I remember is the callousness of this famous South Side cop, named Two-Gun Pete.* He was there acting as though he was a tour guide. I wanted to tell him, 'Would you shut your damn mouth.' He says, 'Now, don't feel sorry for this guy because he deserved it. He had it coming – he asked for it.' Then he said, 'Now what you're going to see is, they're going to put these cathodes or whatever on his legs and something on his arms and head, and you may see a little smoke come up from the side.' He just talked his tail off all the moments prior to the execution. When they brought that boy in, they set him down in a hurry, buckled him up. I remember there was this pause in between. It seemed like hours, but it was a split second. He sat there, buckled his chest, heaved twice, and he went limp. I said to myself, 'What is this all about?' The guy, Two-Gun Pete, almost bragged about killing the man. My mind had to go all the way back to people in civilized France where the crowds enjoyed the guillotine – where they put a head under there and they see it chopped off. There was a whole audience in here, about twenty people. They remained quiet. I looked around and there were some people shaking their heads. Then the doctor came out and gave him a check to see if his heart was still beating. Then they took him out.

I saw another death. Remember the old Bacon's Casino which the packinghouse workers union bought, at 49th and Wabash? This was the first place Joe Louis ever fought. I remember walking out of that place one evening and a car sped around the corner. It had too many cylinders for that little-size truck. The thing turned over and the driver was trapped under it. I looked in there and saw this man

*Sylvester Washington, a black police officer, was feared in the community. He was proud of his brutal behavior and was praised by the 'higher-ups.'

dead. I was always perturbed by the suddenness with which death can occur. The guy was just driving a car. We heard the screeching. And there he was dead with all these cylinders over him. Then somebody on the street says, 'That was God's will.' This is when you almost turn God into a cop-out, to explain everything. Yet people need something . . .

I wish I were wrong about my doubts. That I'd never, never, never see my son again . . . I'll tell you what really gets to me. When I get an honor of some kind, I say, 'Gosh, I wish Bobby was here.' I didn't realize how much I had been living for this boy. If I won the Nobel Peace Prize tomorrow, it wouldn't be the same, because he couldn't be there – because the children are something you dream about before they come. So you know what I found myself doing? I think this is trying to make up for it. I never accept an award; I let one of my grandchildren accept it. I may be subconsciously trying to have my son back.

I remember when my brother got his degree at Fisk and my father cried. He had been a high school principal in Paris, Tennessee. Both his parents were illiterate. The only schooling he ever had was when they were not planting or harvesting. He went to Nashville on his own, without a quarter. And he helped build the chapel at Fisk University. My dad, incidentally, was a strict disciplinarian as a school administrator. *Nobody* talked while the speaker was speaking. He would whip kids in school for what they did on Sunday at church! But here is my dad talking out loud while this distinguished educator, the first black Rhodes scholar in history, Dr. Alaine Locke, was delivering the commencement speech. While Dr. Locke was speaking, my dad started talking and my mother kept punching him, saying: '*Don't do that*. People will think we're from the country!' and I looked up and he had tears running down his eyes, and he was saying, 'You don't know how much I dreamed for a day like this.' He said, 'These wrought-iron seats that are in here, I helped screw these seats down. When they were building this building, I went to the foreman and talked him into letting me be the one to lock up the building every night. I always left one door open or one window unlocked. I used to come in because I had no place to stay. I really didn't have any money to eat.' He said, 'I'd take off my pants at night and roll them up to make me a pillow.' He said, 'I slept right over there in that corner.' He said, 'Look over there now. Look at my son in a cap and gown.' I enjoyed Dad more than I enjoyed the speaker. He just kept talking, he was muttering to himself all the time. You see, if people don't have some dreams to hang on to, a belief in something . . .

I think this was one of the big attractions of Christianity: the fact that He suffered like they had suffered. You have to have a reason to want to live. When I reflect back at the slaves that used to come to my grandmother's house and visit her, I wonder how in the heck they made it psychologically. You saw absolutely no future unless you created it through your religious beliefs.

When my dad died, that was a momentous occasion. I got a telegram from my cousin, Hedda May Thomas. He taught up until the last week of his death. Some way or other they let him stay on. He was a big joke guy. My mother did her ritual of coming in, sitting down, taking off her shoes, putting on some house shoes – 'cause she was a teacher too. She would get up and then fix dinner. He was sitting there having a bit of fun with her. He said, 'You know, there's something you forgot to tell me?' She said, 'What did I forget?' 'You got paid today, you're supposed to give me your money.' He thought that was a big joke, and he just cracked up and started laughing and laughing and laughing. And he caught a deep breath and died – a heart attack.

My father and mother put in together around a hundred and ten years collectively teaching school in those small towns. When he died, it rained all day. The church was filled an hour before the funeral. People drove in from everywhere to say good-bye to him. And three generations of people passed by his coffin. What really shook me up, weeping, were all these little kids and they had to raise up and peek and they were saying, 'Good-bye, Professor Jarrett, good-bye . . .' And I said, 'What the heck am I crying about? This man has lived a *great* life.'

I took a vow at his coffin – just to get the last look – that I had to do something with my life as a perpetuation of his. That's what I think really counts the most. I'm doing the same thing with my son. Much of what I do is on behalf of my son. I do a lot of volunteer stuff with kids, and it's really in his memory. I think of that kid, thirteen, fourteen, walking outside my house – there was a lightbulb,

and he just *smashed* it out. I heard the sound but I didn't know what
it was, so I just grabbed this toy gun – it looked like a real rifle. I
came down the stairs. He used some dirty words: 'Go ahead and
shoot me, mother—' He didn't *give* a damn. A lot of kids out here
have just written off life because they don't see anything to live for.
Despite the emotion you see in the churches, it hasn't passed on
enough down the line. Even if it is fiction, the fiction hasn't worked.
Everywhere you look, it's big fish eating little fish, and little fish
eating shrimp. That's why African-Americans are the most churchgoing people in America, maybe the most religious people in
America: they've had less concrete evidence than anybody else in
this country that they have a place. What's that biblical expression?
Faith is the evidence of things unseen. So you create it.

I remember people used to have the little sporadic prayer meetings up and down the street where I lived in Paris. Religion is a way
of people relying on each other too for sustenance. It's not just
God, it's God together with us – the 'us' thing prevails. You may be
white, and you may be powerful, and you may have the capacity to
take life without any degree of contrition, but *I'm* connected with
God. If I didn't hear that once, I heard that a million times. 'God is
on our side,' 'It's just a matter of time.'

When I was a kid, a lot of people didn't believe that tornadoes
went through black neighborhoods. [*Laughs*] They'd be the last ones
to get off the front porch when a storm was coming. 'God's looking
out for us.' Every group that wants to can anoint itself as God's
chosen people. Our species, we damn humans, forget that we're just
a little globe amidst millions of stars. Yet we're acting as if we are the
beginning and the end. Maybe we've had to believe this in order to
justify the acceptance of the fact that this body is going to die – like
other animal life has died and will continue to die. To show how we
get caught up in our own importance as humans, I plan to write my
own program for my funeral. [*Laughs*] Who I want to be there, who
I would like to make remarks. Then I say, 'I'm acting like this is a big
deal.' Mine is just another minor passing. But I am caught into this
assumption that we are not insignificant, that there's something to
our having been here on this Earth. We don't want to go around
here accepting the fact that this is some evolutionary accident. So we
give all this importance to it.

I have a tombstone. I want my name on it! I want to be buried next to my son. There's an old black spiritual that says, 'This little light of mine, I'm going to let it shine . . .' Right now! Since we don't know the *truth* about any of this, you better let your little light shine right now.

Country Women

PEGGY TERRY

During the sixties, when many Southern whites – especially
Appalachians and Ozarkians – had come to Chicago, she had
become one of their most passionate voices. She became a
fervent advocate of the civil rights movement. She is retired and
lives in a northwestern suburb of Chicago with her daughter and
grandson.

I'm trying to figure out a way to get buried without putting my
children in debt. [*Laughs*] I'm from a Klan background –
Pentecostal, speaking in tongues, and all that. I've fought my way
out of that. I don't know how, but something sparked me. It's like I
was in a big deep hole and I climbed out up into the sunshine. My
granddad joined the Klan in Kentucky. It was tobacco farmers band-
ing together to protect themselves against the buyers and sellers of
their crop. But then it turned into a racist thing, and they started
lynching black people. Grandpa got out of it. He was kind of racist,
but he wasn't *that* racist. He talked about that a lot. There's a tree on
White Rock Road in Paducah, where they had lynched this young
man. Grandpa took me down there and showed me that tree. The
most he said was black people have a really hard time. He might have
said *niggers*. I learned later in life that Grandpa was nursed by a black
woman.

My father died a deep racist. That makes me sad to think of it too,
because he was such a wonderful guy. He was this Irish guy, full of
blarney. He was a good union man, too. In church, we used to sing
the little song: 'Jesus loves the little children, all the children of the
world, red and yellow, black and white, they are precious in his
sight. Jesus loves the little children of the world.' We sang that at least
once a month or more. But somehow they managed to instill a deep

racism. My dad wouldn't go near any church. He said they were all full of blarney.

My mother was very religious. When my grandma went from the Catholic Church to the Pentecostal movement, Mama went with them. She became Pentecostal, too. My aunt and my grandmother both spoke in tongues and danced around. I don't understand tongues. I would say it was gibberish, but you can go from California to New York and from Canada to Mexico and you hear this talk and it sounds the same. I don't know how that came out of my aunt, because she could barely read and write.

We were all going to go to Hell unless we admitted our sins and accepted the Lord Jesus into our hearts as our savior and leader. To me, it was a contradiction because, on the one hand, they tell me that Jesus died for my sins, but yet I was going to Hell unless I admitted them. So Jesus must have known I was going to sin – or he wouldn't have been willing to die to save me and all the others like me! I believed in Heaven and Hell until I was around ten, twelve years old, and then so many things just didn't make sense to me.

When they would have revivals, it was church every night and three times on Sunday. Sometimes revivals lasted two weeks! All my girlfriends would go to the altar every night and get saved. I thought it was just *silly*. You'd lay there on the altar crying and screaming and begging for forgiveness. I would go the first couple of times, but after that it just seemed silly. It seemed pretentious to me. I felt the girls were wanting attention, which was the reason they kept going down to the altar. At that point I still believed in God. My questioning at that point was just questioning the Church and the things that went on – the things that I could see. Later on, I stopped believing *any* of it. I lived in deep fear that when I became twelve years old, I would be responsible for my own sins. Until you're twelve, you're not responsible, your parents are, for any sins you commit. But when you turn twelve, you become responsible. I lived in absolute fear of turning twelve. I wanted to stay eleven.

I remember Blanche Ryan. She was just beautiful to look at. She was Black Irish, had coal-black hair that just hung in ringlets on her shoulders, and she had bright blue eyes. She had danced in a showgirl revue on the stage. She'd come to church – her family had been Catholic. I've noticed in the past few years that a lot of Catholics turn Pentecostal because they're starved for a way to express themselves. In the Catholic Church they don't express themselves very much, except maybe to a priest in confession or something. They snubbed Blanche in church. I felt if she was such a sinner, where else would she belong more so than in the Church? I wasn't allowed to associate with her. I'd wait till Mama was busy with her babies, because she always had a baby in her lap. There were seven of us. I'd sneak away and go behind her back and go sit with Blanche. Blanche would let me look in her purse, and oh, that was exciting because she had lipstick and all kinds of things. I was about eleven. I didn't fear being with Blanche because she was so full of love and life and such a beautiful singing voice. She was like a light in the darkness. I never felt any fear of going to Hell over her – it never occurred to me. But it occurred to me that they didn't treat her right.

I didn't lose the fear of Heaven and Hell until I was grown. I had children of my own before I really kicked it. When I really kicked the chains that kind of held me was about the same time I joined the civil rights movement. It didn't have anything to do with what I learned religionwise – it was *in spite of* what I learned in religion. I was living in Montgomery when the bus boycott there started, and all the women in the neighborhood were talking about Reverend King. 'Course, that wasn't what they called him! He was in jail. These were white women. At that point I didn't know any black people. They were talking about this smartass nigger being down there in jail. So we all went down to look at him, to see what he looked like, the troublemaker. We were standing on the sidewalk watching when he was released on bail. He came out of the side door of the jail, and the minute he was going to walk to his car they were waiting there for him. And about six or seven guys jumped onto him and started beating on him and kicking him. It just flashed in my mind. There's an old saying in the South, two on one is nigger fun. It means white people are above jumping onto another person like that – only niggers do that. White people are too honorable, they fight man-to-man, one-on-one. I thought, here's white guys jumping onto him. I don't know . . . I started seeing things in a different way.

I was in the grocery line, and this very small black woman had her cart full of groceries. She started out the door, and the guy that was in front of her, he started to hold it open, and then he looked around and saw she was black, and he just let the door slam on her. And pushed her back with the cart and everything.

I'm originally from Oklahoma. The only church that I went to in Kentucky was the one where the minister felt up my breast. When I told my mama, she slapped me and told me that he wouldn't do a thing like that. Well, I knew he *did*. So that was another nail in their coffin. [*Laughs*] I don't believe in the hereafter now, not the way it's taught. I'm not sure what happens to us when we die. But why should we be so concerned about it? Think of it as a flower, or a tree that dies and adds its whatever, vitality, to the earth. Flowers die every year. Trees die. All living things die. So why are we so much more than the animals of the Earth, or the foliage, or any of it? We're all part of nature. I don't know why we should all be so afraid of it. It's a nuisance knowing you won't be here anymore. The one thing I hate about thinking about dying is I won't be able to read. If I could take books with me, I wouldn't care. [*Laughs*] I never was so proud of being who I was until I read *The Grapes of Wrath*. I was forty-five when I read it. I have a fifth-grade education. Actually, I graduated, if you want to call it graduated, from grade school after five years. I just read everything I could get my hands on – no matter what it was, I'd read it. I used to know football like crazy because my cousin read football stories.

I don't want to die, but I'm not so afraid of it. What concerns me is the grief of the ones I leave. That is the bad part. You *know* they're going to be heartbroken, just like I was when my mother went. I wish I could do something about that, not being here with them. Of course that concerns me. It happens to everyone. Death is a leveler. I think if we spent more time being kinder to our fellow man than all the time we wasted in churches and grieving about dying, it would be put to better use. I wish that everyone could just go peacefully. But of course, you have to picture death in many different ways, because some people die violently. Some people are lucky and go, *zip* – heart attack or brain hemorrhage and they're gone. That's lucky. I've worked in hospitals enough that I know what it's like to lay there. I worked as a nurse's aide for five years at Mercy Hospital in Jackson, Michigan. I remember taking care of cancer patients who smelled so bad when you'd go in the room that you'd just have to paste a look on your face to keep them from knowing. But this one little man I took care of, he was nothing but skin and bones, and he put his hand on mine and he said, 'You don't have to pretend with me.' He said, 'I know it smells terrible in here.' And I said, 'Well, we won't talk about it.'

The first death I remember is when my baby sister died of pneumonia. She was three years old. We went to Oklahoma from Kentucky in January of 1929, before the Crash in November. My sister died in May – my baby sister. I was about seven. I didn't understand the full implication, because I was excited about this dress our neighbor had made for me to wear to the funeral. It was a beautiful little dress. Of course, everybody made their own clothes back then. Mama took me over to the side and told me to sit down and be quiet, my little sister was dead.

I felt a grief again in a hospital near Waco, Texas. My sister and I worked there. Her husband was at Camp Hood. I saw young soldier boys die – that was real grief. It was like they were kin to me. Soldier boys of World War II. I remember the wonderful guy I wrote to for such a long time. He got the bottom part of his face shot off. He always signed his letters to me, 'the chinless wonder.' [*Laughs*] So that was grief . . .

As for me, I'm for burial. It's somewhere where your folks can go and communicate with you. They can pray and sing and talk to the dead me. I think I'd rather like that. I've already got a place in the Symsonia Cemetery in Paducah. It's where all my folks were born, it's a suburb of Paducah. The graveyard where I bought my grave goes back to my great-great-grandfather. And there's, oh, at least a hundred, maybe more, of my people in that graveyard.

My little baby sister, she died in '29. My sister Elsie died in '79. And my brother Lon died just a few years ago. I have two sisters left. I was born in '21 – I'll be seventy-eight in October. We went there to my grandmother's grave and my cousin, Willie Helms Draffen, was my mother's age and he remembered all those people. He remembered Grandma. He told many things about her, and my sister talked. We had a tape recorder with us, the three of us. We were searching. I was working on my family tree. Willie, of course, knew everybody out there because that's where all the Draffens come from.

Being at that grave is consoling to us, that's it. I don't believe there's anything like Heaven because if there is a God, in my opinion, He's not worth worshiping. If He was what I was taught, a loving God who sees the fall of the sparrow, why are so many people in the world in such horrible, miserable conditions? If He is all that caring, why do so many people suffer so terribly? Why are people who go to church every Sunday still deep racists? Maybe they don't care that there are people that fought for this country sleeping down under the thing on Wacker Drive, no homes, no place to go, no medical care, no nothing. If God has his eye on the sparrow, why doesn't He have it on us people? I love sparrows, but . . . [*Laughs*]

I think Hell is right here on earth, absolutely. Look at the misery. My heart is heavy every day because every— I don't listen to television anymore, I seldom turn it on. It's horror story after horror story. I mean, they're starting to put *children* in jail! Those two little boys they had for raping this child, they had them charged with *murder*. Six and eight years old, for God's sake!

All I can say is, He's the most ignorant God that's possible. I have more respect for the ancient gods of Rome. At least, you know, they didn't claim to really care about us mortals. They cared about themselves and made no bones about it. They were the gods and we worshiped them, but they didn't promise us anything.

I'd love to believe in reincarnation – that would be *such* a sop. Wouldn't that be wonderful if we could believe that? I think one reason people are so desperate about dying is they haven't lived yet. All we do here is we try to see who can get a little higher up the ladder than the neighbor. That's what we spend our time doing, that and driving to work and back, polluting the air and all of that . . . I think life is so miserable for most people. All the time they're racing around like mad, drunken ants, they're fearing dying. That's the way it got this way, that's what keeps it this way, is *greed*. To teach people from the time they're little to have respect for each other, maybe not love, but at least respect and kindness toward each other, care more about each other than you do about getting a new car. Then we might have a different attitude toward death.

I don't think there's anything after. If we've fulfilled ourselves as human beings – not as *collectors* of stuff, money and bank accounts and all that, but as human beings – then I don't think death would be as frightening. I don't think most people understand that their lives are completely empty. Or maybe they do: they know it in a way, because they get up in the morning and they go to work, they work all day like hell and then they come home at night. They get up the next day and do the same thing. Maddening traffic, people who are getting nastier to each other day by day. And they watch the TV news and they think, *My God, they're all a bunch of animals, and here I am living in a zoo where all the animals have gone wild, but I'm above that because I'm out here in the suburbs or I'm somewhere in Chicago where those animals can't get near* . . . And they look with contempt and fear. What kind of living is that, that you live in fear?

How would you like to be remembered?

[*A long pause*] As a symbol for the have-nots that, if given the right opportunities, can find their way out of their holes of misery and ignorance the same way I did. I'd like to be remembered as one that tried to push that as far as I could, to do as much about that as I could. I'd like Fran Ainsley to sing 'Ain't You Got a Right to the Tree of Life.' And no holy words said over me. [*Laughs*] My favorite Irish war song is 'The Minstrel Boy':

> The minstrel boy to the war is gone, in the ranks of dead you
>   will find him
> His sword and shield he has girded on and his wild heart slung
>   behind him
> Land of song, said the warrior bard, though all the world betray
>   thee
> One sword at least thy right shall guard, one faithful harp shall
>   praise thee.

You're the minstrel girl. Any epitaph?

'I did my best.'

Postscript

Never have I heard an ovation equal to the one she received after a speech she made at Operation PUSH in 1968. The audience was overwhelmingly

African-American. Reverend Jesse Jackson introduced her. As I remember it, she spoke of her arrest after a civil rights demonstration. A fellow Southerner had asked her, 'What were you doing inside there with all those niggers?' She replied, 'Where else could poor white trash like me be greeted with respect by a Nobel Prize-winner like Dr. King?' The audience let out a roar, rose to its feet, cheered, laughed, stamped its feet, and shouted amens, on and on and on.

BESSIE JONES

Among the performers at the University of Chicago Folk Festival of 1969 were the Georgia Sea Island Singers. Their home, St. Simons Island, was seven miles off the Georgia coast. Their work was fishing, loading and unloading boats, and housework on the mainland at white people's homes, while they were remembering the oft-told tales of their elders, many of them slaves. They celebrated these memories and histories, as well as their daily lives, in song.

I first met Bessie Jones in the early sixties. The musicologist Alan Lomax had introduced me to her and her fellow islanders. She was, at the time, in her mature years, and, though her companions told their own stories vibrantly, she was obviously their oracle.

It was at the 1969 festival that she met Almeda 'Granny' Riddle, an elderly white singer of olden folk songs and hymns from Heber Springs, Arkansas. During Bessie Jones's reflections, she invited Almeda Riddle to offer her own reminiscences.

We couldn't get out to the mainland much, and that kept us like it was. We do the old work songs, the old rain shouts and prayers. My grandfather, a hundred and five years old, he was a slave and he told us the many things that he did and what did happen. He would get out and pray with us, sing with us, with vim, do it right.

They'd be singing a work song, a shout song, a chantey, or a spiritual. They'd be doing the work while they were singing. They wouldn't be singing one thing and doing something else. If they're rowing, they're singing a rowing song. If they're washing, they're singing a washing song. If they're working in the field, they sing a hoe song. If they're loading a ship, they're singing a longshoreman's song. If they're pulling a rope, a sailor's song. Something to lift, they'd say, 'Boys, let's pull.' Everybody pull at once. So you got vim when you're singing like that. That's why you always see us moving, because you have to feel like the person who you're singing after or else the song wouldn't be no good.

You'd see boys go to the woods, they'd have two, three loads of wood. Make a big fire and sing all night. We didn't have no moving pictures to go to or nothing. We'd just sing and make ourselves happy. Like the church song 'Let Me Fly' – just the hard times they had, and they realize what God would do for them and they feel like flying. Help you survive the day.

Same thing with sad songs. The sad songs is not to make people sadder, it's to make them gladder. Even if he is in jail or on a chain gang, he's singing something out there to help himself to forget the feeling. They sing to make them forget about the hard tasks and this treatment that they was going up against.★

We'd sometimes sing and play in the moonlight. They got that way back in slavery. They wanted to say something to white people and they couldn't – so they'd sing, 'I'm going to rule, I'm going to rule the ruler.' They wanted to rule, sometime, sometime.

There was nightwatch songs to help you out of trouble. When you're in trouble, you'd sing about Moses leading the people out of the land of Israel and Pharaoh pursued them. The night was falling and they found out they was going out on a cliff. They had rock on either side of this entry and the Pharaoh behind them, so they started talking to Moses. We'd sing 'Moses, Don't You Let Pharaoh Overtake Us.'

That was the way they used to tell people about their own selves.

★When I once asked Edith Piaf if she really felt sad when she sang a sad song, she replied: 'Oh no, I feel happy when I sing a sad song and feel bad when I sing a happy song. When you sing a song that is up, where can you go but down? But if you sing a song that is down, where can you go but up?'

When they would die, the colored people would be put away most anywhere: some behind some old bushes or whatnot. And not very decent like the white people was. They used to call them coffins in those days, but they had a rough box and put them away. You know, these colored people had feelings for their bodies and the people that was gone as well as anybody else. So they made a song about it: 'Throw Me Anywhere in That Old Field.' They just made it up with their self and God: just throw me anywhere in that old field, because they didn't care because they knew that Jesus would be with them, go down with them. They arrived with Jesus. That was in their heart, soul, and mind – you can just throw me anywhere.

And they made this dance called a Buzzard Lope. [*She acts it out.*] You'd see the buzzard coming to its prey that's dead. He dances around it, sees that it's really dead, and he'd get it. Take away their bones, their body, but it's all right with them since their soul would be safe. [*Sings*]

> *You may beat and hang me*
> *Since my Jesus save me*
> *Throw me anywhere, Lord*
> *In that old field*
> *Don't care how you treat me*
> *Since King Jesus meet me*
> *Don't care how you do me*
> *Since King Jesus choose me*
> *Throw me anywhere, Lord*
> *In that old field.*

The buzzard could choose a horse or a mule, same thing. That hope will still be there.

[*Almeda 'Granny' Riddle speaks.*] I was a widow in '26 with three children to support and had nothing but just my hands to support them with. There was that great tornado. My older son I had to keep four months in the hospital and I got splattered. My face you see is not mine: it's plastic surgery, most of it. There was twelve places on my face that had to be grafted. After this, I went back to work on the farm. I bought a house and then brought the three children up, got them through school, being on the farm.

I commenced singing when I was six years old. The first I remember was 'The Blind Child's Prayer.' Singing is part of me. If I'm unhappy, I sing. If I'm happy, I sing. If I'm in need of inspiration, I sing.

Bessie and I are entirely different types of singers. I'd be glad if I could sing her style, but I can't. I can only be myself. But, like Bessie, we oftimes sang songs about death. 'Come Angel Band and Around Me Stand' . . . People lived within that song and they died by that. I remember in my childhood people asking me to sing it to them in their last hours. One time I had to do that. The lady got better, but she thought she was dying. So did the doctor. She asked me to come sing 'Angel Band.' [*Softly, in a treble, she sings a line or two.*] 'My last sun has set / My triumph has begun . . .'

[*Bessie Jones resumes.*] That is like the song of the dying sinner. A person that's dying without the Lord and it's 'O Death in the Morning' . . . He's begging death to spare him over another year, begging death to have mercy. Also, it helps that person that is in sin to try to live up and do better. If he hears this song sometimes it helps them to change their ways. It's a spiritual. The song of the living sinner, as I foremost told you, someone that's dying out of Christ.

I was standing at the bedside of a man that was going. I didn't see the thing, but he seen it. I was to the side, and he see that somebody come in that door. I could tell he seen it come right around him. I wanted to touch him but the people wouldn't let me touch him. I knew somebody seen something. Whatsoever it was, he died, and I was on the backside of the bed. Brother! I wanted to come out from there but I couldn't. He was drawing his fists back, saying, '*Unh-unh, unh-unh, unh, unh* . . .' He was just drawing back and hitting at the thing with his fists, you know. Without saying a word, you could tell when it caught him. It got him and then just laid over that way. He went on and just died, he laid on the bed and died. Brother, I tell you he seen something, he really seen it. I could see his eyes . . . when it transferred, his eyes went right around with it in and out that way. Then the windowpane broke. [*Sings*]

Yeah, Death walked up the sinner door
Said, 'O, now, Sinner, you gotta go'
The sinner looked around and began to cry
Said, 'O, no, Death, I'm not ready to die
Death, consider me age and do not take me at this stage'
All my wealth is at your command
If you just remove your cold, icy hand
'O, Death, O, Death in the morning
O, Death, spare me over for another year'
He cried, 'O Death, O, Death in the morning
O, Death, please now spare me over for another year.'

Death is a thing we never have seen but we can be acquainted with him. [*Suddenly*] I don't know why I did that – to call it a he. We don't know whether it's a he or not or a she. [*Laughs*]

I see it this way, whatever it is. The Lord speaks of a man this and a man that. He means she, too, 'cause you can't spell 'woman' without spelling 'man.' So that's why it must be a he. [*Laughs*]

I was once praying, and I wanted to know something I had no business to know – wasn't none of my business. I wanted to know how the Lord looked and what kind of man He was. I prayed so hard, I fasted a long time and I prayed so hard with this. I figured if you mean what you're doing, He'll give you satisfaction, some way, somehow. But He left me in a condition that I would never try it again.

'Cause you see, at one point, the Scripture said that his face was like polished brass. Anyhow, I see this great huge head, the biggest head I ever seen in my life. I was in this vision, and in his head it was just like the flowers in that chair. It had every head, every face, every kind of face that can be under Heaven. He just turned it slow and I seen millions of faces and it looked just like me. I looked every which way and everywhere you could see was a face of every kind of creature, every human being. I worried over that. I said, 'Lord, I want to know what it means.' Then He said, 'I'm the God of every nation.' And that set it with me. [*Laughs*] I ain't tried that no more. But I advise anybody, if you want to know something, ask God. He'll give you that satisfaction. Oh yeah, faces, no bodies, just heads, turning slowly. So that's a mystery.

POSTSCRIPT

Almeda Riddle joins Bessie Jones in singing 'Amazing Grace.' It was the most singular interpretation of the hymn I had ever heard, their styles and tempos being somewhat at variance. Yet, call it what you will, they wound up amazingly and gracefully as one. Unfortunately, the impromptu performance took place after the tape had run out. So it is not to be heard except through my memory of that moment.

ROSALIE SORRELS

She is a traveling singer of folk ballads, though she has composed many of her recent songs.

> I don't fear death. I've already had two really close encounters with it. I had a cerebral aneurysm in 1988 and I was in a coma for eight days. And I did not see any bright lights, nor did anyone come. [*Laughs*] It was a big black hole and I have no memory of it. And three years ago I had breast cancer — and it certainly would have killed me if I hadn't been doing self-examination. Although I was getting a mammogram every year, it never showed up. But it became very aggressive at the point I found it. If I hadn't discovered it, I would have died. I had to go through a very aggressive chemotherapy, and I lost all my hair and all my skin and my fingernails and everything. And it was massively unpleasant. But look at me. [*Laughs*] It made me more stubborn and it made me love life more.

You know, I've never thought of death as unfriendly. I was raised on a farm by a family where, when someone died, we all took turns sitting with them till they finished doing it. I always thought it was the last thing you do, and you would want to do it as well as you could. This was in Idaho. My dad was a road builder, an engineer for the state highway department, so he was gone a lot. My mother went with him, and they often left me with one set of grandparents or the other. My mother's father had a self-sufficient farm, which we know is an oxymoron in Twin Falls, Idaho. [*Laughs*]

My father's mother was a photographer and a journalist. She wrote for the newspaper. She wrote the church news. My father's father was an Episcopal missionary. He had a cabin, about thirty miles out of Boise that he bought. That came into our family before I was born, and I'm fixing to be sixty-eight. And he lived up there. It wasn't a farm, it was a mountain dwelling. They grew their own food and hunted. They mostly lived off the land. There was very little money in the family and no money to put anybody in a fancy sanitarium. You died at home.

The Depression lasted a long time around Twin Falls. [*Laughs*] We had to do that ourselves. Which, I think, was a blessing. A lot of people are afraid of death 'cause they don't live with it. It's like birth: they put you in a hospital and try to make it so you don't notice anything unpleasant about it. They take it away from you. I think they do better now, but for a long time death and birth were removed from the people. They think, well, we can't let the kids see this because it's hard and it will scare them. But they're more scared if they never saw it. I know people who are fifty or sixty years old who've never sat with somebody who died. They're scared to death of it.

I remember when they died very well. We sat with each person. I was expected to spend time just the same as anybody else in the family. That's when I got to know them the best. My mother's mother, it took her a year to die. I sat with her a lot. She wanted to talk. She told me lots of things I didn't know. My mother's father died when I was eight. That's the one I didn't get to talk to – but I remember him better than almost anyone I ever met. He was the Irish atheist, and he was *very* forthright about it. No one told me he was sick. He seemed really strong. He died in his late sixties. I loved this man more than anyone I've ever met. Probably I've never met a man I thought was so powerful. He had fantastic eyes. We call them raven eyes; they could look in your soul. I was in the second grade, and he came into the room where I was in class. He just came and took ahold of my hand and looked at me, and he never said anything. And then he went out of the room. There was this tiny window in the door. And the last I ever saw of him was his eyes looking at me through the door. The next day they told me he was dead – and I didn't even know that he was sick. I was really angry. I mean, I was angry for *years*. When I did that little book of my mother's I showed you,* she comes to me with it and says, 'Why did you say you didn't know how my father died?' I said, 'You never told me. You didn't tell me he was sick. You didn't tell me he was going to die.' She said, 'No one ever told you?' I said, 'Well, years later my father told me he died of a petrified pecker.' [*Laughs*] I said, 'I took

*A diary of family memories and reflections.

that to mean he didn't get any loving and he died of a broken heart.' She gave a big harumph and she said, 'Well, he died of prostate cancer – he died on the table.' He definitely knew he was dying. He never wanted to be buried, he wanted to be cremated. But my grandmother was a Methodist and she was *very* religious. They hired mourners. Oh, he would have been *so* mad. [*Laughs*]

My father, Walter Pendleton Stringfellow – we called him Walt – was wonderful. He drank too much. He lost his job. I think he lost it because he supported Henry Wallace.★ He worked for the state of Idaho. He was also a chemist. He was well-educated. I know that he always liked to drink, and he liked to fight. He was Irish. [*Laughs*] He began to drink too much when he wasn't working. For a while he picked apples – he did this and that. My mother went to work when I was in junior high school. She ran a bookshop in Boise. She did that for twenty years. She made the money and he began to build the house which I now live in, which is a log cabin. He built it with his hands.

[*She shows me a photograph.*] This is the house. He cut every log, he made all these bricks. My mother lived there after he died in 1971.

I think that was the first time I was old enough to be involved in making the arrangements. It was 1971, so I was in my late thirties. He was only sixty-three and he looked strong and healthy all the time, but he'd been drinking a lot. He died of a bleeding ulcer. Partly because he was up there at the cabin and he didn't get medical attention soon enough. It was a hard death. My brother and I went to see the mortician, who was unbelievably unctuous, or as my father would say, an oily son of a bitch. This was at a time when you were required to have a coffin, whether you meant to cremate the body or not. You *had* to buy a coffin – it was a law. We asked for a plain pine coffin. So this guy says, essentially, that we're really cheap

★Henry A. Wallace was President Roosevelt's secretary of agriculture, 1932–40 and vice president, 1940–44. In 1944, during the tumultuous Democratic Convention, Roosevelt, ailing and weak, was persuaded by the powerful city bosses to drop Wallace as his running mate and choose Senator Harry Truman. In 1948, as the Cold War was getting under way, Wallace ran for president on the Progressive Party ticket and became a controversial figure. Many who supported him were considered unpatriotic and, as a result, suffered the consequences.

because we're only going to have a plain pine coffin. And we said we were going to have him cremated. He said, 'Well, how are you going to feel at the viewing?' And we said, 'We're not going to have a viewing – we *know* what he looks like!' [*Laughs*] And then he said, 'Well, what florist do you want me to call?' And I said, 'We're going to bring pine boughs and dried weeds down from the cabin to the memorial service' – it was fall, and that's what my father would have liked. And he said, 'Oh my God . . . Well, what organist do you want me to get?' And I said, 'Oh, I'm going to sing for my father.' And he said, 'Well, you'll need an organist to back you up.' And I said, 'No, I'm going to sing unaccompanied' – and I did. I sang 'Bright Morning Stars Are Shining.' [*Sings*]

> *Oh, where are our dear fathers*
> *Oh, where are our dear fathers*
> *Oh, where are our dear fathers*
> *Days abreaking in my soul*
> *Some are down in the valley praying*
> *Some are down in the valley praying*
> *Some are down in the valley praying*
> *Days abreaking in my soul*
> *And some have gone to Heaven shouting*
> *Some have gone to Heaven shouting*
> *Some have gone to Heaven shouting*
> *Days abreaking in my soul.*

I thought I couldn't do it because I would break down. But I figured out if I didn't look anybody in the eye I could do it. I stood in the back of the church and sang so I couldn't see anybody's eyes. I got through three songs fine. Afterward I was a mess . . .

Anyhow, this guy was distressed that he couldn't talk me into an organist or flowers or anything. So finally he says, 'Well, one of our services is that we write the obituary. Now tell me something about Walter.' I'm feeling very hostile toward him by then, so I said, 'We called him Walt.' [*Laughs*] And he said, 'What did he do for a living?' And I said, 'He hadn't worked in a long time.' And he said, 'He was retired?' And I said, 'Well, you can put it that way if you want.' And then he said, 'What was his religious affiliation?' And I said, 'He didn't go to church much either.' And he said, 'Well, did he belong to any fraternal organizations, anything?' And I said, 'He used to sing for the Elks Glee Club.' So he says, 'Oh, good, I'll put that.' And then he says, 'Now, tell me something else about Walter.' And I'm just looking at him thinking, my father could walk on his hands for two blocks. He could walk all the way to the top of the capitol steps and back down on his hands and *never* get off his hands. He could jump over a card table from a standing jump. He was a piece of work! [*Laughs*] And he was incredibly literate and he used to make up dirty lyrics that I loved and write them to me in letters. [*Laughs*] He wrote me letters all the time, beautiful letters.

My mother's father, the atheist, taught me all the soliloquies from *Hamlet* before I went to school. Before I went to grade school I knew: 'Speak the speech trippingly on your tongue.' I knew: 'Oh that this too, too solid flesh would melt.' He used to swear in Shakespearean language . . . at the horses! 'The devil damn thee black thou cream-faced limb.' [*Laughs*]

My mother wanted to die up there at the cabin. She'd been living there all alone since my father had died, which was 1971. I actually went back home in 1983, 'cause she got really sick and I thought she was going to die. I wanted to stay with her so she could be up there. But eventually she got too weak to stay and had to move into an apartment in town. It was one of those high-rises that the government supports for older people. She was on Social Security. She got better during that time and lived another eleven years. I just stayed at the cabin, and I'm going to stay there!

When you come into the place there's two great big pine trees that my father planted when they were just little babies. They're huge. They're two stories tall, and they're like guards. He used to go down and stand between them in the morning and sing. I always thought he was like Orpheus and he made the morning happen, 'cause he would sing and then the sun would rise into the canyon. He made the morning happen. So we put his ashes there around those trees.

My son died in 1976. My son committed suicide, and we put his ashes there. My brother and I did this, each time. We didn't have a lot of people around for that. We did that ourselves – we sang and we came back. And each time we had a memorial for all the friends up at the cabin. We didn't let anybody bring cut flowers – we planted things each time, trees and flowers. My mother, when she died, we put her ashes up there too. Even my old dog, I put up there. I had him fourteen years. I had his ashes for a long time after he died. I wanted to put him out on the Day of the Dead. My old dog's name was Dominick the Enforcer. I wanted him to be a watchdog. Now I got a new dog. His name is Lenny Bruce Peltier. I'll be there. My brother. It's where those trees are I was describing. Near where the old house used to be. And up into the spring, and in the creek. My mother wrote a poem about it. This was her instruction to us. We followed it faithfully and it'll get read anytime anybody goes. My mother's name was Nancy Ann Kelly Stringfellow.

So this is what my mother said. It's called 'Scatter My Ashes.'

> *Down by the sweet curve of the river*
> *Down where the twin pines reach to each other across the lane*
> *Their branches embracing*
> *Scatter my ashes*
> *Scatter the ashes of my old bones*
> *My tired bones*
> *Let them float free and weightless*
> *Calcium burned away*
> *Pain gone*
> *Dissolved in healing waters*
> *Pitying rain*
> *Nurturing earth*
> *Other ashes*
> *Ashes of those I have loved*
> *Will welcome mine*
> *Smell the sweet wild roses*
> *Gather the sweet wild blackberries*
> *And when a vagrant breeze touches your cheek*
> *You will feel our love and our peacefulness*
> *Down by the river.*

I had five kids. David was nearly twenty-three when he died. He was the oldest. I like to think about him now. It was very hard for a long time. Probably four years I think I was just crazy from it, but I learned to live with it. I don't think you have to get over it – you just have to learn to live with it. He was a wonderful kid. I *adored* him. That was the worst of all the deaths, because I didn't get to say good-bye at all. I did go and get his body and take his ashes to the common ground and put them there. But I didn't get to say good-bye – and that's very hard . . . Some people are afraid to confront it, and they don't say good-bye and it just messes up their whole life for the rest of their life. I'm still saying good-bye.

I wrote a song about him not long ago. It's called 'Hitchhiker in the Rain.' [*Sings*]

> *I saw him yesterday, standing in the rain*
> *His thumb hung low, his back half-turned, his eyes as far away*
>   *as Spain*
> *And though he looked all worn out, and near as old as me*
> *His eyes still held some innocence, like nineteen sixty-three*
> *But I hurried, turned my head and drove by faster than a*
>   *midnight train*
> *I left the aging innocent, just standing in the rain*
> *And their anger grows as their hopes fade*
> *And my nerve goes and I am just afraid*
> *And you and love and fear and memory tangle in my brain*
> *And I leave the children standing, God I hate to leave them*
>   *standing*
> *I leave the aging children standing in the rain*
> *And you told me once I mustn't pass the rain-soaked thumbers by*
> *Or I'd spoil your hitching karma and you'd never get a ride*
> *And maybe somewhere in Wyoming the devil deputy*
> *Might cut you down and end the life that started out in me*
> *Well, the word came to me in Vermont that you had truly died*
> *You took yourself away, my son, for anger and for pride*
> *You just spun out one night by the Pacific ocean side*
> *And for years I drove from coast to coast with the eagle and the*
>   *crane*
> *Searching for your angry ghost among the aging children*
>   *standing in the rain*
> *And their anger grows as their hopes fade*
> *And my nerve is gone, and now I'm just afraid*
> *And you and love and fear and memory tangle in my brain*

> *And I leave the children standing, God I hate to leave them*
> *   standing*
> *I leave the aging children standing in the rain.*

[*A long pause*] He used to hitchhike back and forth across the country all the time. He left me a letter telling me that he in no way meant it to be my fault. He really wanted me to know that he had not committed suicide because of anything I did. But that didn't help a whole lot . . . [*A pained laugh*] It really doesn't. You just feel like there must have been something you could have done to change it . . .

I've seen my father, literally seen him standing in the lane with his hand out to me. I talk to him all the time. I talk to my mother. I saw my son standing by the road waiting to be picked up a couple of times. And then it wouldn't be anybody there, or it would be a post, or it would be someone who looked like him. I don't think you go away. To me, it's not in my mind. [*Laughs*] I mean, they're palpable to me. And God is to me in the spirits that stay, the spirits that live with you. That house is like a ghost almost. The whole house literally holds my family. I live in the house my father built. I'm not home enough, but I live in it. [*Laughs*] Every stalk, every plant . . . there are raspberries . . . I think I'll be there for my children in my songs, in my house. My idea of Heaven would be something like what my mother describes in her poem. It would be gathering the roses and the blackberries and being with people I love, and making music, and not having to worry about health care. Hell is the damnation of innocent people. You get plenty of it on Earth, you don't need any more punishment. [*Laughs*]

I feel more in love with life than I ever did. I want to leave you with a poem. It's by a woman named Judith Kuchen. She's a ranchwoman, maybe from Nevada. It sums up the way I feel.

> *I want to live to be an outrageous old woman who is never*
> *   mistaken for an old lady*
> *I want to live to have ten thousand lovers in one seventy-year-*
> *   long loving love perhaps*
> *There are at least two of me*
> *I want to get leaner and meaner, sharp-edged, the color of the dirt*
> *Until I discorporate from sheer joy.*

The Plague
I

TICO VALLE

A former assistant dean of students at Holy Trinity High School, he is now its director of development.

AIDS is very much alive. I'm scared that what we have seen is the end of the beginning of this epidemic – that many, many more deaths are yet to come. There isn't really any national policy at all. Until AIDS personally impacts our leaders, nothing will ever happen. When the floods happened in the Midwest, our government moved quickly to allocate millions of dollars of emergency funds to help people by a stroke of a pen. Why can't they do that for AIDS? We're the outcasts, the marginal, the people always thrown to the side. That's what's wrong about our society: people imposing their value systems on other people.

I'm also very, very involved in the quilt.* People bring pieces of quilts to be submitted to the larger quilt. This is national, but we started a local chapter here to help people create panels. We have fifty thousand panels, exhibits all over the country. It's names of the gays and straights who have died of AIDS. The quilt represents only thirteen percent of people who have died from AIDS in the United States.

---

*The AIDS Memorial Quilt runs wall to wall in the public halls where it is exhibited in many cities.

I am Latino American, gay male, thirty-six years old. I am one of five children, all raised here in Chicago in Old Town – when Old Town was artsy and fun, not what it is today. I'm the only child that was born on the Isle of Puerto Rico. My parents are from San Juan. They wanted one child to be born on the island. Both my parents worked in factories. They wanted the best for their kids, left the island to make sure that their kids got an education and would succeed in life.

I went to Catholic school all my life, St. Michael's in Old Town, then went to Holy Trinity. I joined the Brothers of Holy Cross at Notre Dame University. I went to Notre Dame for two years, and then I left and went to DePaul. My family raised us to have faith, but I wouldn't say I'm devout. I disagree with a lot of things in the Church. I sang in the church choir for many years, and still do – that's what brings me spiritual guidance.

My mother taught us to help others, to never judge anyone for who they are. My mother and father were very much that way. They would give the shirt off their back. My father died about three years ago from AIDS. It was very hard for the family. But when he was diagnosed, we didn't ask how he got it, we just took care of him. I played a major role in that.

I think it was his sexual promiscuity. It wasn't a shock to us that he had a secret life – it was a shock that he was diagnosed. We hear so much in the media that AIDS is for gay people, and seldom do we hear that it impacts a heterosexual man, like a father. It was very, very difficult. This was the eighties.

What's interesting is my best friend was diagnosed back in 1984. His name was Jay McKinley, a descendant of President McKinley. He said to me, 'I've been diagnosed, will you take care of me?' I said, 'Jay, you have a family, you have friends, everyone will take care of you. But I will be honored to take care of you.' He said, 'They will not be there for me when the time comes.' Because it was a scary time, back in '84. He ended up dying, and I took care of him. It was a long battle. At that time there was very little in the way of drugs. The sickness destroyed his body, destroyed who he was, destroyed his mind. I felt it was an honor to take care of him – that he chose me to end his final days on his Earth.

I was just a very good friend. His lover ended up leaving him. His family came towards the very end, but they were pretty much help-less. They didn't know what to do. People were scared to touch him, people were scared to even be in the room. So very few people came around. I was living at home at the time. I was so exhausted from going to work and not sleeping at night and giving him his medications that I called my mother and said, 'Could you come and help me?' She did – and that's when she first got the awakening of what this disease was doing to our community and to our people.

Jay chose to die at home, and I would pray for him to die because of the pain he was in. He was thirty-six years old, my age today. He was losing his mind. He was a brilliant person. He worked for the stock exchange, a very intelligent man. It's one thing to see the body be destroyed, but when you lose the mind . . . I guess that's every-one's fear, to lose the mind.

He didn't want to go to the hospital. His care was at home. We went to the doctor's a lot. I learned how to give him injections, I learned how to change his IVs, and I learned how to just try to cope with it day to day.

Two years later, my partner was diagnosed. I really believe things in our life happen for a reason. And the powers that be prepared me for what was to come later in life. And that was my partner's death and then my father's death. All from this epidemic. It's made me a stronger person. It's made me who I am today, wanting to fight for the people who live with this disease. My family has lost a lot to this epidemic. I have a younger brother who's gay, and he lost his part-ner two years ago. So all around us is death. It has become a way of life for us.

I am HIV positive. It frightens me. What frightens me more is I don't want to see my friends and my family suffer because of me. I want to be able to live a good life, give back to life until the very end. I don't want to see my loved ones suffer because I'm suffering. I think we all fear the unknown. So part of me fears death and another part doesn't. I have lived a good life. I have been blessed with wonderful, wonderful people in my life. We're on this Earth for a very, very short time. I hope to try to change people's ways of think-ing, to make the difference in someone's life. It always comes back to my mother. She had no education. I've always said, if she had an education, she could have been president of the United States.

I think it's part of my faith, too, that things happen on this Earth to prepare you for the next moment in life. I don't believe there's a Hell – not with what goes on in our world, not when people suffer and die. These *awful* diseases. Not when there's poverty on this Earth. There is no Hell. We live through Hell on this Earth one way or another. But I believe there is something there. When my partner, Jeff, was dying, he and I would always joke about if there is a way for us to communicate in the next life, let's do that. On the anniversary of his death, a year later, I was very depressed and I was at home. I wouldn't go out. I went to bed early that night and the phone rang at two in the morning. I said, 'Well, who in the world is calling me at two in the morning? This is absurd.' I picked up the phone. There was no one there. I hung up the phone and for that moment I felt this sense of peace, and I looked at the clock and it dawned on me, it was the hour, the moment he had died a year before . . .

I never have asked for another sign after that. I felt so content with that. It was almost as if he was telling me he was fine. If there is such a thing as Heaven, it's a place of peace, it's a place of beauty. I feel that I go through this life and the people I've lost are always looking out after me, taking care of me. They're almost like my angels. It is my faith that there is another world out there, whether it's a Heaven or another universe or whatever. I believe in God.

Every day of my life, though, I get angry at God. [*Laughs*] Did He create us? Did He or She create this pain? Does He or She have the power to take it away, and if so then why isn't it taken away? I believe that there has to be something better after this world. For years, I believed that we needed to be buried. But, as I've gotten older and studied Catholicism, I think cremation is the way to let go the spirit so that the spirit is set free.

I think it's the Buddhists who believe that we go through this life, that it's a cycle, and that each time we come back we are learning a lesson in life, until we break out of that cycle and we have understood the meaning of life. I very much believe in that, that there are lessons for us to learn and that each time we come back, we come back as a better person. You know how you meet people and you feel that they're old souls. I think they've been around and they are finally at the peak of life.

Sometimes I wish I could have done more. When I took care of Jay, the last day, the last couple hours, I was giving him shots of morphine, and I knew the last shot of morphine that I would give him would be the final shot. That was so hard for me . . . to know that yes, he would be at peace, and there would be no more suffering – but that it would be at my hands. I feel that I've been honored to hold these people and to let them die in my arms. I think that is a big, big honor.

LORI CANNON

She is an unlikely cross between Sophie Tucker and Olivia de
Havilland. We are at a food bank she runs: the Open Hand
Society, in Uptown, Chicago's multi-everybody community. Its
clients are people with AIDS, although nobody up against it is ever
turned away.

We started on Christmas Eve, 1988. I am the sole survivor of its founders. We serve gay men, white and black,
women, gay and straight, Asians, Native Americans,
Hispanics, Jews – this virus does not discriminate. Our
clients are on disability, Social Security, or just bad luck.
Wonderful people who at one time had thriving careers
and interesting lives and dear friends. Unfortunately, they
lost everything when they got sick. That wasn't the
greatest tragedy, though. They were allowed to die
because the government didn't care. The mistaken thinking in the early eighties is the very same mistake that is
going on in Africa right now, as the devastation of this
epidemic claims generations. It's unconscionable and
shameful. The attitude of the American government in
those days was, 'Gee, who cares if a few faggots or junkies
die?'
    We felt, here in Chicago, the one thing we could do was
feed people. We were taking care of our own friends, but we
knew there were others living in isolation, in shame,
shunned by family, friends, their church. We couldn't do a
lot, but we could figure out a way to prepare meals. These
were the gays and lesbians who responded to a crisis when
no one else would. Lesbians and gay men were the care-
givers. I often wonder, if AIDS had first hit women instead
of men, would the gay men have been as supportive to their
gay sisters as the lesbians have been to the gay men? My gut
feeling says I doubt it. If I'm wrong, I owe everyone an
apology.

What happened in the mid-eighties – people became transformed seeing their contemporaries dying in their arms. Young people, well-built people, professional people. What was killing them, killing my friends? In the year 2000, I liken myself to a medieval woman, totally out of touch with the modern world because death has become a constant companion. I'm fifty years old. I never in a million years expected my midlife to be spent alone. I thought we'd grow old together.

We live with rage. Fortunately, we at Open Hand are able to channel that rage and grief into doing something positive – knowing that we're relieving one burden from the day-to-day life of someone who is struggling. When we started Open Hand twelve years ago, people were in the final stages of HIV. We delivered to the Gold Coast, to Cabrini Green, anywhere there was a need. Especially when you're dirt-poor and too weak to stand at the stove and make a cup of soup, you call Open Hand. Some people have no history of ever reaching out and asking for help because *they've* always been the one to offer help. Now, they're saying, 'I can't do anything. How am I going to get to the grocery store? I'd ask my friends but they're all dead.'

My best friend, Danny Sotomayor, was Chicago's leading AIDS activist. Half-Puerto Rican, half-Mexican. A child of sexual abuse. When he sero-converted to HIV positive, he turned his rage from a tormented life into something positive. He used his talent as a political cartoonist to zero in on the homophobes. He zeroed in on the government. He zeroed in on the drug companies that were making huge profits, blood money, off the backs of our dead friends. He was this little spitfire who would disrupt city council meetings. We were demanding more funding. I can't tell you how many times we were arrested.

One night we broke into the budget office of Chicago. We stole the records, we reviewed the numbers, and guess what? We found *two million dollars* that was unused in the city's health budget. We ran to the alderman, Helen Shiller. She made a stirring, stirring speech on the floor of the Chicago city council, saying, 'Mayor Daley, you cannot kid us, you cannot lie to us.' In an impassioned plea, she revealed the truth to the entire city council that magical day: 'How do you explain these figures? How is it that this money has been unspent? And why are you telling the health department and the people with AIDS in Chicago there is no money for services like affordable housing, transportation to clinics, groceries. How *dare* you! This is *unconscionable*.' The mayor was flabbergasted because I'm sure he's thinking, *How the hell did you get this information?* The vote was unanimous, the bill was passed, and two million dollars that we discovered was indeed available went to the organizations that were involved with the day-to-day life of people living with AIDS. The Chicago Department of Public Health is our number-one funder. Specifically for people living with HIV, Chicago has offered a huge budget. Had it not been for our moles – gay men and women who were willing to work with us, after hours, late at night, in the city hall – and our break-in, we would not have had this funding. When your friends are infected, you are affected. If you know somebody in health, you know them in sickness. And you honor that friendship.

I come from a crazy middle-class family. My dad became a dynamic salesman with the motion pictures and TV shows. And in the middle of everything, he moved to a Navajo reservation and became the executive assistant to the nation's tribal chief. He lived on the reservation for twenty-five years. Because of his public relations background, the tribe offered my father a job. My mother, my brother, who's handicapped, and I stayed here. My dad was very proud of all the work I did. He passed away in 1996.

I worked as a bus driver and then a coach driver – I drove a school bus for the marching band of Northwestern [University], of which the tuba section would always ride with me – and that was *crazy*. I was led to this work when my friends got so sick. I've been involved primarily with the gay community by way of theater, by way of getting my hair done, by way of having the apartment decorated. The gays have been discriminated against forever, and yet they did the humane thing by offering agencies to perform services for all people, not just gay people. To their dying breath, these wonderful activists who were my friends made sure that these agencies did the right thing. They blazed a trail. In Chicago, the legacy is: people with AIDS have services now. With dignity, with respect. I can't say the same at Public Aid, and I can't say the same at Social Security. They don't give a damn. In the

early years, the attitude was: 'They'll be dead before they have to
worry about their benefits, I don't have to rush.'

I'm here seven days a week, fourteen to sixteen hours a day. This
is my life right now. Open Hand. Death is my constant companion.
People aren't dying as often and as frequently as they did in the early
years; 1980, '81 – that's when it started. For those long-term survivors who are fortunate enough to still be here, they remember how
it was back then. You know what our social life was? We would meet
at the memorials. When you go to seven, eight a week, that is your
social life. You worked your job, you went to the homes of your
friends because they had to have clean linens, the kitchen had to be
cleaned up and spotless because you can't have bacteria. When someone is too weak to stand up and make a meal, you have to help. So
you multiply that by the hundreds and thousands of people that
we've been able to serve, and I guess I thought about all of them last
week at the Gay Pride Parade. For me, it was just the memory of the
ghosts, not so much the people who were there but everyone who
wasn't. That was the corner where Bob Adams used to stand and
wave to me . . . and then I'd look at another corner, and that's where
my friend Christopher Richardson would dance shirtless in his cam-
ouflage pants. I'd look at another corner and all I could remember
were all the people who weren't there. I often have these visitations.
So for me, it's a day of pride, but it certainly is bittersweet.

Sometimes you worry, am I going to forget the ghosts? That's disrespectful. You're supposed to remember. Which is why, when
people come to groceryland and they see Lori Cannon, they know
that they're going to get a story about all their friends that are gone.
But the underlying commonality is the heroism. Your diagnosis
meant you had to come out again. Would people want to talk to
you? Would landlords rent to you? Would your job keep you? And
somehow this strength . . . superiority. Who else but the gay community could tolerate it. It's almost like the Jews at the camps. It
requires a culture and a group that grasps that the whole thing is
about *survival*. And if at a certain point you understand you're not
going to survive, then hopefully you're surrounded with friends.
What would motivate somebody who's dying of AIDS to still get
up, write a symphony, design a ball gown, be an architect for a
great building? There is a gene, I think, within the gay community,

that allows them to survive challenges in a way that still offers whimsy, still offers humor, and still offers love. And I've seen it.

My friend Scott McPherson wrote the play *Marvin's Room*.* It was a black comedy, a kind of sneering at death and its challenges. He knew he was dying of AIDS. He wrote the play just shortly after being diagnosed. He was my best friend, Danny's boyfriend. That was my family, Danny and Scott.

It's close to the end. The doctors want to do more testing on Scott. He's a little wisp of a thing – a little body with a big head. His lymphoma had traveled up to his head. It's now misshapen. The one last test came back. The doctor went to find me because he knew I knew everyone on the AIDS unit floor. He didn't want to tell Scott the bad news without me being there. I could tell from his face the news wasn't good. So I go into the room, I'm sitting with Scott, he clutches my hand to his bony little chest, and the doctor tells him, 'Yes, it's lymphoma, Scott. It's quite advanced – doesn't look good.' And without missing a beat, my little sweet friend Scott looked at the doctor and he said, 'I'm sorry that you had to go to the trouble. I know how hard it was for you to tell me.'

My first thought after Scott McPherson died, when we were all gathered in his bedroom . . . I called all the relatives in, because I knew the moment he would take his last breath. I don't know how it comes to me, but when I know it's getting close I beckon people to please join us, let's surround the bed in a circle of love . . . Scott was famous for his glasses – he wore those goony glasses like they wore in the fifties. Couldn't see a thing without them. They had picked up his body and I thought, *If he's lucky enough to hook up with Danny now, how will he find him?* The glasses are on the nightstand. He would need those. And then someone said, 'Well maybe they don't wear glasses.' I said, 'Scott will always need his glasses.' How could he find Danny? 'Cause I'm sure they're going to be searching for each other.

I accept death, but the dying part worries me. Will it be agonizing? Or will it be just going to sleep one day and not waking up? That's not a bad way to go. Something quick, because we've seen

*The play was critically and popularly acclaimed at the Goodman Theatre, Chicago, and later made into a movie (directed by Jerry Zaks [1996]).

the horrors of a lingering death. That's not joyful for anybody, and it's *not* poetic. But I look forward to joining all of my friends, and my dad, and all of my heroes.

There's no reason to prolong pain. Traditional medicine says, 'Wait a minute, let's try this, let's try that ...' But when the person says, 'Hey, I'm tired of being sick, I'm *sick* of everything – I want it to be over,' you *must* listen to him. You can't get that support currently from traditional medicine. It's only with alternative medicine. Look at marijuana. I'm getting it for my friends all the time. Why isn't there a civilized approach to that in Chicago? Legalizing it. It lessens the pain, it helps with chemotherapy.

If you and your doctor have talked about how you want things to happen, that's great. Oftentimes, doctors can't hear that – they don't accept it. They've taken an oath to preserve life and that's it. Some doctors are extraordinary, they understand it completely, and if that means that morphine is upped a little bit every day so that eventually the heart stops, they'll do it, and there is no investigation. It's happening. It's humane. If that person understands that there is just no hope, give them the dignity of deciding how it's going to be and you'll see a peace comes over them, a tranquillity comes over that person. They can count on people to come through and assist.

I had one situation, the guy *wouldn't* die! He called me: he says, 'Help me end it.' I went to New York, I brought all of the medication. The one thing I *couldn't* do was put that plastic bag over his head, tie a belt around his neck. So I'm sitting there, I'm watching his chest go up and down. He is suffering so, it's *killing* you to watch it. I thought, *How could this be?* There's a formula of what kind of narcotics to offer, how to do it. These are young people with young hearts. Normally, a young heart won't stop. I thought, *Goddamn you, Steve.* I go, what is this? So you know what I did? I closed his mouth, I pinched his nose, and that was *it.* I said, 'Well, I gotta go, everybody.' It was in Brooklyn, so I went to Nathan's for a hot dog. I thought, *This is a hell of a thing.* I knew the next morning the sister was going to come by because she would come and check, make breakfast. She knew nothing. He didn't want to include too many people. The next morning, Steve's sister did come into the apartment. When she found her brother dead in bed, it didn't shock her. She knew he was sick, and she would just expect that to happen one day – no reason to implicate her in any of the plans. You could tell she was relieved. She still doesn't know. The police didn't have to investigate, there wasn't anything unusual. The ironic thing is, she called me that night to tell me the news and I offered my condolences. I said to her, 'Daisy, you were a wonderful sister to Steve. You should be proud of yourself.' I made her feel good. She reconnected with her brother only when he became very, very sick. I said, 'I'm sorry for your loss – condolences to your family. I'll never forget your brother.' She said, 'Well, thanks for being a good friend.' I said, 'You bet.'

It's a war. We consider it a war. I consider Dr. Kevorkian to be a saint. I resent it when people attack him, because I think they just don't get it. I respect the sanctity of life. When my friends never got past twenty-seven, or twenty-eight, or thirty-one, those thirty-one years to me were golden. But to end the suffering is also important.

I have had visitations from my friends who are gone. When I see them, I take something to puncture or wound myself, to draw blood, so that I make sure it's not a hallucination. So I can say, *wait*, I was *quite* conscious. A lot of people who have lost friends to AIDS, we all talk about the visitations that we get. One of our volunteers, David, who's now gone many, many years, called me in the middle of the night from St. Joe's Hospital – and he was crying. I knew he was sick. He called me because he was scared. This was a year after Danny died, so it was 1993. David says, 'Lori, I'm at St. Joe's Hospital.' I said, 'I heard. I thought I'd come up and see you this week.' He goes, 'The reason I'm calling is Danny came to visit me tonight.' I said, '*He did?*' The first thing I asked was, 'How did he look – did he have his hair?' 'Cause Danny in good health, before chemotherapy, had the most gorgeous head of Latino hair – thick, wavy, romantic. He said, 'He had hair and he was sitting on my bed. Danny came to visit me to say, "David, it's not your time yet. As sick as you are this week and you think you're dying, it's not your time." And then Danny left.' I said, 'David, did you have a relationship with Danny, did you know him?' David said, 'No, I only knew him in the newspapers.' He never met him. I said, 'Really? Danny found time to come visit you.' He said, 'He wanted me to be at ease.' I said, 'Well, then I would take his word for it.' He got well – he was able to get home. David died one year later.

Oh, I've had visitations often. Even here at 3902 Sheridan, I will look up at the CTA bus that goes by our window, I will see friends of mine who have died sitting on that bus looking. I can't help but when I run outside at the bus stop, thinking they'll get off the bus, but they don't. I feel they're visiting me and they're watching to make sure I'm OK.

BRIAN MATTHEWS

I first encountered him when he appeared at the Open Hand
Society headquarters to pick up his food package. Lori Cannon
had to persuade him, because he felt he might deprive someone
who might need it more.

> I'm a gay male, thirty-seven years old. I have a degree in
> business from Indiana University. After I got out of college,
> I did some graphic design for a few years, and got lured into
> the bar industry. I worked as a bartender for the last ten
> years. For a time, I worked at a leather bar, a bar mostly for
> men who enjoy dressing up in leather. They're the fringe of
> gay, hyper-macho.
>
> I grew up in Munster, Indiana. It's about forty-five
> minutes from Chicago. Upper-middle-class. When I was
> about five years old, I realized I was gay. I didn't know it
> was a sex thing, but I knew that I was different. I was
> fourteen when I had my first gay experience. I came out
> to my family when I was seventeen. My dad was the
> manager of the Amoco refinery in Whiting. I am the
> oldest of three. My brother is an engineer at Amoco. My
> sister is also an engineer. They're all supportive of me,
> very much so.
>
> After the leather bar, I managed Big Daddy's, another
> gay bar, and then tended at Bucks Saloon, right in the
> middle of the gay strip. Finally, I decided I had enough. It's
> a rough life.
>
> I'm now an editor of a gay weekly – irreverent and, hope-
> fully, funny.

I was diagnosed three years ago: HIV. And I became sick within a
couple of months – I became almost deathly ill. In fact, there was
a point when I looked at myself in the mirror in the hospital and
they were running all kinds of tests on me, I didn't know *what* was
wrong, and I was running hundred-and-five-degree temperatures

constantly. I looked at myself in the mirror and said, 'Oh my God, you're going to die . . .' It was really strange, but it wasn't really scary, just matter-of-fact. Then the next day they did a bone marrow puncture in my hip and discovered that I had Kaposi's sarcoma – it's a type of cancer. Usually you get spots with KS. It's usually found in the elderly or people with weakened immune systems. It was HIV-related. With me, they found it in my bone marrow, and I was the first person in the country diagnosed with this type of cancer in the marrow. This was three years ago. So they started chemotherapy the day after that and about a day after that my fever stopped and I just turned around like that and recovered. I had gone on the cocktail medicine prior to that. It's pills, but they call it a cocktail because it's a mix of different medicines. I take thirteen pills a day. I carry a little pill thing. I've taken all my pills today. Here it is. Orderly, all named. Noon. Tuesday morning. Evening and bedtime. We're having a martini and I'm enjoying my life.

I was scared at first, then all of a sudden I wasn't scared. It was just kind of like I accepted that I was going to die. Two days later I was drastically better, much better. Now I'm feeling pretty good.

I've lost many friends. The first friend I had died when I was five years old. We were out playing in the springtime in Munster, and he decided to walk across a bridge that didn't have all the wooden slats on it. He fell through into a river that was raging. He drowned when I was with him. The most wonderful thing that anyone has ever done for me in my life was my grandparents. They lived out in rural Indiana. They took me out to their farm and bought a dozen baby chickens and taught me that there's a continuum of life. They taught me with those baby chickens that although there was death, there was also new life. And they made me responsible for those lives. The ironic part is, when I was eighteen years old, they were joking around with me about eating my chickens, and I had *no* idea what they were talking about. They had told me that the chickens were too big and had to go to a farm. Of course, they butchered the chickens and I ate them.

I was raised Methodist. We went to church every Sunday. I'm not really sure what it is, but I believe that there is something bigger than us and I believe that this isn't it – that there's more than this plane that we exist on. I had a very close friend of mine die about five years ago. He died of AIDS. I took care of him up until he died, and he told me that after he was gone, he would look out for me when he was in Heaven. He would watch over me. The night that he died I was working at Buck's, and somebody came in, I don't exactly remember what happened, but I just had the feeling that my friend had sent this person in to tell me he was OK, that he had passed on to Heaven. I just had this feeling. He had worked for me. He was my assistant manager when I managed Big Daddy's. It was not a sexual thing at all. We were just kindred spirits, we really connected. He started getting really sick and went to the Bonaventure House, which is run by the priests across from Illinois Masonic. It was a house for people living with AIDS. I would go by and visit him every day. I saw his deterioration. He had a parasite in his intestinal system that now is treatable, but back then they couldn't.

With AIDS, each one may have something different. The immune system is knocked out, so it could be any damn thing. The protection is knocked out. I remember now, he had crypto-sporidium – it's something you can get from drinking water. Most people can fight it off, but some people with weakened immune systems develop it. He had a central line that went right into his blood and he had two feedings, called hyperalimentations, that kept him alive. He had chronic diarrhea. He went to the bathroom every fifteen minutes. Barely could keep water down. So he and his doctor decided that they were going to stop treatment and put him on morphine. I promised him I'd be there, and I was until two days before he died. I called him up and he didn't know who I was. He was on morphine and starting to get delusional. But I really feel that I fulfilled my promise to him, that I was there for him.

I wish I could remember what that guy said the night that my friend Tommy died. People don't come to a bar and want to hear stuff like that from the bartender – you're supposed to put on a good face. So he died, and I went to work and I was just trying to be strong. I had broken down a couple of times and I had to go down-stairs to the basement. The people that I worked with were very supportive. When I would start to cry, I would go downstairs. I came back upstairs and I was serving drinks and somebody came in and said, 'It's going to be all right.' They didn't know me, they didn't know what I'd been going through – it was like he sent this person in to tell me it's OK.

When I was like in my late teens, I questioned everything. Anything I believed had to be proven to me. I was like a scientist. Doubting anything that I couldn't hold in my hand. But having lost as many friends as I have . . . Maybe I'm comforting myself, maybe that's all it is is my brain, my psyche defending itself. But I really think there is something, that this being on Earth isn't the end.

Postscript

Recently, he had a relapse. At the hospital, the diagnosis was the dreaded one. He was dying. His family came, last rites were to be offered. But something startling happened. Brian said, 'While I was out of it, I heard a voice that said, "Brian, your time is not yet. You still have work to do."' He recovered somewhat, only to have another setback. He did get out and volunteers at the Open Hand Society.

JEWELL JENKINS

I'm a black woman trying to succeed. I'm sixty-one. I work for Cook County Hospital. Housekeeping. I take the job serious, as though I'm doing it for a family member at all times. I consider most people family members, because I want to do the best job I can. I come from a lower-class black family. I was raised only by my mother. My father was in the service. I was born in Cook County Hospital. I feel my mother did the best she could. She raised us in the Catholic Church. The religion was *very* strict. You went to church in the morning before you went to school. You had to be respectable, you had to obey your parents. When I get home, like Sunday morning from Saturday night working, sometimes I don't get right to sleep, so then I'll go to church. But if I lay down and go to sleep, sometimes I sleep past the Mass. I work forty hours a week. But this past weekend, I worked sixteen hours a day.

I get a joy out of doing things for people, I don't know why. I don't work with AIDS patients anymore, but I worked strictly on the AIDS ward for nine years. When I got hired, the ward was opening up and they didn't have a housekeeper because a lot of people were afraid. That was 1989. People are still afraid of it. I used to tell my co-workers that it was the safest ward to work on. You knew what you were dealing with. This was one specific disease. As I learned more about it, this disease hits the nervous system, it kills the immunity system. So I told my co-workers, *you* are more of a death threat to these patients than they are to you. You can bring in a germ that won't bother you but will react on them. You can have a cold and it's just a cold, but if they're exposed to you, they can pick up the cold and it can turn into pneumonia, also turning into PCP [pneumocystis carinii pneumonia] and that can be fatal. My co-workers always felt like I was going to catch something: 'Oh, you've got to wear your gloves, and you've got to wear this and you've got to wear that.' I found out that the AIDS patients that I worked with were more concerned about me: 'Don't forget to put your gloves on,' 'Be careful when you pick this up,' 'Don't touch that.' They were caring for me.

When I first started, there were mostly gay men. There were one or two of them I got friendly with. I met the family. After work and days off, one particular guy that died, I went to his home. I had dinner with his family. It was like, 'Nobody wants to be my friend but you. Why do you want to be my friend?' I said, 'Well, you ain't never done nothing to me. You're all right with me.' This one particular guy that I went to see, his parents were like feeding him with a long-handled spoon. He was in a wheelchair. When I bent down and I hugged him, they were like, 'You would *hug* him?' This was their attitude – his own family! They didn't say anything, it was just the looks that I got. They had like a small apartment downstairs for him. He was allowed upstairs, but he lived downstairs in the basement. We sat down there for about an hour and a half until his mother called us up for dinner. I could tell by the way he reacted, it was like he felt shoved away. They didn't want to be close, and he felt this. While we were sitting downstairs he was saying, 'They really don't want me here.' I said, 'They brought you home – they evidently want you here.' 'They just brought me home because it was time for me to be released from the hospital and I had no other place to go.' I said, 'No, it's not like that.' I was trying to convince him that his parents still cared, but I could see from the reaction they cared in such a way, like, it's more of a duty than something I want to do. This is something he was starved for, love and affection.

Sometimes people don't have to say things, you just watch their expressions. This is why I like to watch people's body language, their facial expressions. The mother and father and a sister. It was like, 'You're doing some of the things that maybe we should do but we're afraid to do them.' He used to always tell me he loved me. While he was home, every morning he would call back on the floor and talk to me. 'What's happening? Who's up there? What are they doing?' He was up on the ward for about three straight months. He left for home, and he got sicker. He came back and he stayed for another three months. The second time that he went home, he was doing pretty good and he would call the ward every morning. He would always talk to me and I'd say, 'I've got to get off the phone 'cause I've got to start working.' But he just wanted to talk.

He died. The killing thing about that was his father didn't have a phone number for me. The kid was only twenty-two. What he did was he wrote my phone number down, but he didn't put a name at it. I hadn't heard from him for about three days and I got worried so I called the house. His mother answered the phone and she said, 'I'll let you speak to his father.' In the back of my mind: 'I don't want to talk to his father, I want to talk to your son.' So his father got on the phone and he told me the kid had passed. They had had the burial and everything.

God is the person that I can go to no matter what. Whether I speak out loud to him, whether I go to a church, or whatever. He knows how I feel, He knows what I think. I don't have to ask, because He knows exactly what's going to be in my lifetime for me. Because in my life, I've had a lot of problems. When I was down and out, it was like nobody can help me. I had that time. And as things went on they got better and better. I get in the car and I say, 'Let me get to work on time, safely.' I say that every time I get in the car.

My mother was my influence in life. She ran the elevator in a hotel, she was a cook, she was a salad girl. There were four kids, and I was the last.

I believe there's a Heaven. I believe we're in Hell now. On Earth we are in Hell. [Laughs] Me, as a black woman, I've encountered a lot of things that I've learned how to just shrug them off and say, 'OK, that's the way the ball bounces. Tomorrow, I'll bounce it a different way and see what happens.' I try never to let things get me down. I have high hopes for myself – I have high hopes for my children.

I've decided life is for me now, I'm going to live it to the fullest. But there's got to be something better than this. [Laughs] I don't worry about dying, because I know that the life I have is over with. If I die tomorrow, I will feel like I have achieved and done everything I'm supposed to do. Like, OK, when I finish here, I'm going home. And home is where I'm struggling to hold on to. I seriously started thinking about donating my organs to help someone. I don't know if out of my eyes that someone would see what I see. With my heart, would they feel like I feel? But I'm seriously thinking about doing it because to me there's no need of leaving it and letting it deteriorate and not do any good. Maybe the heart that they might be losing would be a bad heart, a lot of animosity in their heart. And getting mine, maybe it would change the way they felt.

I've had grief when my nephew who had AIDS died and the guys in the ward I had gotten friendly with. It hit me hard – but I worked through it. I hope that they lived a good life, that they achieved some of the things they wanted to and didn't leave a chaos here on Earth with the people they left. The family members that come that lose people, they, like, 'Oh, they're gone, oh what am I gonna do?' Well, to me, sure, you're gonna grieve, sure, you're gonna miss them, but you get loud and to a certain extent rowdy with their death because you didn't do what you were supposed to do.

It's guilt. And that makes me mad. Oh, I wish they'd hurry up and leave. Because they've got to wash the body, they've got to wrap the body, they've got to send the body to the morgue. Then I can do my job, I can clean the room. There's very few people I've noticed that will die quietly and family members won't clown in the hospital. Like I tell my kids, when I die, don't cry and be sad, rejoice. 'Cause my problems is over. You're still going on. Rejoice. Hey, she's going to a better place.

JUSTIN HAYFORD

He is a journalist as well as a musician. His current work is as a
case manager at the AIDS Legal Council of Chicago. He performs
weekly at a local piano bar, playing standard show tunes in the
manner of Bobby Short.

We provide legal service to those who are HIV-positive, who can't
afford attorneys. We do a lot of discrimination work – folks who
have been fired from their job or doctors who refuse to treat them.
We help people who are trying to get Public Aid or Social Security
who have been wrongly denied, which happens all the time.

Social Security and Public Aid are full of idiots. They don't know
what they're doing half the time, and they make mistakes. If you're
really sick, it's very hard to negotiate that system. It's *so* bureaucratic, *so* confusing. Folks with HIV very often have a lot of mental
impairments from the virus, so we need to help them go through
that system. We do a lot of work with parents who are HIV-positive,
to plan for their kids when they pass away. We do a lot of confiden-
tiality work. If someone discloses another's HIV status publicly, that's
illegal. It can really harm their lives. A lot of wills, powers of attorney, things like that. It's trying to arrange a guardianship for that
child of HIV parents. Guardianships are particularly terrifying and
awful because here's this twenty-five-year-old mother who is planning to be gone in six months, and she's got a three-year-old. She
looks at that child and you can see in her eyes: *I will never see this child
grow. This child may not remember me.* It's just heart-wrenching. We try
to find if there's somebody in this family or a friend who would like
to be the guardian. The other problem is you've got that father out
there somewhere. Legally, he's got a right to that child. So you've got
to somehow get him involved. Often the father has not been around
forever – maybe he's a junkie, maybe he's unemployed, who knows
what he does? When the mother passes away, her Social Security
benefits go to the child. So this child is now income. Whoever gets
this kid, gets a Social Security check. That makes people *really* ugly.

I'm thinking of a woman, Charlotte, which is my mother's name.

She was just twenty-five, African-American. She grew up in the projects. She was staying at a resident's house in Chicago, a house only for people with HIV. I went over there to see her. Who actually met me at the door was the three-year-old. She instantly ran over and threw her arms around my legs in this big hug. This was so amazing, that a three-year-old, meeting a total stranger, was this affectionate and loving. She spent a lot of time in the hospital with her sick mother, so she needed lots of affection from all the nurses and all the staff and all the doctors – and they gave it to her. Now she thinks any person that she approaches is a loving hug coming her way – which was beautiful. So I went to talk with her and my sick client's mother and father; they were going to become the guardians of this child. They were in their fifties as I recall. They were just lovely people. They had not turned their back on their daughter, knowing what she had. I've seen that happen too many times to count. It's unbelievable that people can lose their families, lose their houses, lose the affection. It's *really* awful. Her parents were there for her. I discovered through the conversation, they were really her aunt and uncle. She had been raised by them because her mother had died quite early in life. They said to me, 'We think of her as our daughter because we raised her, really.' It was just this very long and pretty awful discussion: 'Sign all these papers.' It's forty million court papers you have to sign – this really, really impersonal dry bureaucratic process they have to go through.

Charlotte was terrific. She seemed very calm, very wise. She knew enough to call us and say, 'I better do this now.' She went very quickly after this meeting. We thought she would last for much longer than she did. She was very calm, she was very stoic, but every time she looked at the child, there was this very deep, profound sadness, mistiness, absence in her, just watching what she was about to lose.

At the same time, there was in her eyes this enormous sense of pride that she was doing this very difficult, heroic thing. It's the last thing you want to actually face and make legally true: giving your child away. I also think making the decision to finalize the legal arrangements for the child gave her permission to let go . . .

I grew up in the classic cloisters of suburbia, upstate New York, just outside of Rochester. A very quiet, very conservative upbringing. My passion was science – I went to Northwestern as a physicist. And then just on a lark I took this strange class called the Analysis and Performance of Literature. Which was about getting up in front of a class and performing a poem, a short story, a novel. And I was thrilled! So I switched my major to this thing called Performance Studies. [*Laugh*] I did that, and when I finished my master's at Northwestern in '87 I did a lot of directing and writing for the theater. One of the first things I did, in 1989, was a big show called *The Bride Who Is a Stranger*, which was all about our changing identities because of the epidemic of AIDS. I had done a ton of reading about the epidemic.

As a gay man, it was hard to avoid: it was happening to my community. Every social justice issue intersected this epidemic, right? If you could look around, you could see that this is all about racism, this is all about homophobia, this is all about poverty, this is all about lack of access to health care. They were all there. That has always been one of my greatest interests in life: social justice.

If the cure for AIDS was one clean glass of water, half the people in the world with this problem couldn't get it. So the cure for AIDS is not medical, the cure for AIDS is *political*. Why do so many people every year die of tuberculosis? Because we don't have the political will to get them what they need to be healthy. That political fight will never end. I hope I will have the stamina to maintain the energy to keep it up, because it's very discouraging. You can't end AIDS until you end every social illness out there. You can't end the epidemic until you end the social problems which allow it to spread, right. Why do black people have a high rate of HIV infection? Are black people more susceptible to a virus? *No*. It's racism – period. They don't have access to the resources that I do. Why are women in domestic violence so often affected? Because they have no power over their sexuality. So we have to end violence against women to end the epidemic. For us to go into poor black communities and say, 'Your problem is HIV,' they say, 'No, my problem is the crack dealer on my corner and getting shot at as I walk to school. What are you going to do about *that*, Mr. White Social Worker?' How dare we set the terms for their problems? We need a constant overhaul of how we fight these battles.

We all sort of forget about the early days of the epidemic. Whether you were sick or not, everybody had this thing – because you didn't know. There was no test for it. The way that we all thought of it was: the community is under attack by a virus and by a conservative political regime which doesn't care if we live or die. There was this *amazing* galvanizing effect of that. We weren't fighting just a health problem, we were fighting a *political* problem. We had to fight the system, because there was nobody else to take care of us. The HIV tests began in March of 1985 – fifteen years ago. Until then, no one knew what the hell was going on. There was no way of telling who had what, right? It didn't matter if you were sick or not, or even afraid you were going to be sick, it was a problem which affected a whole community. That, to me, was extraordinary.

I remember one of the early Act Up demonstrations that I was part of – Act Up, the AIDS Coalition to Unleash Power. It was the big street-action group. I was never a member. This great crowd of mostly gay men shut down the street, threw all these mattresses in the street to scream about the lack of beds for women with AIDS at Cook County Hospital. There were only sixteen beds. I thought: *When, ever, in the history of America, have gay men screamed in the streets to give women access to health care?* I thought: *I have arrived in utopia.* This is extraordinary! That coalition, that sense of we are fighting for social justice, was extraordinary and empowering – and we've lost that. That is what got me involved.

As far as I know I do not have HIV, and I don't feel any closer to death from having done this work. About five years ago, I remember, I was driving along on I-55 towards St. Louis: if you look to your right, there's the entire skyline of Chicago from the south, you see the whole city at once. And I had this moment. I was about thirty and I said, 'That city will be here whether I'm here or not, and it doesn't particularly *care* if I'm here or not.' There's something very beautiful about that.

I was walking home from work the other day, down my street, which is a beautiful little tree-lined street in Lakeview. And I thought, *How will I ever be able to leave this?* I'm hearing somebody's television, I'm hearing a dog bark, I'm seeing a couple guys walk by – this is nothing, but this makes me *so* happy. There's this nice cool summer breeze. How will I *ever* leave this? How will I ever be prepared to say, 'I don't ever need to walk down that street again'? I can't imagine. Knowing you won't be there . . . it's terrifying. Just the other night I woke up at about two in the morning, which is the only time when you can really feel what it's like that you're going to die. All your defenses are down maybe – you're in that strange state. And I just had this feeling of . . . I looked around my bedroom which is nothing special – I've got a little one-bedroom apartment. There's my little computer, my little brand-new bookcase which I put together myself . . . And just this terrible, terrible sinking feeling: *I don't ever want to leave this.* I'm given so much comfort by this strange little room which is nothing special whatsoever. But it's me. I can't imagine leaving it behind.

I think of a particular friend of mine, a guy named Larry Sloan. He died almost ten years ago – I think it was 1992, '93. He was a great guy. I remember one night we were going down way south to see a show. I had a little Vespa scooter. It was a lovely summer evening, he's sitting on the back. You have to put your arms around the guy or you'll fall off the scooter. So we're driving along on this scooter down Michigan Avenue, and we're singing all the songs from *Chorus Line* that we can think of at the top of our lungs while we're driving along. Here was this silly, ridiculous moment of riding along and being silly, being goofy, and, boy, I would give anything, *anything* to do that again. *Anything.* He told me that when he was very sick in the hospital, that's the moment he would think of to try to keep pleasant thoughts in his brain when he was feeling awful.

The thing that's so awful about this is that you get used to it. Oh, another gay man died of AIDS – OK, that makes sense, that's reasonable. I realized this about five or six years ago when a friend of mine went to the hospital. He had what looked like pneumonia. I thought, *OK, well, he's got it, he's gonna die* . . . Sure enough, he didn't have pneumonia, he had a staph infection. It's a germ, a virus. When you get a sty in your eye, that's staph. But you get a staph inside you, it's *serious* business. We didn't know this at the time, we thought: *Oh, phew! It's not AIDS – let's have a party!* A week later, he's dead. The shock that we all felt was extraordinary. We couldn't make any sense of this death the way we are used to deaths from AIDS. A death from AIDS is like, well, of course, that fits into a slot, we know that, we're used to that . . . But this thing, we couldn't understand what was going on. We didn't know how to grieve for this person. It was awful. I am now so used to an AIDS death, I'm not shocked any-more. He actually died of a heart attack because the staph infected his heart.

There's a common story that people with HIV assume a certain level of pride and confidence and wisdom, which I don't think is true, but it's a narrative we tell ourselves. For some people it's true, but not for all people, absolutely not. We really have sort of lionized people with HIV in the gay community – they're sort of our heroes. Which is *very* troubling, because why do you have to have HIV to become a hero? The real terror is that there are guys these days who see becoming infected as a very *good* thing.

This is something that I've thought about a lot, working in my job: if you're a gay man and you want to get a will done, we can't help you. If you're a gay man with HIV and you want a will, oh, we'll do it for you *for free*. Any number of things you get for free once you're HIV-positive. You can get housing, you can get food delivered to you, you can get a social worker, you can get a support group. You can't get that stuff just because you're gay. Which is a commentary, really, on how we have delivered social services in this nation from day one. It's not enough to just help people who need help – you have to first be in a crisis situation. Then we'll give you as little as we can get away with.

The amazing thing about the way the gay community set up HIV services in the beginning was: you *didn't* have to be in a crisis to get help. You got HIV, let's get you in here and let's think about what we can set up for you. Maybe you don't need meals delivered to your house, maybe you don't need anything right now. But we'll offer you all these options and all these things, and we're going to keep you going; we're going to keep you integrated into the fabric of gay culture.

Now it's a lot of government-funded agencies. Once the govern-ment funds you, you have to do things certain ways. You've got to provide very specific kinds of help to specific kinds of people and show specific kinds of results. There's nothing terribly wrong with that, but the early model to me was a much more helpful one. It showed people what was wrong with the social services that are already established in this nation. The community, the gay commu-nity itself, set up a *much* better model. And I think we've lost it.

I wish what we had said to America was, 'Learn a lesson from us.' If you've got HIV in this town and you're trying to get Public Aid, you've got a boatload of people who will help you do it. I'll sit with you in the awful, terrible Public Aid office while you wait for three hours to be treated like dirt. I'll get you through this, I will make you feel OK about this, I will make *sure* this worker does what he's supposed to do.

I went to a Public Aid hearing with a client once. The guy submitted all this paperwork. They had made a mistake. I'm talking to the hearing officer and I said, 'Well, everything submitted is in his file.' He said, 'Well, that file is upstairs, I can't get that, so you have to resubmit everything.' And I thought: if this poor client was here by himself – say, a high school dropout from Puerto Rico or a former substance abuser, a very quiet and timid man, he would have been *crushed*. Luckily, I was there in a suit and able to say to this guy, 'Your regulations say I don't have to resubmit this.' That's a system we should have. Everybody in a Public Aid office should have somebody next to him or her who knows what's going on. In serving folks with HIV, we made this great system where we treat you like one of us – like you're my brother, you're my mother, you're my sister.

I do performing on the side, just to keep me creative. Something we forgot is that HIV-negative men can have serious social and psychological problems because of this epidemic. Uninfected men have been left behind. They've watched fifty, sixty, a hundred men die, right? They live in this world where they're told over and over again, your being gay is your problem, you've brought this epidemic on yourself, *blah blah blah*.

A few years ago, remember, there was a Fourth of July celebration in the suburbs and a car slammed into the crowd and killed a couple of kids? The next day they had crisis counselors on the scene for anybody there who had a problem. When the first support group for HIV-negative men in Chicago opened a couple of years ago, they got bomb threats saying, 'How dare you help HIV-negative men – they don't have the problem.' There was a big outcry from people with HIV saying, '*We* have the real problems. The rest of you are all so lucky not to be infected, you should just be thankful.' That is how this community has split apart. I was just infuriated by this response.

So I went to this HIV-negative support group to write about it. I met this man who was just about to turn fifty. This was about three years ago. He said, 'All my problems would be solved if I were HIV-positive . . .'

His story is extraordinary. He was born and raised in the fifties, in the suburbs – repressive Catholic household. He said, 'Every time I masturbated, I ran to the priest to confess. If I died before I did, I would go to Hell.' He believed this to be *true*. The terror of damnation every time he masturbated! He gets drafted to go to Vietnam. This is 1967. He meets a buddy. The two realize they're both gay. So they get out of the army and they begin their journey through the hippie, gay-lib movement of the seventies, which was in Chicago. He was in the very first Gay Pride Parade. He was big in the whole gay revolution. He said, 'The bathhouse was not about sex, it was about changing the consciousness of the planet.' For a good many, it was more about sex, but to Frank, my buddy, it was a political place. He lived through the seventies, and he said, 'For the first time I had this big community, I had this big politics which told me I'm a good person, I'm worthwhile. Then this epidemic starts. People start dying. Everyone is telling you, "Your being gay is your problem."' This is the Reagan Revolution.

Frank becomes celibate and remains celibate until I meet him sixteen years later. It drives him crazy, as you can imagine. He's so traumatized, he can't imagine intimacy with *anyone*. And he said to me, 'If I got infected, I would no longer have this terrible fear of being infected, because I'd be *infected* – the fear would be over.' He said, 'I'm beginning to think that would really put my life back.' What he realized was: in being celibate, he'd wait until AIDS was over. And then he realized: *I was waiting for the world of the seventies to come back and tell me I'm an OK person.* When he realized the politics of the seventies are dead and never coming back, that's when he thought, I may as well get infected. My world is gone. It reminds us of the power of the gay movement in the seventies. That was how we became worthwhile, self-respecting human beings.

Now the mainstream gay community is fighting to become legally married and get in the military, which are the two most conservative and repressive institutions in society. As opposed to saying, 'Let's think about new ways of structuring relationships and families.' In the seventies, we were about to make a new society. Now we're about how to fit into the society that already exists and has long excluded us.

The conservative swing in the nation hit everybody, including gays. We used the epidemic to say: 'See, all that sexual liberation – that got you, didn't it? You all had too much sex.' That's become a very quiet background conversation. It's not stated overtly, but . . . *If we hadn't had so much sex in the seventies, we wouldn't have this epidemic.* We forget what was the *good* of all of that revolution, what we *accomplished*. We would not be a community ready to handle this epidemic were it not for that revolution, right? That put us on the political map. We have Gay Pride Week, but it's become part of the mainstream, too, almost like a Rose Bowl parade. And we march through our own neighborhood, which accomplishes *what?* Who's going to argue with us in our own backyard? *Nobody.* We should be marching down Michigan Avenue. We forget, it was the *freaks* who led the Stonewall riot, right? It was the drag queens, it was the crazy people, it was the people that we now say, 'Oh, they're not part of our community' – the outcasts. What a betrayal of the people who led our revolution! The *bankers* weren't in that Stonewall Bar that night. I used to have the terrible fear: Am I going to have as miserable a death as my client just had? Many, many times I would go to the hospital to execute a document for some guy and there he is in bed. He is literally a concentration camp victim. It's exactly that image. He is just skin and bones. And he doesn't know it. He still thinks, *I'm getting out of here.* He's just doing this for temporary.

I remember, I went to Illinois Masonic Hospital to see this guy whom I'd worked with through many different issues over the years. He's lying in bed – I hadn't seen him for probably a year. Until that point, he'd looked fine. But now he was in the bed just wearing a diaper, because he was incontinent. If he was eighty pounds, I would be amazed. And he was a good five-ten. He couldn't move very well, either, because he was so weak. We were talking about his adopted daughter, that he had to make sure someone was going to take care of this kid. He wanted his partner to have the kid. We thought: *Oh my goodness, the family is going to raise a stink if his partner has the kid.*

I remember, there he was in the hospital in such terrible shape, and the nurse stood behind him the whole time and just ran her hands up and down the sides of his head and his cheeks. Just this inordinately affectionate gesture to this man. Here's this nurse who's seen this a thousand times before, right? She's on the AIDS ward, ten years into this thing. That is the kind of moment that you realize we'll *never* be done fighting this thing. If she can do that, then I can fight whatever fight I've got to put up. Whatever fear there is, maybe that person will be there for me, stroking my cheek in that terrible situation. That's all you've got to hang on to.

MATTA KELLY

She works at the University of Illinois Community Outreach Intervention Project, School of Public Health. She has the amiable appearance of an attractively mature housewife we might see in a television commercial. It was the casual manner of the *gemütlich hausfrau* with which she told her tale that was so startling and yet so natural. 'I have actually been pronounced dead once when I was using drugs. I actually woke up on one of them gurneys outside of the morgue. They had already tagged me – they had already put a tag on my toe.'

'Who is Matta Kelly?' I don't really know because I'm so many, many, many different women through my life. I was born in Reykjavík, Iceland, in 1946, so I am fifty-four. I was raised in poverty by a stepmother and a mother. My mother had seven children. I lived in a very dysfunctional household. I have been the frightened child, I've been the abused child, I have been the frightened teenager, the inadequate teenager, insecure, low self-esteem, and I have been the woman, the mother, the drug addict, the prostitute – I've been all these different things. Now I am a woman with independence, self-esteem, a career. I'm still a mother and a grandmother, and I'm a caretaker. The frightened child was in Iceland. The insecure woman with the low self-esteem came to America.

I left Iceland in 1967. I was twenty-one. I had met a man stationed in the service, an American soldier, Robert Kelly. When he came back to America, he would write me letters. I didn't speak or read any English, so I would translate the letters through the dictionary. My understanding was that he was in love with me and he wanted me to come to America. He said America is great, there's money in the street, everybody is rich. I got a one-way ticket. I had twenty dollars, and I came to America, to Chicago, with a little piece of paper with a name and an address on it. And I'm still here.

When I got here, everybody was very surprised. He was not rich – his family was poor. He didn't have a job. He didn't know I was coming. I sent him a telegram from New York that arrived the day *after* I got there. So everybody was very surprised, angry, upset. They couldn't afford to send me back home. His mother wanted us to get married finally. There was a lot of arguing going on, but I didn't speak any English, so I didn't know what they were saying. My name was mentioned often. We did get married, and we had two children together – and divorced. Actually, I have a son in Iceland that I left there when I came to America. He is probably thirty-five. I have a daughter who is thirty-one and another son who is thirty, and my youngest daughter, who is twenty-six. Our marriage didn't go well. He was young. There was a language barrier. I'm quite sure that I was difficult. There was a child. I got a job, I had an affair. And the marriage was over.

I started working for Bally Manufacturing right after my oldest daughter was born in 1968. They make the slot machines. This is while I was married. After we separated, I moved further up north. I took my two children, but while I was living by myself I ran into some people that didn't work – people that were into music and going to concerts. And I got involved with people that did drugs and started using heroin. I became a heroin addict. Of course, life was difficult because you have to make money to have heroin. From using heroin, I got introduced into prostitution – and stealing, and selling drugs. I lost my children because of that. My two oldest children, I lost to my first husband, Kelly – which, in hindsight, was a good thing. I used drugs until maybe 1987. I finally stopped. But my life was Hell in between.

People think you're having a good time when you're getting high, but you're not having a good time because you have a physical addiction, which is *very* painful. If you don't have your drug, you're in a lot of pain. It was maybe close to fifteen years I lived this way. From late 1973 to '87. I was twenty-eight when I started, and I think I was forty-some years old when I finally finished. There was just *so* much going on. I lived in a housing project, Lathrop Homes. I lived there for ten years, and I did drugs and I sold drugs there. My daughter Michelle, the youngest one, was the only one that was with me then. I dragged her with me though all my misery. She was not Kelly's daughter, so nobody could take her away from me. She was six months old when I started using drugs. I had her by somebody else.

It took a long time to detox off all the drugs. There were people in and out of my house. The police was breaking down my doors almost every week. There was just so much chaos in my life. I was in a car accident, and I was sick.

What happened with me was that every day I started thinking: *God, I hate this so much*. I could see a different place where I wanted to be. One day, I just got rid of everybody out of my house, including my boyfriend, and told them that I wanted to stop and for everybody just not to come back. That was the start. There came a point where I started quitting. It took a long time. I was on methadone, but I was doing every other drug: I was drinking methadone, shooting heroin, shooting cocaine, taking pills – you name it, I was doing it. From that point I started cutting everything down. I quit the cocaine, I quit the pills, I quit the heroin. Finally, I was just on the methadone.

I knew I was going to die, otherwise. I knew I was not going to see my daughter grow up. She has no family but me. I knew that if I died, she would be left alone. She was in her early teens when I started quitting. It took me two years to completely quit. I was afraid for her. I was afraid for her because she has no family. Her father was nowhere around – he was just some guy. I was afraid for my child. She was an early teenager, she was starting to get in trouble. She was hanging with the gangs. I didn't even realize that she had become my mother until I got clean from the drugs. She went through a horribly difficult time. Because all of a sudden, when I became clean off the drugs, the person *she* had been caring for all these years, was now giving *her* orders and expecting her to do what I said.

When I was very high, she would make sure I came home; she would go get me in bars. She would wake me up when I was burning up the couch with my cigarette because I was nodding out. She would worry about me and cry about me and cook for me and all that stuff. Ever since she was little, from the time she was one or two years old, I was using drugs. I didn't pay much attention to her. If I was at the bar, she'd go look. She was at home when the police busted down the doors. She would worry about me going to prison. When I went out, she never knew if I was coming back home. I didn't do any prison time, but I *was* arrested a couple of times.

The guilt, the guilt, the guilt . . . The guilt is what drives most people insane. It was an everyday thing: *I should do it differently, I shouldn't be using drugs today. If I get money, I'm going to buy something for my daughter.* But you never do, you never do – because the drugs are the priority. Every time I shot drugs into my veins, I *knew* I was taking a chance of dying. But the need for the drug is more than the fear of the death.

It took me two years to get clean off the drugs because I had to detox off the methadone. I had to go to a clinic to get methadone, but they didn't have a lot of counseling. They would have, like, a group once a week or something. But usually the groups were given by a very young person that was writing a paper for college. They couldn't really relate to anybody. If you're twenty years old and just out of college, how can you relate? When I finally came off the drugs, I had a horribly, horribly difficult time because I wasn't numb anymore from the drugs. I wasn't in a fog. So what happens is, you are constantly overtensed. Everything is hyped up. Your nerves are *shot.* You have forgotten all your social skills.

I was on Public Aid, and now Public Aid is telling me to go get a job. I'm a person with no American education, I just got off of fifteen years of substance abuse, I didn't write very well, and I had *no* self-esteem at all – none. I was going to places, to like fast food restaurants, and trying to get a job. I was being interviewed by twenty-year-olds. I couldn't sell myself . . .

Then I had heard about this research project and they were targeting intravenous drug users. They were looking for people to do outreach. I was coming from downtown one day and I was on the bus, I had gone to look for a job and I couldn't get it, I just couldn't. So I stopped at a methadone clinic where I knew one of the counselors. I was crying and I was telling them how I couldn't get a job and I didn't know what to do, and that I would probably end up going back out on the street. He handed me a Post-it note with a telephone number on it, and he said, 'Call these people – they're looking for a woman your age that is in recovery.' I called them, they gave me an interview. The University of Illinois, Community Outreach Intervention Project, at the School of Public Health.

This is thirteen years later and I'm still there! I just got a promotion. [*Sounding pleased and proud*] I just became the Quality Assurance Coordinator for the *whole* project. But I started out as an outreach worker. I worked here on the North Side. My job was to walk the

street with literature, with bleach, with little bottles of bleach –
bleach to clean the syringes so as not to spread the HIV. And little
bottles of water. And literature. And condoms. Free condoms. And
talk to everybody that would talk to me.

I'm an addict, so I can find an addict ten blocks away. I can feel
them. [*Laughs*] It's something in the behavior. I used to buy my
drugs in Uptown. I used to turn my dates on Broadway and Irving
back in the seventies. [*Laughs*] You can *feel* other addicts. I think it
has something to do with maybe a little bit their body movements
and the way they talk. Everybody talked to us, like drug addicts do.
They always want to be nice just to get a couple of bucks. That's just
the way it is. People got to know me because I was out here every
day – every single day. There were three of us outreach workers: me
and two other guys. We would walk the streets of Uptown every
day. Most people thought it was great. They wanted the education.
Back in the eighties, everybody was *so* afraid of HIV. But people
thought it was only the gays that had it, and it was a gay disease.
People didn't understand how it was being spread by syringes.

I was an outreach worker for six years, and during that time we
became also case managers – because when you're dealing with
people who are poverty-stricken and sick and they're addicts, a lot of
them were reaching out for help. Help with drug treatment, help
with medical care . . . Once people knew what we were doing, all
of a sudden we had all these people on our hands that were HIV
positive and weren't telling anybody because they were so ashamed.
A lot of these people had no medical care, had no income, were
living in the street or living in some rat's nest somewhere, or in a
shelter, and were too ashamed to seek help. HIV has a stigma
attached to it. The first time I went outreaching, the first person that
walked up to me and leaned up against me and told me they were
infected, I jumped straight back. It was automatic. I didn't mean to
do it. I was scared too, back then.

Most of the people that sought my help back in the eighties are
dead. Back then, there was so much paranoia about HIV that the
families of these people didn't want to be bothered, they didn't
want to *hear* about it. So me and my co-worker sometimes ended up
doing a funeral service ourselves at the Roland Funeral Home, up
here by St. Mary's. Most of these people, by the time they died, had

burned every single one of their bridges. So the family didn't really want to be bothered – the family was *angry*. And they didn't have to pay for anything. When you're on Public Aid, they will pay for the minimal. So we would have a two-hour service in the morning, early morning, and early afternoon if there was more than one person that was being buried that day. We would call around and get flowers donated, and we would make up the coffin ourselves and fix everything, and light the candles, and do the service and read from the Bible, and read from *The Prophet*. I had a funeral kit in the trunk of my car. My funeral kit was two shopping bags. One of them had a tape player and some tapes. And the other one had candles, patchouli oil, ribbons, purple, always purple – I don't know why, it was just a fitting color.

I would play some very soothing music, not religious music, but more spiritual, like chanting, or you could hear the waterfall or the rain. It wasn't sad, because I couldn't stand it when it's too sad. Out of *The Prophet*, Kahlil Gibran, I would always read that chapter on death and dying. My co-worker would read out of the Bible, maybe one little chapter. So we covered all bases. My co-worker would hand-make an obituary. We would have a picture of the client if we could find one. Sometimes we could find one in their wallet. We would do a beautiful service.

A lot of my clients would tell me, 'Matta, please, *please* make sure that I am not hooked up to no machines.' One of my clients, he always wanted a Viking funeral. That's when you put the body on the boat and you burn it and you sail it. I couldn't do that, so I would do the closest thing to it – well, it's actually illegal . . . But what I would do, I would take the ashes down to the lake and I would . . . [*she acts out scattering them on the water*]. But I must tell you the story about Norma Sanders. Norma was one of my earliest clients. She was a woman, a black woman that was born a man – but she always lived her life as a woman. Back in 1989, when I first met her, she told me that she was already HIV-infected. I don't know anything about living wills. But I knew there was a form that all the case managers had that was like, 'I don't want to be hooked up to a machine.' So we filled out this form. So Norma – she was a trans-vestite – used to come in the office all the time. But she would always come in and say to me, 'Matta, do you still have my papers, my living will? I want to make sure that you take care of me when I'm dead. I don't want to be hooked up to no machines. When I'm buried, I want to look my best. Make sure that I have a nice wig, make sure that I have a nice dress.' We knew how the HIV makes people suffer. It progresses into loss of weight, all kinds of bad, bad illnesses . . . We talked about it, that maybe it would be better if she took a really, really nice picture when she's all dressed up, and I would keep that picture until she died. And she did that. She got a picture, she was all dressed up with a red dress. Around Christmas-time she had taken the picture – *very* nice.

So I get a call one day. She's in a coma. This was just last year. So I go to the hospital. Norma had a boyfriend, Wayne. Now, it was my job to figure out a way to sell the boyfriend onto what Norma wanted – because Norma never told the boyfriend that she didn't want to be hooked up to machines. She, Norma, was a nurse's aide at one time in her life, so she knew a lot about being hooked up to machines. When I got to the hospital, I met the boyfriend, and Norma was all hooked up with tubes and all swollen. The doctors told me that she was in liver failure, but she had a chance to come out of it. This went on for almost a month. I would go up there a couple or three times a week, when they needed me to sign papers. They were trying this, and they were trying some other thing too. They always had to ask my permission when they wanted to do something because I had the power of attorney. In the meantime, I had gone into her room and I was standing next to her and she smelled very bad around her head. She had a hairpiece on. I was smelling around her to see if I could find where the smell was coming from, and it was coming from the hairpiece. I know the nurses and the doctors could smell the same thing I did. When I lifted up the hairpiece, Norma had obviously glued it on with glue, and it was all molded and rotted. And I had to get scissors myself and cut that piece off the top of her head.

Then I started thinking Norma would not want this, she would *absolutely* not want this. So I started talking to them about taking her off the ventilator – pull the plug. She had three different doctors: the head doctor, the doctor in the middle, and then the lowest one on the totem pole. All of them were telling me different things. One of them said, 'If we unplug her, she will die.' The other one said, 'If we

unplug her, she might live and she might continue to breathe.' And
the third one was telling me, 'If we unplug her, it's going to be a
really ugly death and she's going to be gasping, and she's going to
suffer.' So I had to think some more about this. This was such a difficult decision. This was a decision to take a human life. And I am
not a trained person. The only thing I can go by are my instincts and
my compassion – and what she wanted.

Without my knowledge, they moved her to a coma center. It's
where everybody is hooked up to machines. First, I called to see
how she was. When I called I asked about Norma Sanders, and they
are telling me, 'Oh, you mean *Norman* Sanders?' I said, 'No, *Norma*
Sanders.' They kept telling me, 'Oh, there must be a misunder-
standing on the computer.' I think I heard them giggling in the
background. So when I went to the hospital, I was *very* upset. I
asked to speak to the head nurse. I brought a picture of Norma with
me, that beautiful picture of her. And I said, 'This is the person that's
lying *in that bed*. She always lived as a woman. She wants to be
treated as a woman. And she wants to die like a woman.' [*A pause*]
They all were laughing, showing it around, 'Look at this, look at
this.' I was *very* upset. I asked to speak to the head person, and I told
him: 'I'm really upset. This person wants to die, number one, with
dignity.' So what I did, I stuck her picture above her bed in that
coma center. And I asked them to take her off the ventilator because
I wanted to allow her to die. [*Infuriated*] And they're still arguing
with me. 'Oh, we have to get the ethics committee together' and all
this crap. I had a *living will* and they wanted to talk about ethics, OK?
They had told me, 'She will never come out of this. Her kidneys
have failed, her liver has failed, her heart is failing.' But they want to
keep her there on that ventilator thing. I met with the social workers, and I told them that I wanted her unplugged and they were
supposed to unplug her the following day. I had the right.

So I went into Norma's room. I stuck my finger in her hand . . .
and I told her, I said: 'Norma, I have promised you for ten years that
I would make sure that you died with dignity. I would make sure
that you wouldn't have to be in pain. And I'm here to take care of
your wishes. If you understand me, squeeze my finger.' And she
squeezed my finger. And then I told her, I said, 'Norma, your cats
are OK. Your rent is paid. Wayne is fine. Everything is taken care of.

Your house is clean. Phone bill is paid. Everything is OK. You can just let go. I know you're in pain. I know you want to stop this. If you still want me to do what I promised you, squeeze my finger.' And she squeezed my finger. The next morning she died from a heart attack. And that was the story of Norma.

[*Long, long silence*]

Oh, she was a rough old broad. She used to beat her boyfriends up with a frying pan all the time. And I had a service for her. We had a closed casket. She wasn't all that bad – it's just she didn't look like she would have wanted to look. She always wanted to look her best. We had the service. Maybe there were four people there, that's all. Her boyfriend couldn't wait to get out of there because he needed a drink, so he was already hunting for somebody else.

The only way I can understand my life and accept it is that there is truly a plan for each and every one of us. I had to come from Iceland. I had to go through everything that I went through as a child, sexual abuse, worked too hard . . . I had to become a drug addict and a prostitute, lose my children – to be able to sit in front of my clients and be able to relate. How can I tell a woman that has just lost her children, 'I understand how you feel, I understand your pain.' How can I relate to somebody that's shooting drugs unless I've done it myself. So it's all a plan. I'm not a religious woman, but I have a strong belief in God. I call him God because that's all I know to call him. He's almost like a big daddy. I'm not afraid of him, but I want to do the right thing and I want to do a good thing. Because then He will reward me. [*Laughs*] He is my overseer. And He protects me. And He has handed me so much, He has given me so much . . .

I am also one of those people that don't like to talk about death, especially not my own. That is just a little too scary, because when you're gone, you're gone – and nobody can come with you to keep you company. I would like for all this experience to be a part of the continuum. So all this education that I've had through my life, I would like to be able to take it somewhere else and continue. I don't care if it's a big computer in the sky and my energy goes to that. I just want to know about it. Things would be easier if I knew for sure.

The Old Guy

JIM HAPGOOD

He is a librarian, who retired in 1993. He had worked in the
Chicago College System as well as at the University of Chicago
libraries. He, a big man, appears frail and obviously weary.

I feel as if I'm a hundred and one. [*Laughs*] I'll be sixty-eight. Since
retiring, my friend, Edward, and I used to go to the racetrack quite
a bit. I wasn't the slightest bit interested, but one of his friends took
us to a visiting day at Arlington, and I was hooked. [*Laughs*]

I realized I was different when I was very young. I would say
probably as early as ten. I think people thought of Edward and me
as just a couple of friends who got along quite well. I don't think
anyone had any idea. Back in those days, it was just assumed that
everyone was heterosexual unless they were proved otherwise. We
didn't do anything to prove it otherwise. We were together from the
summer of '53 until this April, when he died.*

He died of different things. He actually died of prostate cancer –
it had metastasized. And so they put down that he died of stepsis. He
had had severe diabetes also. When he finally died, I didn't realize that
he was that close. For the last two years it had been a sequence of
having to take him to the hospital or the doctor, usually on an emergency basis. In the course of two years he probably went from home
to the hospital half a dozen times at least. The day before he died he
had some symptoms. He was admitted to the ICU and I talked with
him quite a bit. The next day, he had on an oxygen mask, so it was
hard to talk. They said, 'He really is not doing well. His whole
system is shot and he's getting organ failure. His kidneys are not
doing anything.' He died on the 20th at 2:30 in the morning.

We lost so many friends from AIDS, it was really discouraging

*1999

while we were both alive. Actually, he was carrying HIV through the whole thing, but he went to good doctors who used the minimum amount of medicine, so he actually survived. It was listed as the fourth cause of death. It was blood poisoning, prostate cancer, coronary artery disease, and HIV. I could do a quilt for him. I would like to do that, a quilt for the NAMES Project.

I feel very confused. I was hoping I would die first so I wouldn't have to go through the ordeal of being a survivor. [*Laughs*] I think the one who shoves off first is the best.

You lack the companionship that you had. And I was so used to saying, 'Don't you think thus and so?' Every time I would get something in my mind while we were awake, the whole day, the whole evening, I would say, 'Don't you think so?' or 'Why did he say that?,' someone on TV or something. And then I realize he's not there. It's very difficult to get through the head that he's no longer around. Even though I feel him.

Whom do you talk to now?

Anybody I can get on the telephone. [*A laugh*] I have a great number of people to call, but I don't want to wear my welcome out. I try to spend time eating with friends . . . It's just a little over a month that he's gone.

From what I've seen about near-death experiences, I think some of them, if not all, do survive and could be hanging around the apartment or the house or whatever. A number of people nowadays have come forward with accounts of surviving death, near-death experience and all that. I think that kind of gives credence to some thought about survival.

Edward was cremated. We both chose that a long time ago. The idea of a rotting body doesn't appeal to me.

There's a Buddhist sutra that I chant every day. It's called the heart sutra. It's the sutra of transcendental knowledge or something like that. One of my friends said, 'It's all bullshit anyway,' but that's a bit crude. He actually was saying: even this intricate psychology is not the truth, it's simply an attempt to understand. I chant several times a day. The altar is over there and I go over and light the incense. I sit in a chair and then I take out the printed sutra, it's probably twenty lines long. [*He chants.*] It means the jewel is in the lotus, but it's supposed to give people consolation. I do it at least once in the morning, sometimes two or three times. [*Softly*] I don't have anything else to do. It only takes about five minutes.

After repeating it several times, I think I understand it better too. I first started reading it about ten or fifteen years ago and it didn't make a lot of sense. But now it does, so practice makes perfect I guess.

Aside from the Buddhist phrases do you talk to him too? Like, 'Hey, Edward, what do you think of this or that?'

I do, yes. I'll tell him I came over to be interviewed by you. I sometimes go to ceremonies at the Zen Buddhist temple near the Lincoln Belmont Y. I just started going at the time he died.

As a kid I went to a Presbyterian church. I got so annoyed that my father didn't insist that I go if I didn't like it. It was too materialistic. As for the hereafter, I don't know what it is. It really doesn't concern me one way or the other.

Since Edward's gone, I watch TV quite bit. I try to phone people that I haven't been in touch with recently, just to chat. I haven't been going to movies. I just don't feel like going out. I tend to hold on to friends I made years ago.

Do you think of death often, you yourself?

No, not really. I'm probably coasting on the feeling from his absence. I tell Edward everything on my mind for about the last fifty years. When we met in New York, we were know as 'Jim and Ed,' we were a couple, Jim and Ed. Now it's only me.

The Plague II

Nancy Lanoue

It is early morning at Thousand Waves, a martial arts and self-defense center. With her close-cropped hair, T-shirt, and jeans, she is waiting for me.

I used to be a journalist. I worked at the *New York Post*. Unfortunately, I was there right before Rupert Murdoch bought the paper and trashed it. I signed up for an eight-week self-defense course because I lived in New York City and I had to go all around the city all hours of the day and night. I didn't feel safe. I signed up for the class and *loved* it. I was just fascinated by this whole way of moving. It felt right to me.

Martial arts is so myth-laden. It's what we see on TV and the movies. My being drawn to martial arts came out of doing antiviolence work in the mid-seventies, when I was just out of college, and we were starting to speak out about rape and sexual assault, and all the kinds of violence done to women. We were creating some institutions of support for that kind of plague, right? I found a way to enact my feminism through the body by believing we could teach women, so that they could possibly stop a rapist, instead of only providing support after the rape. We could actually work on preventing rape by making individual women unable to be raped. That was a very radical idea at the time.

This is a place I opened. In 1985, this karate program began. I had a special mission, I guess: to bring these skills to women who might not have felt comfortable going into a traditional martial arts school dominated by men. I had to close it in 1989 when my partner – my life-partner and my business partner – died of pancreatic cancer. There were fifty karate students at that time, and they kept the program going. They just refused to give up, because it meant something to them. When I came back and was ready to work again, there they were. We expanded the karate school. We've gone on for ten more years. I think it's actually a way for people to practice nonviolence.

Some martial arts have an incredibly beautiful history, like the art of Capoeira, the Afro-Brazilian martial art. It was developed by slaves. In a lot of the movements you don't use your hands. That's because their hands were in chains. So there's a story of liberation associated with a lot of martial traditions that I relate to very much. Then there's the horrible, Green Beret branch of the family which is something altogether different.

Cancer came into my life like a bomb. I was in no way prepared for it. Both my parents died of heart disease. I was young, athletic, strong. The thought that I would get cancer was the furthest thing from my mind. I was diagnosed on my thirty-fifth birthday – relatively young for getting breast cancer. Usually, people are diagnosed after age fifty. Even women in their sixties and seventies. But I was diagnosed young. I think my martial arts training helped me have the strong spirit needed to fight that, and to do the treatments and keep open, and talk to people about it and not feel ashamed at having had cancer.

A lot of people feel very isolated with cancer. They don't dare tell anyone. In particular breast cancer, because it's so altering to the body. At least in the old days it was. Cancer is a very hidden subject, still. People don't talk about it. When you get cancer, the first question people ask you is: Do you smoke? What do you eat? All these questions that you think: *Ah, I did something wrong to cause me to get cancer.* Guilty. Blame the victim. I found this very irritating. Why aren't people asking what toxic-waste sites were in your neighborhood when you grew up? What chemicals? What companies polluted the rivers around where you lived? What kinds of environmental carcinogens were you exposed to? I believe we have to look at a much bigger picture of cancer than just what this one individual did. I think it's the luck of the draw which one of us gets cancer. I think we avoid the hard questions.

When I was first diagnosed, I thought it was a death sentence – my very first reaction. I was very low and just paralyzed with fear, fear of death. The first time I confronted my own mortality. When you're young you don't think you're going to die. Death happens to other people. And cancer just . . . [*claps*] . . . came like that, and said: 'You know what? Your life is limited. It's going to end. Maybe it's going to end soon.' So that's where I started – fear of death right in my face. But you can't stay there, otherwise it's going to be true. If you don't climb out of that psychological place, you *are* gonna die. So you have to go inside yourself and say, 'Well, now's the time to fight.'

The way that I fought is the way we now teach women to fight. We started a group called the Lesbian Community Cancer Project. What we learned from our battles went into helping other women advocate for themselves. My own recovery from cancer inspired me. I think I'm recovered. I'm thirteen years in good health – I'm forty-eight now.

I had never thought of death before. I'd lost both my parents when I was young, but I never believed it would happen to me. Someone gave me a book that influenced me greatly. It was by Audre Lorde, the black lesbian writer who eventually died of breast cancer herself: *The Cancer Journals*. She spoke about her battle with cancer. It was different than how everybody else spoke about cancer. She talked about it as a battle, and that we are warriors. That you have to be a warrior in how you're going to fight this plague. Her way of fighting it was not to be invisible, not to hide the fact that you had cancer, not to have reconstructive surgery and pretend you still have a breast when you don't have one, not even to wear a prosthesis, which suggested that everything is like it was before. But to be a one-breasted warrior. If you have chemo and you've lost your hair, be bald so that people can know this happened to you. Then they can connect with you and you won't feel so alone and isolated. This went against everything everyone else was telling me: 'Oh, no one need ever know this happened to you. You can wear this, you can have this surgery, and everything will be the same as it was before . . .' Audre Lorde is saying: It's never the same as it was before. Now you know that you are mortal and your life will be forever changed by that. And you should be out there and be open. I was very, very moved by her words, and I tried to live that way. So I did my battle with cancer bald and one-breasted. It was a very good experience for me.

I had women tell me that it was more difficult for them to come out as a cancer survivor than as a lesbian. Can you *believe* that?! It tells you how the dialogue about cancer has been personalized by the powerful forces that don't want it to become a political discussion. They want us to be thinking: *What did I do to cause my cancer?* Because that keeps us busy and guilty. We won't become activists, and we won't get involved in the struggles that need to happen to really solve the health crises that are created by the way corporations run the world. That's my personal belief.

This shame or extreme privacy about cancer is something that didn't feel right to me. I didn't feel safer that nobody need know about my cancer. I felt safer by sharing my struggles with people. And I got support from that. A year and a half after my own experience with cancer was when my partner Jeannette was diagnosed. Hers was a much more grim and hopeless diagnosis. She lived with her cancer for eight months, and she died in the fall of 1989. I was *devastated*. The love of my life. The woman I started a business with. Her loss, seven and a half years into our relationship, was terrible.

Jeannette was Greek and a big character. At her funeral, my sister gave a speech at my partner's request. She said, 'Jeannette knew she was going to die, she accepted it. But she wanted me to tell you that she was mad as hell to be dying of cancer at age forty-seven. And she wants you all to get involved and get busy and do something about it.' After the funeral, people started calling me up and saying, 'What are we going to do about it? How can we start a group? How are we going to act up about cancer?' After Jeannette's funeral, in Chicago, lesbians started to realize: there's more than one plague, AIDS. We should be active in the fight against cancer, too. I was depressed and tired and grieving and I didn't want to start a group. Eventually, enough women contacted me. I said, 'OK, if you send out flyers, we can have a meeting at my place.' The notices were just in the gay papers because it was a bunch of lesbian women who were originally concerned. They were a mixed group who showed up in my living room – about thirty-some. They were lesbian women who didn't feel comfortable going to a traditional, mostly heterosexual support group because they were afraid they might encounter homophobia at a time when they were very vulnerable. There was a straight woman, a very political, activist biologist who herself was a cancer survivor. She was interested in starting a discussion about cancer and the environment and pollution and corporate responsibility. It was a mixed group of all kinds of women.

After it's all over and the terror is past, you can sometimes speak about what was the gift of that experience. What did I get from it? The common thread that we talk about is having your mortality put up in your face. It sounds trite but it's true: it makes you appreciate your life in a more tangible and immediate way. You start to reevaluate: *Am I doing the work that I'm here to do?* If my life ended tomorrow, would I be happy with how I spent today? You ask yourself those questions. Sometimes you make big life changes. Sometimes you go: *Yes, I'm doing exactly what I want to be doing.* If I have one more day or ten more years, I know I'm doing what I'm supposed to be doing. The experience of confronting your death becomes in a strange way a gift.

I feel great. I feel lucky and happy and great. I still have fear that the cancer will come back, but I've learned how to work with that fear. It's no longer a big, gray cloud that covers my whole life, like it was in the beginning, where every single body reaction, every ache, every pain, you're sure it's the cancer coming back. Now I have my checkups. Every year when you go have the mammogram, it's *still* scary. But I feel lucky. Not everybody has thirteen years' good health after breast cancer.

That time, in the late eighties, was when little movements started developing all around the country – women who wanted to become cancer activists. Remember, this was the time before we understood AIDS to be a worldwide epidemic. It was in the context of an epidemic that affected the gay male community. Jackie Winnow, a cancer activist from Oakland, said, 'If I got AIDS right now I would have somebody to bring me meals. I would have a buddy who would support me. I would have all these agencies that have been created to help people with AIDS deal with this tragedy. But as a woman with cancer, I don't have *any* institutional support.' That's a big part of it, the issue of gender. Audre Lorde had an experience when she went out for her first checkup after her mastectomy. She dressed up and felt good and went to her oncologist's office, and the nurse there told her, 'The next time you come to the office, I want you to wear your prosthesis' – because it might scare the other women to see this one-breasted woman, one big breast, the other side flat. Audre was so mad at being told that she should wear a prosthesis to hide her experience. She compared it to the Israeli, Moshe Dayan, with his eye patch. She said, 'Did anybody ever tell Moshe Dayan that he should have an artificial eye put in because it's depressing to people to see him with an eye patch? No. That's a battle wound. He wears that proudly, and it reflects his experience.' She said, 'This reflects my experience. And I don't want anybody to tell me how I should look.'

I had a similar experience. My doctor was a good surgeon, and he meant only the best for me. There is the older surgery of a mastectomy, which is complete removal of the breast. Now there is a newer surgery called a lumpectomy, where they take out the tumor and a margin of tissue around it. It's for the purpose of conserving the breast. This is a new development in the last fifteen years. The science now suggests that the lumpectomy, if you follow it with six weeks of radiation treatment, offers equivalent protection to the mastectomy by itself. My doctor made the assumption that I would choose the lumpectomy and the radiation over the mastectomy because, as a man, he couldn't even imagine why a woman might prefer the other choice. But I didn't want six weeks of radiation therapy. Radiation is dangerous in and of itself – not extremely, but there is a danger associated with it. Every day to go to the hospital for six weeks when I could go back to work? I chose the mastectomy.

He thought I would look better. Even a woman oncologist I visited said, 'You should think seriously about reconstructive surgery because later on, you're gonna not be happy with your disfigurement.' I'm happy that these developments have been created, to make some women with cancer feel better about themselves – I'm happy for them. But I'm worried that so much attention is being paid to the cosmetic issues of cancer, that *that's* taking attention and research and time and money away from figuring out what's causing cancer and how we can deal with it.

I can't say I've overcome my fear of death. I think my practice of martial arts, my meditation practice, my willingness to look at death and see it as an ultimate transformation helps me be ready for it. My fear of death is less than it was before cancer. As for belief in the hereafter, my personal feeling is that the work that we do, the lives that we touch when we're here, is how we live on. Jeannette, my partner, lives on in my memory, and the things she built, and the ideas she put in my head, and the way she taught me things. Her life goes on because it became a part of me, and I'm passing it on to the next person. So that's my spirituality. I believe we exist again through our good work and our unique personality, how we are. I don't believe that I'm going to Heaven, and I don't believe I'm going to Hell. [*Laughs*] And I don't believe I'm going to be reincarnated. My father was a very profound atheist. *Hated* religion. My mother was a Unitarian. In the South, you *had* to be Unitarian because it was the only progressive religious institution. Through my martial arts, I've been exposed to Buddhism, and I'm drawn to it in some ways. The stoicism associated with it has resonance with me.

I'd like to be remembered as a person who had an optimistic belief in our capacity to grow and change. I believe for myself, and for all the people I come in contact with, that we're not set in our ways – that we have the capacity to grow and learn and revise ourselves till we're dead.

Out There

DR. GARY SLUTKIN

He served as an intern and resident at San Francisco General
Hospital and stayed on to run their TB program, eventually
leaving to work in Africa. After a decade overseas, he returned to
the United States.

> I'm the founder and director of the Chicago Project for
> Violence Prevention. I'm working full-time on reducing
> violence. A big piece of this is outreach to the young people
> to try and change their thinking about violence, and about
> the availability of alternatives. We're trying to shift from
> the idea that violence is cool and glamorous and the way to
> respond to anything – whether it's a girlfriend being taken
> by somebody else, he owes me money, or you looked at me
> the wrong way. The kids in the inner city with this vio-
> lence, they have been hurt so much they have had to put a
> shell around themselves so they don't feel. They've been
> insulted so many times that they don't want to feel all these
> insults. So their soul, their heart has a very, very hard shell
> around it, and they're not feeling. We have a hundred and
> twenty-five clergy who work with us: Jewish, Christian,
> and Muslim. We're working with the police department,
> state's attorney's office, U.S. attorney, city government –
> and we're working with the neighborhood groups and the
> residents.

I spent three years living in Somalia, working with refugees primarily. Then I was seven years working with the World Health
Organization and the AIDS epidemic in Uganda and Kenya,
Tanzania, Malawi, Congo, Central African Republic. In Somalia, we
were working with a population of about a million refugees in forty

refugee camps where a lot of death had already occurred. Child death is very, very common in these places.

There was a cholera epidemic where we saw *thousands* of people die in a period of a week or two weeks. Women wailing and screaming and crying for their relatives. The graves being filled as fast as anyone could dig them. This is now fifteen years ago.

Myself, the other medical people, we cried every night. Then we'd go back to work and cry again. Different teams of volunteers from different countries would come in and we'd struggle with it, like cowboys from abroad. I was there with my ex-wife, who's an amazing hero, a doctor too. And a number of people from Holland and Switzerland and Finland. And of course, the Somalis themselves were the primary helping group. We hadn't a clue what to do. I'd never faced a cholera epidemic. We were scrambling to get to phones to call people, to get the U.S. Navy to come in and help. I think we were all psychologically damaged from it. I've not really had death in my family. I've touched it only as a doctor who has taken care of patients and has seen some horrible things.

America doesn't really pay attention. Right now we have very, very long life expectancies here, so we're very, very much disconnected from what is still continuing to happen everywhere else. We're talking about all these millions of people who have died from AIDS in Africa and still are, but we're *totally* disconnected from it. No matter how many times we see it on television, we are unable to respond appropriately.

When I was running the TB program in San Francisco we were taking care of refugees from Vietnam. TB is an *enormous* problem overseas. They carried with them a lot of TB into the city. We had extraordinary success in containing a TB epidemic in San Francisco. At the time, there was a refugee crisis in Somalia. My ex-wife went over there, and other friends of mine went. This was to do basic health care in emergency circumstances. They came back and said. 'There's an awful TB problem. Can you go over and just take a look at it?' Actually, I went over five or six times over two or three years. I'd go back every three to six months. I was having very good luck and success. We were setting up a program in one camp, and then we expanded it to three and then to ten and then to forty. Everything we did kind of worked. I was commuting between San Francisco and

Mogadishu. In East Africa, there were about fifty thousand TB cases. Only about four thousand of those were being cared for properly. I got only five hundred people over here in San Francisco. We've done the job. 'What am I going home for?' So I made the decision to move to Somalia. I stayed there three years: 1985, '86, and '87.

It seemed to be needed. It seemed like it had to be done. There was no one else doing it. Right now, I don't have a lot of money. [*Laughs*] So I've occasionally had my regrets. My mom says, 'You would have been bored being a doctor.' There's plenty of doctors here. These doctors are competing with each other for patients. So I want to be part of that? Over there there's not enough doctors. No one's doing it. When you know that, what do you do?

I'm not exactly sure at this point why I went to medical school. I wanted to figure out how the body worked – I was particularly interested in how the brain worked. So it was really a pursuit of knowledge. I was actually majoring in physiology, and people were saying: 'Get the MD, that's where the better teachers and the better training is.' I also did have some visions of discovering something or being some kind of a hero in cancer or in something. But, frankly, I hit the wall on doing research because it was too tedious. When I went to Mogadishu, I went without a salary. I had zero. I scrambled to get someone to pay for a month, someone to pay for three months, and finally, after about a year, I got someone to give me a two-year contract. But that isn't what we were there for. We had enough money. I was in my late twenties and early thirties – who cares? Now, I just hit fifty.

What we cry about is our helplessness. When there is death, death, death, death, death, and we can't get to enough of them or even know that what we're doing is the right thing, what frightens us so much is our helplessness. You have to realize the extent to which death is prevalent in Africa. There's *always* somebody dying. We had a helper in the house. She herself was a refugee. It was the two of us, my ex-wife and myself, in this one place in Mogadishu. She helped with preparing food and keeping the house clean, for the smallest amount of money, which to her was the largest amount of money. She was asking us for our car almost every day for a funeral. There was always some friend or some family member dying. I attended a *lot* of funerals. What a funeral was like five or ten years ago and what it's like now is different. There's three to five times as many funerals now as there were five or ten years ago – because of AIDS. In most African countries, funeral ceremonies would last from three days to a week: all the meals that are involved and the family getting together . . . Now they're down to a few hours. Because people can't leave work so continuously. Some of them actually are celebrations, with drinking and dancing. If it's an Islamic funeral, they are more solemn, with a tremendous amount of prayer. Somalia is Islamic. Much of Africa south of the Sahara is a mix of Christian and what they are themselves.

TB in Africa has increased almost every year over the last ten or twelve years. We don't see the circumstance of Africa. We see a little bit of Europe, we see a little bit of Asia, but we really don't see the circumstance of Africa. In Africa, most people don't have water in their homes, don't have enough food. Most people don't have jobs. The climate is almost unbearable, the heat . . . And now we have this AIDS epidemic.

I left Somalia in 1987 and joined the World Health Organization. I stayed with them until 1994. They assigned me to the AIDS epidemic in Africa. I worked in Uganda and the twelve or thirteen countries around it, the epicenter. We learned pretty soon that between fifteen and twenty-five percent of the population in the cities were already infected with AIDS. My job was to work with the governments to develop plans and to raise money for public education campaigns, for outreach programs, for condoms, and for treatment services, basically. I'd go to each of these countries two to five times a year. I was always on the road. We'd talk to the U.S. government, Britain, England, Switzerland, Sweden, the World Bank, the European Community. We'd recruit people from the international environment to staff that program. And then we'd push and push and push and push. In Uganda we succeeded in part: the epidemic has been reversed there. This was the only country really in Africa where it's been reversed. I put twenty-five percent of my time into that place, and so did my boss. The other countries never got the money, they never got the support. So Uganda remains to this day the example of how to handle it.

In the other countries, the situation gets worse and worse and worse. You see a lot of skinny people on the street. Absolutely everybody knows someone who is sick with AIDS at the moment. There are funerals constantly, the funeral bells are constantly heard. Most of these small villages have run out of nails for caskets – you can't get *nails.* I remember being on a fishing boat on Lake Victoria, going from one part of Tanzania to another. This is a boat that, by convention, will carry some food and mats and things like this. The whole hull, the whole underneath, was just full of caskets. There are villages that are deserted. There's a place I visited in northwest Tanzania where there's hardly a person living. The few that remain have fled the place in fear of spirits. It requires only money and commitment to reverse it even at this point. Everybody, World Health and the UN, totally understands that this is still a reversible circumstance. But we're not kicking in. It basically requires about four or five things, depending on the size of the country – about fifteen to thirty million a year. That's *all.* Fifteen to thirty million a year per country. It's nothing! We're spending fourteen billion on roads in Illinois. If it were solidly put into prevention, it would cause about a fifty or sixty percent reversal. This kind of money goes into programs for young people, public education materials, posters and leaflets and billboards and training and workshops. And condoms. That's basically all that's required.

Now there's another thing happening. So many people have the disease itself that there's an overwhelming call for the medicines. The expense on the treatment side is very, very large, 'cause now actually we have the medicines to keep anyone alive. In this country it costs about twenty or thirty thousand dollars a year, per person, for the medicines. We couldn't get two hundred dollars a year for TB for Africa. Sometimes we couldn't even get fifty cents for penicillin! It's probably the biggest ethical dilemma on the planet today: the fact that we have medicines that will keep people alive in the worst epidemic ever in history. We *have* the medicines and we *have* the prevention modalities and we're *not doing it.*

The drug companies are mostly here, and the money is by far mostly here. When I was there, half to three-quarters of the hospital beds were all AIDS and TB. I see a hospital room – beds without mattresses. Picture a room of, say, thirty or forty frames of beds, springs, but no mattresses, OK? Some patients two in a bed. About another twelve or fifteen people on the floor, OK? No medicines available, OK? And no food in the hospital either. Some family members bringing food in. That's what you got. That's the rule.

Something comes to mind that I wasn't thinking of when I came here: death is our teacher. It is the ultimate teacher of what we're not doing in helping each other. If there are deaths happening that we can do something about and we're not doing it . . . What could be more in your face as to how we have not grown up?

In the West, we are the experts at the outer world. In the East, they are the experts on the inner world. We have looked at the telescope and the microscope as far as you can, and we're still trying to go further. In the East, they really have been, for four thousand or more years, looking in. They're looking at the way their mind works and looking at all kinds of methods for accessing people who have died. In Tibet, one of their principal teachings is to reflect on death. In the West, no one has *ever* told me, 'Think about death.' My grandmother died – don't think about it. They say: 'Think about it. Face it.' When we touch that loneliness or fear, we immediately go to the television or the telephone or the refrigerator. We don't want to *touch* that fear. They say, 'Touch that fear, go all the way into that fear.' When you go past that fear, that's when you start to see something. But as soon as we feel fear, or sadness, 'Oh, come on, let's go for a walk.' I read and study Judaism, Christianity, and Buddhism, and science – physics in particular. All this stuff about particles, and waves, and energy, and matter, and the interchangeability of energy and matter. Science and Buddhism come close together, actually.

I was brought up Jewish, but my parents didn't practice any Judaism. I'm culturally Jewish. But I pretty much learned that the answers were going to be in science. I married a Christian woman, I moved to a Muslim country, studied Buddhism. I think that all of these have something to offer. I don't like labels, because there's something wonderful in every one of them, and they all kind of fall short, too. I'm open to them all. You need to experience something for yourself. There's something wrong with the word 'belief' with a capital B. Whenever you really say you have a *belief* about something, you have stopped your investigation. We have to be open to death. We won't be able to run away from it, will we? I want to avoid it as long as I can. I think I'm doing something with my own mind and maybe for others too, so let's keep the physical body together. No smoking, good exercise, good diet, do things to put death away for a while. But we should, when it comes, be prepared to go with it. I'm very, very compelled by Jesus and by Jesus' life, as I am by science and by Buddhism and Judaism. I really am in them all.

PART IV

VISSI D'ARTE

Vissi d'arte, vissi d'amore . . .
I have lived for art and for love.
. . . and offered my song to the stars
and to Heaven, and made
them more beautiful.

– from Puccini's *Tosca*

Vissi d'Arte

William Warfield

A baritone celebrated for his work on the musical stage as well as his concert singing. He has appeared in a number of European countries as well as throughout the United States in *Porgy and Bess*, with Leontyne Price. He is perhaps best known as the favorite interpreter of Aaron Copland's adaptations of American folk songs. Eighty years old, he teaches at the Northwestern University School of Music. 'I still sing, but my main function is passing on to youngsters the results of what I have learned. Our profession is much like the laying on of hands, offering inspiration to the young to go further than you've gone.'

I was first aware of death as a little kid, because we had a brother who was two and a half years old – he got pneumonia and died. Death, to me, was that ogre – although I was raised in the Church, where we were taught that our souls live and go on after death.

The first time I actually came to grips with death, the fact that I'm not going to be here long, was in my sixties. I had some prostate troubles and had to go to the doctor and he says, 'We're going to have to do a biopsy because this sounds like it could be cancer.' That word was the *scariest* word I've ever heard. I had all of this on my mind with a concert coming up. We went in to practice for this concert, my accompanist Robert Ray and myself. There was one spiritual called 'My Good Lord Done Been Here': 'bless my soul and gone away.' I was rehearsing that and I got to the second verse which is [*sings*]:

> *When I get up in Heaven*
> *And my work is done*
> *I'm gonna sit down beside Sister Mary*

> *I'm gonna chatter with her darlin' son*
> *Oh, my good Lord done been here . . .*

I said, 'Oh' – just like that. And my accompanist said, 'What's the matter?' I said, 'Nothing, nothing . . .' And it just dawned on me that there *is* something after this and I need not fear it. And I've never feared death since and that was twenty years ago. [*Laughs*] That song. It's just something hit me and I said, 'Oh.' That's affirmation. We were always taught that, but that was the first time I felt it for myself: *This is only a journey to a place that's much, much better.* I never feared death since. It was book knowledge before then, but that was a spiritual experience for me, that moment.

I have not actually figured out in my mind exactly how Heaven and Hell exist, and how they will manifest themselves after death. Whenever I reach a perplexity about that, I just go back to the Scripture in the Bible. I have sung this in the last series of songs of Brahms. The first one goes,

> *Who knows whether our souls are different from the souls of*
> *   animals*
> *We see here only in part*
> *But in that day, we will understand why these things are*
> *   happening. . . . Here is love, charity, and the greatest of*
> *   these is love.*

From *The Four Serious Songs* of Brahms. The text in the last of the four is: 'We see only through a mirror darkly. But in that day we will see clearly and understand all things.'

My father was a sharecropper in Arkansas. He had a calling to the ministry, and he thought he had to educate himself to be a proper preacher. So he came North and brought his family. I was raised in Rochester, New York. All of the time, it was in me that he figured the ministry was my calling. Somewhere along the line, I transferred that feeling toward my art. I said I was called to do this: If I don't do this, I'm going to end up in the belly of a whale and be thrown somewhere, like Jonah. Every time I've reached any kind of a catharsis it's always, 'Well, my goodness, it's not just me. I'm getting this from somewhere else, from a higher source than I am.' I was talking to Leontyne about this. She said to me, 'Bill, we are the closest to God when we are practicing our profession.' And I said, 'Oh, baby, you are *so* right!'

My art and my religion, they're all the same.

My father was a Baptist, he raised us kids, pastored a church in Rochester, went to school at night and ended up educating himself. He had a job with the sanitation department, and they started *very* early – five o'clock in the morning. Then he'd come home, and mother would have his breakfast. We'd all eat breakfast by the time he'd get back home, which was several hours later. Then he would take a nap in the afternoon and he would go to school at night. I remember my father saying, '*Amas, amat . . .*' I didn't know what it was. Sure enough, later on in high school, I was saying, 'I love, you love, he loves. . . .' That's what Dad was doing, conjugating 'I love' in Latin. It was just always there in the home.

I was definitely a church kid. My first learning of music came from the lady in the church who was our organist. I came to her and said, 'Mrs. Edwards, I want to learn piano.' She said, 'Oh, child, you don't want to do *that*. Why don't you just go on and play?' But I was absolutely adamant. I came to Mrs. Edwards and I said, 'I make a dollar a week because I polish my math teacher's car. I'll give you that if you'll teach me.' Years later, when I went back and my life had been successful, and I'd made a movie, Mrs. Edwards was sitting there rocking. She said, 'I'm so *proud* of you!' She said, 'When you came to me that day and offered me all the money that you were making just to study piano, I was so touched I had tears and I had to walk away from you because I was going to cry.' [*On the verge of tears*] She said, 'I figured, I've *gotta* teach this boy.'

My introduction to classical music was through Handel's *Messiah*. As a youngster, we were not allowed at all to bring a jazz record in our house. Jazz was considered the Devil's work: You don't do any jazz in *this* house. Somebody asked me to come and play piano with a little group there, and my father said, 'No son of mine is gonna be playing in a nightclub.' Let me tell you the ironic thing about that. When I got into the army I started learning how to play jazz because our post had a little combo. I was playing piano. When I got out of the army I played jazz for a time. When I didn't have anything in New York, I would do nightclub work. I was in a club in Toronto. I was invited to the table of this gentleman and his girl, and he was telling me, 'My girl says that you've obviously been trained for something other than this.' I told him that I had wanted to get started in the classical field, but you had to make a debut in New York if you wanted to get anywhere. And he said, 'Have your manager draw up a budget. I think I want to sponsor you in that.' Isn't it ironic that the very place my father wouldn't allow me to go was where someone saw me, heard me, and sponsored me, and put me on my way on my classical career. Isn't that wild? [*Laughs*]

I'm in a family in which religion dealt with grief. It wasn't grief in the sense of having lost somebody, but that they'd gone to this place and you were going to be rejoined with them later on. They weren't gone permanently. There's something after this. I'll be there, OK, I'm going to meet you over on the other side. So I didn't have grief as such. It was just temporarily missing the person and sorry that they were not here anymore – but not grief in the sense that I see people just grieve over someone they'll never see again. I want to just put my arms around them and say something from the sermons of J. Rosamund Johnson's 'Go Down Death.' The poem ends, 'Don't weep for her / She's not dead, she's just in the arms of Jesus.' That was the way I was raised. That is the solace of religion. I find right now, for instance, if something is bothering me, I just go and sit at the piano and start playing and singing and at a certain point I get up and I'm all right. Art is my solace as well as belief: the one is tied in with the other.

Burial or cremation, it doesn't matter, because in that day, whatever you were, it's your soul and your spirit that lives on. What happens to the body doesn't really matter. I have a horrible fear of being cooped up. So the idea of being in a casket under the ground just makes me go – [*gasps*] . . . On the other hand, I don't want to be burned up either! [*Guffaws*] I think I'll take my chances of laying in the ground because, being burned, that represents a certain awful pain to me.

Even though I miss my friends, the worst thing for me is reminiscing and memories. My nature is: *OK, I've got to adjust, and I go on*. But every once in a while . . . [*pause*] . . . when someone, like my brother just died recently . . . I was the eldest of five boys, and he was the one next to me. I was completely calm at the funeral, I've accepted it intellectually and he was suffering so . . . I was relieved that he wasn't going through that suffering again, and accepted it. [*He is deeply moved and has difficulty speaking.*] But then every once in a while, even now, something from childhood will come back that has to do with Robert, and I just break down and cry. If that's what you call grieving, I don't think any of us ever forgets that. There are times that the memory of something that exists no more makes you weep.

God is everything. He's my art, He's my mother, He's my father, He's love. He's all of these things to me. And God is in me – yes, yes, yes, yes. Many times when I'm singing, I feel that I'm a vessel which this talent is going through. The only thing that I can brag about is the fact that I just didn't sit and let it go to waste, that I did something about it and learned how I could be this vessel which God flows through. I pray before I go out on a concert, every time. I say, 'Lord, be with me tonight and let me sing not for myself but for thy glory and thy honor.' That's my constant prayer before I go out to sing.

Jesus is mine. When I go out on stage having done that prayer, I don't think that I'm out there alone. Marian Anderson used to always say, 'We did this and we did that,' and she was of that belief too.★ She said: 'I don't do this on my own. When I'm out there singing, God is with me and is helping me, and that's why I don't say, "I sang a concert" – I say, "We sang a concert."' She felt that she was being helped by a divine source, that she had a calling to do.

I knew Paul Robeson. He helped me in so many ways by advice. As a man, he's the hero as far as I'm concerned. But as an artist,

★When I interviewed Marian Anderson for my radio program on WFMT Radio, Chicago, she constantly referred to herself in the third person singular – 'she.' Never was it 'I' or 'we.' Speaking of her early influences, she told me 'she' was inspired by Roland Hayes, the very first of African-American concert artists. He fused art songs, lieder, and troubadour songs with spirituals. As to her debut, as the first African-American artist to sing at the Met, Miss Anderson reminisced, 'When she sang Ursula in *The Masked Ball*, she was not nervous as much as she was thrilled.' I was bewildered, at first. I occasionally looked behind me: was there a third person in the room? I've got a hunch that Mr. Warfield would have said, 'There was.'

Roland Hayes and Marian Anderson inspired me the most to do the kind of singing that I do, because they were slaves to the art. They worshiped and performed the art for itself. Robeson went a step beyond that. He was a humanitarian and for the rights of people. He used his art to further that, which is a different aspect than being the artist whose art and God are one.

To me, Heaven wouldn't be Heaven unless there was music. A friend of mine introduced me at a dinner in New York. He said: 'Bill went to Heaven and he told the Lord he wanted a thousand sopranos, he wanted a thousand altos, and he wanted a thousand tenors so that he could form this heavenly choir. He asked Bill, "How many basses you want?" Bill said, "Oh, I'm going to sing bass."' [*Laughter*] I don't think of Heaven as a place of milk and honey. A friend of mine said, 'I don't like honey and I can't *stand* milk!' That's not true with me, I do like honey and I do like milk. I think of Heaven as being an ethereal, wonderful place where you feel happy and are content and whatever it is that you are, music abounds . . .

I think not having those things is Hell. [*Chuckles*] Did you ever hear the one about the mountain climber who had a reputation for being quite an atheist? As he was climbing this mountain, the rope broke and he started sliding down and there was a precipitous drop. There was a branch of a tree that had grown out of the side of the mountain. He grabbed on to this branch, holding on for dear life. He called out, 'God, help me! God, please help me! God, help me!' And this voice out of the sky said, 'You calling on me?' He said, '*Yes, yes, yes.*' God says, 'But you're supposed to be an atheist. You believe in me now?' He says, 'Yes, yes, yes, yes – God, I believe in you!' God says, 'Well, then just let go of that limb.' There was dead silence for a minute. And then he yelled out, 'Anybody else up there?!' [*Laughter*]

UTA HAGEN

She is an actress and has won two Tony Awards: one for her performance in *Who's Afraid of Virginia Woolf?* and the other for her role in *The Country Girl*. She was equally celebrated as Shaw's St. Joan, as Desdemona to Paul Robeson's Otello, and as Blanche DuBois in *A Streetcar Named Desire*. In her later years, she was acclaimed as Mrs. Klein, a drama based on the life of a renowned child psychiatrist. In her younger years, after an appearance in 'a terrible play' in Brooklyn, she was described by Alexander Woolcott, drama critic of the *New Yorker*, as 'the Duse of Brooklyn.' She has appeared in a few television plays and 'once in a while in a movie.' She is the founder of the HB Playwright's Foundation,⋆ a drama school and theater in Greenwich Village.

I think about death all the time. Then I pretend I'm not thinking about it and I pretend it doesn't exist. The notion that when we get old death doesn't bother us is baloney, because it bothers me a *lot*. It bothers me that I watch my body disintegrate slowly but surely. When people say, 'Oh, but you have so much vitality and you're so alive and look so young,' I always say it's because I love to work. If I'm allowed to work, I feel younger and I forget that I'm going to die.

I only stopped working in October of this year. I played in Canada for three months and was unbelievably alive and vital and feeling wonderful. I always think it's my swan song, and I'll never get another job, just because I'm so old and it's hard to find parts that are interesting and challenging to me. I just found one and overnight I was rejuvenated! I started exercising, I started dieting, I started working on my role. And I felt now there's hope again, because I have a part and love to work.

I have faced death often in my life. I had huge emergency surgeries

⋆The foundation is named after her late husband, Herbert Berghof, a noted drama teacher and director.

when I was twenty-three. I had mastectomies. When I was through with it, everybody said, 'You're so lucky.' I said, 'Why am I lucky? I lost a breast! What's nice about that?' They said, 'But you're alive.' I said, 'I had no intention of dying!' I never for a moment thought I would die, but everybody else thought I would. There's a kind of blankness in my feeling about death, that I ignore it. I don't know if that's good or bad. To this day – I'm eighty-one – I have never seen a corpse. Not of a dog, not of a person, not of my parents. Everybody whom I lost. I never saw a dead person. I have a terror of it. If I see a dead rabbit in my backyard, I run the other way. If I see a dead mouse, I run the other way. I finally can face that I see a dead bird because they knock into my windows in the country. That aspect of death is to me terrifying. And I've never faced it. I've never had to yet.

I don't believe in funerals because they're so loaded with hypocrisy. When I've had to go, on the two occasions when there was an open casket, I wouldn't go near them!

I was against funerals, memorials of all kinds, from the time I was nineteen. I was in a play by Maxwell Anderson, with Paul Muni, called *Key Largo*. One of the actors in it, whom everybody detested, died – set himself on fire, drunk, in the Brevoort Hotel here around the corner. We had to go to his funeral. *Nobody* liked this man. I remember Joe Ferrer calling up people to say he had died, and every single person said, 'I'm not sorry he's dead.'* He was forty-nine. I thought: you spent forty-nine years of your life and everybody's glad that you're gone! The church was full. All the people were talking about how glad they were that he was dead. I thought: *this is grotesque.* Then I went to an awful funeral for my old vet whom I loved. The minister kept talking about hellfire and how he had sinned. I thought, *He never sinned in his life!* In Broadway, memorials were always so much, 'Did you go? Were you seen? Who was there?' That's why I say this is the most hypocritical reminder of death that I can think of. It's ugly.

So I never wanted anything like it for myself or anybody I loved. Then I had a student whom I was very close to – he was like my son – Hal Holden. He died at a very early age. The first thing I thought was:

*Jose Ferrer, her former husband.

I have to have a memorial for him. I became obsessed. I had a memorial at our studio,* and it was beautiful, and people spoke. And it comforted me, most of the people who were there. It was a very, very genuine occasion. From then on, I changed my mind about memorials. I had a beautiful memorial for my husband.† I have it all on tape. With the most magnificent speeches by some of the most gifted people in New York, about what he had meant to them. Forty-four years we were together. It was unbelievable. I'll never forget it!

My husband died in this apartment, where we're sitting right now. He died while I was in the country. The police called me, and I drove in. Friends were here already waiting for me. I said, 'Do I have to go in?' And they said no. I'm not sure I shouldn't have. I might have accepted his death more readily if I had seen him. I just heard every detail: that he looked relaxed, that he had not died in pain. He died, thank God, without tubes and without all the horrible things that medicine keeps us alive with now. But I could not look at him. [*Suddenly, she weeps.*] I wish I had, but I . . . I don't know. I really don't know whether I should have seen him. I still dream that he's alive. The other person whom I loved most in my life was my mother. And when she died, I was in the hospital and they said I couldn't see her because if she knew I was there, she would be alarmed and know how seriously ill she was. So I had an excuse. But I also dreamed for years and years that she was still alive. Maybe if I had seen them dead I would have been able to accept the death more readily. I don't know . . .

I remember when Alfred Lunt died. Thirteen years later, somebody said to Miss Fontanne,‡ 'Do you miss him?' She said, 'No, I talk to him every day.' My husband's ashes are right in his study. And if I die, I want mine and his sprinkled in our yard at the studio. Or out over the water.

I have a funny story. When my daughter was eight, I was playing a comedy. She had seen me before in plays like *Othello*. I said to the nurse, 'Please, if she makes any noise or rambunctiousness out there,

*The HB Playwright's Foundation.
†Herbert Berghof.
‡Lynne Fontanne, wife of Alfred Lunt. They were the most popular and revered acting couple in the history of the American theater.

take her out, because if I hear her, I won't be able to play.' During the intermission, the nurse brought her back. In the funniest scene in the play, I heard out front [*mock sobs*] . . . this sobbing sound. I thought, *Oh my God, what is the matter?* Backstage, I said, 'Lettie, what is the matter with you?' And she said, 'When are you going to die?' And I said, 'Lettie, I *don't* die in this play.' And she said, 'You do, you always do.' [*Laughs*] She'd seen me as Desdemona – she was terrified that I would die any minute.

When I'm rational, I fear death. I guess I'm not rational very much. [*Laughs*] Oh yes, I think about it a lot because, as you age, everything falls apart. Your scalp starts to turn pink, and you lose your hair, and your teeth ache, and your bladder gets weak, and you have big brown ugly spots all over your body, and you get skin cancers. It's a never-ending gradual diminishment of all the correct bodily behavior. [*Laughs*]

I have had fourteen dogs in my life. And the loss of a dog is immediate. A person takes time to grasp the loss. With an animal, it's the immediate loss of something you love that's close to you. Feeding them and getting them water and their dependence on you. I find that sometimes immediately as intense as the loss of a human being. It's frightening.

Right now, seated between us is a dog.

My dog is GB – George Bernard Shaw. A toy poodle. I got deliberately a small one, so that I could hold it close. He's been to Europe twice, to California – he's a great traveler. He's my constant companion. He's a rescued dog, so he was neurotically attached to me from the beginning. I can't leave him alone. Right now he's deaf and blind and is losing the use of his hind legs. I'm housebound. My life is just around this dog.

You were Shaw's Joan. You were Desdemona. I saw you in both roles. Your deaths were so real to me. How did you, at those moments, envision death?

A fear of death, if I analyze it as an actress, is a fear of the unknown. The fear of the unknown we experience a lot. We experience it when we're waiting for surgery. We experience it when we're waiting to have a tooth extracted, for God's sakes. And the terror that comes in when we don't know what is going to happen to us is, to me, exactly the same as the fear of death. So it's a very unrealistic, strange terror. It's what I don't want to face. Because I don't think we *can* realize what it means to die and really not be here anymore. I don't think we know. I think the Lord protects us from that.

I'm not at all religious. My father was an agnostic, although I was baptized and all sorts of things like that. I do believe that there is a power way beyond our comprehension, that is bigger than all of us, but I don't believe in organized religions at all. I don't think I need it in my life because my faith — maybe that's religious — has to do with art. I think that the passing on, if I go . . . Michelangelo with Adam touching God's finger . . . that passing on of art is so enormous to me. If I hear a Bach cantata or chorale I'm transported into a spiritual world. So I have belief in the spirit, but I don't believe it has to do with an organized God.

When you say God, you're referring to art . . .?

I am, I am. That I am truly religious about. Oh my God, I think that the faith, the miracle of creation is what a human being is capable of communicating. It's not a private thing, it has to be *communicated*. Which is what I love about art — that you pass on, you make an offering of your spirit to somebody else hoping that it will help them, enlighten them, make them laugh, make them cry. These are things that make our lives worth living as far as I'm concerned. To me, that's art. That's my religion.

What I've never understood is people who have survived, let's say, the Holocaust or any experience of suffering, of deprival, of terrifying loneliness. My life has been so rich, and I demand a lot of it — so that I think if I really lost what is important to me, if I were incapable of enjoying what is meaningful to me in life, I don't think I would want to live. I've never understood people who want to live in spite of . . . that is, to me, amazing. I've always prayed to God that I will die fast: in a car, or an airplane, or in my sleep. That would be the loveliest.

What do you think happens? After . . .

I think it's over, period. It's the end. But I do believe, and only really since my husband died, I do believe that there is something in the spirit surviving, and being near and being around. I also think that nobody is really dead until nobody remembers you anymore. I think somewhere my mother is still alive because she's still so important to me and so alive in my memory.

I've found more and more with my peers in age, and we're all dying, that it becomes important to evaluate what our life has meant. I used to resent that when I was young. There's something already dead about thinking *What did my life mean?* But, as I am getting really old, it's something that occurs to me. Will that have meant anything? Will it still be around? Will our studio still be around? I've just finished a documentary on my teaching. Will my teaching go on because I've made that film? This is the thinking that ten years ago I would *never* have thought about. I have a friend who's a painter and she's just doing a catalogue of all her work. All she thinks about is this catalogue. That summing-up of your life. That you say there was a reason for it. We weren't just here and passed on. We had some kind of influence, some kind of value to the world we left, to somebody we were useful . . .

I was in a car accident once. I thought I'd lost my eye. My flesh was hanging down over my face. I made jokes. Everybody else around me was screaming, but I wasn't. I was just fighting for normalcy. I sat for three hours in a car with glass from the accident. My whole body was covered with cuts. I didn't even know it, I didn't feel it. I think it was the first time I ever understood soldiers having half their heads blown off and still continuing in action. There is something in nature that puts you in a trauma until you can cope with it. I hope death is the same.

Right now, as always, my work is my life. If I could no longer work, I wouldn't care to live.

But you care now.

Because I've got a job! [*Laughs*]

POSTSCRIPT
In April 2001, three months after this interview took place, she was to begin rehearsals for Six Dancing Lessons in Six Weeks.

The Comedian

MICK BETANCOURT

I'm afraid that when I die and go to Heaven, I'll walk in and the lights will be off. All of a sudden the lights come on and all my dead relatives yell, '*Surprise!!!*' As I'm crying with overflowing joy, the Devil walks out and says, 'That trick *never* gets old. All right you bastards, back to work!'

I just turned twenty-six. April 14th. I m married, no children. I'm a professional stand-up comic, and a writer, and an actor. I think you're always looking for that big break. I've performed in Canada, all across the country, in the Chicago Comedy Festival. I think I'm getting ready to move to New York. I think once I move, that'll really define who I am, because now I'm taking all my chips, putting them in one basket, and saying, 'All right, I'm going to bet my life and my family on being who I am.' I'm betting on me.

I've had every bad job you can possibly imagine. But I've wanted to entertain since I was a little kid. I did every play in grade and high school, and I wrote sketches and cast the other kids in them. I wrote comic books, poetry – but making people laugh, that's my drug of choice.

It just occurred to me that I've never lived with any member of my family for more than five years. My father died when I was six. Then I moved in with my mother. She went a little nuts, so I moved in with my grandfather. I lived with my mother for, like, four years – then with my grandfather for three years, and then he died. Then I moved in with my aunt and uncle for the last three years of high school, and then I moved out. So everything seems very temporary to me. My father died and I didn't really know him that well, but my grandfather was the most important person to me. He still is, to this day, in my life. When he died, that was *crushing*. I was thirteen, fourteen. I grieve for him every day.

Death is an odd thing. My wife – nobody has died in her family. To me, I'm not too afraid of life. Because my whole family is dead. I don't have any brothers or sisters. My mother's been missing now for almost a year. No one knows where she's at. I guess death has made me impatient about things that I want to do and making sure that what I get done in my life will carry over into my kids' lives. It's just that you think you can do everything you want, but it's hard to think that every day. It's hard to believe in yourself enough to go, 'I can do anything I want,' because the exact opposite of death is life. Every day you're alive it reminds you that death's coming so let's get something done here, let's do something with what we have.

I feel that the older you get, the less you're willing to take the risks, and I think that's because of the fear of death. Even though death is at the end, it just seems like it casts a shadow that makes you afraid of life. You just fear it so: you start to slow down and you don't want to do anything. You don't want to go out there and attack the world.

I feel old. I feel like I'm about forty-five mentally with all the shit I've been through. [*Laughs*] My grandfather died in my arms. I was the only one in the room. It's a recurring nightmare that I have. He was seventy-two. He had a two-flat building on 26th and East Avenue, and we lived upstairs. It was the scariest thing ever. When my dad had died, it didn't check in that it was death. I was six. And he was missing for three days before anybody even thought to go looking for him. So then someone decided to go down to see if he was in the morgue, and he had been in there for three days. He was electrocuted on the El. My parents were divorced, they didn't live together. So then I moved back in with my mom – she lived downstairs from my grandfather, and I just started spending time with my grandfather and wound up moving in. When I was six I didn't know what death was, I just knew that my dad was gone. I remember the wake, when they were showing the body, I walked up and I tried to open his eyes. Of course, everybody ran up and grabbed me and they were crying . . .

But it really kicked in the morning my grandfather died. It happened early, like seven o'clock, he had a heart attack. It was a very hot night. I slept in the sunroom, and he had his own bedroom. But I would go in and sleep in his bedroom. I'd crawl into bed at night. I remember it was one of the hottest days of the summer, and I got into bed with him and I remember thinking how hot it was, how I should go back and sleep in my bed. We used to wrestle, so when he was having a heart attack, I was woken up by me thinking that he wanted to wrestle. So I was kind of wrestling with him and then I realized he was having a heart attack. He was blue and they couldn't resuscitate him. It happened so fast, like that. [*Snaps fingers.*] It was the fastest life-changing event that I – I can never experience that again. Even if my wife were to die, I would be devastated, I would be heartbroken, but it can't happen that fast because now I know that she has to die sometime. Of course, you always wish that you go first.

You know what death does? It makes you impatient and hesitant at the same time. I don't know if that makes any sense. I'll give you an example. I'm impatient to love my wife. I want to do everything for her, but then you think, *Man, do you* remember *that experience?!* How much I loved my grandfather and how much that hurt when he was gone? It's irreversible – it's a done deal. Here's his license I keep for good luck. I still have his mass card from the wake in my pocket. Here's a card from the wake: [*Reads*] 'In loving memory of Thomas McDonnell. At rest, June 15th, 1987, Mass of the Resurrection, St. Odilo Church, burial at Mt. Carmel Cemetery, June 19th, 1987, 9:30 in the morning.' And this is a mass card: 'May thy soul and the souls of all the faithful departed . . . God rest in peace, mercy of God.' I had it laminated. Gone except for memories.

So I want to love my wife and give her everything that I can emotionally, but will I be able to go through that again? Can I do *that* again? Can I *possibly* mentally deal with that and go through that whole thing again? But you have to.

I think that's partially why I enjoy comedy so much. Laughter is a quick fix of somebody loving you for a moment. It's an intrinsic response and you get that, you get an association with people, but you don't need to have an emotional connection with them. You have a relationship for ten minutes, half an hour when you're on stage, and then you're done. You could still be by yourself and you're not emotionally invested in anything. I love making people laugh.

Even at work, I'll fall off a table in the middle of a meeting just to have that shock laughter. It's addictive.

You know how people are so afraid how if they die and that's it, and there is no Heaven or Hell – that petrifies people. To me, I don't care. If this is it, that's fine. I can't imagine Heaven and Hell – there's too many questions.

There's a dead squirrel in front of your house, I don't know if you know that. Is that squirrel in Heaven or Hell? Does that squirrel have a soul? Can that squirrel tell the difference between good and evil? If so, does he go to Heaven? There's just too many questions that you can't possibly answer.

I was an altar boy and was taught that the altar is the most holy of places, it's the window to God's soul. The priest is the mediator. So if that's the case, then why do you have eight-year-old kids up on the altar? They are the *farthest* from the most holy sanctuary. I mean, you're making fart noises by the tabernacle. It just didn't make *any* sense to me. It made almost like a joke of it. I tried to be very serious, but you know, you goof around with your buddies. It was like seeing *The Wizard of Oz*: pay no attention to the man behind the curtain! Now that I do shows and I perform in front of people, I know what's behind it. You know how to inflect your voice to manipulate somebody. So I just saw the incense and I'm like, *This is a lot of smoke and mirrors going on here. Bring out the dancers . . .* [*Laughs*]

When I was a kid, I would write out these arguments to test myself and talk to people. I'd bring them to teachers, especially in high school, the religion teachers. I went to Fenwick High School on the West Side – Dominican Brothers. It's never that I stopped having faith in God or anything like that. I have no problem testing that faith and talking with people and saying there's no reason that we're hurting anybody's feelings, especially God's, by delving in deeper and trying to find out what's going on. One of the people that I would argue with and have these debates with was Father Peddicord, at Fenwick. I asked him the same question that you asked me. This is somebody that's devoted his life to God. I said, 'Father Peddicord, what do you think is going to happen to you after you die?' He said, 'Hopefully, I'm going to go to Heaven.' And I said, 'Well, what if there's no Heaven.' And he says, 'I'll be pretty pissed.' [*Laughs*]

I love life more than anything. I want to be one of the greatest comedians ever. I want to be up there with Martin and Lewis, and Richard Pryor. I don't want to have a stupid TV show, I want to be known as a great entertainer. I want to make people's lives fun, give them a little break from their busy day. I see a lot of people are complacent, but because of my grandfather's death I just feel like I've got to do these things because death is there.

I don't live my life recklessly, although I did get boozed up last night. [Laughs] I don't live my life like tomorrow's never going to come. I work basically eighteen, nineteen hours a day, pretty much usually six days a week. So I'm working hard at what I want, I'm investing a lot in life, but I'm not afraid to die. I wouldn't want to, but I'm not afraid of it. I work for the city of Chicago – I'm a teamster. And when I get done there I usually take an hour nap and then I'll write, and then I'll go out to the nightclubs and perform. I'm thinking about moving to New York in a couple of months. I just got offered a really nice apartment here, three bedrooms, new floors, carpeting. My wife's a travel agent, but she doesn't have something burning in her heart that she has to do. She wants to have a family. But I have something that I feel I *have to* do. I'm going to put everything on the line. I'm going to quit the city job, which is the best job that I've ever had in my life, and I'm moving to New York. I'm betting my family's life that I'm going to make it as a comedian.

A friend of mine who was a great painter, an artist, when we were in high school together, always said that he was going to move to France to paint and write and live his life like an artist. To live to be an artist, not to be a waiter who wants to be an actor, that's what I want to do. I ate dinner at his house the other night; he's married and he has a kid. He works as a mechanic where I work. We were all eating dinner and his hands were filthy. He cleaned them, but you know, as a mechanic you can't ever get all of that off. And the food that he was eating was getting dirt on it and his daughter was watching this. What he had let come into his life was now in his life permanently. He can't get it out of his hands. It's in the food that he eats. That's not the life he wanted to live, but another life crept in there because he wanted to play it safe and not go after what he wanted – no risks, no nothing. Now it's in his skin. He can't get it out. It's taken him over. I saw it and I said, 'I don't want that to be me.'

I gotta beat the clock. Yet I play it safe. What am I sitting around another year for? You may think I'm nuts saying twenty-six is getting up there in years. If you're a smart kid when you're nineteen or twenty, they go, 'That kid is smart, look at him.' Maybe he's driving his car across the country just trying to see what's going on. 'That's great, that takes a lot of balls. Look at that kid, he's going out there . . .' But you take that same kid who's twenty-nine and they go, 'This kid is a bum. He doesn't have a job, he's driving across the country. *Why?*' Why the big difference of opinion on that? They call the kid of nineteen a prodigy: 'He's sucking the marrow out of life – look at him go!' Not even ten years later, that kid's a bum, he should get a job, he should get whatever he can to put food on the table, he should start saving up for retirement.

Here I am, working for the city. When I tell my in-laws I'm quitting the city job and I'm going to move to New York and not get a job, but every day go on auditions and try to make it as a professional entertainer, most likely they'll be very supportive of me – but I'll *still* be a bum because I'm married and I should be staying at this city job, maybe getting another part-time job. But I want to be with the best of the best.

Death has been around me since I was a little kid. I had a friend in college commit suicide. Two of my good friends, both of their sisters killed themselves – it was a double suicide in Oak Park. Everybody's thought about killing themselves at one point in their lives. You feel like you're backed up against a wall. It's easier for people to commit suicide that don't really care about this life. They don't feel like they fit in, they don't want to fit in, they don't need to fit in. Suicide, that's it. When you're dead, it's over. When I first got married I thought, man, I'm *never* going to be able to . . . For me to provide an average life, after what I feel that I've gone through, would be an injustice to me and an injustice to my wife. It would be stupid because I *know* I can do more. Now I would never do it, but this is just the mentality of saying: *Get out now before you hurt anybody.* My wife's going to invest her life in mine . . . Get out before she does it. Let her find somebody else and live the life that she wants to live. Get out of town by knocking yourself off. But that's a fleeting thought.

My friend whose sister killed herself and I went out drinking last night. He was really angry. She was sixteen or seventeen. His dad died when he was a junior in high school. Death surrounds him too, so we have kind of the same opinion. We lived very carelessly from, like, eighteen years old. We both got kicked out of college. We drank our skulls off for three, four years, just boozed it up, didn't care about anything. We were going to die anyway. Just because the fragility of life, it was exposed to us at such an early age. My wife, she's never seen death ever, which is *great*. It's weird, too, because I always say, 'You know, your parents are going to die.' Which is a weird thing because, why should I tell her that? I don't need to remind her of that – but to me that's always there.

People should be allowed to do what they want. You can't judge people. It's too big of a place that we live in to try to judge. When you die, I hope you go to a place full of strippers and cold beer. [*Laughs*] My father-in-law had a good point. Say you're married and you get in an accident and you die. You're in Heaven, your wife remarries. Now both of them die. In Heaven, who does the woman spend her time with? The first husband or the second husband? What happens? Questions like that, you can't answer them. That's why there's faith. People don't want to have that insecurity of not knowing what's going to happen – they can't deal with it. There's such a void in their lives. They denied themselves their passions and they're trying to find . . . Some people don't even have passions. These are the people that have faith because they think there's got to be something other than this *because* I wasn't given a passion, I wasn't given a talent, I wasn't given something. So who can give me something? God, God can give me something. What can He give me? Eternal salvation. I'll go to church four times a week and I'll put my money in that bank, and hopefully it'll pay off.

Day of the Dead

CARLOS CORTEZ

He is a painter and poet living in Chicago. 'I'm seventy-six, going on seventy-seven.'

I remember when I was a little kid, it bugged me, the idea of death. My mother said to me, 'Hey, just think if you never did die, if you lived forever, that would be worse!' After all, nothing lasts forever – and it's a good thing too. I remember my wife grieving over the death of her mother. An old friend said, 'We have to make room for the next generations.' I've said to people, 'Hey, don't be afraid of death. If you're afraid of death, you shouldn't have been born.' I was somewhere between five and seven years old when I first realized what it was. People don't like to accept the finality, but nothing is infinite.

I spent some time with the Jehovah's Witnesses during the war when I was incarcerated for my draft refusal – this was World War II. They would say, 'How would you like to live forever, never die?' I said, 'No, I don't think I would care for it.' To see everything there is to see, know everything there is to know, and have nothing new, that would be terrible. I hope to be conscious when the time comes, because I've had a good life. I'm going to hate to leave it, but I think I'm better being sorry to leave it than saying, 'Oh, at last it's come, it's over with.' I want to feel that there's still more. If we live a good life, we will live on with those who remember us.

Mozart had a short life, what, thirty-two years? As an old conductor said – it was on your radio program – 'He was but a moment in eternity.'* Well, that's what all of us are. We're but moments in eternity. But we've been a part of it. People have many ways of facing the prospect of death. Some don't want to think about it. When you get to be in your upper seventies, you realize you got more behind you

---

*Maestro Josef Krips, founding conductor of the Salzburg Festival.

than you got ahead of you. There's no time to be afraid of death any-more – you know it's coming.

Among the Mexicans – my father was a Mexican Indian – they sort of celebrate death. It's a way of honoring the recently departed and honoring one's roots. Without death, there's no life: they're mutually dependent. It's just a process of the circle. The great print-maker José Guadalupe Posada used the death image a lot as a matter of caricature. He would depict the politicians and big people of his day as skeletons, which underneath they are. There's a date now, the second of November, which is called *el día de los muertos*, the Day of the Dead. When the Spanish priests came over, it happened to coin-cide with All Souls' Day, just the way it coincides with the Anglo-Saxon Halloween. It happens at a time of year when the last green has disappeared, and people are reminded of the imperma-nences of existence. At the same time, there's a continuity to it. It's a celebration that we've lived and that we've had a good life, that we've done our part. I would not know about the hereafter. The idea of the Heaven, the garden of Allah, the Happy Hunting Ground, is a reluctance to accept the finality of things. Everything has its limitation. As we say: even the mountains fade away. For the better, for the worse, life is what we make of it. Personally, I would not like to spend eternity on a cloud plucking away at a harp. I think I'd rather be where the gang is.

Bliss you can't understand unless you've had a little rough bumps. The person who says, 'Oh, I've always been happy.' *B.S.!* If you haven't known the opposite, how can you know what happiness is? I think I have paradise right now. Despite this messed-up human world that we live in, I think it's a very interesting world. Remember old Cholly Wendorf, the one-armed soapbox orator? He was saying he died once and was sent up to Heaven. St. Peter said, 'Oh, you're an *agitator*,' he sent him down to Hell. The Devil says, 'I don't want you!' He says, 'You only got one arm. You have to shovel souls into that fire there and you have to toss Christians around in the fire. So I'm going to send you to purgatory.' *So here I am, back in purgatory!* Existence is a great thing. We hang on to it as much as possible, no matter how rough things are.

When they celebrate the Day of the Dead, they build their home altars and put offerings for the departed there, and photographs of the recently departed. And on that night they go to the cemetery. First they clean off the tombstone and whitewash it, decorate it with flowers. Decorate it with the marigold, because that's the one flower that still grows at that time of year. And then they sit down and have lunch with their departed, and spend the night with them. Sometimes you'll see musical groups out there, mariachi bands. And they spend the night with their departed. This is not only Mexico. I know the cemetery where my wife's mother is buried here on the northwest side of Chicago, a lot of Greek Orthodox people are there, Russian, Serbians, and what have you. And people will come out and have their lunches with them, sit down by the grave site and have lunch with their departed. Or they'll be carrying a case of soda – Coke, Pepsi, or whatever – everybody he sees goes and gives them a can of soda because it's a part of remembering their departed. In Mexico it's become an annual holiday.

You see dry twigs and dry branches, and you're reminded of the impermanence of existence. The Protestants, who settled the northern part of the hemisphere, when they saw the old practices, they said, 'Oh, that's stuff of the Devil. We have to stamp this out.' The Spanish padres said, 'Well, wait a minute, this is el día de – the day of St. Gerónimo. From now on this will be the Fiesta of St. Gerónimo.' St. Jerome – Gerónimo, the way the Apache chief was named . . .

I recently returned from California, where I picked up a lot of silkscreen posters and a lot of these used the image of death. The image of the *calaverismo*. *Calavera* means skull or skeleton. It was the practice for thousands of years. You have to consider that in Mexico, people lived next door to earthquakes, volcanoes, pestilences, and bad economic conditions, so death was no stranger. It was something that was accepted philosophically. The poet Octavio Paz says that in the capitals of Paris and London the word 'death' gets caught on the tongue, burns the tongue, but in Mexico they embrace it, they play with it, and they celebrate it. It's illustrated in the toys that are found around the Day of the Dead. Skeletons, little pushcarts with skeletons are given to the children: *This is what you'll become someday.* Don't be afraid of death. What's more important: *Don't be afraid of life.* There's a verse from a traditional Mexican song. '*Nadie debe lamentarse por muerte de sus amores,*' 'Nobody should lament the passing of one's loves.'

I build an altar for my parents or my wife's parents and for recently departed friends. And of course what interests you is the composition of this altar. You put on things that you associate with the departed's life, be they cigarettes or a can of beer or a bottle of wine, but always there's a glass of water. And the idea behind that is the souls, after making the long journey to visit the altar, are thirsty, so they have the water. And of course the water stays there, it evaporates – and so, you know, the souls are drinking it.

The altar is made out of many things. It's usually a platform or a table in a corner of the room that you decorate with flowers, candles, and such. I decorate my altar with skulls made out of sugar candy, besides the toys and such. And there are the various breads they make to represent dead people. And pictures of the departed. Friends come over and add their bit to it. I go over to friends and add my bit to their altars. I'll take a drink and raise it up to them, to the altar, to salute them. Life is a celebration, and death means you're reminded of the life you no longer have.

VINE DELORIA

'I'm an old Indian politician, observer of events, and a writer.' His most celebrated book is *Custer Died for Your Sins*. He taught for many years at the University of Colorado and is now retired, though still writing.

I grew up in a border town of about seven hundred people in Martin, South Dakota, right on the Pine Ridge Reservation. I had classmates die, get run over by tractors, drown. A good friend of mine died in those polio epidemics.

On the prairies, death was a quite a big event. When I was a child, we had wakes, and they would last quite a while – maybe a couple of days before the actual burial service. A custom they started to do was very comforting: to have a giveaway a year after the funeral. They recognized that you can't observe all that grief in a two- or three-day period. So people set themselves aside for a whole year, and go out of their way to be helpful to other people, and people come in to comfort them. About a year after the person died, they have this big giveaway. They hold a big feast and they give things to everybody in the community. That's to mark the end of the mourning period. They recognize that losing a mate or a family member, a child, is very traumatic. In the old days, they used to cut their hair and gash their skin and go into mourning. Today, they announce that they're going to be mourning for a certain period of time. During that period, you're not supposed to talk harshly to them. Usually, the people in the community will help the grieving family to start accumulating things so they can have a big feast and giveaway a year afterwards. Some people very severely affected by a loss will have giveaways four years in a row.

That was the most comforting thing for me when my father died, looking forward to having a giveaway – that I could feed the people in that community, give them blankets and jackets and scarves and things like that. During the giveaway, I had to pass muster from the medicine man that I knew enough about the culture and language, that I was sincere in what I wanted to do. He used the anniversary of my father's death as an opportunity to tell all of the people what life meant and what death meant. He didn't spend his time talking about my father, so he didn't pull me back into the grief at all. He made me feel like my father, as all the other people who died on that reservation, had moved on. And we should move on too.

The women up there loved these little blue porcelain, blue enamel bowls. So I just bought all kinds of 'em, handed 'em out. [*Laughs*] You accumulate goods, but all of your friends also contribute a quilt or a blanket. You basically are celebrating the life of the person who died, and you're thanking the community for their support during this whole year. You're really celebrating the life. [*A gentle chuckle*] You're a year away from the immediate shock of losing someone. At these giveaways, they always tell funny stories about funerals, or about someone dying, but they enable you to feel very good that you've really accomplished something by doing this. There's feasting, of course. They cook turkeys, hams, buffalo, whatever.

My family converted to Christianity. My grandfather was a very famous missionary, and he really forced my father to follow his footsteps. He was a chief of the Yankton Sioux. He was an Episcopal missionary. My great-grandfather was a very famous, very powerful medicine man. He had this dream about our family. So he encouraged my grandfather to not become chief but to become baptized and become a priest. So he turned Christian, and now I'm turning the family pagan again. [*Laughs*] My grandfather was then reelected chief by this band, and he was chief right up till he was so infirm he couldn't do anything.

He wasn't *abandoning* beliefs so much as looking at where would the leadership possibilities be *once you're confined to the reservation*. He said you've got to get an education because they are now outlawing the traditional religion. So if you're going to fulfill the vision I have of our family as religious leaders, you're going to have to do it in this other religion. I've talked to modern medicine men who say in their visions they're offered a choice: you can be a Christian minister, you can be a peyote. You can be a traditional Sioux, or you can be something else. The spirits say you can choose any of those. We work in all of them.

I grew up as an Episcopalian. Everything's changed quite a bit for me, and I do a lot with traditional people now. Most of them will go right back to the medicine man when they're in a crisis and find out what to do. He performs in many ways like a priest or a minister. A lot of times, he makes up the ceremony by watching the grieving people and adapting their statements and feelings. They sometimes use a sweet grass to smudge everybody and put smoke on them. They use a pipe sometimes. There's a lot of visitations by spirits.

When I was a kid, a young Indian boy got bucked off a horse – he hit the corral and broke his neck. They had a big wake for him. This was summertime. It was a log cabin, and they had opened part of the wall to let the breeze through. In the middle of the wake, this horse stuck his head in the cabin. He was foaming at the mouth, and the water from his mouth was dripping down on the floor. One of the men said, 'That's the horse that bucked this kid off and killed him.' And so they said, 'Let's capture that horse!' So they ran out and they got on their horses with their lariats and it was pretty close to dark, so they had lanterns. They chased that horse about five miles into the badlands. In a box canyon, they had the horse trapped – it couldn't get out. And there was the horse laying dead, and it had been dead for about three days, same time as the boy. But we had people back at the cabin wiping up where the horse's saliva was. This was a real visitation. You have that quite frequently. Instead of saying that the world is material and it evolves into spiritual, what the Indians say is that the world is spiritual and it manifests itself in the material. So if there's a strong spirit, the spirit can take on physical form.

Just in the last four or five years, people on the reservation have been wanting to be buried up on a scaffold, like the Plains Indians did. They would wrap the body up very carefully and put it up on a scaffold. It would be just a little higher than a person's head. They would let the body disintegrate until it was just bones. They'd visit it every year, make sure that the thing hadn't fallen over. When it was just bones, then they would take the bones and hide them. This comes from the old belief that we are high on the food chain, and all our lives we've benefited from the bodies and lives of everything below us. So then we have to return our bodies to the dust, so that the buffalo can feed off us. Scaffolding is coming back among reservation Indians who are reasonably well educated. They see the spiritual connection.

There *definitely* is a hereafter. There have been numerous near-death experiences, visions, which tell people about the hereafter, with valleys and game and everything. It's painted as a very pleasant place. It's not radically different than the life we have here. You just continue on. Your relatives who have gone before you come and visit. You can stay there for a while and visit them, but you can't drink any of their water and you can't eat any of their food. If you do, you have to stay.

Right now, there are studies going on that Indians were reincarnation people: they believed they would come back. Every now and then, a rumor will go through one of the reservations that one of the famous chiefs will be reborn and will lead the people. At funerals sometimes, if there's an unusual disturbance, people say, 'This person must have been the reincarnation of someone else.' One of my very best friends, who had been chairman at Standing Rock, died and it rained and thundered for five days – you could hardly go out. It scared all the people on the reservation. They said, 'He had the power of the thunders. They're welcoming him home.' It was very moving to a lot of people. The most common figure for God is this very old Indian man. I don't think it's God in the Western, European sense at all. It is power in everything that is alive.

In the old days, when they used to kill their favorite horses and dogs to go along with them to the next world, it wasn't just a sacrifice. What they were saying is that the horse and dog are so much a part of me that we all have to go on together. I would be incomplete without them, and they would be incomplete without me. It was a rare occasion because your favorite horse was probably a well-trained buffalo hunter. Your son would get the horse. You wouldn't kill an animal that valuable.

I hope I'm rational right until the last minute, that I understand what's going on around me. I had a terrible staph infection about four years ago – I thought I was going to die. My son videotaped as much as I could tell him. I was like the old man in *Little Big Man*. I laid down on the floor in our rec room. [*Laughs*] I got my cigarettes, and my wife made me a big thing of coffee, and I got my little tape recorder, I put on my Hank Snow tape and I listened to that for a while and smoked a cigarette, and I thought, *All right, I'm ready to go.* But I wasn't ready to go. [*Laughs*] I *didn't* go. I got to a point where

I was just totally paralyzed, and then they called an ambulance and took me to the hospital. I almost waited too late, but I really thought, *Well, I've done the best I could* . . . I've done some bad things and I've done some good things. It's a toss-up. If there's a big judgment day, I'll say, 'Look, if I'd had more information, I would have done better, but you didn't give me a very good shot.' [*Laughs*]

When I was about nine years old, there was a very famous Indian who lived about nine miles west of us, Billy Fire Thunder. He woke up one morning and he said to his wife, 'I'm going under the earth tonight at midnight, so I want you to fix my favorite breakfast. And then I want you to take me to town to say good-bye to my friends.' He had a nice breakfast and sat and smoked his pipe with a coffee. He went to town and said good-bye to storekeepers and some of the Indians who lived in town. He was very energetic. He didn't say he was going to die, he said, 'I'm going on a trip, so I want to say good-bye to you in case I don't come back.' Then he went back home and they fed him a real nice meal, and he just took little bites of it, just to get the taste of all these things he liked. Friends from the community came in, and finally, about ten-thirty, he said, 'Now I just want my family around because I'm ready to go.' He planned out this whole day. It was the talk of the reservation for weeks and weeks and weeks. People just kept saying, 'How could a guy *know* all of this?' Then old-timers came and said, 'Unless you were killed in the war, this is the way you did it. You knew that your end had come.' So you made all these last-minute good-byes and 'Give my horse to this person' – like that. They said that's the way you're supposed to do it.

Almost all the tribes taught their young people that this is a hard world. You have to be brave in spite of what happens. But you can't have a false courage about things, or a bravado. So they weren't really afraid of death. They like to tell the old stories over and over again. An Osage chief, his son killed some white man and the soldiers came for him. 'We're going to take him and execute him.' The father says, 'If all you want is a life for a life, why don't you take me? I've lived most of my life and this young person might have made a mistake, but he still has a whole life to live and he could do something with it.' Here you have the elder saying, 'Well, if you really want to kill somebody, go ahead and kill me.' You have people who, when they're outnumbered, sing their death song. A song summing up their life: *This is the way I live.* A lot of times they said it's far better to die in battle or to be killed by someone than to get so old you can't do anything.

I thought that was a general attitude of Indians for a long time. And then we held a conference in Arizona. We asked this ninety-year-old Navajo medicine man, 'What do you attribute your long life to? Explain your life to us.' He said, 'Our people taught the rank and file that it's good to die on the battlefield. But if you were a brave warrior and you lived through that, as you got older, you began to understand more and more. By the time you're in your eighties, you understand that you've been one of the people who's been blessed,' he said, 'because you're gonna live to your nineties and you're gonna know what prayer really means before you die.' So we've got two levels of interpretation. Now there's no battlefield. They took that away, and so you lost a lot of the focus on that higher thing: that you could live to be very old and you would understand what prayer was. That's why you have such confusion on Indian reservations. There's no way that young men can measure themselves against anything. Tribes valiantly try and reinterpret it: go get an education, or learn a skill. That's the equivalent of going on the warpath. But deep down, people know it isn't the equivalent. They're trying to make, in this hundred years, that transition. That it's just as important to live for a long time and take care of your family as it is to die on some battlefield.

When I did my father's memorial, he had left me this beautiful pipe, which is a sacred ceremonial pipe. It had a red buffalo carved on it, with a nice stem and a beaded bag. I had about three pipes, and you're supposed to give the medicine man a pipe when he does the memorial. I'd feel chintzy if I didn't give him the best pipe, my father's. He made this speech and then I gave him this pipe. He's holding the pipe with the bag and he said, 'I want to tell people what this means.' He said, 'When I first looked at it, the bag looked a little familiar.' He said, 'I made that pipe thirty-two years ago, and I gave it away in a ceremony.' And he said, 'Look . . . this pipe has never been used.' And he said, 'This pipe has passed from ceremony to ceremony all these years and now you're giving it back to me, a pipe I made when I was a young man.' I thought it was *incredible* that no one had ever smoked that pipe, and it had just been a present from one person to another. He's gone, I don't know who has it now – he died this summer. I'm sure he gave it to somebody else. In those ceremonies, those Indians always give the best they have, they don't hold back. [*Wistfully*] 'Cause it was a beautiful pipe . . . While you're giving it away over here, someone's tapping you on the shoulder to give it to you. It just kept getting given away, all those years. Each time, the person said, 'I don't want to give this away, but I can't be a slacker, I can't hold back.' So they gave it. No one ever took it out in public and bragged about themselves, 'Look at my beautiful pipe,' and smoked it. They all treated it with dignity. My father got it – and you'd think once a Christian minister has a pipe, you're never gonna see it again. And then I got the pipe, and I gave it back to the man who made it. The circle of life and death.

HELEN SCLAIR

She is sixty-nine. She is a cemetery familiar. She had been a public school teacher for twenty-seven years. 'Now, I spend my time visiting and tracking cemeteries. It is my full-time occupation.' She arrives with bags full of pins, ribbons, cards, jewelry, and other funeral artifacts.

I was born into death. My mother died a few days after my birth. I grew up in a foster home out in Lake County, Illinois. The first thing my foster family did was take me to visit my mother's grave down in southern Missouri. It was a Sunday afternoon. I remember very distinctly that visit. I had baking-soda poultices on my two-and-a-half-year-old knees – I'd been bitten peeking into a beehive . . .

My grandparents began dying. This was back in the days when funerals were at home. I remember one of my grandfathers laid out in the living room. I tried to crawl into the coffin with him to pat him, to wake him up. 'Grandpa, I want to be read to.' He's the person who introduced me to reading. Every Sunday morning he'd read the comics to me.

I lived for Saturdays because my mother's sister-in-law would pick me up and we'd go to the cemetery. With scissors, on my little knees, I would trim around every one of the grave markers of the family. It wasn't even my family – it was my foster family. It didn't make any difference. This was my job and I loved doing it, because you could see what you had done. All those little weeds or leaves or whatever were cleaned away. I was probably about four when I first did that. When I got a little bit older, I'd go down to the spring and bring up buckets of water to water the flowers. Those were my jobs.

There was no movie theater in the town that I grew up in, so you went to funerals. That was the thing to do. My goodness, you had to get the paper because it would be *terrible* if you missed a funeral. My foster mother would read all the obituaries and she'd take me. The cemetery was my thing. [*She begins to open the bags and display the artifacts.*] See these medallions? Ribbons – red, white, and blue on one side, black and silver on the other side. It was of the Grange

Society, a rural group. The red, white, and blue side was worn at the regular meetings, the black and silver at the funerals. There were various fraternal orders. Everybody belonged to something.

All would have worn something like this or variations when some comrade or relative died. It was communicating, 'I feel lousy, I feel terrible, I've lost somebody.' It was stipulated that you wear this for X number of years, months, however long. The community knew how to respond to you. They knew you lost somebody of importance to you. Here's a black-bordered hankie and all these envelopes, edged in black.★

Here's a size-fourteen ring: a black cameo with a woman's face.

[*She displays her necklace.*] It's onyx, with my aunt's hair woven in the locket. This jar lid on a chain was made by somebody who had little money – see, it's brass with human hair inside. The chain was made with four-penny nails. It was a laborious job. It's a souvenir having more to do with memory than death itself. Today we go to the funeral home and we get little-bitty cards. They used to have cards intended to be put in scrapbooks or framed on walls. Here's a card in black: 'In loving remembrance' – and see that circle? – 'Kinsey Drake, Died March 19th, 1914, age seventy-eight years. Gone but not forgotten.' See this poem beneath:

A precious one from us is gone
A voice we loved is stilled
And though the body slumbers here, the soul is safe in Heaven.

These cards were possessions. People collected them. These are what I call the accoutrements of death. Wearing one of these ribbons or

★'The Letter Edged in Black' was a familiar sentimental song at the turn of the century; others were 'Put My Little Shoes Away' and 'The Baggage Coach Ahead.' In Eugene O'Neill's play *Moon for the Misbegotten*, Jamie Tyrone's guilt-ridden soliloquy, as he rides the train, about his mother's death refers to the baggage coach ahead. Other such dirges as 'Flee as a Bird' were parlor songs, offered by art singers. This one was often played by African-American marching bands on the way to the cemetery, along with the hymn 'Just a Little Walk with Thee.' On the way back, as a tribute to the living, they'd play something upbeat like 'Didn't He Ramble.' A popular Southern hymn was 'O Lovely Appearance of Death.'

medallions, people understood that you were grieving. Today we have grief counselors because people don't know how to express themselves. They have to go to somebody to tell them that, yes, it's OK to feel terrible . . .

In the nineteenth century, everybody knew about death. In the twentieth century, nobody knows about death. People die in hospitals now. In the nineteenth century, nobody knew about sex. In the twentieth century, everybody knows about sex. Death has become the new pornography. We don't talk about it.

I would describe myself as an advocate for the dead. I don't see anyone else worrying about where cemeteries are, where people are buried. I can't separate death from life. It's just as much part of life as anything we might do.

My mother and father were Presbyterian missionaries – they brought back Bushman.* I grew up in a Methodist home and finally became an Episcopalian. My husband was Jewish. I claim myself to be absolutely nothing now. No, I don't believe in the hereafter. When you die, you die. It's not something that bothers me. I'm not afraid of death. Oh, heavens, no. I've got so much to do, I don't have time for it today. But when it happens, it happens.

*Bushman was the celebrated gorilla her parents bequeathed to the Lincoln Park Zoo in Chicago.

The Other Son

STEVE YOUNG

He and his wife, Maurine, raised four sons. In June 1996, in Chicago, their eldest, Andrew, was shot and killed by Mario Ramos, eighteen.

I have trouble sleeping at night because I have just too much energy running through my veins. I was a piano technician for many years, I was a speed-skating coach for my son and his friends. Back in the days when they were skating in the national championships, we used to travel in a station wagon to god-awful, distant frozen ponds all over the northern woods.

After my son Andrew died, I decided to get involved in the issue of gun violence, because it was an illegally trafficked gun that took his life. I knew that the industry bore some responsibility for his death. That led me to a life of advocacy.

We have four children. Andrew's a twin. He was the oldest by ten minutes. His twin is Sam. We have Philip, who's probably still downstairs sleeping – he's in bad shape these days. I'm on his case. And Clinton, who's twelve, who's off at school right now.

It happened in June of 1996. Andrew and Sam and two friends went out to cash a check and some kids in a gang started throwing gang signs at them and they took offense and words were exchanged. Andrew drove off about two blocks north of this grocery store. And these two kids in the gang were on a bicycle – two kids, one bike – and they chased after the car and one of them had a gun and Andrew was caught in rush-hour traffic. It was about five-thirty on a Monday night in June – bright daylight. And this kid just walked up to Andrew and shot him in the shoulder from about point-blank range. And he later admitted to a Catholic priest that he was only trying to scare Andrew and shoot him in the shoulder. This is what I'm finding out now is that these kids, they don't understand how powerful and lethal these weapons are. He shot Andrew in the shoulder and it went clear through his body, right through his heart. And Andrew basically passed out in Sam's arms inside the car. The damage to his heart was too severe. The doctors could not save him.

Everything's been different since then.

The shooter had never been in trouble with the police before. He received forty years. The other kid who handed him the gun and said, 'Do it' – the one who instigated the whole series of events, throwing the insults and the gang signs – he got fifty-five years because he already had thirteen priors. He was fifteen. Mario Ramos was eighteen, he was the shooter. The other kid was Roberto Lazcano. Andrew was nineteen. A couple days later, Maurine and I were leaving the funeral home. I'd just chosen a casket and I was in a complete state of bewilderment. My knees buckled. I was there on the sidewalk, on my knees, crying, and I knew if they'd let me inside the cell with Ramos I just would have walked in there and snapped his neck. I was just so *filled* with grief and anger . . . I'd lost my son. He was my best friend in many ways. Andrew. He was the one that loved to skate, and I've loved to skate ever since I've been a little boy. I probably would have, at the very minimum, if they'd let me into a room with Mario Ramos, beat the living crap out of him.

We've usually gone to church most of our married life. I was raised an Episcopalian. I grew up, I moved away from that. Christian or non-Christian, I don't differentiate that much. My wife wanted me to come to some of these Bible churches, and some of the people there were kind of extreme. I always felt a little uncomfortable, especially when people started rolling on the floor and speaking in tongues. My spirituality is an internal dialogue with myself and with my God.

I was self-employed at the time as a piano technician and I couldn't work – I was just too devastated. So the bills continued coming in: I still had to pay for the mortgage, I still had to pay for the lights and everything else. I didn't care. I just started tossing bills into the corner. I just didn't give a damn. I couldn't work. I'd wake up in the morning and I'd have a few appointments and I'd just say, 'Screw it.' My income was probably cut by about two-thirds at the time. The people at this church, they passed the hat for my family and they came over with a couple of checks. I remember one was around eight hundred dollars, another around nine hundred, and it really helped. The bills really started adding up, and after about six or eight months I owed a *lot* of money. I had a customer up in Glencoe, this sweet little old lady. Whenever I worked on her piano, it would be like seventy-five dollars, but she'd always want to pay me twice as much. I'm not going to take advantage of some old lady just 'cause she's too generous, so I'd charge her the regular price.

About six months after Andrew died, there was an incident in one of the courtrooms with one of the boys that shot Andrew – the one who handed the gun to Mario. We went to the sentencing hearing and the judge said fifty-five years. The boy's father was this very short Mexican immigrant man, and I heard somebody repeat to him *fifty-five* in Spanish. He had a cousin with him who was interpreting. And the man put his head in his hands and he started sobbing. And I really felt sorry for the guy because his son was going to prison for basically the rest of his life, fifty-five years. He had just lost his son. I know a tiny bit of Spanish, so I went over to him and I said, '*Yo siempre su niño*' – I think that means I'm sorry for your son. I put my arm around him. He literally came up to my shoulder, he was so short. I really felt sorry for him in my heart because I knew this man, he was an immigrant, and he never came to this country to raise children to be murderers. My picture was on the front page of the *Sun-Times* the next day, the front of the *Tribune* as well. The TV stations called me. It was my first exposure to being in the media. This little old lady I was talking about read this story and realized that I was the same person. She sat me down and said, 'How are you doing?' I said, 'It's very, very difficult. It's not just me – it's pulling my family out of this, getting my other sons to get back on track with their lives.' And so she gave me the money I needed to cover all my bills.

In my mind, my son is in his grave, and I believe in the afterlife. We're Christians, and we believe that when this body dies, it doesn't end. Your spirit goes on. I believe my son is out there, might even be aware of what we're all doing down here. And to me that's a better situation than if I had a son who was sitting in the belly of the beast down in some god-awful prison where unspeakable acts are happening all the time. I looked at this guy who was just silently

weeping. I felt like he needed to be comforted. It's not complicated.
I just felt sorry for him.

One night I had a dream about Andrew. I was standing on a
footbridge over a frozen lake and Andrew was skating under the
bridge. I was afraid the ice was so thin that he was going to fall
through in the middle and drown. I ran down to the end of the
bridge and motioned for Andrew to come over. And I said, 'If you
just hear me out on this, you won't have to die, you won't go
through the ice.' It was all nonverbal communication: he could tell
what I was thinking, and I could tell what he was thinking. It was
like: *You don't have to die, you won't fall through the ice and drown.* And
Andrew just said, 'I'm OK, I'm fine, I'm in a good place. Don't
worry about me. I'm safe. Take care of my brothers, take care of
Mom.' That's the message I got out of the dream.

I've quit my job as a piano technician. Now I'm in advocacy.
The Million Mom March. It's a national organization working for
sensible gun laws to protect our kids from guns. The church that
raised a little bit of money for us, they were very sympathetic
right after Andrew died. But when I started getting involved in
advocacy, I noticed that all of a sudden I was dealing with some
pretty conservative, right-wing people. I go to church one
Sunday and here's a Christian Coalition voting guide sitting there
on the information table. I go to the pastor: 'What the hell is this?
This guy's NRA. This is blood money.' The pastor got very
uncomfortable. A couple of the women in church said to
Maurine, 'We don't talk about gun control in this church.' I found
myself drifting further and further away from the church at the
same time as I was being approached by Father Oldershaw –
Mario Ramos's family went to his church. When Father
Oldershaw found out about Andrew's death, he said, 'A member
of our parish has murdered a member of our community – we've
got to do something.' He had written a letter in the parish
newsletter when he heard about this kid who just walked up to a
car and shot point-blank. He said, 'Lock him up, throw away the
key. Worthless individual has no value to society.' But then he
found out it was Mario, a kid who had been an altar boy in his
church and somebody he had known since he was a small boy. It
just completely bewildered him. Mario, in his memory, was a

pretty gentle kid, but he'd been sucked into this gang lifestyle. And he got pushed over the edge so that one day there was a gun in his hand and it cost my son his life. The parish started praying for the family of Mario Ramos. The family was so ashamed they went back to Mexico for a couple of months. The parish started praying for my family, too.

One day, Father Oldershaw ran into my wife and talked to her for a few minutes. He left his phone number. She said, 'Who's this guy? Should I trust him?' I was just so black and angry and depressed that I probably would have bit his head off if I had seen him. In my mind, I would have held him responsible in some way because it was his kid from his parish. I called him a couple of nights later, about ten-thirty at night. We talked until one in the morning. About a week later, I was over at the rectory. I tried to tell him about who Andrew was and about my family. And it was the beginning of a beautiful friendship. I belong to that church now.

I'm not overtly devout, but I am inwardly. I say a little prayer every day. A prayer that my mother taught me when I was a little boy. I can say it for you: 'Jesus dear, my friend and guide, please be always at my side. In my work or rest or play, Lord be never far away. Tell me what I ought to do, let me often think of you. So shall I be safe from wrong, happy as the day is long.' I've been saying it ever since I was a little boy. I say that prayer, and I say the Lord's prayer, every day.

Clinton, my little one – he's twelve. He was eight at the time. He used to stand in the street and wait for cars to hit him. He'd start fires on the stove. He'd start fights with kids twice his size, hoping he'd get beat up. He'd say, 'I'd rather be with Andrew.' He'd scare the *hell* out of us. We didn't know what he was going to do to himself. I remember one of his teachers at school called me up – she was *so* concerned about him. He was living in a netherworld. I was in such shock myself that I wasn't noticing everything that was going on. Maurine was at a grocery store and all of a sudden she became disoriented – and she didn't know where she was. Fortunately, P.J., my middle son, was with her and he was able to get her home. P.J. went into abject depression. He was fourteen at the time. He shut down for quite a long time. I noticed that everybody grieves on different schedules. Sam, he quit school, he quit his job, he basically holed up in his room. Sam has got artistic talents, and so he sat in his room and drew a lot of bizarre, dark, very demonic type of images.

Everybody's doing better now. They're not out of the woods, but everybody's still feeling the aftereffects. Maurine's liberated because of her act of forgiveness. I'm liberated because of my activism. I think Sam's doing okay. P.J. was the last to crash, and he went into an abject depression through most of his high school years. He's starting to come out of it. Clinton has got some emotional disorders, and so that compounds the situation. He sees therapists. He's getting a little better. He'll be thirteen next month, and so all these adolescent hormones are kicking in and that makes the situation more complicated. But he's getting better – the whole family's getting a little better.

And a lot of people are praying for us. Mario Ramos prays for us every day in prison. I have not written him, I have not visited him. Even though I finally have come to a place in my heart where I've forgiven him for what he's done.

Being able to forgive has cleared my mind to be able to focus on the things that I have to work on. I'm not rooted down in hate or the need for revenge. I've seen victims that can't get past utter rage and the need to strike back, and it's eating them *up*. They're going to get cancer. It was just so obvious to me when I saw a couple of victims that couldn't get past the hate, and I realized that you will go downhill if you let it consume you. Maurine has helped me to see that.

Maurine Young

In contrast to her husband's introspective nature, she is outgoing, a large-boned woman, overflowing with gusto and ebullience. She frequently laughs out loud.

I'm a forty-six-year-old woman of Jewish-Gentile descent – my father's a Jew, my mother's a Gentile. My parents divorced when I was young, and I was raised by my stepfather – raised Catholic. He was a truck driver. My younger brother, Mark, became a truck driver. I went to public school. But I went to the Catholic catechism every Wednesday. I did the confirmation and all that kind of stuff. I got close to age twelve, thirteen, and I began to see what I was saved from. I was saved from Hell. But what Catholicism wasn't teaching me was what I was saved *to*. They didn't tell me how to live with God and experience a taste of Heaven on Earth, *now*. So I began to pull away from the Church. It just didn't meet my needs.

If I read my Bible I saw that it said very clearly to worship God, then why were people worshiping statues? To me that looked like idolatry. So, as a young teenager, I started asking questions. Then I began to wonder what is this all about? I know that there's a God, and I know that He loves me, but what else is there? How do you live now? I lived in a very difficult, alcoholic home, and early in my teens began to experiment with drugs – do whatever I felt like doing. In the one sense, I had the Ten Commandments ingrained in me, so I knew what was right and wrong – but I didn't really care about the consequences. I didn't really understand the value of a God who loves me, and that because He loves me, I should act loving towards him, which means act loving towards everybody else. I was very, very selfish.

I had been working part-time jobs since I was fourteen. A couple of weeks after I graduated from high school, my dad said, 'Get out of the backyard, sitting in your bikini, and get your butt downtown and find a job.' So I went downtown and found a secretarial position. I was seventeen. And then I moved out when I was eighteen, to live with my boyfriend. That didn't work out. Moved back home and met Steve not that long afterwards, in March of 1975. We moved up here to Rogers Park and had a family. We had twins in May of 1977, Andrew Needham and Samuel Richard, born on different days – May 7 and May 8. And then in 1982, in August, we had Philip; and then in 1987, December, we had Clinton. I was working as a floral designer, part-time, in Skokie. Steve was tuning pianos.

Andrew went out to cash a check with his brother and didn't come back. He was shot by a young man who had easy access to a handgun and who had graduated from high school the day before and was looking to move up in the gang that he was in, the Latin Kings. He shot Andrew, probably because Andrew didn't back down with his mouth. He knew that gang members were idiots and didn't mind telling them what he thought of them when they made signs at him. He was in our car.

When I got to the hospital and found out that he was gone, and I asked the boys what happened and they told me, I said, 'Well, you know what? There'll be no retaliation for this. I just want to make that clear.' Men usually want revenge; women, too, but men usually much quicker. Women will stew for a while. I knew that revenge was wrong, but I also knew that I hated what these kids had done and knew that they deserved to be punished. I pulled out some old journals from that time. These notebooks. Here's an entry that I wrote July 13th of 1996. Andrew was murdered June 10th of 1996. It reads: 'It's been sixty days since Andrew left us. Forced out of his body by Mario and Roberto. Please, Lord, let justice be served. Plus, punish them. Let them not have a free life.' That's how I felt. I did not want them to be free, and I was real glad that the police had seen what had happened.

I'm going to backtrack a tiny bit. My twins were three months old. I was sitting on the beach with them. Somebody came up to me and said, 'Could we talk to you about Jesus?' And I said, 'It's a public park, it's a free country, you can sit down.' So they started talking to me about Jesus. This lady turns to me and she says, 'So how's your life?' And her words shot into my chest like a sword. I'm thinking, *Oh my God, what does she know?* I had just had the twins. I was *not* coping. I was smoking massive amounts of marijuana. I was up twenty-four hours a day, not knowing how to keep these little babies on a schedule. I was fantasizing throwing one of them out the window. I was having what now I understand to be severe post-partum psychosis. I didn't have any help. I was really just trying to hold on ... So I began to tell this lady and her friends how poorly I was doing. She said, 'Would you like to commit your life to Christ again?' And I said, 'I really would. Because I realize I'm not doing very well by myself. Something is missing.' So I did that and I prayed that day. Since that day, I've been learning how to parent, and to let God love me, and to love and forgive others.

Nineteen years later, when this happened with Andrew being murdered, I said, 'OK, I know who I'm following.' What would Jesus do? It was pretty clear. He says: Love your enemies – I consider these little guys my enemies that killed my son. Pray for those who use you, forgive as God has forgiven you. So I thought, *OK, what does that mean?* Looking back at another journal ... this is from January of 1997. I wrote: 'What are the obstacles to forgiveness? How can forgiveness free us? How can it free me? Well, first I needed to know that I must face my own pain and grieve. And not keep anger on, sort of as a suit of armor. Admit the wrong that was done to me and experience the rage. But be honest with God about my pain and why. Releasing my anger to him and pardoning the offender makes me feel vulnerable, even out of control. But what's my choice? If I hold my anger, it will destroy me.' And then I also wrote, 'It's OK to be afraid of being hurt again.' So, obviously, the whole idea of forgiveness was there in the back of my mind the whole time, and I kept thinking: *I want to kill them, I want to see them fry.* But God says forgive ... And I kept going back and forth thinking, *How do you do this?* Scratching my head. Then I realized I could make the choice and trust that the power to do it would be there. Because I know that my faith, which is just my yes, is the glue that holds God's power to his promises. And He's promised that He would do what I ask, He would do the right thing in my life. I'm going to have the faith and forgive and trust that He's going to take care of it all. So I finally did that about July of 1997, about six months after what I just read to you. I forgave and wrote Mario in prison a letter. He was eighteen, my son was nineteen. I told him about my life. I just wanted him to know how I was raised, and that I had done plenty of things that needed forgiving and God forgave me. So how could I withhold forgiveness from him? I couldn't. That I love him and God loves him and I forgave him.

I didn't know that at the same time, he was writing me a letter. As I remember, he was begging forgiveness, saying how sorry he was, how he wished he could bring Andrew back, even trade places. And I believed his letter was sincere. But his letter was unnecessary for my forgiveness. I had been asking to see him.

It's one thing to write to someone and say you forgive them – it's another to physically touch them and say you forgive them. It would help me in my healing and him in his, I knew. I felt *compelled* to do it. I had been asking through his priest when was a good time. Mario kept saying, 'I'm not ready. Mrs. Young is pushing too much. I'm not ready.' He was terrified. He thought I might hit him or something. He was not ready to face me. That was July of 1997. I didn't get to see him until December 17th of 1998. So it took more than a year and a half before he was ready. And I waited. We did correspond. And then I went to visit him with Father Oldershaw, and a retired schoolteacher by the name of Arlene Bozack. She had been visiting him.

When we first got there, the assistant warden, who was Hispanic, was crying. He said, 'Mrs. Young, *why* are you here?' I said, 'Well, I'm here to offer forgiveness to the young man who killed my son.' And he said, '*Why?*' And I said, 'Because I care about him, I love him. It's the right thing to do. I want to do it in person.' He said, 'In all my years, this is the first time I've ever seen this happen. I really commend what you're doing.' He was this big, tough-looking Hispanic warden.

I see Mario for the first time. He couldn't look at me. He had his head hanging down. They sat us around a small round table with four attached seats, told us where to sit. Everybody kept looking at me very suspiciously, like I was going to just jump on this kid and beat the hell out of him. Mario's got his head hanging down, and all of a sudden he kind of looks, and he can't make eye contact. I saw that his whole body was starting to shake. All four of us prayed. It was me, Father Oldershaw on my right, Mario was across from me, and Arlene Bozack was to his right.

I grabbed both Mario's hands from across the table, and I looked at him in the eye, and I said, 'I just want you to know that I'm glad to be here.' I knew I had to go first. He just shook his head. Slowly, but surely, the conversation started. Little chitchat, we all took turns talking. I wanted to know about his family and how they were doing. Because the shame that he brought on them – especially being an Hispanic family – that's so important. And then the conversation changed a bit because I felt like, OK, it's time for this little guy to hear what he's done to us. The consequences of his actions. I began to tell him the difficulties that each of our family members was having. As I went through, person by person, saying, one young man's suicidal, the other one can't focus, or whatever the problems were for each of us, he listened. He held Arlene's hand and he trembled and he wept, but he listened.

At some point in the conversation I said, 'I love you like you're my son, like you're one of mine.' And I was like, 'I can't figure out how this happened!' [*Laughs*] I thought I was *nuts*. I didn't tell him that. I was thinking, *I gotta be crazy*. So I said, 'I love you like you're my own son. You got into my heart violently, but you're there. So this has to be a miracle. God did this. Because I didn't do this. But, as a son, you have responsibilities to know what's going on and to pray for us, to communicate with us regularly. You're part of the family now.' Then he pulled out his Bible. I said, 'Mario, there's a Scripture that meant a lot to me and helped me take this step. I wanted to tell you what it is. It's in Romans, in the twelfth chapter. It says, "Never pay back evil for evil to anyone. Respect what is right in the sight of all men. If possible, so far as it depends on you, be at peace with all men."' I said, 'My reaching out and extending and forgiving was my responsibility, and it didn't depend on whether or not you accepted that forgiveness. I had to do that.' It also says, 'Never take your own revenge, but leave room for the wrath of God.' Then I said what was really important was when I got to verse 21. It says, 'Do not be overcome by evil, but overcome evil with good.' I said, 'Mario, that really meant a lot to me. Because I wanted to win. I did not want this evil thing that you and Roberto did to us to win. I wanted good to win. So that's why I forgave you and that's why I love you.'

He was speechless. He looked at me like I had two heads. [*She roars with laughter.*] He stared at me like: *I don't know what she's talking about – she's from another planet.* It wasn't quite sinking in. But he was listening. I heard later that he was confused and didn't understand it, but it was beginning to make sense. He was actually holding his Bible open to this spot, looking at it over and over and over again. We talked, and then I got to hold him. That was really, really special. Here's another reason I thought I was crazy: I'm sitting across this little table from him, and it's all I can do to stay in my seat. I'm thinking: *What's wrong with me? Am I having a nervous breakdown?* Everything in me wanted to leap over the table, grab hold of this kid, and rock him like a baby, just *hold* him. The urge was so overwhelming. The compulsion was so overwhelming, I was afraid that if I couldn't keep control, I'd be in really big trouble with the guards and the warden. So I resisted that urge the whole time.

On the way back home, I was thinking about it, and then I talked to Arlene and Father Oldershaw. I said, 'I've got it! I know what was happening. I was getting a taste in my body of how much God loves us. He loves us so much that He wants to leap over the table, grab hold of us, and just rock us because we're his children.' That love, that forgiveness – I got a taste of what it must have been like for Jesus when he was here and walked the Earth among people that he loved so desperately, so wonderfully. I got a taste of it!

As time went on and we kept corresponding, I did go see him again there, and it was good. I really began to see him maturing, through his letters and through visiting him. I was training him, I was mentoring him – to help him to grow up, to help him in his spiritual walk. His letters changed. They became clearer, he became more willing to take total responsibility. I saw no excuses anymore, I saw a person that was squarely saying: *This is where I am and this is where I should be, and God's changing me right here, and probably being here saved my life.* He's working as a chaplain's assistant now . . . [*Sighs*] . . . I'm convinced that if I did not forgive and I held on to my anger, that I probably would have become mentally ill. Maybe killed myself, maybe hurt someone else. I felt like God's hand was on me and he was squashing me into a pancake: *You gotta do this – this is the right thing.*

I knew that there were great things ahead, although they terrified me, the thought of going out into new territory. Because, I'll tell ya,

I was not a very forgiving person most of my life. I used to hold things against whoever did what to me. It really took the murder of my son and the forgiving of his killer to teach me how to forgive everybody around me. I began to realize: My husband's not going to be Mr. Perfect. My parents haven't been perfect parents. My children are not perfect children. My friends are going to let me down. That's a given. Because they're human, like I am. There is one perfect, that is God, and He loves me. And that's good enough for me. So, by forgiving them, like I did Mario, it freed me to really love. My love was, like, stopped up in a bottle or something. It came out in little bits. But for the most part, it was stopped up until I forgave this kid. And then it was like *whoosh* – this is what I've been missing my whole life. [*Belly laugh*]

I saw Mario just this last month. I've met his mom and his dad. They don't speak any English, but usually one of his sisters is there to interpret. Most of the time, all his mother can do is hold on to me and cry. She's a very sweet person.

The Job

WILLIAM HERDEGEN

A semiretired funeral director in Chicago. He once had five such places in the city. Now, there is only this one. 'We have two chapels here – fifteen units. We have visitation usually the night before. Down at the other places, there were two night wakes, sometimes three.'

After high school, I attended Worsham College of Mortuary Science in 1948. It was actually a two-year course in one year. We went to school from eight in the morning until five at night. If you were working in the morgue on a body, you had to complete it, no matter if it took you till six o'clock. We learned embalming, of course: removing the blood out of the body and replacing it with embalming fluid to preserve the remains.

I waited till I got my full license before I went into the service in 1952, the Korean War. I was with the 92nd Armor. I was there only thirty-nine days, and we were shelled about thirty of them. The battery commander finally says, 'I see here by your records you're a licensed mortician. What are you doing in the artillery?' So they transferred me into the 40th Infantry Division, and that's where I worked myself up to head of the burial detail. I was in the Division of Graves Registration. The bodies were all taken to an airfield and then sent back to Japan, where they were processed for shipping back home. We had no morgue set up for preparation of the bodies. We were only a couple of miles behind the lines. We just had to get them out of there, fast. It was very scary at first. Our company buried over three hundred enemy dead right there on the spot.

I came back home in 1954, and for three years worked in several funeral homes in Chicago. Old established ones. I went on my own in March of 1957. I bought out George Westphall, who was there since 1907. Three years ago, I gave my son the business. I'm semiretired now, but I still come in on weekends so he has a couple days off to be with his family. I remember my first case when I started my own business. It was Mr. Knights, a good friend of my mother-in-law's. He lived on Clybourn Avenue. Since then I think I've buried most of that family. They stuck with me.

It was a little scary at first. I did everything myself. In fact, I still do, even when I come in on the weekends. If we have a death call, I go out on it, and I come back and embalm the body. If the person dies at home, then we go to the home. We have to call the doctor to sign the death certificate. Then we go and pick up the remains, bring it back to the funeral home. Most of the time it's two or three o'clock in the morning, so they'll come in about nine o'clock the next day and make funeral arrangements. By that time, I've got the body all embalmed and everything. I work all night, all hours. Seven days a week, 365 days a year we're on call. Now I'm on call Friday night till Monday morning when Joe, my son, comes.

The main thing was, you try and comfort them and help them – especially if it's a woman. A lot of times the man did everything and the woman didn't know what to do, so you would help. If the man had been a veteran, I'd take them to the veteran's office, over on Belmont, when it was there. Billy Duffy – I buried him when he died – would fill out all the papers for them so they'd get their benefits. Then I would take them to the Social Security office, sign them up for their benefits. Then I would take them – if they had insurance – I would take them to the insurance office. People would talk about how nice I was and everything. Of course I had the time. I didn't have that big a business.

At first, many funeral directors were afraid to handle people with AIDS. We were the first. I think my first case was in 1985. The man was a very good friend of mine. I said, 'You don't look good.' He said, 'I can't go to the doctor – I don't have any money.' I talked to a friend of mine and he says, 'Take him to the hospital and just leave him there and they'll have to take care of him.' I took him to the University of Illinois. I went to see him the following day and his door was closed. The nurse says, 'You can't go in there.' I said, 'What do you mean?' She says, 'You gotta put on a gown and mask, we think he's got tuberculosis.' I put on the mask and the gown. The next day I came, there's a sign: YOU MUST SEE THE NURSE

AT THE STATION BEFORE YOU CAN GO IN TO VISIT. I went there and they said, 'You've got to put on full gown and mask.' And I says, 'Yeah, I know from when I was here yesterday.' 'No, he's got AIDS,' she says. 'Be *very* careful.' That was how I first started.

I was on the board of directors for Chicago Funeral Directors. I was put on the infectious disease committee. I talked to the different doctors. They told me what to do. I had a funeral director from Libertyville call me and he says, 'I got an AIDS case. I don't want it. Do you want it? I'll send it down to you.' I says, 'Yeah, no problem.' So the people come in and they said, 'We've been to three funeral homes. None of them would take him. I want to tell you right now, my brother's got AIDS.' I said, 'No problem.' They couldn't get over it, that they finally found somebody that would take care of him. The others were afraid of catching it. The word got around that I was very sympathetic to people with AIDS, so I started getting calls from all over the city and the suburbs. They'd all come down here. I went to the Howard Brown Clinic and talked to them,* and they said the main thing you have to watch out for is the blood – that's where the AIDS virus would be. You can't catch it from just kissing somebody on the cheek.

I just thought we'd had every walk of life and just because some of them were gay . . . what's the difference? They're human. I felt that somebody had to do it. When they'd come in, you could just see the *relief* on their faces. My son, he had no problem with it either.

I've seen so many things. I prayed when I went for prostate cancer, and I had everybody in church praying for me, and I come out with flying colors so far. I pray every night. I think that's maybe why God saved me, because I helped other people like that.

My wife gave communion to the AIDS people at Illinois Masonic for fifteen years. Nobody from the church wanted to do it. They were afraid they would catch it, giving them communion. It never bothered her.

I was the only one for three years, till '88. Then it was mandatory under the American Disabilities Act. They *had* to start taking them. One case sticks in my mind. This man came in and he said, 'My partner died.' He had durable power of attorney. He wanted to go

*The Howard Brown Health Center for Gays, Lesbians, and Bisexuals.

back home after his partner died. His partner's mother says: 'We don't need you. We don't welcome you no more.' He went home and the following week he hung himself. So we had the two within a week's time. I'll never forget that.

I've had actors, florists, caterers, the organist from church here died of AIDS. Like I say, I've had every walk of life. The one case I had, a boy was in Vietnam and his father was, I believe, a colonel. The boy stepped in front of a train and the train hit him. My son and I worked about eight hours on him, putting him back together. The father insisted he wanted to see him. One arm was tore off. We sewed it back on. The father took a look at him and he says, 'It don't look like . . .' I said, 'It wouldn't.' There was nothing missing; it was just that from the impact his face was twice the size as normal. We fixed him up the best we could. He says, 'I want to thank you,' he says, 'that's him. But it don't look like him . . .' We worked from a picture.

The hereafter? Yes. I feel that when I get up there I'm gonna see all my friends and relatives and everything, and we're gonna have a helluva time. I really do. Before I go to sleep at night I pray and thank the Lord for giving me another year. And I've done good. From a little place down there where we never broke a hundred cases a year, and we moved in here. The first year we did two hundred and six. It's fallen down a little bit because a lot of people are going through the Cremation Society. And the AIDS cases have dropped quite a few too because they're living longer.

Most of your cemeteries are all full now. Take St. Boniface on Lawrence and Clark, that's full. St. Henry's on Ridge, it's full. The only burials they have are the ones that own the lots. St. Joseph is full. That's where my grandparents and parents are. I've got my name on the stone already. When my mom died, my dad remarried and his second wife wouldn't bury him there – she wanted him next to her family at St. Boniface. So I asked if I could have that grave. It'll be a double internment. Whoever dies first, my wife or I, they go down eight foot, and then the other one will be put on top. There was another grave on the other side of my mom and my brother died very suddenly. I'd asked him if he would like that grave, and he'd said he would.

I don't fear death. No. In this business, a couple of times I've shaken hands with a man coming out of church and I get home and I get a call, 'Mr. So-and-so died.' 'I just saw him a little while ago – I shook hands with him at the church.' 'Yeah, he's gone. He come home, into the house, and down he went.' It's all over with. My wife and I both have the living will. We don't want to be hooked up. I've seen so many people come in where the body is rotting already, but they keep 'em going with the machines. I think that's so wrong. They're rotting before the heart stops, put it that way.

I took over in 1957 in March, and my mom died in '58. We were all laughing and joking – she'd baby-sat for my children the night before, and the next day she was gone. I had taken out a baby to be buried, and I got home and my dad called and he says, 'Come over quick – something happened to your mother.' She had diabetes bad and she went into a diabetic coma. We got her an ambulance, got her over to Masonic, and in an hour and twenty minutes, she was gone. She was only fifty-one. And then I lost a sister in '53 – she had cancer of the throat, esophagus. I lost a sister in '57, she also had diabetes. My dad was seventy when he died in 1975. I lost my brother, the baby of the family. We just buried him two years ago – he was sixty-five. I'll be seventy in December, and I was glad to get out of my fifties. My grandmother, I think, was fifty-two when she died.

My mom, I had my friend do, because I just couldn't handle it. My sister that died of cancer, I used to go every week to talk to her. She was at home. She was resigned that she was gonna die and she said, 'Bill, I want you to promise me that you'll embalm me. I know your work is beautiful.' She too had lost a lot of weight. I says, 'Oh, Cheryle, that's a big promise.' She says, 'Bill, please do it.' And I did. I embalmed her. In fact, all the rest of my family I took care of. My mother I couldn't handle. All my aunts and uncles . . . they didn't bother me as much as my own siblings. That's where it gets a little sticky, when you have to do your own family. It's kind of hard.

I want my son to do it for me. Like with my sister, he said, 'You're asking a lot of me, Dad.' I said, 'I know but I respect your work.' Everybody that comes in there that he's taken care of, the family says, 'Oh, your son, he did a beautiful job. My mom looks so nice.' A lot of these boys that died of AIDS, sometimes they wither away to just about nothing. I go and rebuild them from a picture. I use silicone. People come in, especially their partner, and they say,

'Oh, that's how he looked before he got sick. Thank you, thank you.' That's what makes you feel good. Joe is the same way. He goes out of his way to try and get that likeness again. I've been to some funeral homes, they don't take the trouble. Where the coat was like this, careless, I went up and straightened it out. Or if he wore his hair straight back and they've got it parted to the side, I say, 'No, he wore it back, give me a comb.' And the family goes, 'Thank you, thank you. We didn't want to say nothin'.' They were afraid to say anything.

I buried two of the boys that were found under Gacy's house.* One, the funeral directors all got together. I had six funeral directors for pallbearers. There were no outsiders. I was so proud of the Funeral Director's Association that time. I think there was thirteen or fourteen unclaimed bodies. The cemeteries donated the plot and the monument dealers donated a stone. The one I had went to Irving Park Cemetery and the stone read, 'Only known by God alone.'

They all went out of here fully dressed, and most of them in tuxedos. When the tuxedos went out of style, a friend brought me in a whole carload of them. So when they had nothing, indigent – veterans that we got out of the TB sanitarium or the VA hospital – they would send them over to me and I would bury them for Veteran's and Social Security. Whatever I got, that's all I got. I put them all in tuxedos. People would say: 'I thought he was penniless, I didn't think he had any money.' I said, 'I took care of it.' I gave him suit, shirt, tie, underwear, everything. They went out first class.

*John Wayne Gacy murdered scores of young men, whom he buried in and around his house.

Rory Moina

He has been an AIDS-certified registered nurse for fourteen years at the Illinois Masonic Hospital, Chicago. 'My parents were divorced when I was seven or eight. I have a sister who lives in South Carolina. My father remarried when I was about thirteen years old. He moved to California, and I have two half brothers and two half sisters out there. I lived with my mother here. Working-class family. I had a loving relationship with my father, but he wasn't a good role model. That was the reason my parents were divorced. My father was a compulsive gambler.'

In 1986, one of my first patients was a young man, his name was Bobby. I had just finished my six-week orientation. As I walked by a patient's room there was a young man laying across the bed and he was crying. I didn't know him, I wasn't taking care of him at the time, but something pulled me into the room. I sat down and we started a conversation. He told me about his life growing up outside of Detroit, being sexually abused when he was a child and running away to California and just kind of doing drugs and leading a wild kind of lifestyle. He'd come to Chicago, settled there, and started to get his life together when he realized he had AIDS. He had had PCP pneumonia, which was very prevalent back then. He had had it about five times, which is amazing. I knew him for about a year before he died. It took him a while to build some trust in me, having been abused by men when he was younger. He was a gay kid. He lived in a third-floor walkup and because of these pneumonias and the condition of his lungs, he wasn't able to walk up all three of those stairs. So right before he died, he came to live with me and my partner, Stephen, so I could give him IV medicine. Back then there were really no other places. There weren't hospices for people with AIDS. You've heard of Bonaventure House, Chicago House – there was nothing like that back then. Not only myself, but a lot of the other staff who worked there took people home with them.

What I realized – maybe it took about a year, two years, after he died – was that he was my teacher. I was a novice nurse, out of school. With him coming to live with us, I learned what it's like to have AIDS on a day-to-day basis: the pain, the neuropathy, the pain in his feet, the lung pain that he had. Not being able to sleep because he could hardly breathe. And also the personal stigma of what it was like to have AIDS back then. He had developed some Kaposi's cancer lesions. He was only twenty-five years old, and people would stop and stare. Sometimes people just don't think.

After Bobby died, people would say to me, 'Bobby was so lucky to have you in his life before he died . . .' I felt *very* uncomfortable hearing that, even though I realized that in a lot of ways it was true. It was about two years later, I was going to Unity Church in Chicago. The minister was giving a lesson, it was the first time I ever heard the phrase, 'When the student is ready, the teacher appears.' I burst into tears because of what I realized, what made our relationship reciprocal: Bobby was my teacher back when I needed a teacher because I'd embarked on something that I knew nothing about. I knew nothing about taking care of somebody with AIDS. With Bobby as my teacher, I was learning firsthand, without actually experiencing it, what it was like to live with AIDS. It was a big event in my life. There were so many things after that that just came intuitively to me, but it was based on what I had come actually to know. So I was able to care for other people better with this little bit of inside information.

Was I scared of contracting? No – actually, I remember two instances. One time I got a splash of blood in my eye, and another time I got stuck with a needle. I had to go through a series of testing. I remember initially being shocked. When something like that happens to you, it just throws you off for a minute and everything rushes before you. I just don't remember ever being concerned about it after that initial incident happened. I remember getting tested and maybe for an hour before I had my results I would be a little nervous. But, other than that, I have to honestly say I never really thought, *Oh, I'm going to catch AIDS.* There was something inside of me that just told me I had a purpose. I have a book at home about the quilt. It explains what the quilt was and shows some of the quilt panels. Over the years, I've slipped little things into the book to jog my memory of certain patients. A card that I might have got or just something. There's all sorts of little mementos, little things that patients wrote to me or their families wrote to me. When I think of the fourteen years, about the devastation of lives and the stories there and the families that I met, the supportive families, the not so supportive families – the not so supportive families who came around to end up embracing their child . . .

I came to know Laurie Cannon through Danny Sotomayor, the political activist, and his partner, Scott McPherson, the playwright who wrote *Marvin's Room*. I remember Danny's mother, whom we loved dearly, but who was just so unaccepting of her son being gay and being this political activist and out in the mainstream.

Unlike Danny Sotomayor, I'm not somebody who would go out and chain myself to fences. When he was first hospitalized, I was aware of a little bit of like anger inside of me because I thought, *This isn't the way I do things.* After a while – again, he was my teacher – I realized that *I* don't have AIDS. How the hell do *I* know if I wouldn't be chaining myself to fences if I was in his position? So I ended up dropping all of that crap because I realized that was just my stuff, and I learned to love this young man. He was this adorable little Irish–Spanish cherub of a person. I remember once after he had had surgery, he was sitting on the sofa in one of our lounges and he just looked up at me with so much love in his face. Just because of my caring and my being there for him as a nurse. I remember he got up from the sofa, which was just so hard to do because he had stitches in his stomach, and he just put his arms around me and gave me the biggest hug. I was like, *Wow!* That's the kind of stuff that kept me going. I get goose bumps when I think about experiences like that.

When I look back, I had no particular role models in my life. I had people who loved me dearly, my family, but who didn't have a clue as to how to raise a young man, a young boy. Anything I did was fine with my father. My father loved me unconditionally. That's something that I learned without a doubt before my father died. We never had any arguments, but we ended up not seeing each other for fourteen or fifteen years, and only had one or two phone conversations. When I found out he was close to death out in California, I dropped what I was doing just to make sure that if he did die, he knew that I loved him. I became reacquainted with my half brothers and half sisters who live out there. I know before he died he was very happy because he saw the five of us together again, which circumstances prohibited over the years. I'm becoming aware of how much my father did play a role in what I feel, even though he really didn't play a role in how my day-to-day growing up went. My mother did the hands-on. When I was younger, I remember my father, who was this very macho Sicilian guy. He grew up in Little Italy here on the South Side. You could pick a character out of one of those gangster movies and that was my father – the black curly hair and all that. Yet I remember when I was little he was holding me and all that macho stuff was lost. I remember taking baths with my father. He just adored me and loved me unconditionally. I grew up with that. I missed not having my father around, but I was always content to know that my father loved me dearly.

My mother – when I told her that you were going to interview me for this book, she didn't say anything. But I talked to my sister in South Carolina a few days later and she told me our mother was uncomfortable with the idea. There's been a lot of discomfort. My mother loves me dearly. She accepted my being gay; she didn't have a problem with that. When I did tell her this, about ten years ago now, even though I had been in two nine-year relationships with men, it never was spoken. After the breakup of that last relationship, with Stephen, I remember we were out shopping one day and she looked at me and said, 'When are you going to start dating women?' And I'm like, 'Oh my God . . .' So we found a bench, we sat down and I was ready.

I was at a point in my life where I couldn't have been more happy or proud of who I was as a person. So we sat down. Initially she was like, 'Well, oh my goodness! Was it because we got divorced?' She was trying to blame herself. I tried my best to expel all those fears. Finally, I bought her a book called *Loving Someone Gay*,[*] which was one of the first books written about coming out to your parents. I gave it to her and it helped her tremendously. After that, she was just totally fine with it. But my working on the HIV unit is still scary to her.

Things have changed now because of the HIV cocktail. There are different medications that can keep the amount of virus in the body at an undetectable level. These medications are hard to tolerate, they have

---

[*]Donald H. Clark, *Loving Someone Gay* (Millbrae, Calif.: Celestial Arts, 1977).

lots of side effects, but the majority of people taking these medications are able to live normal lives. Occasionally there are complications, but some of those complications are from the side effects of the medications because they cause renal problems, kidney problems, and liver problems. Sometimes that's why people are hospitalized.

We had twenty-three full beds on our unit for at least the first ten years, from 1986 to '96. We had people waiting to come down to the unit because we didn't have room for them. Last year in July, our census dropped down to between two and seven occupied beds. The unit actually closed for a few weeks. When it reopened, it was an HIV/Medical Unit, which is what it is now.

Most of the people who have died or are living with HIV now are people in their twenties and thirties and maybe forties. 'Hospice' isn't a word that people in their twenties, thirties, and forties want to hear, but hospice work is having people die with dignity. And having their wishes met. When people get to the end stages of their disease, stop any unnecessary treatments and give them the pain medication that they need to carry them over to the next world or the next wherever.

Just to give you an idea. Danny Sotomayor and Scott McPherson were partners in life, OK. They were frequently in the hospital together. We had some double rooms at the time with two beds. We wanted to be respectful of the fact that they were partners. So we would move their beds together and they would share a room together. Just little things like that. The staff was so in sync with this. People worked there only because they wanted to be there. There were a lot of female nurses, more than male. Everyone was in total agreement. In other places, if you had AIDS, if you had HIV, then you were shunned, you were locked off in a room somewhere. That was commonplace. I had so many people come from other hospitals and they told me how they were treated, and they were literally put in a room and people wouldn't even bring their dinner trays in. They would put it outside the door. Like in prison.

I first experienced grief with Bobby. I had worked until eleven o'clock the night before he died. He died about six in the morning. While he was in the hospital, I would go to his room after I finished my shift. He would usually have the TV on. I would rub his feet. People with AIDS have something called peripheral neuropathy, foot pain. I learned how to massage his feet, to bring him comfort without hurting him. I would do that for half an hour, just spend some time with him.

This night, just before I was getting ready to leave, I noticed he was having breathing difficulty. He became alarmed, but he didn't want me to do anything about it. I wanted to respect his wishes, so I left. I was tempted to go to the nurse's station and turn the intercom system on so I could listen to his breathing, but I knew that that was an invasion of his privacy. So I told the nurse who was going to be taking care of him that night, I said, 'He's developed some difficulties but he wants to be left alone, and I want to respect that.' I didn't know if this was serious or not. But I didn't want to inform a doctor, because it was Bobby's wish that I not do that.

We're talking end stage here. This wasn't like we could do some heroic thing. He'd already had pneumonia five times, his lungs were ravaged. Anyway, I left, went home, I went to sleep. At six o'clock in the morning the phone rang. The nurse taking care of him said, 'Bobby's dying, why don't you come to the hospital right now.' I threw on some clothes, I went to the hospital. The head nurse of our unit, a very compassionate person, and another nurse I graduated from nursing school with were working up there. They knew the scenario. They knew how close I was to Bobby. When I came off the elevator on the unit, they both put their arms around me and hugged me and opened the door to his room and let me go in. I remember him laying on the bed there. He was actually waiting for me to show up, so close to death. He couldn't really speak anymore. I remember going over to him and sitting on the side of the bed and holding him and a big tear came up in the corner of his eye, the biggest tear I ever saw in my life. I remember I had a lot of difficulty with this because going back to that time, people weren't even sure if you could contract HIV from tears – I didn't really know. Part of me thought, *Oh my God, I shouldn't do this* . . . But I saw he had a tear in his eye, and I thought, *That's my tear* – and I kissed it away, even though I, you know . . . that's what I did. I kissed it away. And he died right then. I remember not feeling sad, not feeling anything. If anything, in some ways, I was joyful. Because I knew that he was released from this worldly suffering. And I was able to quickly move on.

Now people are seeing that it's not just gay men. Look at all the people in Africa, men, women, young people, old people, children. It's changed dramatically. People don't see this as a gay disease anymore. A year or two down the road, I see HIV as a manageable illness, like diabetes or certain heart conditions. Right now, medications that keep you alive are so potent they can kill you. But I know that on the horizon are medications with less side effects, so a few years down the road HIV will be a manageable illness as long as you can afford the medications. I think the important thing is getting these medications to Third World countries right now. That's where we need to start working, helping people in Third World countries – because we're so privileged here and we can have all these things and there are people who don't.

I think about all the people I've treated through the years, who, in the face of death, stood out in my mind. Especially in the early days: if you had AIDS, you died, period. I mean, there was *really* no medication. You had a death sentence. Especially if you came down with an opportunistic infection – a pneumonia, for instance, certain kinds of skin cancer, or Kaposi's sarcoma. In spite of that, some of those condemned-to-death patients were able to go on with their lives. I was often amazed at their ability to do that. Because occasionally, there would be people who were so scared they would literally be frightened to death, and they would die shortly after this scare. But there were a couple of people who had what I call grace, who come to mind.

One in particular I remember. His name was Matthew. When he would come into the hospital, he would bring a couple of suitcases with china. He would bring a silver service, cloth napkins. In fact, he even brought a candelabra. He would set this up on his bedside table in the hospital. He would bring flowers and set things up in his room just as if he was at home. He was quite a character – everyone was very fond of him. He was very flamboyant: he wouldn't wear the hospital gowns, he would wear caftans. I'm trying to think of somebody well known he reminded me of . . .

. . . A caftan? Like a sheik? Peter O'Toole – Lawrence of Arabia?

No, not a sheik. Given Matthew's personality, more flamboyant – [*suddenly*] Tallulah Bankhead!

Matthew had developed Kaposi's sarcoma. So there were these

large, blotchy purple lesions all over his face. He found somebody who was good with makeup and covered those as best as he could. What was so outstanding to me was in the face of all this, knowing that he would eventually succumb, that at any time he could die – there were no medications that could turn this around – he was always in the best of spirits and always happy to see you. In fact, he invited me and one of the other nurses to his home. His home was just filled with treasures from his travels: beautiful antiques and tapestries and different things. In spite of all, he lived life to the fullest. He didn't succumb just like that. He'd go out in style. He was his own hospice. He didn't live very long. I don't even think it was a year, but he went in his own way. On the other hand, there were people who were so scared that, even though they weren't as sick as Matthew had been at times, died within weeks. I would occasionally put myself in Matthew's place, and I don't know if I could do that. I would be *so* scared. I had never been ill in my life. So I'm amazed at people's courage.

There was another gentleman, Tommy. He was one of my first patients. Tommy was an entertainer – he had traveled all over the world. He sang and danced and he appeared with many famous people. He was just a really outgoing, effervescent human being. Tommy had gotten quite ill and had been in the hospital numerous times. No matter how sick he was, Tommy always had a smile for you. He would often sing at services at Unity while he was ill. Tommy was gay. His wife, Irene, knew that, but they fell in love. A lot of Tommy's gay friends were very upset when he got married. But Tommy loved Irene very, very much. I remember when Tommy was dying, this one day he was taking a bath, and he was in a lot of pain. There are people when in pain who just kind of shrink and succumb to it. Tommy just wouldn't let that happen. He was in the tub and got these stabbing bursts of pain – but he was singing in the tub. Occasionally he would get these stabbing bursts of pain, so he'd have to stop singing for a while. I remember the song that he was singing. He'd be going, '*Ow-ow-ow-ow-ow-ow-ow* – it hurts, it hurts, it hurts!' But then as soon as the pain subsided, he'd get back into singing the song.

Do you remember the tune?

Yes. 'God Bless the Child.'

The End and the Beginning

MAMIE MOBLEY

> . . . *But there was something about the matter of the Dark*
>   *Villain.*
> *He should have been older, perhaps.*
> *The hacking down of a villain was more fun to think about*
> *When his menace possessed undisputed breadth, undisputed*
>   *height,*
> *And a harsh kind of vice.*
> *And best of all, when his history was cluttered*
> *With the bones of many eaten knights and princesses.*
>
> *The fun was disturbed, then all but nullified*
> *When the Dark Villain was a blackish child*
> *Of fourteen, with eyes still too young to be dirty,*
> *And a mouth too young to have lost every reminder*
> *Of its infant softness.*
>
> — *Gwendolyn Brooks*★

She is a retired Chicago public school teacher. In 1955, her
fourteen-year-old son, Emmett Till, was killed while
visiting relatives in Mississippi. He was her only child. Two
white men, Roy Bryant and W.J. ('Big Jim') Milam, were
accused of the murder. Though the evidence against them
was overwhelming, they were acquitted by an all-white
jury.

★From 'A Bronzeville Mother Loiters in Mississippi. Meanwhile, a Mississippi
Mother Burns Bacon' by Gwendolyn Brooks, *Blacks* (Chicago: Third World
Press, 1987).

The case had international repercussions, and it is still considered a significant prelude to the civil rights movement that followed.

This conversation took place in September of 2000, forty-five years later.

Emmett just barely got on that train to Mississippi. We could hear the whistle blowing. As he was running up the steps, I said, 'Bo' – that's what I called him – 'you didn't kiss me. How do I know I'll ever see you again?' He turned around and said, 'Oh, Mama,' gently scolding me. He ran down those steps and gave me a kiss. As he turned to go up the steps again, he pulled his watch off and said, 'Take this, I won't need it.' I said, 'What about your ring?' He was wearing his father's ring for the first time. He said, 'I'm going to show this to my friends.' That's how we were able to identify him, by that ring. I think it was a Mason's ring.

I got four letters from him in a week's time. My aunt in Mississippi wrote me a long letter in praise of him – how he helped her in the kitchen, with the washing machine, preparing the meals. The way he did things at home. He'd say, 'Mama, if you can go out and make the money, I can take care of the house.' He cleaned, he shopped for groceries, he washed. Do you remember when Tide came out? It was in 1953, two years before he went to Mississippi. He told me about the advertisement: 'Tide's in, dirt's out.' All the neighbors knew him.

I didn't know what happened to him until the following Sunday.

I'm a seventy-eight-year-old woman. I have lived all my life being brought up in the Church. I feel that I'm a very strong woman. When I lost my son, that's when I found out that I really had two feet and I *had* to stand on my own feet. I had to stand and be a woman.

There was nobody around who could really help me. Everybody was so in tears. I had to calm them down. They couldn't help me if they were going to be hollering and screaming. So I found out, in 1955, that I was very capable of getting the job done, even though I couldn't see for the tears.

I was able to get it done.

The spirit spoke to me and said, 'Go to school and be a teacher. I have taken one but I shall give you thousands.' I have to identify that as a spirit being bigger than I am. I was the only one hearing that voice.

I had ordered Emmett's body brought back to Chicago. It was in three boxes. He was in a box that was in a box that was in a box. Each had the Mississippi seal and a padlock on it. It was the biggest box I'd ever seen in my life.

I said to the undertaker, 'Give me a hammer. I'm gonna break that seal. I'm gonna go into that box. I don't know what I'm bury-ing. It could be a box full of rocks. It could be cement. It could be dirt. I've got to verify it is my son in that box.'

They had laid him out on the cooling board. His body was still in the body bag. [*She has difficulty, weeps. A long pause.*] The undertaker unzipped the bag. And that's when I saw all that lime. They hosed him down. And, oh, my God, I knew what that odor was by then. It was not the lime, that was my son I was smelling.

I glanced at his head and it was such a mess up there, I just had to turn away. I started at his feet. I knew certain characteristics about him. I knew how his knees looked, I knew how his ankles and feet looked. I made my trip from his feet up to his midsection, identify-ing what I could.

And then I saw this long tongue hanging out of his mouth. What on Earth! They were looking for me to fall out, and I told them, 'Turn me loose – I've got a job to do.' I said, 'I can't faint now.' I began a real minute examination. I looked at his teeth and there were only about four of them left. He had such beautiful teeth. I moved on up to the nose. And it looked like somebody had taken a meat cleaver and had just chopped the bridge of his nose. Pieces had fallen out. When I went to look at his eyes, this one was lying on his cheek. But I saw the color of it. I said, 'That's my son's eye.' I looked over at the other and it was as if somebody had taken a nut picker and just picked it out. There was no eye. I went to examine his ears. If you'll notice, my ears are detached from my face and they kind of curl on the end. And his did, too. There was no ear. It was gone. I was looking up the side of his face and I could see daylight on the other side. I said, 'Oh, my God.' The tears were falling, and I was brushing tears away because I had to see.

Later, I was reading the Scriptures. And it told how Jesus had been led from judgment hall to judgment hall all night long, how he had been beaten – and so much that no man would ever sustain the horror of his beating. That his face was just in ribbons. And I thought about it, and I said, 'Lord, do you mean to tell me that Emmett's beating did not equal the one that was given to Jesus?' And I said, 'My God, what must Jesus have suffered?'

And then I thought about some of the pictures we see, where he has this neat little crown of thorns and you see a few rivulets of blood coming down, but his face is intact. And according to Scriptures, that is not true. His visage was scarred more than any other man's had ever been or will be.

And that's when I really was able to assess what Jesus had given for us, the love he had for us.

And I saw Emmett and his scars. Lord, I saw the stigmata of Jesus. The spirit spoke to me as plainly as I'm talking to you now. Jesus had come and died that we might have a right to eternal life or eternal Hell or damnation. Emmett had died that men might have freedom here on Earth. That we might have a right to life.

That was my darkest moment, when I realized that that huge box had the remains of my son. I sent a very lovable boy on a vacation – Emmett, who knew everybody in the neighborhood. They'd call him whenever they wanted something done. 'Mom, I gotta go help Mrs. Bailey.' He was the block's messenger boy.

What might have been? He's never far from my mind. If Jesus Christ died for our sins, Emmett Till bore our prejudices, so . . .

DR. MARVIN JACKSON

He is a neurosurgeon at the George Washington Hospital, Washington, D.C. He is thirty-five. In 1965, I had visited his grandmother, Lucille Dickerson.★ She was, at the time, a hospital aide, who spent most of her off-hours reading paperbacks. Among her favorites were Charles Dickens, Theodore Dreiser, Richard Wright, and Nelson Algren. Toward the end of the evening, she motioned to her pregnant daughter, who was seated on the divan. 'The only thrill left for me is to see my grandchild come to life and see what I can do about him. Won't that be fun? I'll be able to afford things that would give him incentive to paint, music, literature, all those things that would free his little soul. What counts is knowledge. And feeling. You see, there's such a thing as a feeling tone. If you don't have this, baby, you've had it – you're dead.'

You and I were in the same room together, but I'm afraid I don't remember it. [*Laughs*] I still had about a week or two to go before I was born. My grandmother spoke of it occasionally.

We lived over in the projects off Roosevelt and Loomis. My grandmother was interested in one thing more than anything else: education for the kids. Because money for black kids was not coming into the schools.

She died May 9th, 1984. I had just turned nineteen – I was a freshman at Stanford then. I had come back from a chemistry exam and there was a note on the door: CALL HOME. THERE'S AN EMERGENCY. My uncle said that she had died. It was like the bottom had fallen out. My whole life . . .

Early memories of her? Oh, so many. I'd go to Malcolm X College with her. She was taking courses. [*Laughs*] I would sit in the back of the classroom while the class was going on, and I would doodle and draw. She'd take me along everywhere – 'cause my mom was working.

★She was 'Lucy Jefferson' in *Division Street: America* (New York: Pantheon, 1967).

We had a kitchen table, and she'd read the paper while I was doing my homework. Everything was done at the kitchen table.

When I went to St. Ignatius,* my life really changed. I became very, very busy. [*Sighs*] I was headed out the door for my final exams as a freshman when my grandmother had a heart attack. I wanted to see her, but I *had* to go to school. I *had* to take those exams. It was what she wanted.

She stopped smoking, stopped drinking, she retired. She was slowing down. She was just living to see her dream come true in me.

When I went to Stanford, she wrote me pretty much every week. She would send me all sorts of clippings from Chicago newspapers, just so I'd feel at home. She sent me stuff pretty much every week.

My birthday was May 6th. I was taking my midterm exams that day. She had another heart attack, probably on my birthday – but they didn't call me and tell me she had died until the 9th. I have a feeling that in her last moments – she knew I was taking those exams – she told them not to call me. She was seventy-four.

I flew back . . . I can't describe my ache. It hurt so badly. It was two years before I got over it. I finished out the school year, but I was never the same after that.

I felt like I was wandering. I felt like I was out in the wilderness by myself. I didn't feel connected. I didn't feel like I belonged any-place. I just plugged through Stanford as best I could. It was not a good time. Even academically – I didn't perform well. But it was good enough. By the time I was a senior, I had an idea of what I wanted to do. I wanted to be a doctor. I wanted to change the world in that way, one person at a time. After five years at the UCLA Medical School, I knew what I wanted to do with my life – be a neurosurgeon.

My experience at the medical school was difficult. I really believe I was expected to fail, not to succeed. There were about thirty African-Americans in the class of two hundred. The attitude of the faculty as well as some of the students was so clear to me. But I was thinking about my grandmother all the time. I had to make it.

Since my grandmother died at seventy-four and I'm thirty-five, I

*A Chicago Catholic school celebrated for its high scholastic standards. He was a scholarship student.

feel that half of my life may be over. But something else is beginning. My marriage is beginning. My career is beginning, my wife is
a doctor, too.

The grief about my grandmother never goes away, but you find a
way to put it in a place where you see the good things. She's gone,
but somehow, some way, I know she plays a role. There's this con-
nectedness, this level of understanding, the *feeling tone* that my
grandmother told you about years and years ago. *And I was in the
room when she said it.* [*Chuckles*]

She had a feeling for me, wanting me to live out a life that no one
in our family ever lived before. And I believe she still plays a role in
what I do, where I go, how I do things. She's very much alive in my
memories: the way I see and remember, the way I try to conduct my
life. Hopefully, one day I'll have a son or a daughter and teach him
everything from medicine to changing oil to cutting the grass.

I think it also helps me as a neurosurgeon. I've had to tell people
their loved ones are no longer here, even though they're looking at
this shell of a human being. The person they knew, the mind they
knew, is no longer here. Once you say that, people understand.
And they may be comforted, I don't know . . .

I look at the nurse's aides who work in the hospital, and I remember a long time ago when my grandmother was one of these people.
I speak to them. I know their names. I see my grandmother, and I
see the struggles that these particular women – most of whom are
black, single, with children, trying to raise their families – are trying
to provide. I see the path that they're on, because I'm at the other
end of the path: I know where they're trying to go.

And when they bring their little sons or daughters to the hospital, I remember being brought to the hospital by my grandmother to
see the hospital and the patients and the physicians.

I see this hospital aide in another family, who is just as important
to her child as my grandmother was to me. Someone who has the
same dreams for their children and grandchildren and would do
anything to set their souls free.

Epilogue

KATHY FAGAN AND LINDA GAGNON

They are lesbian mothers. Each has an eighteen-year-old son. They are visiting Chicago because Linda's son is about to enter Elmhurst College, located in a western suburb. They are celebrating the occasion. We are in my kitchen. It is a dialogue. Each listens intently and with obvious affection as the other speaks. Kathy, the upper-middle-class daughter of a Cleveland salesman, is the first to speak.

I am forty years old, a physician. I did my residency at Cook County Hospital. That was an exciting time – there was a lot happening. I met Ron Sable there. He was a gay doctor who was quite active politically. He was outspoken on many matters – civil rights, peace, and gay rights, of course. He ran for alderman and almost won. I discovered I was gay at medical school. It didn't click until then. Cook County was a wonderful training ground for many gay doctors. It was at that time that I decided I wanted a child. I was looking for someone to donate sperm.

It was unusual then. This was 1981. I began talking with friends and looking for someone who would be willing to be a sperm donor. This is the whole turkey-baster concept. You obviously need sperm and you need an egg. The joke was that a gay woman would get a turkey baster and have the sperm in the turkey baster and insert it. So first I needed to find somebody who would be willing to do this. I just started asking around, and what was wondrous was that Ron was very open to the idea of donating sperm. He felt strongly that lesbians should be able to have children. The one way he could support that idea was to donate his sperm. So Ron's sperm and my egg made a child. He's a boy, now eighteen years old. He's a neat guy. His name's John Gabriel Fagan. He's entered college – he's at Northeastern in Boston, studying computer engineering.

We continued to live in Chicago for a couple of years before I moved back to Cleveland with John. Ron came to visit us in Cleveland a few times during the course of John's growing up, so he came to know Ron as his dad. They didn't spend a lot of time together. I think Ron wasn't that used to being around kids.

Ron died of AIDS in December of 1993 – seven years ago. John was eleven. There was a celebration of Ron's life. It was a tribute to him. His lover was there, his mother, his sister. Hundreds of us were there. We came together: Linda, her son, John, and myself.

Linda and I had started to know about each other a few years before that, through Ron. He told me Linda had a son of his sperm, too. We talked a little bit and wrote some letters to each other. Linda and Matt were living in Florida. I actually met Linda for the first time in April of 1993.

[*Linda picks up the story.*] I was born in western Massachusetts, Northampton, in 1950. I have five brothers and two sisters. I came from a working-class family. My father was a crook. He was a gambler and a crook. He spent five years in jail.

You asked who I am, that's who I am. I was the youngest. I grew up in public housing in Northampton. My mother worked. We were never on public assistance. When my father got out of jail, we moved to Wheaton, Illinois – partly for a fresh start.

I knew I was gay when I was in high school, when I was sixteen, seventeen. I went to college for a short while, but I didn't graduate. I was really kind of footloose and had wanderlust – it's very prevalent in my family. We had to find our own paths. So I went back east, to Northampton, Mass. I was nineteen, twenty. I lived there for a long time and worked and spent all my money on women and booze. [*Laughs*] Then I came back to Wheaton to see my mom. I was twenty-six, and I needed to get some kind of occupation. She taught me how to be a neurotechnologist, and that's what I do. She knew I was gay. She just wanted me to be happy. I wanted a kid. I had a strong desire to have a child, but I wasn't ready to have a child until I could justify bringing a child into this world. It really took me a long time before I could find a positive reason to have a child.

I worked in WICCHA – Women in Crisis Can Help Act. It was a hotline. I was involved in the women's community. It wasn't particularly that I didn't want male interference – I love women. [*Laughs*] I wanted a child, and I wanted a long-term relationship. That was maybe selfish of me, but I thought I could have that with a child. A friend of mine who lived in Chicago knew Ron Sable. They were good friends. She said he might be interested in doing this. He said he'd be glad to meet with me. We talked about it for a while, and if there were any medical reasons why we shouldn't do it. He wasn't ill at the time. That was just when HIV and AIDS were getting public attention. He said, yeah, he would do it. I had a significant other, I was in a relationship at the time. We would find out when I was fertile and we'd call up Ron, and Ron would say, 'OK, I'll come over.' He'd come over, go into a spare bedroom, drop the stuff off, and then he'd leave, and we would do the rest. That was 1982. My son is two months older than Kathy's – he's eighteen. His name is Matthew Gagnon.

Where did you have the baby?

Here, at St. Luke's–Presbyterian. I worked there, so I had him for free. Then I left Chicago because my son was getting to be five and I just couldn't see raising him in Chicago. I went to Florida and took a job in a hospital down there. Ron visited on occasion.

When did Matthew discover that Ron was his father?

Shortly after Matt was born, I called up Ron and asked if I could put his name on the birth certificate – because I was freaking out. He said fine, he said OK. Kathy and I had known about each other and actually met very briefly. She called me up one day and said, 'We have these kids that have the same father. Would you like to get together?' I said, 'No, I don't think so.' People in my life at that time were telling me that it wasn't a good idea. I had a lot of pressure that the boys shouldn't meet until after high school.

Then Ron called me and said that he was coming down to visit, and he would like to see us. I thought that was great – because Matt had gone to spend a weekend with him. We had a nice visit and he left. Ron had meant to come down to tell me that he was HIV-positive. He wanted to tell me, but he just couldn't. He wrote me a letter. [*Her voice breaks.*] Which was . . . it was just really sad. I called Kathy up right away and said, 'Let's meet.' Then I really was ready to meet.

KATHY: It was Easter weekend, 1993. We decided to meet in Chicago. Ron rented a house on Lake Michigan. We all stayed together for the weekend. We knew Ron was dying. That's when Linda and Matt and John and I first met. It was electric – it was just beautiful. It was one of the most beautiful weekends in my life.

LINDA: That was it.

KATHY: Everybody got along great. Ron watched his kids play. We all had dinner together, Easter dinner.

LINDA: We had fireworks. I brought them up from Florida.

KATHY: That was one of the things John remembered best, the fireworks.

Is that when something happened between you two?

LINDA: Absolutely.

KATHY: We couldn't put it in words yet, but, boy, did I *feel* it.

LINDA: Nothing physical happened.

Was it love?

TOGETHER: Yeah.

KATHY: It was, it was. It blew me away. I had no expectations that that might happen.

[*After a long pause*] LINDA: I wasn't prepared for it. I mean, it was *wonderful* – it was just . . . We knew that we needed to spend more time together.

KATHY: Oh yeah, it was just *so* strong.

Was Ron aware of this?

LINDA: I drove Ron back to Chicago and he asked me, 'How did you and Kathy get along?' And I said, 'Well, she already wants to take me to California to meet her sister.' [*Both laugh.*]

KATHY: The next time we got together was when school ended for the boys and you drove up. It was in June of '93. They came up to stay at our house.

LINDA: Oh, yeah. [*More laughter*] I remember that.

KATHY: And it was still electric between us.

By this time you had decided to live together?

KATHY: No, no, no! We just decided to be intimate. Ron is getting sicker. We were alerted that there was going to be this big tribute to him in July. So again we met. It was just a stunning tribute – it was very emotional. One of the things I was thinking about was how were John and Matt taking this in? They were only eleven years old.

LINDA: By this time, they were calling him Dad. He was writing cards and letters, 'Love, Dad.'

KATHY: It was quite emotional for John. I could see that he was somewhat blown away by that event.

LINDA: One of the really nice things that we remember, I think, is that we had an intimate dinner with Ron, all of us – his mother, his sister, and José* was there, too. And we were able to connect with his family. The sad thing was we tried to continue that connection and they didn't – but at least we had that one time.

We rented a really expensive hotel room, and we asked Ron and José if they would take the boys overnight, because I thought it would be good for them, you know, for all four of them. It was that same weekend as the tribute. And then we had dinner with them and they took the kids. And then we spent the night together at the hotel. That was it, that night.

KATHY: Linda and I have been together since then. She and Matt moved up to Cleveland so that we all lived together that next year.

LINDA: In '94. We now live in Cleveland Heights. [*Haltingly*] My sister just died last week. I was really close to her. But when I think of death, I think of Ron and I think of when he was dying. I was really sad, because I had wanted Matt to be able to get to know him. I had a long time ago told Ron that when Matt asked who his dad was, I was going to say, 'Go talk to that man over there.' So there was this loss of opportunity for them to know each other for a long period of time, which made me very sad. At Ron's deathbed, I had made a promise – that I would care for Kathy and for John and for

*Ron's lover.

Matthew for the rest of my life. When I think of death, I think of that time.

KATHY: I guess I still believe in the hereafter . . . We have my mother living with us. She has Alzheimer's, so we're taking care of her. Her Alzheimer's is at a point where she does a lot of talking, and you think maybe she has hallucinations. But she'll say people's names and she talks about my uncles who've died, or my dad. And we get this feeling that we're getting visited by all of them. [*Laughter*]

LINDA: And after my sister Chris died . . .

KATHY: My mom was talking to Chris.

LINDA: And she didn't know Chris that well . . . Who knows?

KATHY: I feel that my dad is still with me, that Ron is still with us, that they're there watching out for the boys.

LINDA: Since Ron died, I became aware that suddenly you start seeing these people in other people. I would see Ron in other people. I would see his nose or I'd see his jaw or I'd see his shoulders. I would see him, in some ways, far more often than when he was alive. I don't know what that means, but I think it means something. Another thing that's interesting to me about death is that while Ron was actually dying, time slowed down dramatically. It continues to move, but it is so much slower.

I remember sitting in Ron's apartment – he died at home – and thinking about all these cars that were just going by, and that life was just continuing on outside these doors. To me, that was comforting. Because I knew that I could, when it was time, go and join that world again. Death was much different than life out there. If there's life hereafter, I feel that if it's just sleep, it's the best sleep that I've had in years – and who wouldn't want that? And if you meet all your friends, or you get to be absorbed by this great space, who wouldn't want that? I find a lot of comfort in that, and it's OK.

KATHY: As Ron became ill, I think that our boys became a different thing for him. Originally it was political. He wanted lesbians to be able to have kids if they wanted to. He was interested in the boys somewhat, but he had his own life. But when he became sick, the specter of death broadened his view of life and he really wanted to know those boys better.

LINDA: He grew into it. It's very bittersweet, this memory. Our love came from a hard time. I think it made it very strong.

But you've had no social difficulties?

KATHY: That's not totally true. When Matt and Linda first came up to Cleveland to live, we enrolled him in a Catholic school because we thought it might be better. They figured us out right away and they did *not* want us in that school. They drummed him out of the school. Here's a kid who just lost his father, just moved to a new place, and they gave him all Fs! They didn't want to talk with us. They wanted us out of that school.

LINDA: We had our two separate families and we forged them into one. It is one now. They feel as brothers.

KATHY: They were worried: Gee, are we gay because we have gay parents? Does that mean they're gay? They went through thinking about that and talking about it. So far they both think they're not, they both think that they're heterosexuals. One of the things that we see in both of them, they're very tolerant of diversity, and that's nice.

LINDA: Ron gave me my entire life. He gave me everything. He gave me my whole life. [*Near tears*] He gave me Matthew, who is someone I would go through a burning building for. I would die for him. Unless you've had a child, you can't imagine the love that you feel for a child. Ron gave that to me. And he gave me Kathy. She is the love of my life. We will be together until death parts us. So he's given me everything. And he never asked for anything. He gave me Matthew because I asked him. And he gave me John. He gave me my family. He gave me Kathy because I think he knew I needed her. I think he knew we needed each other. It was difficult being a single parent. He knew. He was involved in both our lives. So he engineered it. He wanted this, he wanted us to be together. And we accepted his gift.